STANDING: GRANDPA JONES, UNKNOWN, WANDA JACKSON, EDDIE HILL; SEATED: HANK THOMPSON, STONEY COOPER, THE EVERLY BROTHERS, HANK SNOW, MERLE TRAVIS. COURTESY OF THE CHARLES K. WOLFE COLLECTION.

Classic Country

LEGENDS OF COUNTRY MUSIC

CHARLES K. WOLFE

ROUTLEDGE • NEW YORK • LONDON

c-1

Published in 2001 by

Routledge
29 West 35th Street
New York, NY 10001

Published in Great Britain by
Routledge
11 New Fetter Lane
London EC4P 4EE

Routledge is an imprint of the Taylor & Francis Group.

10 9 8 7 6 5 4 3 2 1

Library of Congress Cataloging-in-Publication Data

Wolfe, Charles K.
Classic country : legends of country music / Charles K. Wolfe.
      p. cm. —
   Includes index.
   ISBN 0–415–92826–5 — ISBN 0–415–92827–3 (pbk.)
      1. Country musicians—United States—Biography. I. Title.

ML385 .W64 2000
781.642'092'2—dc21   00–044638
[B]

Contents

Introduction

In an age when country music seems to be shooting off in a dozen different directions, it is important to remind ourselves that there was once, and still is, a broad mainstream that genuinely defined the genre. It was not called "power country" or "alt country" or "retro country" or "country rock" or "cowboy country," but just "country." It was the home of a large number of performers who shared a range of values and beliefs about the music, and who shared a common body of tradition and history. This great unifying, nourishing stream runs through the history of country music, from the pioneer Appalachian harmonies of the Original Carter Family through the varied vocal styles of Roy Acuff, Bill Monroe, Grandpa Jones, Kitty Wells, Martha Carson, the Statler Brothers, and dozens of others. Some have taken to calling this broad mainstream tradition "Classic Country," in the same manner that we speak of "classic" rock or "classic" jazz. This book is a collection of some fifty profiles of musicians, past and present, who were part of this great stream.

Though the subjects seen here range from pioneers of the 1920s—the first generation of professional country musicians—to stars of the present, they all have certain things in common. First and foremost is that each artist has serious ties to country music's past, and to the country music tradition. It is true that most of these stars have created their own distinct style and image, and this has made them unique and worthy of interest; but most have accomplished this by building on older, earlier traditions. And many of them are willing and even anxious to pay homage to their teachers. Roy Acuff could not get out of his head the sound of the old mountain ballad singer in eastern Tennessee; Lefty Frizzell stuck his head inside the old Victrola to try to better hear the archetypal recordings of Jimmie Rodgers; fiddler Tommy Magness was obsessed with the old fiddle tune he learned growing up in the north Georgia hills that people later came to call "Black Mountain Rag." Bill

Monroe never missed a chance to pay homage to Arnold Schultz, the black guitar player who introduced him to the blues; the Louvin Brothers often returned to their native Sand Mountain to sing the old Sacred Harp songs at their country church. These musicians all felt connected to some earlier music, and in some special way, felt that they were a part of something. And, for better or worse, they had to deal with it.

Another characteristic most of these musicians have in common is a willingness to talk seriously about their work and their influences. In an age of sound bites, spin control, publicists, and superficial radio interviews, it is becoming rare to find an artist who is willing to sit down, one-on-one, and talk at length about his or her career. These profiles, generally, have been based on such personal interviews; in the case of older artists who have long since passed, an attempt has been made to speak directly with their close relatives and friends, or to find taped interviews in archives. This personal aspect is what makes these profiles different from an encyclopedia entry or a formal history. I have always been convinced that a good anecdote or an insightful quotation can tell us as much about a performer as pages of discography or lists of awards.

Though we have in recent years lost a number of key artists in this Classic Country mainstream, the tradition is by no means extinct or even seriously threatened. One can look at the work of modern stars like LeAnn Rimes, Alan Jackson, George Strait, Vince Gill, Marty Stuart, Steve Earle, Asleep at the Wheel, Bryan White, Patty Loveless, and many others. For these artists, the past of Classic Country is no hollow, dusty museum where people tread quietly and stare at glass cases with reverence, but a vibrant, pulsating, nourishing force that infuses their own work in manifold and surprising ways. Though few of the artists profiled here have a record on the current *Billboard* charts, their influence continues to make itself felt in dozens of new records that do make the charts.

Nor does this collection represent a complete roster of all the performers in this genre; for a variety of reasons, I was not able to do interviews and profiles with many that I had wanted to. I did not get a chance to talk at length with George Jones, or Merle Haggard, or Minnie Pearl, or Eddy Arnold, but these particular artists have found their own biographers and collaborators. I did not deal much with cowboy or western swing music, since that area had its own enthusiasts and experts. But in general, there was no rational master plan guiding my writing of these profiles. Some were targets of opportunity, and the result of specific writing assignments or record projects. This should be considered as a representative collection rather than a comprehensive one.

The profiles themselves span a number of years, but most of them date from the decade of the 1990s and first appeared in a publication of *Country Music* magazine devoted to vintage performers and songs. This bore the unwieldy title *The Journal of the American Academy for the Preservation of Old-Time Country Music,* though it was often called simply *The Journal.* Though its editor in chief was *Country Music* founder Russ Barnard, many of the day-to-day duties belonged to Helen Barnard and Senior Editor Rich Kienzle. It was under their tutelage that many of these profiles were conceived and written; all three editors gave me a wide berth to write about whatever parts of Classic Country that I wanted to, and were generous in making room when an article ran a bit long, or took an unexpected direction. Other articles appeared in journals and periodicals now defunct: the legendary English quarterly *Old Time Music,* the short-lived tabloid *Country Sounds,* and the lovingly crafted Georgia publication about gospel music, *Precious Memories.* A handful of pieces appeared in *Bluegrass Unlimited,* then as now the leading chronicler of that protean field, and a few others started life as liner notes to a record or CD set. Some of the profiles have never appeared in print before, and were written expressly for this volume.

A depressing number of the artists included here have died since I did my interviews and wrote the stories about them. They include Pee Wee King (d. 2000), Hank Snow (d. 1999), Grandpa Jones (d. 1998), Bill Monroe (d. 1996), Curly Fox (d. 1995), Roy Acuff (d. 1992), Lew DeWitt (of the Statler Brothers) (d. 1990), Bradley Kincaid (d. 1989), Jimmie Riddle (d. 1982), and DeFord Bailey (d. 1982). In other cases, my subjects had been gone for years: I never got to meet Fiddlin' John Carson, Riley Puckett, Lew Childre, Vernon Dalhart, Karl and Harty, Tommy Magness, Seven Foot Dilly, Arthur Q. Smith, Albert E. Brumley, and others. But I was able to talk to their friends and relatives and get some sense of what kind of people they were, some sense of personality to flesh out the bare bones of discography and chronology.

I have divided these profiles into seven sections. The first comprises probably the best-known names here, those who are in the Country Music Hall of Fame. These are, in every real sense, legendary figures whose careers have spanned generations and have established themselves as seminal figures in the development of the music. The second category, "From the Victrola," celebrates the first generation of country recording stars from the 1920s—names that are familiar to most country fans, but that are lacking in any sense of identity. The great age of live country radio is reflected in section three, "From the Airwaves." During the 1930s and 1940s, virtually every country musician had to establish himself or herself by doing live radio work. (I have chronicled one particular show from this era, the Grand Ole Opry, in my *A Good-Natured Riot* [Country Music Foundation/Vanderbilt University Press, 1999])

Next comes a series of tributes to "Unsung Heroes," figures who played significant roles in the music, but have been neglected or ignored by the formal histories. "From the Stage" chronicles the mainstream artists who found their best venue to be the live personal performance, the touring show. These were the old-time "showmen," whose dynamic performances transcended any individual song or style—Stringbean duck-walking across the stage to get to the mike, Martha Carson whirling through the audience during a driving gospel song, Bill Carlisle leaping four feet straight up into the air behind a microphone and telling an audience to "Shut up!" "From the West" includes portraits of our first genuine singing cowgirl, Billie Maxwell, as well as other performers in this style. Finally, there is a section devoted to modern acts who have a special affinity for the older styles, "New Fogies," to remind us that this tradition remains in good hands.

Charles K. Wolfe
Murfreesboro, Tennessee
February 2000

Classic Country

PART I   *From the Hall of Fame*

The Carter Family

It was the granddaddy of all country music success stories, the pattern on which dozens of Music Row Cinderella tales would be founded. A local group, used to singing on front porches and at country churches, wanders into what today would be termed a talent call. More by accident than by design, the group gets an audition; the big-time talent scout can't believe his ears. A contract is signed; records are cut; in a matter of months, the group hears its records playing from the Victrolas rolled out in front of the appliance stores in its hometown. Across the country, millions hear the same music, and are charmed by its feeling, its simplicity, its soul. A career is launched, and soon the little country group is making it in the big time, on national radio, continuing to produce great music but struggling to ward off personal problems, divorce and changing tastes. It is a story almost as familiar as the music of the group or the name of the group: The Carter Family.

The interesting thing about legends is that some of them are true. Back on that hot August day in 1927, the big-time recording scout from Victor Records in New York was really not impressed with what he saw at the door of his studio. There were two women and a man, he recalled. "He is dressed in overalls and the women are country women from way back there—calico clothes on—the children are very poorly dressed. They look like hillbillies." The man in overalls was Alvin Pleasant Carter, but they called him A.P. He was a lean, hawk-faced young man, with a pleasant, bemused expression not unlike that of Gary Cooper in *Sergeant York*. With him was a woman holding an odd little instrument called an autoharp that she had ordered from Sears' mail order catalog and a seven-month-old baby named Joe. She was A.P.'s wife, Sara Carter. The third woman, the one holding the big guitar, staring around the studio with a surprising confidence, was Sara's cousin, Maybelle. They had spent the entire previous day driving an old Model

A Ford down mountain roads and across rocky streams to get to the audition. They'd had three flat tires, and the weather was so hot that the patches had melted off almost as fast as A.P. had put them on. But they were here, and they were wanting a record tryout.

"Here" was the sleepy mountain town of Bristol, straddling the state line between Virginia and Tennessee. In an empty furniture store at 408 State Street—the street that was actually the state line—the Victor Talking Machine Company had set up a temporary studio. It was late summer 1927, and country music didn't even have a name yet; Victor called its brand "Old-Time Melodies of the Sunny South." The company had only recently decided to get into the country music business. Field teams had been sent into the South to find authentic material and singers who would sound more soulful than their current big singing sensation, Vernon Dalhart. Heading this team, in fact heading all the teams that summer, was a fast-talking, moon-faced young man named Ralph Peer. Several years before, Peer had helped American record companies discover the blues; now he was doing the same with "hillbilly" music. For two weeks he had been at work in Bristol, auditioning talent and recording them on the spot in his studio; he had already recorded classics by the Stoneman Family, harmonica player Henry Whitter and gospel singer Alfred Karnes; soon he would produce the first sides by a young man named Jimmie Rodgers. Though he didn't know it at the time, he was in the middle of what Johnny Cash would later call "the single most important event in the history of country music."

The family auditioned for Peer on the morning of Monday, August 1, and that evening at 6:30 he took them into the studio. In those days, it wasn't uncommon to cut a session of four sides in three hours—and there were times during the course of the Bristol sessions when Peer managed to cut as many as twelve masters a day. Though the Carters were relatively young (Maybelle was only eighteen), they were full of old songs they had learned in their nearby mountain home of Maces Spring, Virginia. The first one they tried was "Bury Me Under the Weeping Willow," an old nineteenth-century lament that both girls had known since childhood. Peer at once realized that he had something. "As soon as I heard Sara's voice," he recalled, "I knew it was going to be wonderful."

And it was. Peer cut three more songs that night and asked the group to return the next morning to cut two more. These six sides became the start of one of the most incredible dynasties in American music. For over sixty years now, some part or offshoot of this Carter Family trio has been a fixture on the country music scene. The family's musical contributions have ranged from the pure folk sound of the original trio to the contemporary, rock-tinged sound of Maybelle's grand-daughter, Carlene. "Carter Family songs" is a term that has become almost synonymous with old-time country standards, and parts of the Carter repertoire are revived in almost every generation by a wide range of singers and pickers, including Hank Williams (who toured with Maybelle and her daughters), Hank Thompson and Merle Travis (who added a honky-tonk beat to "Wildwood Flower" in the 1950s), Roy Acuff (whose anthem "Wabash Cannonball" was first recorded by the Carters), Johnny Cash (who married Maybelle's daughter June), the Nitty Gritty Dirt Band (who recorded the classic album *Will the Circle Be Unbroken* with Maybelle in 1971), Emmylou Harris, and dozens of others. Though their recording career lasted only fourteen years—from that day in Bristol in 1927 until the eve of World War II in 1941—the Carters managed to work for every major label and make some 270 records, among them some of the most influential recordings in country music history. "They didn't have gold records in those days," said modern publishing giant Wesley Rose. "But if they had, the Carters would have had a wall full." What the industry could do was vote them into the Hall of Fame, which it did in 1970.

After they made the six sides for Peer that day in 1927, the trio drove back to their mountain farm, and A.P. returned to his old job of selling fruit trees. In September the first batch of recordings from the Bristol sessions was released in the new "Orthophonic Victor Southern Series." Big ads appeared in the Bristol papers. As A.P. scanned the list, his heart sank; no Carter records had been selected for release. Another batch appeared in October; again, no Carters. A.P. had about given up hope when, in November, the local furniture store dealer who had the Victor franchise hunted up A.P. to tell him that "The Wandering Boy" had finally been issued, and that he had a nice royalty check for him. A few months later, a second record, "The Storms Are on the Ocean," came out. At this point, Peer realized that Carter music was catching on; soon their records were outselling all the others recorded at the Bristol sessions, including those of Jimmie Rodgers.

Not long afterward, Peer sent the group expense money to come to the New Jersey studios for more sessions. Here they cut twelve more songs, including such standards as "Little Darling Pal of Mine," "Keep on the Sunny Side" (an 1899 Sunday school song adapted from *The Young People's Hymnal No. 2* that eventually became the Carter theme), "Anchored in Love" (another taken from an old church songbook; it wound up selling almost 100,000 records), "John Hardy" (a famous bad-man ballad), "Will You Miss Me When I'm Gone" (a latter-day favorite with bluegrass bands), and a simple piece called "Wildwood Flower." In this one, Maybelle figured out a way to pick the melody on the lower strings of her guitar while she strummed the chords on the higher strings. This technique, soon known as "the Carter lick," became the single most influential guitar style in country music. It wasn't hard to master, and soon every kid who could get his hands on a guitar was being told, "First you've got to learn to play 'Wildwood Flower.'" The song itself was another old one A.P. had learned in the mountains; though he didn't know it at the time, it was actually an 1859 sheet music song that had been a vaudeville favorite since before the Civil War. At Peer's suggestion, A.P. filed copyright on this and dozens of other older songs he arranged, rewrote, or adapted. Many of them still appear in the Peer-Southern catalog.

If there had ever been any doubt about the Carters' popularity, "Wildwood Flower" ended it. Not only was it sold by record stores around the country, it was peddled by Sears, Roebuck in its catalog and later issued on the Montgomery Ward label for sale in that company's catalog; a later 1935 remake was sold in dime stores across the land on labels such as Conqueror, Melotone, Vocalion, and others. It was easily the best-selling of all the Carter records and one that remained in print well into the LP era.

Unlike Jimmie Rodgers, Peer's other big find at Bristol, the Carters seemed oddly unable to capitalize on their record success. In the late 1920s and early 1930s, while Rodgers was playing the big RKO vaudeville houses in Dallas and Atlanta, the Carters were setting up plank stages and hanging kerosene lamps for shows in remote mountain coal towns. While Rodgers was in Hollywood making films, A.P. was nailing his own homemade posters to trees and barns announcing Carter Family concerts and asserting, "This program is morally good." While Rodgers stayed in deluxe hotels, the Carters went home with fans who invited them to spend the night and "take supper."

Things got so bad in 1929, at the peak of their recording career, that the Carters were not even performing together full-time. A.P. went north to find work in Detroit. Maybelle and her husband moved to Washington, D.C. Tension began to grow between A.P. and Sara. For a time, in 1933, they even separated, eventually getting back together to perform with the group. Both women, who did most of the actual singing on the records, were busy raising their young families, and nobody was really making a living with the music. At times it was hard to get together, and A.P. would on occasion use his sister Sylvia to replace Sara or Maybelle if one of them couldn't get free.

The great records continued. There were "I'm Thinking Tonight of My Blue Eyes" and "Wabash Cannonball" in 1929; "Worried Man Blues"

("It takes a worried man to sing a worried song") and "Lonesome Valley" in 1930; "Gold Watch and Chain" in 1933; and then, in 1935, "Can the Circle Be Unbroken?" This was the first recording of the classic song in the form we know it today. The Carters had actually recorded it for Victor in 1933, but the company didn't think enough of it to release it. After they signed with the American Record Company in 1935 (the company that eventually became Columbia), the Carters re-recorded it, with much better results. The song was a textbook case of how A.P. could take an older song and make it relevant to a new audience. This one started out as a rather stuffy gospel song copyrighted by two famous gospel songwriters, Ada R. Habershon and Charles H. Gabriel, under the title "Will the Circle Be Unbroken?" A.P. took the chorus to this song and grafted onto it a new set of lyrics about death and bereavement. The version was issued and reissued throughout the 1930s, eventually appearing on ten different labels. When singers like Hank Williams and Roy Acuff began singing the song in the 1940s, they reverted to the use of the word "will" in the title and the chorus; their usage stuck. But in every other respect, the song was the Carters'.

A.P. was officially the leader of the group, but his real role was that of manager and song-finder or songwriter. He also did emcee work for most of the stage shows and acted as front man, cutting most of the deals. Most of the music, however, was really the work of Sara and Maybelle. Years later, Maybelle recalled of A.P.: "If he felt like singing, he would sing, and if he didn't, he would walk around and look at the window." In one sense, then, the Carter Family could be thought of as country music's first successful female singing group, since most of the records focused on Sara and Maybelle's work. A.P.'s great talent was finding songs; he would travel far into the mountains looking for them. For a time, in those days before tape recorders, he hired a black blues guitarist named Lesley Riddle to go with him; A.P. would write down the words to songs he liked; it was Lesley's job to memorize the music. His association with Lesley gave A.P. a love of the blues, evidenced in hits like "Coal Miner's Blues."

In 1938 the Carters hit big-time radio, moving from the Virginia mountains to the dusty border town of Del Rio, Texas. Here, every morning, they would go into the studios of XERA, a radio station whose transmitter stood across the border in Mexico, and do a show for the Consolidated Royal Chemical Corporation. Border radio stations like XERA aimed their broadcasts into the southern and midwestern parts of the United States, blasting out with a power of over 100,000 watts—a far stronger signal than any legally authorized United States station. The Carters could now be heard throughout much of the country, and their fans multiplied by the tens of thousands. By now, the children were getting old enough to join the act. Sara and A.P.'s daughter, Janette, began her career here, as did Maybelle's three little girls, Helen, June, and Anita. Many of the recordings of these radio shows—known as transcriptions—have since been issued on LP. They give a fascinating picture of wonderful, informal, music-rich broadcasts, replete with commercials for tonic medicines.

Thousands of fan letters poured in, and record sales skyrocketed. By now the group was recording for Decca and doing some of its best work. But bad luck set in again. In 1939 A.P. and Sara split for good; Sara moved to California. Then, in 1941, XERA went off the air. One last chance arose to get together—a six-month contract with radio station WBT in Charlotte. A photographer from *Life* magazine came down to do a major photo spread on the threesome. For a moment, it looked like the big national break might come after all. The photographer filled up a wastebasket with flash bulbs, but the Carters waited in vain for the story to come out. The story, they eventually found out, had been displaced by an even bigger one: the bombing of Pearl Harbor. This was the final disappointment. Sara really called it quits, and A.P. went back to his home in the mountains of Virginia, where he eventually opened a country store. Maybelle started up a new act featuring herself and her daughters, eventually finding her way to Springfield, Missouri, where she teamed up with a young guitar player named Chet Atkins. All the Carters would keep their hand in the music for another twenty years, and all would eventually make more records, but none of these recordings featured the original trio. The act was history. A.P. died in 1960, Maybelle in 1978, and Sara in 1979. Their legacy was a hundred great songs, a standard for duet singing, and a guitar style that helped define the music. As music historian Tony Russell has put it, "Whenever singers and pickers gather to play 'Keep on the Sunny Side' or 'Can the Circle Be Unbroken,' Sara, Maybelle, and A.P. are there, benign and immortal spirits."

THE CARTER FAMILY ON BORDER RADIO

It was October 1938, and another hot afternoon in the border town of Del Rio, Texas. A few miles away was the Rio Grande, and across it the Mexican town of Las Vacas; off to the northwest ran U.S. Highway 3, the "scenic route" that led through Devil's River. To the east, Highway 3 turned back into gravel and dirt—what the maps called an "all-weather road"—and wound some 150 miles to the nearest large town, San Antonio. On the steps of Del Rio's biggest hotel, the Grand, a man named Harry Steele stood waiting, looking up the road toward San

Antonio. He was a radio announcer, working for the Consolidated Royal Chemical Company out of Chicago, a company that made various patent nostrums like Kolorbak (a hair dye) and Peruna (a cough medicine). He was a long way from Chicago now, though, down here in this arid corner of Texas, working on a strange new radio station called XERA. His bosses had found that they could sell boxes and boxes of their products by advertising on the station, especially when the programs featured country singers. Steele was waiting for the newest act on the Consolidated roster, a trio from Virginia named the Carter Family.

The leader of the group, a man named A.P. Carter, had just called to say they were just a few miles out, and Steele had gone out on the porch to wait. Consolidated had sealed its deal with the family by buying them a big new Chevrolet, and eight days before they had started out for Texas from their mountain home in Maces Spring, Virginia. Their first broadcast was scheduled for this evening, and to meet the date, A.P. had been driving ten hours a day over chunky, Depression-era roads. Steele knew they would be exhausted. Finally he saw a big Chevrolet driving slowly down the street, stopping in front of the hotel. It was the dustiest car he had ever seen—much of the road to San Antonio was not then paved—and strapped to the back was something that looked like a motorcycle. (He found out later it belonged to shy little Maybelle.) Steele was not sure this was the right car, but a tall, lanky man got out and squinted up at the hotel. Two women got out of the other door, and a teenage girl from the back. Then Steele was sure who they were. He started down the steps with his hand out to greet them. The Carter Family had arrived in Texas.

It had been just about eleven years before that the odyssey of the Carter Family had begun, with the release of their first Victor record. It had come from that famous session in Bristol, where talent scout Ralph Peer had auditioned both the Carters and Jimmie Rodgers within the space of a few days. Now Rodgers was dead, and the contract with Victor only a bitter memory; they had done over 120 sides for the company, seen some handsome royalty checks, and were still seeing those tunes reissued on Victor's new Bluebird label and through the Montgomery Ward label. But the record checks had been about their only dependable income; the big-time vaudeville and motion picture contracts that had come to Jimmie Rodgers had eluded them; while Rodgers was headlining RKO, A.P. was still booking schoolhouse shows in the mountains, and tacking up posters on trees and barns. Ralph Peer, who was still serving as their personal manager, had been aced out of his job with Victor, but still had a wealth of contacts and was determined to get the Carters a decent gig. He got them record deals with ARC (the American Record Company, now Columbia) and with Decca. Shortly after the last Decca session (in Charlotte in June 1938), Peer called A.P. with the best deal yet; as good as records were, the real money now was in big-time radio, and Peer had an offer from Consolidated to work six months on the border radio station—from October to March, the coldest and most bitter months in the mountains—and then have six months' vacation. For this each member would get $75 a week—both working and on vacation. As a bonus, there was the car. Not only was it decent money, Peer reminded them, but it was a chance at a national radio audience—a chance to expand their audience beyond the Southeast. In spite of the relocation problems, and the growing families of both women, no one had to think very long. Texas it was.

Just why South Texas had become the country music radio capital in the mid-1930s was another story. It all started with a "radio doctor" named John R. Brinkley, who got in trouble in Kansas for selling a goat gland remedy (for virility) over the air. In 1932, to escape prosecution, he set up a new radio station, XER, with studios in Del Rio, Texas, but with a transmitter across the border in Mexico. At that time, the Federal Radio Commission had a limit of 50,000 watts for all American stations; Mexico did not, and XER had soon boosted its power to an incredible 500,000 watts. With this, it could blanket most of the continental United States, drowning out and overriding many of the domestic stations. XER changed its call letters to XERA in 1935, and was soon joined by a host of other "X" stations using a similar technique; by the time the Carters arrived in 1938, there were no fewer than eleven such stations. They became outlets for dozens of American companies offering a wide range of dubious mail-order products: cancer cures, hair restoratives, patent medicines like Crazy Water Crystals ("for regularity"), baby chickens, "Resurrection plants," and even autographed pictures of Jesus Christ. It didn't take the advertisers long to figure out that their long-winded pitches worked best when surrounded by country music, and by the mid-1930s a veritable parade of record stars were making the long drive down Highway 3. The Pickard Family, formerly of the Grand Ole Opry, came down in 1936; Jessie Rodgers (Jimmie's cousin) came, as did Cowboy Slim Rinehart. J. E. Mainer's Mountaineers, fresh from their success with "Maple on the Hill," came down to work for Crazy Water Crystals.

The Carters soon found themselves at the center of this hectic new world. The very night they arrived, they were asked to make out a list of songs they could do on the spot, and then were rushed into the studio. At 8:10, the *Consolidated Chemical Radio Hour* took to the air live; it ran for two hours, and was filled with a bizarre variety of singers, comedians, and announcers. The Carters were not on mike the whole time, but they were the stars, and they carried the lion's share of the work. Their sound was pretty much the way it had been on records: Sara played the autoharp, Maybelle the guitar. Now, though, there were fewer duets between Sara and A.P.—the pair had been separated for several years and would get a divorce in 1939—and A.P. himself sang more solos and even began to feature his own guitar playing on the air. There was more trio singing now, and more plugging of records, including the recent Decca sides like "Coal Miner's Blues" and "Stern Old Bachelor" and "Little Joe." Janette, A.P. and Sara's teenage daughter, began to do an occasional solo. (Later, Maybelle's children would join them as well.)

The family soon found that they would be earning the salary, and that, regardless of how glamorous it sounded, regular radio broadcasting could be grueling. Their contract called for them to broadcast twice a day, six days a week; afternoons were taken up with rehearsals, and some mornings were given over to cutting transcriptions for the station to play for their early morning show; one hard morning's work would yield enough recorded programs to allow the group to sleep in the other days. Then, every evening at 8:10, there was the live show to do; "You hardly had any time to yourself," Maybelle recalled. Though Maybelle's husband, Eck, was able to come down and join them later that year, Maybelle missed her children, whom she had left with relatives in Virginia. The first year in the big time was rougher than they had ever imagined.

It was doing wonders for the Carter Family music, though. For a time, it was hard to tell just how well the shows were going over. At the end of their shows, however, announcer Harry Steele reminded listeners to send in box tops from Consolidated products to get free gifts, such as a Bible or a picture. (The idea was to build a mailing list.) Soon the Carters were generating some 25,000 box tops a week—to the delight of the company. June Carter later recalled that during this time you could hang a tin can on any barbed-wire fence in Texas and hear the Carter Family. But the signals carried far beyond Texas; when the group got back to their home in Virginia after that season, they found 5,000 fan letters waiting for them. Their Decca and ARC record sales boomed as never before; tens of thousands were sold on the dark red Conqueror label through Sears catalogs. Suddenly, the Carters were America's singing group.

Delighted with these results, Consolidated quickly signed the family on for a second season, to run from October 1939 to March 1940. This season saw a host of changes. For one thing, both Maybelle and Sara decided they wanted their children with them. Before the end of the first year, Maybelle's youngest girl, Anita, had joined them, as well as

Janette, then fifteen. In an era of child stars on the radio (like Little Jimmie Sizemore), six-year-old Anita had emerged as a special favorite with fans, and letters had poured in praising her. The older kids back in Virginia were understandably jealous. June recalled: "At night we listened to the powerful signal coming up from Texas, lying on our stomachs with our chins in our hands, me and Helen. Then Anita's voice would come over the air, and at first we didn't believe it was her. . . . It didn't seem right that Anita should be down in Texas with Mother, singing so well on the radio." Both June (now ten) and Helen (now twelve) wrote letters to Del Rio, begging to come down, and now Maybelle agreed. June would play autoharp and guitar, and Helen guitar, and all three of Maybelle's children would sing together as an act. The only problem was that June didn't really want to sing, and Maybelle was not sure she could carry her share; June remembers her mother saying, "If you're gonna be on the world's largest radio station with us—we'll need some kind of miracle."

But the second season was a miracle of sorts, and all the Carter children found parts on the show. A new announcer had arrived, Brother Bill Rinehart, and it was he who emceed the shows and often delivered a moral at the end of the songs. A typical show would start off with the whole family opening with their theme song, "Keep on the Sunny Side," and then go into a favorite like "Goin' Back to Texas," with A.P., Sara, and Maybelle. Then Maybelle and Sara might do a duet like "Cowboy Jack," and A.P. a solo like "Diamonds in the Rough." Then June, Helen, and Anita would do a piece like "I've Been Working on the Railroad," and Janette a solo like "The Last Letter," then a current hit. There was usually time for an instrumental—Sara and Maybelle doing "Shortening Bread" or "Red Wing"—and then another gospel standard like "What Would You Give in Exchange for Your Soul."

By now the family was putting more and more of its programs on big sixteen-inch electrical transcriptions. This gave them a little more time off, and allowed Maybelle and her daughters to live in San Antonio. This was convenient, because most of these transcriptions were recorded in the basement of the San Antonio home of Don Baxter, the station's engineer. From a thirty-minute show on disc, Baxter could then dub off copies, and send the transcriptions to other border stations such as XEG and XENT. This helped "network" the Carter music even further, and their fame continued to rise. (After the demise of the border stations, many of these big shiny transcriptions were tossed out, and for years farmers in the area used them to shingle their chicken houses.)

For the family itself, though, things were becoming as uncertain as the war clouds that were gathering in Europe. The break between Sara and A.P. had become permanent, and on February 20, 1939, Sara married A.P.'s cousin, Coy Bayes, at Brackettville, Texas. Family tales tell of A.P. standing at the back of the church, staring vacantly at the ceremony. As Sara's new husband prepared a home for them in California, she boarded with Maybelle and her kids. A.P. and his children lived in Alamo Heights. Though he still arranged songs with his customary genius, he began to take less and less interest in choosing repertoire for the shows; for a time, he got involved in directing a choir for the local Methodist church, sometimes even arranging old Carter Family songs for it.

By March 1941, XERA was off the air, and the colorful era of border radio was coming to an end. It also meant, for all practical purposes, an end to the original Carter Family. A.P. would return to Poor Valley, never to remarry, never to match the fame he had had on XERA. Sara would retire from the business and go to California. Maybelle would remain in radio, working her children into her act, and eventually make her way to Nashville. There would be an aborted comeback in 1943, but basically the Carter Family was ended. But the border radio years had been invaluable for them—and for country music. It was here that their wonderful harmonies had made their impact on a national audience, and helped spread classic country singing styles across the land. It was here, too, that the Carters passed the torch to their next generation, and set the stage for later careers of Joe, Janette, June, Helen, and Anita. Though the old transcriptions with Brother Bill Rinehart might be rusting on dilapidated chicken houses, the Carter Family sound would live on.

THE CARTER SISTERS AND MOTHER MAYBELLE

It was the winter of 1942–43, and the Original Carter Family was making its last stand over radio station WBT in Charlotte, North Carolina. Since 1927, when they made their first recordings at the famous Bristol sessions, A.P. and Sara Carter, along with their younger cousin Maybelle, had dominated the new field of country harmony singing. They had recorded their classic hits like "Wildwood Flower," "I'm Thinking Tonight of My Blue Eyes," "Keep on the Sunny Side," and "Gold Watch and Chain" for every major record label, and since 1938 had spread their music all around the nation over the powerful "border radio" stations along the Rio Grande. But times were changing; Sara Carter had divorced A.P., remarried, and moved to California. Maybelle had married at sixteen to A.P.'s brother, Ezra (Eck) Carter, and had started her family: three daughters named Helen, Anita, and June. The big border stations had closed down, and the record business, beset by shellac shortages from the war, was a shadow of its former self. Small wonder that when a company called Drug Trade Products offered A.P. a twenty-week contract to work the winter at WBT, he accepted. WBT was a 50,000-watt station with a huge coverage and a good cast of other musicians, and the money was too good to pass up. For the last time, the Original Carters gathered together again, moving into the Roosevelt Hotel on South Tryon Street in Charlotte because of the housing shortage.

Maybelle Carter was forty-five that year; she had blossomed from the shy, small, dark-eyed guitar player into a seasoned and confident musician and songwriter, and had even contributed several original songs to the last Carter Family Victor session the year before. Her husband, Ezra, had recently taken early retirement from his job on the railroad (due to low blood pressure) and was interested in seeing Maybelle form her own group with her girls. By now the two oldest, Helen and June, were in high school, and Anita, the baby, was barely eleven. All three had gained entertainment experience when their mother had brought them onto the border radio shows in 1939. Helen sang and played the guitar, June the autoharp, and even little Anita would sing and play guitar. The old radio transcriptions from XET showed the kids doing their own specialties on the show—June strumming the autoharp and singing "Engine 143," all of them together doing "Give Me the Roses While I Live" and "Somewhere a-Working for My Lord." The Carter Sisters, as they were starting to be called, had decided they wanted to try for a career as they finished school, and Maybelle was agreeable. All this took on a new excitement when *Life* magazine sent down a photographer to document the family's music at Charlotte; for a time, it looked like a cover story and a chance for the Original Carter Family to get the national publicity it had been needing. But after doing a long series of photos, both in Charlotte and back home in Poor Valley, the magazine decided war news was more pressing, and the project was scrapped. The last hope of keeping the original group together had vanished. Thus when the contract at Charlotte expired, A.P. decided to return to Virginia, while Sara went back to the West Coast with her new husband. "It really wasn't all Dad's decision," recalls A.P. and Sara's son, Joe. "Maybelle had been wanting to strike out with the girls for some time. When she got that offer to go up to Richmond and be on the radio, they thought it was a good deal."

Maybelle's group returned to Maces Spring that spring for some R&R, and then in June 1943 headed for Richmond. At first they did a commercially sponsored program for the Nolde Brothers Bakery over WRNL as "The Carter Sisters." Then, in September 1946, the group was asked by WRVA's leading star, Sunshine Sue, to become members of a new show that was starting up, to be called the *Old Dominion Barn Dance.* Sunshine Sue Workman was a native of Iowa, and had won a solid reputation appearing on various Midwest programs through the 1930s. She had arrived at WRVA in January 1940, and was a natural choice to be host of the new barn dance program; in doing so, she became the first woman emcee of any major barn dance show. Her music featured her own accordion and warm, soft voice doing songs like "You Are My Sunshine." Like Maybelle, she was juggling being a wife and mother with being a radio star; she also, by the late 1940s, was planning the *Barn Dance* shows and organizing touring groups.

By March 1947 the new barn dance was doing daily shows from a local theater from 3 P.M. to 4 P.M.; soon, though, it moved to Saturday nights, where WRVA's 50,000 watts of power sent it up and down the East Coast. In addition to the Carter Sisters, who were now getting headline billing, the early cast included Sunshine Sue's husband, John Workman, who with his brother headed up the staff band, the Rangers; Joe and Rose Lee Maphis (with the fine guitarist being billed as "Crazy Joe"); the veteran North Carolina band the Tobacco Tags; and local favorites like singer Benny Kissinger, champion fiddler Curley Collins, and the remarkable steel guitar innovator Slim Idaho.

By 1950 the cast had grown to a hundred, and included major national figures like Chick Stripling, Grandpa and Ramona Jones, Toby Stroud, and Jackie Phelps. The station's general manager, John Tansey, worked closely with Sunshine Sue to make the *Old Dominion Barn Dance* a major player in country radio. At the end of its first year, it was filling its 1,400-seat theater two times every Saturday night, and by December 1947 it could brag it had played to 100,000 "paid admissions." The Carters realized they were riding a winner.

As always, success on radio also meant a bruising round of week-night concerts in schoolhouses and small theaters. Eck Carter did a lot of driving in his Frazier, and on the way there was time to rehearse new songs. June Carter recalls: "The back seat became a place where we learned to sing our parts. Helen always on key, Anita on key, and a good steady glare to remind me that I was a little sharp or flat. . . . Traveling in the early days became a world of cheap gas stations, hamburgers, tourist homes, and old hotels with stairs to climb. We worked the Kemp Time circuit, the last of the vaudeville days, and the yearning to keep on singing or traveling just a little further never left." And in spite of their growing popularity, the sisters continued to hear the border radio transcriptions of the Original Family over many of the stations—proof, it seemed, the old Carter sound was not yet as passé as some thought it was. By now Helen had learned to play the accordion (à la Sunshine Sue), and Anita was standing on a box and playing the bass fiddle.

The early days at Richmond were especially hard on June. Helen had already graduated from the high school back in Hiltons, but June was just coming up on her senior year, and she would be spending it in a large Richmond school called John Marshall High School. She was self-conscious about her accent (in which a touch of Texas drawl had been added to her Poor Valley dialect), her looks, and the way in which she would be hoofing across some theater stage at night instead of doing homework. She remembers: "I took a good look at myself. My hair went just where it wanted to go, and I was singing those hillbilly songs on that radio station every day and somewhere on a stage every night. I just didn't have the east Virginia 'couth' those girls had." In response to her problems with singing on pitch, and her natural volubility, she began to turn to comedy. "I had created a crazy country character named Aunt Polly Carter, who would do anything for a laugh. She wore a flat hat and pointed shoes and did all kinds of old vaudeville bits." She also sometimes wore elaborate bloomers, since in her dance steps her feet were often above her head. And for a time, part of the act had her swinging by a rope out over the audience. But she managed to have a great senior year at her new school—she learned to read "round notes" and to sing in the girls' choir, and to make new and lasting friends. But in 1946, when it was all over, she cried because there was no way she could follow her friends off to college.

The Carter Sisters spent five good years in Richmond, and by the time they left, the girls had all become seasoned professionals, and the group was no longer being confused with the Original Carter Family: it had an identity, and a sound, of its own. In 1948, they took a new job over WNOX in Knoxville, Tennessee, where they played on the evening show, the *Tennessee Barn Dance*, and the daily show, the *Mid-Day Merry-Go-Round*.

Though the former dated from 1941, and the latter from the 1930s, the station was hitting its stride in the late 40s and was being thought of as a AAA farm club for the national shows like the Opry. Regulars included Archie Campbell, Homer and Jethro, the Bailey Brothers, Wally Fowler and the Oak Ridge Quartet, Carl Smith, Pappy "Gube" Beaver, the Carlisles, the Louvin Brothers, Cowboy Copas, and such strange novelty acts as Little Moses, the Human Lodestone. One of those who was amazed at the popularity of the Carters was a young guitar player named Chet Atkins: "They were an instant success. Crowds flocked into the auditorium every day to see them; the crowds were so heavy at the *Barn Dance* on Saturday night that you had to come early even to get in." He was thus surprised and pleased when Eck came to him one day and offered him a job traveling with the group. "We'll cut you in for one-sixth of what we make," he said. "That's equal shares for each of us."

Soon Atkins was crowding into the back seat of Eck's Frazier as they headed out after the Saturday Knoxville show to play in one of the big music parks in Pennsylvania. During all of this time, the Carter Sisters and Mother Maybelle, for all of their success in radio, had not recorded on their own. This was finally remedied on February 2, 1949, when the entire ensemble traveled to Atlanta to record a double session for RCA Victor. They produced eight sides; the first two issued were "The Kneeling Drunkard's Plea," which was credited to them, and "My Darling's Home Again," which they had gotten from Johnnie and Jack. More popular were "Why Do You Weep, Dear Willow," from Lynn Davis and Molly O'Day, and "Someone's Last Day." June added a couple of novelties, "Root Hog or Die" and "The Baldheaded End of the Broom." The sales were above average—some of the sides were among the very first to be issued by RCA on the new 45 rpm "doughnut" records—and the band was quickly scheduled for another session later that year. In the meantime, on May 17, 1949, June lent her comedy talents to the first RCA session by Homer and Jethro. In New York City, they did a takeoff on the pop song "Baby, It's Cold Outside." It got onto the charts, established Homer and Jethro as comic "song butchers," and established nineteen-year-old June as a comedienne in her own right.

June 1949 saw the troupe once again uprooted, this time headed for KWTO in Springfield, Missouri. The small towns around southern Missouri and northern Arkansas offered new audiences for personal appearances, and the Radiozark company was making the station into a center for transcribed shows. Helen recalls: "We did two or three radio shows a day, worked every night, and got up in the morning and started all over again."

Chet Atkins was still with them, though the girls were increasingly concerned about his debilitating asthma attacks. June remembers: "Chester and I set up the public address system, and he'd have those asthma attacks and I'd have to lug the stuff in." But two things of lasting interest happened in the year they stayed in Springfield: they cut a series of thirty-nine fifteen-minute transcriptions which featured a good cross-section of their repertoire, as well as some fine Atkins solos. (Copies of these have survived, and deserve reissue.) And Helen, the oldest of the girls, got married, in March 1950, to a young man named Glenn Jones.

In June 1950 the group, with Atkins, got an offer to join the Opry and moved to Nashville. Things got complicated in the next few years, as the other two girls got married as well. Anita chose a young, hot fiddle player named Dale Potter, while June said yes to a young singer she had met in Knoxville who had just joined the Opry, Carl Smith. While the three sisters still got together with their mother for recording sessions and radio shows, each began to be interested in a solo career. June created a band called the Bashful Rascals and made her first solo try on RCA in August 1950 with a single called "Bashful Rascal." At the same session, Anita tried her first solo with a song called "Somebody's Crying." Helen tried her hand with the new independent label, Tennessee, cutting a duet with Opry announcer Grant Turner ("Heaven's Decision"), another one with Don Davis ("Sparrow in the Treetop"), and a couple of solo efforts (including "Fiddling Around"). In February 1952, all of them signed with Columbia, where they would largely remain for the next two decades.

In 1951 Anita also began working as a duet partner to RCA's hottest current star, Hank Snow; their version of "Bluebird Island" reached Number Four on the Top 10 charts. A little later Anita would become duet partners with singers like Johnny Darrell and Waylon Jennings. In 1955 RCA producer Steve Sholes paired her with Rita Robbins and Kitty Wells's daughter, Ruby, to form a rockabilly trio called Nita, Rita, and Ruby. No big hits resulted from the experiment, but they did some of the earliest female rockabilly, and recorded songs that ranged from pieces by the Everly Brothers to Cindy Walker ("Give Me Love").

Mother Maybelle continued to work on the package shows, including several of Snow's, where she met and took a shine to a young Elvis Presley. June recalls: "She'd drive all night getting us in from somewhere and we would be exhausted, but she was wanting to go bowling at some all-night lane." By the early 1960s, Maybelle had been discovered by the young college audiences of the "folk revival," and she began to make some solo appearances at places like the Newport Folk Festival, performing the older songs and conducting guitar and autoharp workshops. (She had begun to play the autoharp after moving to Nashville.) June, for her part, took her solo career in a different direction: she moved to New York to studying acting with Elia Kazan, and eventually landed acting roles in TV shows like *Gunsmoke* and *Jim Bowie*. By 1963, after a second marriage to Rip Nix, she had joined Johnny Cash's show.

Throughout the 1950s, labels like Columbia and RCA kept cutting singles of the Carter Sisters and Mother Maybelle as a group and as individuals. When A.P. Carter died in 1960, Maybelle felt comfortable in taking the name "the Carter Family" for her organization, and in 1962 used it on the cover of their first real LP, *The Carter Family Album* on Mercury. Many of these early LPs were filled with versions of old Carter songs from the '20s and '30s, though a superb 1963 solo album by Anita contained a bevy of new songs done by modern Nashville tunesmiths—including the first recording of "Ring of Fire." In 1963, the Carter Family as a group joined Johnny Cash's successful road show, and celebrated the event by cutting their first Columbia record, "Keep on the Sunny Side" (with Johnny Cash). June and Johnny married in 1968.

Albums of all sorts now began to flow during the late '60s and '70s, many with the full family, some featuring Maybelle, some featuring one of the girls, some featuring other groups like Flatt and Scruggs and the Nitty Gritty Dirt Band. By 1974, yet a third generation of Carters was making its mark, with the Columbia LP *Three Generations*. June's daughter, Carlene, started a solo career in 1978, achieving great success in recent years. Maybelle herself began struggling with arthritis and a type of Parkinson's disease, and by the mid-1970s her legendary energy was beginning to run down. There was time for one last album, *Country's First Family*, cut at the House of Cash studio in February 1976; it was an engaging mix of old Carter songs and new Nashville ones. Maybelle died on October 28, 1978, knowing that there were new generations of Carters to carry on the work.

Roy Acuff

Just how popular was Roy Acuff during his heyday? In the latter days of World War II, Japanese soldiers in the Pacific would try to psych out American Marines by yelling taunts like, "To hell with Franklin Roosevelt! To hell with Babe Ruth! To hell with Roy Acuff!" Back in San Diego, soldiers and sailors from all over the country would hold "Roy Acuff contests," in which the object was to see who could do the best imitation of the singer. Acuff records were so popular that the government had to issue them on V-discs so overseas troops could hear hits like "Low and Lonely." It was not unusual for 15,000 fans to show up at Acuff concerts, and not unusual to see the Acuff name ranking with Frank Sinatra and Benny Goodman in popularity polls among servicemen. Nobody in the music business was really surprised to see Roy Acuff run for governor of Tennessee in 1948.

Modern fans who are used to seeing Roy Acuff as the stately, white-haired elder statesman of the Grand Ole Opry may wonder what all the fuss is about and whether Acuff's role is partially the result of Opry hype. It isn't. Acuff was actually the music's first great stylist after the death of Jimmie Rodgers and was a major influence on younger singers like Hank Williams, Lefty Frizzell, and George Jones. Though he's had only three modest hits since 1950, his continual presence on the Grand Ole Opry gave him a platform from which he continued to influence country music: as a publisher, a media pioneer, a spokesman, and, in later years, a defender of older traditions and performers. His nickname, "The King of Country Music," may sound a bit mawkish and old-fashioned, but, in many ways, it is remarkably accurate.

Acuff actually came from the Smoky Mountains. He was born in Maynardville, Tennessee, on September 15, 1903. He was born at home, "in a little three-room house," he recalled, modest circumstances even though his father had attended a local college and served as a lawyer and as the preacher of the local Baptist church. His father taught him to play the fiddle and sent him to an occasional church singing school, but as a teenager Roy was more interested in baseball and fighting. "There was nothing I loved as much as a physical fight," he said, and though he was small for his age, he soon developed a reputation as a scrapper around Knoxville, where he'd moved. Old-timers still talk about a brawl in which Roy took on seven local policemen at a ballpark melee and wound up in jail.

Though he was a good enough ball player to be invited to a major league training camp for a tryout, he suffered a severe sunstroke on a fishing trip to Florida in 1929. While recovering, he honed his skill as a fiddler and apprenticed himself to a local medicine show man, Doc Hauer. Here he learned show business: the comedy, the hucksterism, the way to work an audience. He did imitations—he had learned to do a neat train whistle while working as a railroad "call boy" as a teenager—and tricks that called for balancing things on his nose. These skills led to a job on Knoxville's WROL with a local band called the Tennessee Crackerjacks. An announcer later dubbed the band "the Crazy Tennesseans," and soon they were playing $25 schoolhouse gigs all over east Tennessee. "Mostly, we fiddled and starved," Roy remembered.

All this changed one day in early 1936. Acuff and fellow band member Red Jones met up with a young Bible college student named Charley Swain, who had been working part-time as a radio singer. Swain had been featuring an unusual gospel song called "The Great Speckled Bird," which both Red and Roy liked. When Roy learned that Swain was moving and would not be singing the song in Knoxville anymore, he offered him 50 cents to write down the words. Swain agreed—though Jones recalled, "We had to borrow an extra quarter to pay him." Soon Acuff was singing the song over WROL; that October it landed them a recording deal with the American Recording Company. In 1938, when Acuff and his band were offered a chance to audition for the Grand Ole Opry, "Great Speckled Bird" was one of the songs he sang. Thousands of letters poured in, and the surprised Opry management realized they had a new star on their hands.

At first, the Acuff band—now dubbed the Smoky Mountain Boys, a name the Opry management thought more dignified than the Crazy Tennesseans—tried to follow the western swing formula, mixing old-time country with pop material like "Coney Island Baby." Roy didn't like this, though, and in 1939 three members left. Among the replacements Roy recruited was Pete "Oswald" Kirby, whose soulful tenor singing and breathtaking dobro work soon became permanent elements in the Acuff sound. Roy's preference for the "mountain sound" over the western sound was underscored when he became the star of the NBC network portion of the Opry in 1939. It was also an issue in the seven Hollywood films he made in the 1940s, when he refused the demands of Hollywood directors to turn his outfit into a cowboy band.

Fans rewarded him with hit records. The lonesome, sentimental songs were the biggest: "Beneath That Lonely Mound of Clay" (1940), "The Precious Jewel" (1940), "Wreck on the Highway" (1942), "Fire Ball Mail" (1942), "Wait for the Light to Shine" (1944) and "Two Different Worlds" (1945). "Wabash Cannonball," an old song that had been recorded in the 1920s by the Carter Family, had been a favorite with Acuff audiences since the Crazy Tennesseans first recorded it back in 1936. Ironically, Roy did not sing the song on that record; Dynamite Hatcher did. It wasn't until 1947 that Roy recut the song for Columbia, able to sing his own theme song on wax at last.

In 1942, primarily to preserve his own publishing interests, Acuff joined forces with veteran songwriter Fred Rose to open the first modern publishing company in Nashville, Acuff-Rose. It was immediately successful, and later became a major country publisher, signing everyone from Don Gibson to the Louvin Brothers to Hank Williams. This business interest helped Acuff survive the hard times of the 1950s and enabled him to take advantage of the folk revival of the 1960s.

By the 1970s he had decided to return to his roots, to the older, acoustic sounds that had first brought him fame. Following his participation in the 1971 Nitty Gritty Dirt Band collection *Will the Circle Be Unbroken* (a project he was initially dubious about), Acuff saw his audience expand dramatically. In the years since, he has continued to follow his instincts, honing his fiddle playing, resurrecting old songs, and defending the faith to a Nashville scene that all too often has a short memory of its music's past.

On June 28, 1940, readers of the Nashville *Tennessean* opened their morning papers and saw something they had never seen before: a large display ad for a film titled *The Grand Ole Opry*. There was a picture of George D. Hay—the Solemn Ole Judge, the show's founder—standing right in front of a WSM microphone, decked out in his best summer skimmer and whitest spats, holding his script, smiling big. "Please don't pardon our southern accent when we say YOU ALL," the copy read. "Secure your tickets now to see Judge Hay, Roy Acuff and his Smoky Mountain Boys, with Rachael and Uncle Dave Macon—on the stage and screen at the WORLD PREMIER of Republic's full length feature picture GRAND OLE OPRY." Nashville's hillbilly radio show had finally made it to the big time. True, the celebrations in Nashville could hardly match the hoopla of just a few months before, when its sister city of Atlanta had premiered *Gone With the Wind.* Republic, which ground out budget films at the rate of two or three a month, was not exactly MGM. But this was still a first, a very big first, and WSM was hoping the film would do for mountain music what Gene Autry's Republic efforts had done for cowboy music—make it a nationwide phenomenon.

The night started with a big "free" square dance at Memorial Square in downtown Nashville. Then the various dignitaries, including Tennessee governor Prentice Cooper, Acuff and the Opry stars, WSM announcers and dozens of reporters from papers as far away as Cleveland, Knoxville, Memphis, Atlanta, Birmingham, and Detroit, assembled for a parade to the Paramount Theater. Attired in top hats, riding in horse-drawn carriages, the procession made its way downtown, where Hay and Acuff were to appear on stage for a brief program before the film rolled. It all worked, and soon the guests were watching a sur-realistic version of how the Grand Ole Opry was founded—as a campaign plot to get "Abner Peabody" elected governor. The Weaver Brothers and Elviry, veteran vaudeville troopers from Arkansas, were featured along with Acuff. Fans got to see a very soulful version of Roy singing "Great Speckled Bird," a stately "Wabash Cannonball," and a rousing "Down in Union Country," sung with the band in an old Model A Ford bouncing down a Tennessee hill. There was also a boisterous scene where Roy fiddled for a square dance and even called a set or two. Though he did not receive top billing for the film—his name was actu-ally listed under Uncle Dave Macon's—Acuff's singing stole the show. In later weeks, as the film toured nationwide, Republic officials sensed they had a new star for more Acuff films.

For Roy himself, that evening in 1940 was an important step on his road to truly national fame. He had been on the Grand Ole Opry only a little over two years, fresh from his background and boyhood in east Tennessee, where he had played the fiddle and organized a string band called the Crazy Tennesseans. Too many stories about Acuff emphasize this past; his debut on the Opry, and then—poof!—he is a living legend and Japanese soldiers are taunting American GIs by saying, "To hell with Babe Ruth! To hell with Roy Acuff!" But a number of very specific and very important events occured in Roy's career during the early 1940s, events that really propelled him from an average Opry star to a national sensation, an earlier generation's version of Garth Brooks. These were Acuff's glory days, and as they changed him, he in turn changed coun-try music.

Even before his Hollywood debut, Acuff had begun to sense that things were starting to go his way. The letters that poured in at the Opry seldom had much to say about his fiddling, but were raving about his singing. "I didn't realize how different my singing was from the rest until mail started coming in," he said. The letters would mention "how distinct my voice was, and how they could understand my words." Early in 1939, he reorganized his band, bringing in Lonnie Wilson, Pete "Oswald" Kirby, comedian Jake Tindell, and a cousin of Sam McGee's named Rachael Veach. This gave the band more versatility and made Roy the only featured vocalist.

Then, on October 14, 1939, the Grand Ole Opry signed a deal with the NBC radio network. The show had been on the air since 1925, but for most of that time it had originated only as a "clear-channel" broadcast live from WSM Nashville. "Clear channel" meant that no other station anywhere in the country was assigned to WSM's 650 wavelength, and that the 50,000-watt WSM signal could be heard widely. But now, with the NBC hookup, parts of the Grand Ole Opry would be heard literally nationwide—at first on some NBC stations, eventually on all. Chosen for the network segment was the so-called Prince Albert Show portion of the Opry, one that featured Roy and his band. Thus every Saturday night Acuff's music was carried into an imposing number of homes, reaching many who knew little of country music, and others who could now hear the Prince Albert portion more clearly than they could the other sections of the Opry. Though Acuff didn't do the kind of announcing he would do in later years (the announcing was handled by Judge Hay, reading from clever scripts), he handled scripts well, was quick with an appropriate ad lib, and displayed an easygoing humility. Fans began to see what Roy was really all about. As he began to specialize more and more in heart-tugging sentimental songs like "Don't Make Me Go to Bed and I'll Be Good," fans were impressed with how seriously he took the songs. On one particular show in early 1940, Acuff began singing an old piece called "That Beautiful Picture," spun it out for a full four or five minutes, and by the end, according to witnesses, tears were literally streaming down his cheeks. The audience went wild with applause. Even on the tight network schedule, Opry management let Roy come back on stage for an encore, to do another couple of verses. It was all part of the magic of his appeal, and now it was being heard on NBC as well.

It was also during this time—the years between 1940 and 1943—that Roy produced his biggest group of hit records. His "Great Speckled Bird" and "Wabash Cannonball" had been cut and made into hits even before he came to the Opry, but now came the second wave—the ones that got on the *Billboard* charts, onto the jukeboxes, onto radio shows across the country. There was the one that started with the plaintive, "Way back in the hills . . ."—"The Precious Jewel." Roy wrote it himself, driving the band car to a show date one evening. "Rachael sat beside me and took the words down," he recalled; the melody he borrowed from an old prison song called "Hills of Roane County." Then there was "Wreck on the Highway," the song "where whiskey and blood ran together," which was recorded in May 1942. As with "Precious Jewel," this one featured a "screaming tenor" by Oswald—no-holds-barred mountain music as its best. (On one such session, Oswald's voice gave out, and he had to reinforce it with a bottle of the song's subject.) There were the other great train songs, "Fire Ball Mail" (1942) and "Night Train to Memphis" (1942). Serious Acuff fans also remember a few chart hits that aren't so well-known today: "The Prodigal Son" (1942), "I'll Forgive You But I Can't Forget" (1944), and a rollicking song about the newfangled Social Security system called "Old Age Pension Check" (1939). Most of these records came out on the old purple Okeh label, then a subsidiary of Columbia.

During his early recording days, Roy had almost lost the rights to a number of his songs to a clever A&R man. As his records now took off, he began to sense that there was money to be made from the songs as well. In 1941 his wife, Mildred, got together a sheaf of his favorite songs, as well as some snapshots of the band, took them to a local printer in Nashville, and came up with a little souvenir songbook. They sold these for 25 cents each to fans at shows in schoolhouses and auditoriums, and even bought time to advertise over WSM, offering them for sale by mail. This was by no means a novel idea—Opry singers had been doing this for ten years—but the sentimental Acuff songs struck such a chord that thousands of fans responded. Quarters—actual quarters, not checks or money orders—rolled in. Mildred had to hire extra help to get the books in the mail, and soon she was carrying quarters to the local bank in bushel baskets.

Now came letters from northern publishers wanting to strike a deal to include Acuff songs in their folios and books. "The fourth New York publisher had offered up to $2,500 a song for nearly anything I could write," Roy recalled. This only made him suspicious that his songs were worth even more. About this same time, he got a letter from a lawyer in South Carolina representing a local textile worker, Dorsey Dixon, who claimed ownership of "Wreck on the Highway," which was becoming popular. Dixon had copyrighted the song as "I Didn't Hear Any Body Pray" in 1938, though he had actually bought the song from a popular North Carolina radio singer, Wade Mainer. As it turned out, Roy answered that he had not tried to copyright the song, and he eventually reached an accommodation with Dixon. But the episode showed him that as his popularity grew, the songs he sang were becoming important properties and needed special attention. The days of casually picking up an old "public domain" folk ballad were over.

Thus in 1942 Acuff made what would be the most important and most lucrative decision of his career: He sought out veteran songwriter Fred Rose and asked him if he would be interested in starting up a publishing company. Rose was a forty-five-year-old native of Evansville, Indiana, who had grown up in St. Louis and Chicago; during the late 1920s, he had been a popular radio singer and pianist and even recorded pop songs for the Brunswick Company. He had been to Nashville in the early 1930s, before Roy came to the Opry, and had then gone to Hollywood to write cowboy songs for Gene Autry films. He knew the big-city publishing business well and had learned how to write just about any kind of song. In fact, in the spring of 1942, Rose's friend Art Satherley, the Columbia A&R man, submitted "Fire Ball Mail" to Roy, a song Rose had penned under a pseudonym. Roy liked it enough to record it, and only later found out Rose had actually written it. This so impressed the singer that, he said, "I went to Fred Rose and made him an offer I hoped he couldn't refuse." Roy offered Rose a partnership in a new Nashville-based publishing company. Roy would put up $25,000 seed money, and Rose would completely run the company. At the center of the catalog would be songs by Acuff and by Rose. Sensing the time might be right for a country music publisher, one located right in Nashville, Rose agreed, and on October 13, 1942, Acuff-Rose was born. (For legal reasons, the actual partnership was signed between Fred and Mildred Acuff.) Within two months, Fred came to Roy and said, "I think we need a little bigger place"—the new company was taking off. Eventually, of course, it would be the most famous publisher in Nashville, with catalogs that ran from Hank Williams to the Everly Brothers.

Going into the 1940s, Roy and the band traveled like any other Opry group, grinding over old two-lane highways in Packards and Fords; their dream, Roy recalled, was to do a show where their gate would crack $100. As the radio, the films, the records, and the songs began to work their magic, the tours began to grow as well. By 1943, some of their shows at southern fairs were attracting as many as 16,000 fans. For a time, Roy decided to travel with his own tent show—a fleet of trucks, the entertainers, a crew of roustabouts to put up the tents, a set of cooks to feed everybody, and a sound crew to set up the sound. "We started out in Georgia in early spring and worked our way up north, up through the Carolinas and Virginias, up to Ohio," Roy recalled.

"And then we worked down the Southwest to Oklahoma and Texas by fall." Three thousand people a night was common. By now, too, Roy had hired his own bookers, and his promotion was getting better. Somebody booking the Acuff band now could get: (1) preprinted window cards and posters; (2) movie trailers in sound for use in local theaters; (3) pre-recorded radio interviews and Acuff records; and (4) press stories ready to go. In some communities, churches even dismissed Wednesday services when the show was in town. Small wonder that by 1943, Acuff was making up to $200,000 a year—a fortune in those days.

Roy's success story of the early 1940s is even more impressive when given the obstacles he had to overcome. His biggest record hits came in the early days of the war, when a shortage of shellac crippled the record companies. The recording ban of 1942–44 meant that he could make no new records then, and had to rely on recycled masters from earlier years. Wartime gasoline shortages soon caused problems with touring, too. Then there was Hollywood. Republic called Roy back for seven more films, including *Hi Neighbor* (1942), *O'my Darling Clementine* (1943), *Sing, Neighbor, Sing* (1944) and *Night Train to Memphis* (1946). The pictures helped Roy's popularity, but he had to fight constantly with directors who wanted him to don cowboy clothes and become the next Gene Autry. Though he did one film with cowboy hats, Roy refused to sell himself as a singing cowboy. "I told them my music was mountain music, not western music," he said. At a time when the cowboy craze was sweeping the country and other country bands were becoming cowboy bands (even on the Opry), it took courage to toe the line, and not sell out. But Acuff did it, retaining his image as "the Smoky Mountain boy," as well as his mountain songs and high, soaring harmony.

By the end of the war, Acuff had moved from being a regional favorite to a truly national star. He was popular enough to run for governor of Tennessee in 1948—only the fact that he ran as a Republican in a Democratic stronghold caused him to lose. He was popular enough to leave the Opry in 1946 and make his move to Hollywood (he soon returned). His partnership with Fred Rose not only made him rich, but helped make Nashville the country music center it is today. And the base for all this was formed in just a few short years in the early 1940s; Roy's personality, his self-confidence, his immense talent, all happened to be in the right place at the right time, and the result was a great leap forward for country music.

Lefty Frizzell

During the summer of 1947, the dusty New Mexico town of Roswell was very much in the news. It was home to the Roswell Army Air Field, where sections of the Eighth Air Force helped continue tests of the new atomic bomb; it was also a growing oil town, where oil riggers were replacing cowboys in the local honky-tonks and clubs. In early July it became something else; local ranchers found parts of a "flying saucer" that had crashed nearby, along with the bodies of several small "aliens." A nationwide UFO scare was triggered, and suddenly hundreds of reporters were flocking to the town, asking the Air Force what was going on and accusing the intelligence officers at Roswell of a massive cover-up. For weeks the local newspapers were full of the scare, and few people noticed a tiny article on the back pages of the Roswell *Daily Record*; a local radio singer from KGFL, "Lefty" Frizzell, had been arrested and sentenced to a six-month jail term.

He was a big, strapping boy with thick, curly black hair and an aw-shucks grin. As he began his jail term—for what he would describe later as "fighting and carrying on"—he was nineteen. He had come to Roswell from Texas to try to make it as a radio singer, together with his young wife, Alice, and their two-year-old daughter, Lois. Times were tough, but the couple scraped by, living in a little trailer on the seedy side of town. They had no car, and when Alice got off work from her part-time job at a restaurant, Lefty would try to meet her to walk her home. Now these precarious arrangements had come crashing down, and the young singer spent his days in the old-fashioned jailhouse, whiling away his hours writing love letters to his wife and wondering whether he could ever pick up his career again.

He also thought a lot about songs. Since he was twelve, he had been trying to write songs—not tough blues or novelties or lonesome ballads, but country love songs, lyrical laments that he could use to show off his singing voice. Most had been awful, and soon forgotten. But now he had more time, and in between the love letters, he started writing love songs and sending them out to Alice. One Friday evening in September, he took out his tablet and began to write down a new one he had just worked out. "I Love You, I'll Prove It a Thousand Ways," he wrote at the top, and started off his prose: "I love you, I'll prove it in days to come." It was a letter, and a promise, and an intensely personal thing, but Alice Frizzell saved it (as she saved all the letters), and when Lefty got out, in early 1948, he added music and sang it for her. Then they went back to Texas, not suspecting that the song would have any effect on their own lives, let alone on the entire direction of country music singing.

Some fans think that the impact of a singer can be measured by counting up the number of chart hits he or she has had, by looking at the highest *Billboard* position a record reached, or by tallying up how many weeks the record spent in the Top 40. By these standards, people like Hank Williams, Webb Pierce, Red Foley, and Conway Twitty certainly had more success than Lefty Frizzell. The bean-counters note that Lefty only had three Number One hits in his whole career—"Always Late" (1951), "I Want to Be With You Always" (1951), and "Saginaw, Michigan" (1964)—and wonder if Lefty wasn't just another colorful Texas honky-tonker who burned out too soon. True country fans, and many country singers, know better. They know that real influence isn't so much a matter of a specific song, but a potent style, and that Lefty was a stylist supreme. Years later Merle Haggard would say; "When I'd get on stage, and I'd wonder how I should do a song, and maybe I'd be in doubt, I'd just mentally try to remember how Lefty would do it." Lefty was, first and foremost, a singer's singer—someone whose influence far outweighed his commercial success.

Testimonials to Lefty's style—what his wife, Alice, once called "Lefty's game"—show up almost everywhere modern singers talk about their craft. George Jones was sent home from his very first recording session because he sounded too much like Lefty; Willie Nelson dedicated an entire LP to his memory. Merle Haggard said, "I feel he was the most unique thing that ever happened to country music," and singers as different as Freddie Hart, Ray Charles, and Ronnie Milsap have cited Lefty as an influence. The late Keith Whitley cut his teeth on a stack of old Lefty records that belonged to his mom. "I can still remember sitting in front of the record player when I was very, very young trying to emulate Lefty's style," he said. Randy Travis won his initial fame by emulating Lefty; he confesses: "In the beginning I would learn Lefty Frizzell songs and try to copy them note-for-note . . . try to learn all the licks and the phrases that he would use in songs." The compact disc era has seen a number of Lefty's original cuts reissued, and Germany's Bear Family Records has released his complete works in a massive box set. In addition, Lefty has been a member of the Hall of Fame since 1982. Nevertheless, he remains a misty legend to many fans. "There's no way in the world that Lefty Frizzell's being recognized as much as he should," insists Hank Williams Jr.

The legend actually started before the traumatic jail term in Roswell. It began in the rough-and-tumble Texas oil town of Corsicana, where William Orville Frizzell was born on March 31, 1928. He was one of eight children born to a young oil driller, Naamon Frizzell, and his wife. Since he was the firstborn in the family, he soon acquired the nickname "Sonny"—a name his family would use for him all his life. As a boy, Sonny listened intently to the old Victrola his dad had gotten in a trade for a milk cow, sticking his head right up next to the speaker to hear every nuance of his favorite singer, Jimmie Rodgers. He recalled, "Instead of going out and playing when I came in from school, I'd go in, and my head would go close to that speaker, and yodel right with him." In 1939 the family moved to El Dorado, Arkansas, and Sonny made his debut on stage singing a version of Gene Autry's hit "South of the Border"; soon he had his own radio spot—on a children's show over local station KELD. "I knew when I was twelve years old what I was gonna do," he said.

Throughout the 1940s we get scattered glimpses of young Lefty trying to carve out his career in music. He wins a talent contest on "Wayne Babb's Stage Show" in Dallas; works with an Arkansas string band headed by Rex "Jelly" Elliot; buys his first fancy cowboy suit at a rodeo clothes store in Dallas and borrows $100 from his mother to pay for it; gets nicknamed "Lefty," not, as later legend would have it, from a Golden Gloves boxing match, but from a fight with a schoolyard bully; gets married at barely sixteen, to Alice, in March 1945; and goes to Roswell in 1947 to sing at local servicemens clubs.

Then came the jail sentence. It would have been enough to discourage many men, and for a time Lefty did quit trying to sing and went back to work in the oil fields with his father. But he couldn't let the music alone. And sometime during this period he began to sense he had a new way of delivering a song, a style that was suited to the new type of country music that men like Ernest Tubb and Floyd Tillman were singing. Some called it "honky-tonk," in deference to the new roadhouses and clubs that were springing up in the Southwest; it was a style that was fitted to the new microphones and sound systems in these places, systems that allowed the singer to get away from the old mountain "shouting" style of Roy Acuff or Bill Monroe. Lefty began to exploit his wonderful sense of phrasing, breaking a simple syllable like "ways" into something like "way-yays" and stringing it out for a whole line. He developed a break in his voice—he attributed it to his "mixed-up" Arkansas-Texas-Louisiana accent—and added slurs and curves to his singing; and it was all quiet, sincere, intimate—and haunting.

By 1950, Lefty had settled in at the Ace of Clubs in Big Spring, Texas. Suddenly he caught on, and began drawing crowds. He began to feature "I Love You a Thousand Ways," finding the song perfect for his new style, and began to write other songs that would give him more opportunities to show it off. One day the jukebox man came in to restock the club's machine, and he and Lefty got to talking. "He was wanting me to go somewhere with him," recalled Lefty later, "and I said, 'Well, if you've got the money, I've got the time.' And it just hit me, that'd be a heck of a title for a song." Word of the new singer soon reached the ears of a man named Jim Beck, a well-connected talent scout and studio engineer who ran a studio on Ross Avenue in Dallas. He sent word for Lefty to come up and cut some demos; if they sounded good, Beck would pass them on to friends at Columbia Records.

In April 1950, Lefty pulled up in front of Beck's studio and unloaded his own Martin guitar. Beck asked him to sing some of the original songs he had been doing at the Ace of Clubs, and Lefty obliged; the old acetate cutters rolled, and soon Beck had rough cuts of "If You've Got the Money" and "I Love You a Thousand Ways." At first, recalls Alice, "Beck was interested in the songs, not in Lefty being on record." And, in fact, Beck soon took the demos up to Nashville with the idea of pitching "Money" to Little Jimmy Dickens, then Columbia's hottest novelty act. Dickens turned it down, but Columbia head Don Law liked the voice he heard on the demo, and a few weeks later was in Texas listening to Lefty's show. By July 25, he had given the young singer a contract and was setting him up in Beck's studio for his first real session. A pickup band was thrown together; featured was a young woman from Wichita Falls named Madge Sutee, who had been a piano player for the Miller Brothers band there. Her romping, barrelhouse piano helped set the Frizzell style on "Money," and Don Law insisted on using her whenever possible for all Lefty's later Dallas sides.

Four sides were cut that first day, and Columbia put two of them ("Love" and "Money") back-to-back on the first single. When it was issued on September 4—after an anxious summer when Lefty and Alice almost starved to death—it became one of the fastest-selling records in country music history. Other artists rushed to record cover versions of "Money"—eventually forty of them, including pop singers like Jo Stafford. Sales were so strong that, seventeen days after the release,

Columbia rushed Lefty back into Beck's studio for some new sides. Throughout 1951 he was producing hits every three or four months: "Look What Thoughts Will Do," "I Want to Be With You Always," "Always Late," "Mom and Dad's Waltz," "Travelin' Blues," and "Give Me More, More, More (of Your Kisses)."

Soon he was on the road with a band called the Western Cherokees and being managed by a Houston agent named Jack Starnes (who later helped discover George Jones). He became one of the first country stars to fly extensively on tour, often flying to dates out of Beaumont; for a time his pilot was Henry Cannon—the husband of Minnie Pearl. Bookings were rolling in, and Lefty, according to younger brother Allen, "did what any Texan worth his salt would do—he bought three Cadillacs." On top of it all came a deal, in July 1950, to join the Grand Ole Opry. While there, Lefty actually shared a dressing room with Hank Williams, and the two hit it off fairly well—in spite of some mutual kidding and ribbing about who was a bigger star.

Things began to go sour in 1952. Lefty and Starnes made one of their biggest mistakes when they decided to leave the Opry, on the theory that they could get more money by doing their own bookings. He then missed a special command performance in New Orleans for a bunch of Columbia bigwigs and wound up getting jailed for drunk driving; fortunately, the sheriff was a fan and let him out. Then in June he and Starnes had a bitter falling out and went to court; in the settlement, Lefty gave up most of his record royalties and came away with a lasting distrust of managers and promoters.

In the fall of 1952, thoroughly disgusted with the Texas and Nashville scenes, Lefty headed for California. He had found a spot on Cliffie Stone's pioneering TV show, *Hometown Jamboree*. Cliffie recalls: "The first night Lefty performed on the show, the mail, phone calls and attendance of the show tripled. Lefty's easy, natural, down-home ways were immediately captured by the cameras, and the viewers at home loved him." For a time, things looked good again, but Lefty began to have trouble getting hits. Finally, he broke up his band and traveled only with his kid brother, David, who had just turned sixteen; he used pickup bands wherever he played—something he would do for years to come. "Those slump years," recalls David, "he'd been used and abused by everybody that could get their hands on him. Lefty played every little dive I've ever seen. Everybody in country music during those years was doing the same thing, trying to survive, trying to get by."

By 1958 things were looking up again. He had gone to Hollywood to cut some sides with big string sections and to Nashville to try his luck with a Marty Robbins song, "Cigarettes and Coffee Blues." The song worked, and he followed it up with a new song by Danny Dill and Marijohn Wilkin, two young Nashville writers, called "The Long Black Veil." It stayed on the charts for weeks, and suddenly Lefty was hot again. In August 1961 he left California and moved to Nashville. Old friend Merle Kilgore loaned the family the money they needed to make the move.

Lefty spent the last fourteen years of his life settled in Nashville, trying to cope with being a living legend, trying to record a few more good songs, and trying to write. The Jim Denny bureau booked him, and Denny's Cedarwood Publishing Company looked after Lefty's new songs and fed him a diet of good Music Row product by songwriters like Wayne Walker, Mel Tillis, and Danny Dill. His friend Buddy Killen at Tree Publishing got him "Saginaw, Michigan," which he recorded—reluctantly—in 1963. In addition, Lefty himself began to write seriously with old drinking buddies like Whitey Shafer, Dallas Frazier, Abe Mulkey, and Doodle Owens. He liked to talk about when he could retire to a farm he had brought down in Wayne County, Tennessee, and just write songs. In the mid-70s he made two good albums for ABC, and he and Shafer produced two final masterpieces—"I Never Go Around Mirrors" and "That's the Way Love Goes"—both recorded by Lefty, but popularized by others.

But years of hard drinking and harder living were starting to take their toll. Plagued by fits of depression and high blood pressure, Lefty couldn't believe his doctors were serious. Given a choice, he would usually prefer a shot of Jack Daniel's to his medication. On July 19, 1975, Lefty was getting ready to leave for the Delaware State Fair in Dover, where he was booked to perform with Skeeter Davis and Stonewall Jackson. Late that morning he suffered a massive stroke, and died that evening.

In one of his last interviews, just a few weeks before his death, he spoke what might have been his best eulogy: "When I sing, to me every word has a feeling about it. I had to linger, had to hold it, didn't want to let go of it. I want to hold one word through a whole line of melody, to linger with it all the way down. I don't want to let go of that no more than I wanted to let go of the woman I loved. I didn't want to lose it."

And to country music's good fortune, he never did.

Grandpa Jones

It was a hot night at the Grand Ole Opry in the summer of 1995. Out front, the crowd in the Opry house was stocking up on Cokes and trying to explain to northern visitors what Goo-Goos were. Backstage the talk was about whether or not the Houston Oilers were serious about moving to Nashville. Announcer Kyle Cantrell was checking over his schedule and getting ready to introduce the host for the 8:30 P.M. segment of the world's longest running radio show. He smiled when he saw who was up next.

Accompanied by his backup band of Joe Carroll and George McCormick, eighty-one-year-old Grandpa Jones came out of his dressing room. The backstage crowd in the hallway reverently parted to let him by, recognizing at once the familiar figure and costume: an old checkered shirt, red suspenders, porkpie hat, bristling white mustache, and big old leather boots that had been given to him in 1935 by singer Bradley Kincaid—boots that were already fifty years old by then. His banjo was strapped on, and he paused a minute to say to his boys, "Let's see if we're in tune," and whammed out a chord almost loud enough to be heard out on stage. There's nothing timid about Grandpa's music— he has for the past two weeks been suffering through the agonies of a root canal, but he is a trooper of the old school, and the show will go on. Someone asks, "Grandpa, they want to know if you're gonna need the drums." "No," he snaps, "we're trying to keep it country!"

Then the big red curtain is rising and Cantrell is saying, "And now let's make welcome a member of the Country Music Hall of Fame, everybody's grandpa, Grandpa Jones!" The band breaks into his theme song, "Eight More Miles to Louisville," and the audience applauds in recognition. Newly energized, Grandpa struts on to the stage and tears into a song called "Banjo Sam," an old-time banjo tune he first recorded back in 1961 and has recently resurrected. After singing the first verse, he holds his big banjo up to the mike and plays a chorus with an energetic downstroke style called clawhammer. This is what the audience has been waiting for, and they applaud again; many recognize it as "Grandpa Jones style" banjo work, but it is really an old mountain style that predates the popular bluegrass style. Grandpa is one of the very few commercial artists who can still do it.

After the song, Grandpa decides to tell a couple of stories. Even before his long stint on *Hee Haw*, where he held forth in comedy duels with the likes of Junior Samples, Minnie Pearl, and his old friend Stringbean, fans and friends alike knew that Grandpa was one of the funnier storytellers around. "I read in the paper the other day about a scientist at this university who had invented this contraption where you put an egg on it and it could tell you if the egg was gonna be a hen or a rooster. Well . . . I don't know. I think I've got a better method. You wait until the egg hatches and take the little chick and put it down in front of some feed. Then you watch. If he eats it, it's a rooster; if she eats it, it's a hen." The audience eventually gets this, and someone on stage tells him, "Tell the one about the bald-headed shoe salesman." Grandpa obliges, launching into a yarn about a nearsighted old maid who goes into a shoe store. The baldheaded salesman bends over to try to fit her with a shoe, and she looks down to see only the top of his bald head. Mistaking it for her knee, she quickly pulls her dress over it to cover it up. "It took that poor salesman three or four days to recover," says Grandpa, in the best ad lib of the night.

Then, after introducing a couple of other guests on his segment, he concludes by doing a fine old Jimmie Rodgers song, "My Little Old Home Down in New Orleans." As he finishes and waves good-bye, a fan watching from the wings says, "You sometimes forget that Grandpa used to be one of the best Jimmie Rodgers singers around—that he did a whole album of yodel songs." A friend nods. "You sometimes forget a lot of things Grandpa can do."

And, indeed, Grandpa's long career has taken him down some trails that typical country singers don't follow. His days were not spent in the Tennessee mountains or the Arkansas cotton fields, but in the rolling hills of northwestern Kentucky, near the banks of the Ohio River. He was born Louis Marshall Jones in the hamlet of Niagra, Kentucky, the youngest of eight boys and two girls in a family of tobacco planters. An early photo shows him and his sisters standing amidst huge leaves of tobacco. When the farm work was done, there was time for music in the family; his father played old fiddle tunes like "Bonaparte's Retreat," and his mother played the concertina and sang old songs like "Daisy Dean." After radio got started, the Jones family bought a crystal set and listened to the *National Barn Dance* out of Chicago; on nights when everyone wanted to listen at once, one of his brothers got the idea of laying the little crystal headphones in a Number 3 washtub so it could amplify the sound.

By the time he graduated from the eighth grade, Marshall (as he was called then) was serious about his singing and wanted nothing more than a guitar so he could sound like Jimmie Rodgers on those Victrola records his brothers kept bringing home. Finally one of his brothers, Aubrey, came home from work one day and told Marshall to look in the cab of his truck. "I expected to find a sack of candy," recalls Grandpa. "But there on the seat lay an old guitar. It was warped a little, but it looked like gold to me. I don't even think it had a brand name on it. Aubrey had brought it at a secondhand place called Cheap John's for 75 cents."

By the time Marshall was in high school, his family had moved up to Akron, Ohio; here he continued to work on his singing and his guitar playing, but he began to hear more pop music and show tunes. One of his first performances in public was singing "Old Man River," the famed anthem from *Show Boat*, for a high school assembly. Then, in March 1929, singer Wendall Hall came to town. Hall was a quasi-hillbilly singer who had had a big hit with "It Ain't Gonna Rain No More." During a weeklong talent contest, he auditioned over 450 contestants, with the winner appearing on his radio show and winning five ten-dollar gold pieces. Marshall practiced his yodel, entered, sang two Jimmie Rodgers songs, and won. His years behind the mike had started.

His first years as a pro were spent in the unlikely locales of Cleveland and Boston. He got his first solo show at WJW Akron (now in Cleveland), where he was billed as "The Young Singer of Old Songs." His specialties in those days were "Eleven Cent Cotton and Forty Cent Meat," "Twenty-One Years," and "That Silver-Haired Daddy of Mine." By 1931 he had met and teamed up with harmonica player Joe Troyan, who would later win fame as Bashful Harmonica Joe. "He was living in Cleveland then," Grandpa recalls. "He was Slavic, and his mother was one of the best cooks I ever met. Trouble was, I never got to talk to her directly. She didn't speak English. Joe had to interpret for me." Soon the pair joined a local radio band featured on the popular *Lum and Abner* show—the Pine Ridge String Band. The show had been started in 1931, and the antics at the Jot 'em Down Store in Pine Ridge, Arkansas, were a national sensation. "Though they dressed up in mustache and goatee, in real life Lum and Abner were nice-looking young men," Grandpa recalls. "In the off season they went on tour, and we provided the music for that too."

In 1935 Grandpa met the one man who was to have the most influence on his career: Bradley Kincaid. A genuine product of the Kentucky hills, Bradley had won fame on the WLS *National Barn Dance,* and by 1935, with the death of Jimmie Rodgers, he was easily the most popular singer in the country. One night Bradley shared a bill with Marshall and Joe at a benefit and stayed around afterward to talk to them. "How would you boys like to join me in West Virginia," he asked, "and then go on up to New England and play on the East Coast for a while?" "We were bumfuzzled," says Grandpa. "We managed to tell him we needed to ask our folks." They did, and when Bradley's wire came, they were ready to go.

For the next two years Grandpa and Joe worked out of WBZ Boston with Bradley, learning that New Englanders had as much a taste for the old-time songs and ballads as southerners. The trio would do their morning radio show and then travel to small towns throughout New England for personals; Grandpa was surprised to find that "reserved" New Englanders were warm and hospitable—often they invited the musicians home to have supper with them. Bradley not only taught Marshall a lot of old songs—and a respect for old songs—but a lot about stage presence and showmanship. And he was the one who turned Marshall Jones into Grandpa Jones.

"I was just twenty-two when it happened," Grandpa recalls. "We were always having to drive back in late from a show and having to do that early morning radio spot on WBZ. We *were* sleepy, and it was hard to hide it. One morning on the air Bradley said, 'Get up to the microphone. You're just like an old grandpa.' And the way I talked made me sound older than I was, and pretty soon people were writing in saying, 'How old is that fellow? He sounds about eighty.' So we decided to play this up. There was an old vaudeville comedian named Bert Swor in Boston then, and he took me down to a store that had wigs, and fixed me up with make-up and a false mustache. I've been Grandpa ever since—though I don't have to have the false mustache anymore."

By 1937 Grandpa was out on his own, working radio in West Virginia and then Cincinnati. Along the way Cousin Emmy, the flamboyant banjo-picking comedienne, had taught him how to play the old-time clawhammer banjo—though he still thought his main instrument was the guitar. At WLW Cincinnati he joined forces with young Merle Travis and the Delmore Brothers (Alton and Rabon) to create one of country music's best-known gospel groups, the Brown's Ferry Four. (In later years Grandpa would use this group as the prototype for the Hee Haw Gospel Quartet.) Singing songs like "I'll Meet You in the Morning" and "I'll Fly Away," the group existed, with several personnel changes, throughout the 1940s. It was at Cincinnati, too, that Grandpa finally got into the record business. In the fall of 1943 he and his buddy Merle Travis went into a makeshift studio in Dayton and recorded two sides for a new label that would be called King. Not sure how their bosses at WLW would like them recording, they released this first record under the pseudonym the Sheppard Brothers. This first release was not all that successful, but a few months later Grandpa began issuing discs under his own name, and soon had a hit with "It's Raining Here This Morning" in 1944.

A stint in the Army, where he served as an MP and led a string band in occupied Germany called the Munich Mountaineers, interrupted Grandpa's recording career, but by 1946 he was back in the King studios. King flew him to Hollywood, where he joined Merle Travis in the studio and cut his next big hit, "Eight More Miles to Louisville." "I wrote that off of an old Delmore Brothers song, 'Fifteen Miles to Birmingham,'" Grandpa remembers. And though Merle wasn't listed on the original label (he was signed to Capitol then), in the middle of his great guitar solo, Grandpa shouts, "Play it, Merle!" In 1947 he went into Nashville studios and cut the two songs that were destined to be his biggest sellers: "Mountain Dew" and "Old Rattler." Both were based on old folk songs. "Mountain Dew" he had learned from his friends Lulu Belle and Scotty, who had in turn based it on an older version by mountain singer Bascom Lamar Lunsford; Grandpa added the verse about "my old aunt June/bought some brand new perfume." "Old Rattler" was a song Grandpa had sung back in Wheeling, and was based on an old folk song named "Calling the Dog." The idea is even older—one of Davy Crockett's famous hunting dogs was called Rattler.

On the original recordings of "Rattler," the backup band consisted of Grandpa's old friend Cowboy Copas on guitar and doing the barking, and a very special bass player named Ramona. She had been born Ramona Riggins, and had grown up in southern Indiana. During the 1930s she had become one of the first full-time woman performers in country music, as she had worked with Sunshine Sue over WHAS in Louisville. She had met Grandpa while both worked at WLW, and the pair had married on October 14, 1946. It began a partnership that would last up until the present; she would play fiddle, mandolin, bass, and sing on many of Grandpa's later records, and would in the 1970s carve out a career of her own. They would also start a second generation of Jones music with their children Mark, Eloise, Alisa, and Marsha.

During the 1950s Grandpa spread his time between the Opry and stints at Arlington and Richmond, Virginia, and in Washington, D.C., where he worked on Connie B. Gay's TV show. By 1959 he had settled in permanently at the Opry, and began a series of albums for companies like RCA, Decca, Monument, and CMH. In 1969 he became a charter member of one of country's most successful TV shows, *Hee Haw*. And when he was named to the Country Music Hall of Fame in 1978, his election was one of the most popular in memory. During all this time, he was consistently one of the music's strongest champions of old-time country, and with Ramona worked tirelessly to keep alive the traditions of Bradley Kincaid, Cousin Emmy, Sunshine Sue, and the Delmore Brothers.

Pee Wee King

Pee Wee King, country music's most famous accordion player, composer of "The Tennessee Waltz" and half a dozen other standards, vividly remembers his first night on the Grand Ole Opry. It was a landmark not only for his own career, but for the history of the Opry and even for country music. "We had been playing over WHAS in Louisville," he recalled, "and our manager, J. L. Frank, said, 'Let's go to the Opry and audition.' We played a theater at Horse Cave, Kentucky, on Friday, and on Saturday we drove on down to Nashville, to WSM. At eleven o'clock that morning we auditioned for David Stone and Harry Stone and an engineer named Percy White. And they said, 'Gee, why don't you just stay over and do the Grand Ole Opry with us tonight?' This was about June 1, 1937. So we did the Opry that Saturday night—then we went back to Louisville, knowing that in two weeks, we were coming back as permanent members of the Opry."

In those days Pee Wee's band was called simply the Golden West Cowboys, and that's how their name appeared in their first Opry radio listing. Almost at once, Pee Wee sensed that his act was different from anything else on the show. Neither Roy Acuff nor Bill Monroe had joined the cast as yet, and though cowboy music was the rage on radio and on movie screens across the country, the Opry hadn't really fully embraced the trend. That summer of 1937, the show was still being broadcast from an open-air tabernacle in East Nashville, and people were still talking about the great Ohio flood and the disappearance of Amelia Earhart. The show's stars included old favorites like Uncle Dave Macon and the McGee Brothers and DeFord Bailey, as well as newer names like the Delmore Brothers, Robert Lunn (the Talking Blues Man), the Lakeland Sisters, Curt Poulton, and the Missouri Mountaineers.

What did the Golden West Cowboys bring to all this? "Organization!" laughed Pee Wee. "Most of them on the Opry were farmers and had jobs and did this on a Saturday night only. We were trying to make our living in the music business. We knew studio work because of our radio work. There was no hesitation, no drawn-out pauses between our tunes. We knew what we were doing because we were organized. We opened up with a novelty tune, followed it with a ballad, came back with a duet, maybe a trio, then a triple yodel, then came back with an instrumental, then a sacred number—we already had our package together." Drawing on their vaudeville experience, the band showed the Opry how to use "play-on music" to introduce an act and "chasers" to accompany an artist as he left the stage. Common enough today in every live country show, these techniques were innovations in 1937. The Golden West Cowboys also dressed to kill, and sought to give what Pee Wee called "a good image. Not only do you do a radio show, you pleased people in the audience, and we were conscious of it both ways: radio and visual-wise." At a time when most Opry artists were still booking out on their own or using the Opry's booking agency for package tours, Pee Wee brought to town one of the most innovative promoters in the business, his father-in-law, J. L. Frank. He also brought his union card. "I believe we were the first country entertainers in Nashville to join the musicians' local," he recalled. Later, he would be one of the first regular Opry acts to use an electric steel guitar, one of the first to try to use drums, and one of the first to use a trumpet—when his horn man sounded taps for President Roosevelt in 1945. But all that was later: What he really brought from Louisville in 1937 was a sense of professionalism—a sense of style.

Though he was to be associated with Louisville and Kentucky for most of his career, Pee Wee was not born in Kentucky. Nor, in fact, was his name really Pee Wee King. His given name was Frank Kuczynski, and he was born February 14, 1914, in the middle of rich dairy country in Abrams, Wisconsin. His Polish-American father led a local polka band, and by the time he was fifteen, young Frank had gotten his first accordion and was soon leading his own band, playing polkas and cowboy songs on local radio stations. One day cowboy star Gene Autry, then appearing on Chicago's WLS *National Barn Dance*, heard the band and hired them as his backup group. It was Autry who gave Frank the name "Pee Wee"; he did so because his new accordion player was, at five foot seven, the smallest member of the band. The King part of the name was borrowed from saxophonist Wayne King, who was a popular radio and recording star in the 1930s, best known for his dreamy "The Waltz You Saved for Me." In 1934 Autry and Pee Wee moved to WHAS in Louisville, but Autry was beginning to get calls from Hollywood, and after eight months he went to the West Coast to work in films full time.

For a time Pee Wee took a job with a local band, Frankie More's Log Cabin Boys, and stayed with them through 1935 and into the first part of 1936. He became a member of a radio show and tour group, the *Crazy Water Barn Dance*, sponsored by the venerable laxative Crazy Water Crystals. Along with Bob Atcher, the Callahan Brothers, and a group called the Arizona Ranch Girls, Pee Wee and More's band toured throughout Kentucky, sometimes playing to tobacco barns and local schoolhouses. When it became obvious that Autry was in Hollywood to stay, Pee Wee officially formed up his own band, calling it the Golden West Cowboys—a name he chose, he recalls, because he "had a crush" on a popular WLS *Barn Dance* duet, the Girls of the Golden West. His original personnel included fiddler Abner Sims, singer Texas Daisy, guitarist Curly Rhodes and, at one time, the comedy team of Homer and Jethro. In 1936, Pee Wee's new father-in-law, J. L. Frank, introduced him to Redd Stewart, a Tennessee boy who had been playing fiddle with another Louisville band called the Kentucky Wildcats. The two hit it off, but Redd was not ready to join the band; later he would, and would enter into a partnership with Pee Wee that would make history.

In the meantime, Pee Wee went about trying to put his own unique stamp on the routines he had inherited from Autry. He was fascinated with the new, sophisticated string band sound that was being generated by groups like Clayton McMichen's Georgia Wildcats, then ensconced over Louisville radio, and Louise Massey and the Westerners, favorites of the *National Barn Dance* in Chicago and purveyors of the hit song "My Adobe Hacienda." The bands used innovations like twin fiddles, intricate harmony vocals, and a swinging beat that owed more to Benny Goodman than to the Skillet Lickers. "McMichen had a *fine* band," he recalled. "They were the Glenn Miller of the country music field." Even more influential were the Westerners. "We copied the Westerners. I figured . . . we could pattern ourselves in the western mold—that way, we wouldn't have too much of a problem getting bookings. Country music had things to do with events and everyday life and people's feelings. And in western music we dealt with the atmosphere—the sky, the wind, the ground, the territory, the hills, the prairies." Soon the band was working over WNOX in Knoxville (where "they really weren't ready for western music" and where for a time they got paid in scrip) and quickly attracted the attention of record scouts. Art Satherley, who had signed Gene Autry and Bob Wills to his giant American Record Company label, heard them and told Pee Wee, "I believe what you have is saleable, but I already have Bob Wills." As a result, the King band never got to record commercially until after the war, and won its early reputation as a radio and a tour band.

In spite of the fact that the the Golden West Cowboys sometimes got a little too uptown for the taste of Opry founder and announcer George D. Hay, the fans loved them. Soon the band became a training ground for a series of fine vocalists Pee Wee discovered and hired. One of the first was Eddy Arnold, whom Pee Wee first met at Kiel Auditorium in St. Louis, where the Cowboys found themselves playing a J. L. Frank gig. Arnold was a west Tennessee farmboy—his later nickname, "the Tennessee Plowboy," was no exaggeration—and Pee Wee sensed that his warm, smooth baritone would fit. He offered him a job, and Arnold jumped at the chance. "He didn't even ask how much we were going to pay him," Pee Wee recalled. Arnold made his Opry debut with the Cowboys, and was their lead singer for five and a half years. Later came the versatile Tommy Sosebee, who was the singer for the group when they began to record, and Milton Estes, who became a fixture on Nashville radio and later recorded with his own band, the Musical Millers. By 1944, the singing star was "Little Becky Barfield," a sixteen–year-old yodeler who was related to the 1930s singing star Johnny Barfield; little Becky had started yodeling when she was only four, and at sixteen was a radio veteran. In late 1945 (Arnold had left the band in 1943), Pee Wee hired Lloyd "Cowboy" Copas, "the Oklahoma Singing Cowboy" who was actually born in Blue Creek, Ohio. Copas was hardly a "discovery"; he had spent years on the radio and fiddling contest circuit (working with a fiddler named Natchee the Indian) and had even recorded what would be his first solo hit record, "Filipino Baby," before he joined Pee Wee. Like Arnold, Copas had such a distinctive style that after about a year with the band he went out on his own. Songbooks issued by Pee Wee in the mid-1940s included the Copas favorite "Juke Box Blues," Bill Monroe's "Dog House Blues" and pieces like "Double Trouble" and "My Main Trial Is Yet to Come." And then there was "Praying for the Day That Peace Will Come," the patriotic song Pee Wee bought in 1944 for $10 from a skinny kid in Alabama named Hank Williams.

During the early days of World War II, the Golden West Cowboys saw their national following take a quantum leap when they began touring military bases as part of an organization called the Camel Caravan. The R.J. Reynolds Tobacco Company, then an Opry sponsor and maker of Camel cigarettes, went in with WSM to sponsor a touring troupe drawn from the show. Pee Wee and his band headed it up; the emcee was Ford Rush (the Opry veteran who had worked vaudeville as part of Ford and Glenn); the comedienne was young Minnie Pearl; the lead singer was Eddy Arnold; Kay Carlisle was a pop vocalist; and a cowgirl singer named San Antonio Rose was a cast regular. From the summer of 1941 until Christmas 1942, the group hauled its cars and trailers from Fort Getty in Rhode Island to Fort Sam Houston near San Antonio. One month they cruised out of New Orleans south to the Panama Canal Zone and Central America, where they did shows for troops on outpost islands like Taboga—and were served iguana for their meal. The tour was good for war morale, and for country music's image, and the free packs of Camels the performers passed out to servicemen won them thousands of new fans.

By this time, Redd Stewart had joined the band, bringing with him talents as a singer, songwriter, fiddler, and guitarist. Sometime in late 1941, Redd began playing an instrumental he had worked up called "The No Name Waltz." Occasionally the band used it as their theme song. Redd and Pee Wee soon found they hit it off, and began to do some songwriting together. "We drove the luggage truck," recalled Pee Wee—the quietest spot in the tour caravan, and the best place to concentrate on writing. One night in early 1946, the two found themselves listening to Bill Monroe's hit "Kentucky Waltz" on the radio, when Redd commented that it was odd that nobody had ever written a Tennessee waltz song: "So we took the old melody we had been using as our theme—the 'No Name Waltz'—and Redd started writing some lyrics on the back of a matchbook cover." The pair took it to Fred Rose, their publisher, who made one change in it and pronounced it acceptable—if not terribly exciting. Pee Wee recorded the song in Chicago in December 1947, with Redd doing the vocals and playing twin fiddles with James Boyd. Pee Wee's first hit was born; and when country-turned-pop singer Patti Page recorded it in 1950, it became one of the decade's biggest hits. Over the next thirty years, "The Tennessee Waltz" would be recorded over three hundred times and sell more than 40 million records.

Despite the song's success, Pee Wee had trouble finding a follow-up. He had minor hits with similarly titled efforts like "Tennessee Tears" and "Tennessee Polka" in 1949, but it wasn't until 1950 that he really had what would be his own personal biggest-selling record: "Slow Poke," written with a Louisville music librarian named Chilton Price. Among the four hundred–odd other songs Pee Wee wrote or helped to write were "Bonaparte's Retreat" (based on an old fiddle tune and put together in the last seven minutes of a recording session to fill out a side) and "You Belong to Me," which became a pop hit for Jo Stafford. Other Victor hits included "Silver and Gold" (1952), "Busybody" (1952), "Bimbo" (1954), and "Changing Partners" (1954). Some Victor sides were not hits, but were rich, complex examples of western swing as it shifted toward rhythm and blues and rock 'n' roll.

At the height of the "Tennessee Waltz" popularity, in 1948, Pee Wee decided to return to Louisville. "The main reason I left the Grand Ole Opry was I wanted television," he recalled. Opry management saw no future in TV; Pee Wee did. His act had always had a strong visual dimension, with snappy costumes and vaudeville-like pacing, and he hit Louisville at the dawn of the golden age of local, live TV. Soon he had a show over WAVE in Louisville on Thursday nights, and before much longer he had added a Saturday show over WBBM Chicago, a Monday show over Cleveland and a Wednesday show over WLW Cincinnati. This incredible pace continued for much of the 1950s; in addition, he ran a weekly network radio show. He finally gave up his TV shows in 1962, after his band had been repeatedly named Number One by *Cash Box* and *Billboard*. By then, he was a major force in music promotion and tour packaging, as well as a warm, friendly, elegant father figure for millions of fans.

In later years, dozens of awards and honors came his way. In October 1971, Kentucky governor Louis B. Nunn issued a proclamation announcing Pee Wee King Day in the state; a huge crowd and dozens of luminaries attended the festivities in Madisonville. In 1974, he was elected to the Country Music Hall of Fame, and later was active on various boards and committees. Currently retired in Louisville, he watches with amusement modern Nashville's claims about crossover hits and "country pop." Fans can understand his tolerant smile: He has been there before.

Bill Monroe

It was a cold February day in 1950, and at two o'clock that afternoon Grand Ole Opry star Bill Monroe was driving down to the Tulane Hotel, on Church Street in downtown Nashville. He was on his way to the Castle studios, a remodeled dining room in the hotel that had become Nashville's first real recording studio; there he would meet Paul Cohen, the A&R man for his new record label, Decca. In fact, Monroe's very first session for Decca was set for 2:30 that afternoon, with a second three-hour session scheduled for 7:30 that night. Monroe had seven songs ready, but even then he knew it would be a long day: He had a new, young band, most of whom had never recorded before, and a new producer to break in as well. And to top it all off, Monroe was in a crisis of sorts in his own career: Though his distinctive music was starting to take off, it was also threatening to get away from him, as young bands around the South began copying the "high lonesome sound." His new bosses at Decca seemed nervous about Monroe tying himself too much to this sound, and had been making noises about a more mainstream country style.

On that day Monroe was thirty-nine years old, and had been recording for some fourteen years—first with his brother Charlie on the old Bluebird label before World War II, then with his own bands for Bluebird, and, since 1945, for Columbia. Both labels had brought him major successes: "What Would You Give in Exchange for Your Soul?" with his brother on Bluebird; "Orange Blossom Special" and "In the Pines" with his prewar band for Bluebird; and "Kentucky Waltz," "Footprints in the Snow" and "Little Community Church" for Columbia. Since September 1946 his recordings had included the singing and guitar of Lester Flatt and the revolutionary banjo sounds of Earl Scruggs. He had won national fame in the early 1940s by landing himself and his Blue Grass Boys a spot on the NBC network portion of the Grand Ole Opry, and the incredible popularity and influence of band members

Flatt and Scruggs had caused crowds at the old Ryman to shake the place with their screams and whistles. Monroe was popular enough to get his own tent show when he went on Opry tours, and for a time he even carried with him an amateur baseball team.

By the end of the decade, though, things were taking a different turn. For various reasons—some personal, some professional—both Flatt and Scruggs decided to leave the band in early 1948, and afterward decided to start their own band. "Bill might have always had the feeling that we had planned it," Flatt explained years later, "but actually we hadn't." Monroe felt he had helped mold the two into the stars they were, and did not take kindly to their departure; he told them there was no way they could make it on their own. The bitterness was strong, and remained for years; it even extended to Monroe's trying to keep them off the Opry in the early 1950s. As they started their new career in east Tennessee, Flatt and Scruggs were careful not to use the word "bluegrass" to describe their music—since it was part of the actual band name used by Monroe, the Blue Grass (written as two words) Boys. But inadvertently their fans conspired against them; not wanting to anger Lester and Earl by mentioning Monroe by name, fans started asking for the "old Blue Grass songs" they had done in the 1940s. The name stuck, and soon other people were using the name of Monroe's band as a generic term to describe the music played in that style.

Monroe was also finding out that fame bred imitation. Over in Bristol—the same place Flatt and Scruggs would go—in the late 1940s was another band called the Stanley Brothers who were becoming adept at copying Monroe's sound. Mac Wiseman, who had worked with Monroe in 1949, recalled: "When the Stanley Brothers first started, whatever Bill did Saturday night on the Opry, they did next week on the Bristol program that they were on. . . . Well, Bill used to see red. He used to hate the word Stanley Brothers." The Stanleys weren't really trying to rip off Monroe—they simply loved his music, and the way he did it. "It wasn't that they were out to steal corn out of his corn crib," says Wiseman. But things came to a head in September 1948, when the Stanleys did their cover of Monroe's famous racehorse song, "Molly and Tenbrooks," and released it on the small independent label called Rich-R-Tone. The problem was that Monroe had not yet released his own record of the song—Columbia had held it back during the 1948 recording ban. To make matters worse, Monroe then learned that his own record company, Columbia, had signed the upstart Stanleys to a contract in March 1949, and had rushed them into the studio before scheduling any sessions with him. And worse yet, one of the first Columbia releases by the Stanleys (June 1949) was a song called "Let Me Be Your Friend," which bore a close resemblance to Monroe's most recent Columbia release,

"It's a Dark Road to Travel"—though it gave composer credits to Carter Stanley. Monroe was understandably furious, and that fall decided to sever ties with Columbia. (He was even angrier with them the following fall, when they signed up his old sidemen Flatt and Scruggs.)

But Monroe was far from feeling washed up on that February day as he walked into the Tulane Hotel. He had always responded well to a challenge, and a couple of upstart bands trying to make it by playing what he considered "his" music weren't about to intimidate him. Two of his new musicians were singer-guitarist Jimmy Martin and fiddler Vassar Clements. Martin, who would later win fame on his own with songs like "Widow Maker," was from Sneedville, Tennessee, and was working as a painter when Monroe found him. "He had a wonderful voice that would really fit with mine," Monroe recalled later, in a memorable understatement. Young Vassar Clements was also destined for bigger things—the 1974 album *Hillbilly Jazz* would help redefine the role of the fiddle in country and bluegrass music. Like Chubby Wise, Vassar was from Florida, and in fact had met Monroe through Chubby; after auditioning with "Orange Blossom Special," Vassar was hired by Monroe to replace Chubby. "We had a number called 'The New Muleskinner Blues,'" recalls Monroe. "Well, Vassar was powerful on that. He put some new notes in it that was fine, that every fiddler went searching for." Monroe especially liked Vassar's ability to play the blues; "there's fiddlers that could beat Vassar on 'Sally Gooden' or old-time fiddle numbers, but Vassar would beat 'em on a number like the 'Mule Skinner'—they wouldn't touch him on that."

In fact, "New Muleskinner Blues" was one of the songs cut that February afternoon, and one that would become one of Monroe's best-known Decca sides. It was a remake of the old Jimmie Rodgers song Monroe had first cut back in 1940 for Victor—and the first song he had sung on the Opry. "We don't do it the way Jimmie Rodgers sung it," Monroe notes. "It's speeded up." Monroe also brought to the session three new original songs, "My Little Georgia Rose," "Memories of You," and "I'm on My Way to the Old Home." All three were autobiographical—almost confessional—in nature; in "I'm on My Way to the Old Home" Monroe was especially evocative at calling up the scenes of his youth in Rosine, with the echoes of the foxhounds running at night. Monroe's mother had died in 1921, when he was ten; his father (who had been fifty-four when Bill was born) had died in 1927, when Bill was sixteen. Now, as he entered his forties himself, Monroe found himself thinking more about his childhood and his old home place.

That night, when the band reassembled for the second session, Monroe brought out two songs associated with his fellow Opry singer Hank Williams. Banjoist Rudy Lyle recalled that during this time "Hank

Williams used to prank with us a lot, especially at the Friday Night Frolic up at old WSM on Seventh Avenue. . . . He used to always kid Bill about where he got his banjo players."

A few weeks before, Williams had given Monroe a song he had written called "Alabama Waltz." It was designed to take advantage of the fad for state-named waltzes—Monroe had done "The Kentucky Waltz," and everyone was cutting "The Tennessee Waltz." Monroe also brought out "I'm Blue, I'm Lonesome," which, though credited on the label to "James B. Smith," was really the joint production of Monroe and Hank Williams. On tour with Williams, Monroe had been fooling around with the melody on his mandolin backstage, and Williams overheard him; he liked the tune, and soon set words to it. For months the pair had sung the song backstage for their own amusement, and Monroe thought it was worth preserving on disc—even though Williams's MGM contract forbade him to sing on the session. Cohen agreed. By 10:30 that night, the session was over, and Paul Cohen declared that the new Decca artist was on his way. Monroe hoped so too.

Unlike Monroe's A&R man at Columbia, the veteran Art Satherley, who tended to let Monroe go his own way, Paul Cohen was younger, more aggressive, and was determined to make Nashville into Decca's country and western center. He was also interested in creating sales, and was disappointed when Monroe's first Decca release, "New Muleskinner" and "My Little Georgia Rose," rushed out in March, fell with a thud; it failed to dent the charts, and was not even noted in *Billboard*. Cohen decided to find more commercial material. One number was suggested to him by Eli Oberstein, the former Bluebird executive who had been A&R man for the Monroe Brothers back in the 1930s. Oberstein had released it on his own independent Hit label: a song called "The Old Fiddler," written and sung by an Arkansas composer and singer named Hugh Ashley. Ashley had written the song to an old fiddle tune played by a local character named Frank Watkins (though the old fiddler referred to in the lyric is called "Uncle Ben"). Cohen got the song to Monroe, persuaded him to record it at his very next session (April 8, 1950), and rushed it into release as his second single. Though *Billboard* noticed this one in its new release column, it too sank like a stone—even with Williams's "Alabama Waltz" on the flip side.

"The Old Fiddler" did have an unexpected effect, though. Six months later, at the very next session, Monroe presented Cohen with his own version of a song about an old-time fiddler—not Uncle Ben, but "Uncle Pen." As Monroe explained years later: "My uncle, Pen Vandiver, was one of Kentucky's old-time fiddlers, and he had the best shuffle with a bow that I'd ever seen, and kept the best time. That's one reason people asked him to play for the dances around Rosine. . . . My last years in Kentucky were spent with him." Monroe had gone to live with Pen Vandiver when his father died, and the teenager spent countless hours traveling with him to square dances and learning the rudiments of his music. Vandiver died in 1932, and during this "confessional" period, Monroe began to write a song about him.

Hugh Ashley always assumed that "The Old Fiddler" had inspired Monroe to write his own song about a fiddler, and this seems still likely, though Monroe himself has denied it. Rudy Lyle recalls that Monroe wrote the song "in the back seat of the car up on the Pennsylvania Turnpike on the way to Rising Sun, Maryland." Fiddler Merle "Red" Taylor, who later worked with Monroe, felt that he had come up with the fiddle part to the song after Monroe had sung some of the lyrics to him one night in a hotel room. Singer-guitarist Jimmy Martin, in his twenties at the time, also recalls helping Monroe work on the song "while riding on the bus and in little schoolhouse rooms." (Taylor played the fiddle on the original recording of the piece, done in October 1950, and Martin and banjoist Rudy Lyle were also on the session.)

Cohen saw at once that this was a much better song than "The Old Fiddler," and rushed it out by Christmas 1950. Though it never reached the charts, it sold well, was played everywhere, and soon was on its way to becoming a country standard. (Porter Wagoner and Ricky Skaggs would each later do remakes of it.)

Even so, Cohen and Decca remained dubious about the "old-time" sound of Monroe's all-acoustic Blue Grass Boys, and decided to try with Monroe what they had done with most of their other Nashville singers: have them record not with their own bands, but with a special team of crack studio men. An opportunity to try the plan came sooner than they expected. In March 1951, Cohen got wind that Eddy Arnold had recorded a version of Monroe's old 1946 hit, "Kentucky Waltz," and decided to rush Monroe back into the studio to do a new cover of his own song. The trouble was that Monroe was on tour, and to fly the whole band back to Nashville was more than the company would pay. Finally Monroe himself was flown back and put in the studio with some of Nashville's best session men: electric guitar player Grady Martin, fiddler Tommy Jackson, even Farris Coursey on drums. On "Kentucky Waltz" Owen Bradley even played a skating-rink organ—on others a romping honky-tonk piano. One track from the session, a souped-up version of "The Prisoner's Song," featured Grady Martin's electric guitar to the point where the arrangement approached rockabilly. The session marked the first time Monroe had recorded with electric instruments and drums; not wanting to make waves with his new producer, he cooperated.

Cohen liked the sound, and in April he scheduled more sessions under the new format. This time he let Monroe use his regular banjo player, Rudy Lyle, but once again added a drummer, an electric guitarist, and bass player Ernie Newton. Oddly, most of the cuts were versions of Jimmie Rodgers songs, cut to cover Columbia's set of Rodgers songs done by Lefty Frizzell. This time, Decca realized the experiment wasn't working. Owen Bradley, who was now Cohen's assistant and actually overseeing many of the sessions, recalled how much Monroe himself disliked these arrangements; many of the cuts were not even issued at the time. Decca's marketing people had even tried advertising some of the sides—such as "Lonesome Truck Drivers' Blues," a shameless cover of Bob Newman's King hit—in *Billboard* with no reference at all to "the Blue Grass Boys." But trying to separate Monroe from his "sound" or band merely irritated his old fans, and won no new ones. By the end of 1951, Decca had given up, and Monroe himself had seen the danger of trying to modernize his style.

A story Owen Bradley tells reflects just how much Decca gave in. At one session later that year, scheduled for 8:30 in the morning—an ungodly hour for most, but one that didn't bother Monroe in the slightest—Bradley assigned an assistant just down from New York to oversee things. About noon Bradley got a call from the new man; he'd been in the studio an hour with Monroe, and had finished only one song. "And I can't understand a word he says," he concluded. Bradley told him not to worry—let Monroe do what he wants, and when he feels the take is right, go on to the next one. In other words, let Monroe be Monroe.

The New Yorker finally agreed, and the session concluded. With it came a production style that would endure for the next four decades and beyond, and that would see both Decca (now MCA) and Monroe through one of the longest artist-company relationships in country music history. For Monroe, it was an important victory, as well as a vital watershed in his own career. He had weathered a serious crisis, and was now ready to embark on the most productive decade of his career.

Hank Snow

On a recent spring morning, Hank Snow was sitting in his sunny office in Madison, Tennessee, talking to a visitor. At the other end of the room his secretary was taking care of some paperwork for Hank Snow Enterprises; on the walls were dozens of plaques, awards, gold records, certificates— all testimony to four decades of one of the music's most enduring success stories. This morning Hank was talking about some of his early 1950s recordings, the kind RCA Victor issued on both 78 and 45 versions. "You know, I'm not sure I can think of stories behind all these old songs," he apologized. But he proceeded to do a pretty good job of it, calling up in wonderful detail memories of long-forgotten songwriters, legendary old-time song pluggers, and recording sessions done in dusty car barns and transcription studios used before RCA even owned a real studio in Nashville. Finally the conversation turned to a song called "I Traded Love," which he recorded in 1953 and again in 1955. Never released, it bore composer credits to "Clarence E. Snow" (Hank's given name). With a grin he reached into his desk drawer and pulled out a handwritten copy of the lyrics. "Steve Sholes liked the guitar work on that, he liked the melody, but he wasn't crazy about anything else. I'm rewriting it now," he said, "and when I get finished, I'll use it in my current act."

In an age when many singers look on their old songs as disposable product with as much value as last month's newspaper, Hank Snow stands out. His discography is one of the largest in the business—it extends from 1936 to 1985 and includes over 840 commercial recordings. He was always committed to revising and reworking old songs, his own and others', and to maintaining the integrity of everything in his repertoire. In his later years, he often put his words on a holder attached to his mike stand to make sure he does the song as it is supposed to be done.

Over the years, Hank has not taken kindly to having songs foisted on him by overeager producers, even if they turn out to be hits. One was the novelty number "That Crazy Mambo Thing," which went to Number Six on the charts in 1954. "I never did care for the song," he recalled. "It was sent to me by Hill and Range, and they had sent me a lot of good songs." Then there was "Mainliner"; it made the charts in 1955. Composer Stuart Hamblen ("This Ole House") ran into Hank in Hollywood and rushed him into the studio, at his own expense, to cut that one. "I never could get into the feel of the song," said Hank. "It died the death of a rat."

On the other hand, Hank could be stubborn and tenacious when he was fighting for a song he believed in, one that had met his standards. His first blockbuster hit, "I'm Movin' On," is a case in point. Hank wrote the song about 1946. "It was inspired by Jimmie Rodgers," he remembered, "though I didn't copy anything from him in it." He tried to record it at his first American recording session for RCA, in Chicago in 1949, but producer Steve Sholes didn't think much of it. "It was turned down in Chicago," Hank explained, "even though it was the song I had most faith in." A year later, Sholes scheduled another Snow session for Nashville, and this time the singer hatched a plan. He told his band, "I've got this song I've been trying to get Sholes to record for two years, and I think I'm gonna be able to do it this time. He's only got three songs picked for our session, and I think we can get it by him." He had the band rehearse an arrangement different from his earlier one, so that Sholes wouldn't recognize the piece. The ploy worked, and the producer let the song slip by at the tail end of a late-night session. As the band was packing up, Sholes told one of them, "I don't think we've got a single side here we'll be able to use." Of course, he was wrong, and Hank's little deception won him a hit that became what today's singers call a "career song."

It had been a long, long road to Nashville. It began up beyond the northeastern border of Maine, in the Nova Scotia village of Brooklyn, where Clarence Eugene Snow was born on May 9, 1914. He and his three sisters led a reasonably normal life until he was eight; that year his parents divorced. Their split plunged Hank into a series of childhood experiences that resembles something out of a Dickens novel. Two of his sisters were sent to an orphanage, and young Hank was sent to his paternal grandparents; he missed his mother, though, and repeatedly ran away to be with her. Finally she agreed to let him stay and moved to the coastal town of Lunenberg, where she remarried.

By now a young teenager, Hank soon ran afoul of his new stepfather, a rough, violent fisherman. As Hank told it, "I was treated by him, mildly speaking, like a dog. I took many beatings from him and still carry scars across my body that were left by his ham-like hands." Years later, these experiences would lead Hank to form a foundation to help abused children; they would also affect him in more subtle ways, making him quiet, introspective, at times almost withdrawn.

To escape from this impossible home life, he began to ship out as a cabin boy on a large fishing schooner. In between battles with the rough seas of the North Atlantic, he entertained the crew by singing and playing the harmonica. To his surprise, he found he was good at it, and that the crew genuinely enjoyed his music. His mother had had him singing in church, and now she presented him with an old wind-up Victrola and a stack of Vernon Dalhart records. At night Hank memorized the words to "The Prisoner's Song" and "The Wreck of the Old 97"; he was especially interested in the guitar accompaniment to the ballads, since he had never heard a guitar before. A little later, about 1929 or 1930, his mother added to his stack of records some new ones by a singer with a different style, Jimmie Rodgers. "After hearing the first record by him, nothing would hold me," he explained. Within weeks he had gotten a "T. Eaton Special" model guitar (Timothy Eaton being the Canadian equivalent of Sears, Roebuck) and was trying to copy Rodgers.

In March 1933 Hank set out on foot for Halifax, the nearest big town, about seventy-five miles up the coast; to make a little money, he peddled housewares on the way, rewarding customers by singing a free song for each purchase. He brashly approached the local radio station, and soon had his own show on CHNS in Halifax; it was at the depth of the Depression, though, and even with a sponsored program, he could not make ends meet. He found himself standing in bread lines, signing up for relief, and on one especially embarrassing day, shoveling snow with a public works crew right in front of the radio station where he was appearing at night.

In the meantime, he met an attractive young Dutch-Irish woman named Minnie Blanche Aalders, who was working at a local chocolate factory. It wasn't a great time to be starting out, but the couple began dating and soon were married; a couple of years later a son came along, Jimmie Rodgers Snow, named after Hank's favorite, who had recently passed away in New York. About this time, Hank finally found a big-time sponsor for his show: Crazy Water Crystals, the wonderful laxative company who had sponsored groups like the Carter Family, the Monroe Brothers, Mainer's Mountaineers, and others. To streamline his act, Hank began calling himself "Hank, the Yodeling Ranger." A tribute to Rodgers, the title was drawn from a song Rodgers had written after being named an honorary Texas Ranger. Later, when his voice deepened and yodeling became less important in his act, Hank changed the name to "Hank, the Singing Ranger." Many of his early records do not even mention his last name: just "Hank, the Singing Ranger" appears on the label.

Other breaks followed as people throughout eastern Canada began to notice the smooth, confident singing and yodeling that would become the Snow trademark. A spot on Canadian network radio helped him build a coast-to-coast following, and on October 10, 1936, in an old church in Montreal, he made his first records—two Snow originals entitled "Prisoned Cowboy" (a prison song) and "Lonesome Blue Yodel" ("a Jimmie Rodgers type thing"). A series of releases on RCA's Canadian Bluebird label followed, and a string of early hits: "The Blue Velvet Band," "Galveston Rose," "My Blue River Rose," and "I'll Not Forget My Mother's Prayer." Between 1936 and 1949, when he began recording for RCA's United States label, Hank had over ninety songs issued in Canada—records that were seldom released in the States. His American fans had to smuggle them in from Canada when and where they could.

Soon Hank was able to hit the road, with his wife acting as "advance man," to take advantage of his radio and recording fame with a string of personals. This approach worked well during the late 1930s and early 1940s, but as time went by, Hank realized it would take more than music to make the big time. Though a short stay in Hollywood in 1946 proved unsuccessful, Hank met several cowboy stars of the day, including Roy Rogers and Jimmy Wakely. Soon his traveling show sported a trick riding component. Through sheer determination, Hank learned to ride and added to his troupe his "famous trained horse, Shawnee." His performances took on some of the daredevil atmosphere of a circus as, unlike many "singing cowboys," Hank really put his horse through his paces. On a typical show, the lights would dim, the band would strike up a fast tune, and the spotlight would swing out to hit Hank riding in on Shawnee. He would sing a few songs, then go into a display of trick riding. Jimmie Rodgers Snow, a boy of ten or eleven by then, recalled: "The one that drew the gasps was the 'death-drag,' where he lay across Shawnee's neck and raced the horse back and forth in front of the grandstand." After more songs came the comedy routines. In one, Hank and Shawnee would pretend to bed down for the night, with one blanket over both. Hank would pretend to be asleep and tug at the blanket as if cold; Shawnee would promptly grab the blanket with his teeth and pull it back. "The audience loved it," said Jimmie.

Meanwhile, Hank kept trying to crack the American market and get his records released in the States. In 1945 he did a stint on the WWVA *Jamboree* in West Virginia, then one at Washington, Pennsylvania, in addition to the junkets to Hollywood. By 1948 he was in Dallas, playing on the *Big D Jamboree* over KRLD and singing occasionally at a place called the Silver Spur, owned by a man named Jack Ruby—the same Jack Ruby who was to make history fifteen years later by gunning down Lee Harvey

Oswald. Hank was offered Hank Williams's slot on Shreveport's *Louisiana Hayride* when Williams left to join the Grand Ole Opry; he turned it down because the money wasn't very good.

During this period, he had been corresponding with Ernest Tubb about Jimmie Rodgers's music. Finally he got a chance to work some dates with Tubb, who was impressed and promised to do what he could to get Snow on the Opry. As Hank remembered, "He kept pestering those people. He'd drag my records from his record store, take 'em up there and play 'em, until he finally convinced them." It all bore fruit in early 1950, when WSM's Harry Stone offered Hank a job. Snow was stunned to find out that Hank Williams himself was set to introduce him on the Duck Head Overalls portion of the show. Williams did, and the two Hanks found themselves side by side. "Let's call it short Hank and tall Hank," joked Williams, referring to Snow's build.

At first, the Opry looked like another dry run. Looking back on his first appearance, Hank said, "I don't mind telling you I bombed. The people just sat there while I sang. And sat. No applause, no nothing, almost. Just sat." The next few months were no improvement. Hank was sure Stone was going to fire him. Then "I'm Movin' On" hit, and suddenly the Singing Ranger was the hottest act on the stage. The American breakthrough had come. The string of Number One hits began: "Golden Rocket" (1950), "Rhumba Boogie" (1951), "I Don't Hurt Anymore" (1954), "I've Been Everywhere" (1962). Others became standards without technically reaching Number One: "Gold Rush Is Over" (1952), "I Went to Your Wedding" (1952), "Fool Such as I" (1952), "Yellow Roses" (1955), "Conscience, I'm Guilty" (1956), "The Last Ride" (1959) and "The Name of the Game Was Love" (1968). In addition, Hank put out a series of trend-setting "theme" LPs and a series of impressive guitar duets with Chet Atkins.

By the mid-1950s, Hank was one of Nashville's most visible and most successful stars. He rejected an offer from Dot Records in order to stay with RCA and weathered the rock 'n' roll storm by refusing to try to beat the rockers at their own game. While other country singers tried rockabilly to impress the teenage audience, Hank turned his attention to albums and went after their parents. He put together Jamboree Attractions, one of the best of the early booking agencies that specialized in package shows and visited the parents of the young Elvis Presley to convince them to allow the singer to sign with Jamboree. He also helped further the career of his own son, Jimmie. He played steel guitar on Jimmie's four RCA sides—Jimmie eventually became an evangelist and the founder of the Sunday evening *Grand Ole Gospel* show.

Through the 1970s and '80s, Hank held the line against the dilution of traditional country music. He traveled widely, going as far afield as

Vietnam, and released his 104th album for RCA in 1977, *Still Movin' On*. A jazzy, blues-tinged set that reflected the then-current Outlaw movement in country music, it was one of Hank's better efforts, though not commercially successful. A series of duets with Kelly Foxton in 1979 fared better; they were Hank's last real fling with singles. His 1985 duet album with Willie Nelson remains his last major commercial recording work.

By the 1980s, Hank Snow stood as perhaps the most articulate and serious spokesman for the classic sound of country music. His passionate attempt to keep the old songs and the pure styles alive has led some writers, reporters, and promoters to characterize him as aloof. His fans know better. His remarkable works speak more eloquently than any reporter or TNN tribute could, and his great songs continue to be revived—most recently, "Yellow Roses"—by new generations of singers, a tribute to his taste and uncanny ability to find good songs. Toward the end, he toured little, recorded little, and was content to do his regular Opry shows. Few would argue that he had earned that right.

Kitty Wells

To be sure, there were other women in country music before Kitty Wells came on the scene. There were Sara and Maybelle Carter, the staid core of the Original Carter Family, who introduced dozens of classic songs, but who seldom sang songs with a woman's point of view. There were banjo-picking girls like Lily May Ledford and Molly O'Day and cowgirls like Patsy Montana. There were novelty singers like the Dezurik Sisters, whose trick yodeling and harmonizing gave them the name "the Cackle Sisters" and landed them a radio spot for Purina Feeds. But history took a dramatically new turn one May afternoon in 1952 when a young house-wife and mother named Kitty Wells stepped before the Decca micro-phones in Nashville and recorded a song called "It Wasn't God Who Made Honky Tonk Angels." Country music—and the role women played in it—would never be the same. As Tom T. Hall later explained, "Kitty was the first lady to come out and tell her side of the story about honky-tonking and cheating and those kinds of things . . . the harsh realities of life. I was fascinated by her music."

In some respects, Kitty Wells was an unlikely revolutionary. In 1952 she saw herself mainly as Mrs. Johnny Wright, the mother of three young children, who had just helped move her family to Nashville and was looking forward to settling down and retiring from the music busi-ness. For ten years she had sung with the band led by her husband and Jack Anglin, specializing in demure, old-fashioned, sentimental songs like "May I Sleep in Your Barn Tonight, Mister," "I'll Be All Smiles Tonight" and "Gathering Flowers for the Master's Bouquet." For a time she had a radio show in Shreveport on which she was known as "the Little Rag Doll" because she sold cloth and piece goods that rural women used to make quilts and rag rugs. On stage, she liked to dress in conservative, full-skirted gingham dresses with frilly lace collars and lit-tle bows. In 1953, Tennessee governor Frank G. Clement presented her with an award which read, in part, that Kitty was "an outstanding wife and mother, in keeping with the finest traditions of southern womanhood." At the time, Kitty was trying to work out ways to have her aunt help keep the kids while she went out on tour, worrying all the time about school clothes, smallpox shots, and birthday parties.

Kitty Wells, of course, was not her real name; that would come some years after she had been singing on radio. She was born Muriel Deason, one of six children in a family from rural Humphreys County, hilly farmland about forty miles west of Nashville. Her father was a local guitarist and singer. "He used to play around at square dances when we were growing up," she recalled. "I guess that is when I took an interest in learning to play music and sing, sitting on the floor watching him play the guitar—he'd sing old-time songs like 'The Preacher and the Bear.' And, of course, I grew up singing a lot of hymns and church songs in the summertime. My sisters, my mother, all of us would join in." Before she was in high school, her family moved into Nashville, where Muriel's father took a job as a brakeman on the Tennessee Central Railroad.

Soon she was singing in the choir at the local Nazarene church, learning more chords on the guitar, and going with her mother to watch the Grand Ole Opry. This was in the mid-1930s, and the first generation of great Opry singers was just coming into its own: the Vagabonds, with smooth three-part harmony on sentimental songs; the Delmore Brothers, with their light, soft, skittering style; Texas Ruby, the big-voiced blues singer who would soon marry fiddler Curly Fox; the Vaughan Quartet, who worked for the famed Vaughan gospel music publishing company and introduced new gospel songs every week. Muriel took all this in, but never dreamed of performing herself; the Depression was on, and she had to drop out of school to go to work at a Nashville factory. She spent most of her days folding shirts and humming songs she heard on the radio.

Then a cousin, Bessie Choate, moved to town, and she and Muriel began singing together at local dances, billing themselves as the Deason Sisters. About 1936 another Nashville radio station, WSIX, decided to mount some competition to WSM's Opry, and started a Saturday afternoon amateur show. The Deasons decided to try their luck and worked up a Carter Family song (later popularized by Minnie Pearl) called "Jealous Hearted Me." One line in the song read, "It takes the man I love to satisfy my soul," and though neither girl realized it, the station management got worried. "They thought it was a little risqué," said Kitty, and they cut the sisters off in mid-performance. To everyone's surprise, angry fans flooded the station with protests urging them to give the girls another chance. The station relented, and soon the cousins had their own 6:00 A.M. show; they continued to build an audience, and in 1937 won an even wider hearing as a result of the disastrous Ohio River flood. "We started singing a gospel song called 'There's a Big Eye Watching You.' We had a lot of people call the station and want to know about that song."

In the meantime, Muriel had met a young man named Johnny Wright. The son of a champion fiddle player, Johnny had moved into Nashville from Mt. Juliet, Tennessee, to work at a cabinet factory. After a courtship that lasted two years and was filled with the pair harmonizing on old gospel songs, they eloped one Halloween night. When they returned, both continued to work at their day jobs, but Muriel and Johnny linked up with Johnny's sister, Louise, to form a new WSIX act called Johnny Wright and the Harmony Girls. By 1939 Louise was being courted by another singer on the station, Jack Anglin, whom she eventually married. Jack also became close friends with Johnny, and by year's end the two had teamed up to form the group that for the next generation would be known as Johnny and Jack.

By this time, Kitty was no longer singing regularly with the band. She remembers: "I was just singing maybe on Sundays. We would sing together Sundays at some of the parks." The couple's first child, Ruby, had been born, and Kitty was nervous about leaving her. "I didn't like to leave her, but we could take her with us to the parks. That way I could work a little bit." By 1940 the group had gotten a manager, George Peak, and hit the road as the Tennessee Hillbillies. "We loaded everything on a homemade, two-wheel trailer, our breakfast suite, bed springs, everything," recalled Johnny. This was the beginning of a ten-year span of almost constant moving around from station to station: Greensboro, Charleston, Knoxville, Raleigh, Decatur (Georgia), Birmingham, Shreveport. A second child, Bobby, was born in West Virginia, and again Kitty dropped out for a while. When she started singing again, she and Johnny found themselves at WNOX's *Mid-Day Merry-Go-Round* in Knoxville; that was where Kitty Wells was really born. Kitty recalls: "After we went to Knoxville, Lowell Blanchard—manager of the show—talked to Johnny and said, 'I think that we ought to come up with a name that would be easier for people to remember.' So Johnny picked the name from an old folk song sung on the Grand Ole Opry—'Kitty Wells.' It was a big hit with The Vagabonds and the Pickard Family."

By 1949 the band had landed a contract with RCA Victor, and cut a series of sides, some featuring Kitty by herself, some featuring Johnny and Jack. The latter were successful enough (one of them was "Poison Love"), and though Kitty had some good sales with "How Far Is Heaven," her fine solos were not making much of an impression. "I don't think the records were promoted all that much," recalls Kitty. The records were generally of older songs, done in a string band style more reminiscent of the 1930s than the '50s. Without much fanfare, RCA dropped her contract.

Johnny wasn't discouraged, though, and had Kitty cut a new demo, which he gave to Paul Cohen, then the head of A&R at Decca. Weeks went by and they heard nothing; in the meantime, the band left Shreveport to move back to Nashville, with Kitty assuming her career was pretty much over. She looked forward to retiring, staying with her children, and going to PTA meetings. Then, one night when Johnny and Jack were playing at the late show at Ernest Tubb's record store, Johnny ran into Paul Cohen and asked him point-blank if he was interested in recording Kitty. Cohen said yes, that he had a song in mind and wanted Kitty to listen to it. A few weeks earlier, Louisiana songwriter J. D. Miller had written an "answer song" to the current top hit, Hank Thompson's "The Wild Side of Life." It was called "It Wasn't God Who Made Honky Tonk Angels," patterned after a line from the earlier song: "I didn't know God made honky tonk angels." A few days later Kitty and Johnny heard the demo, but they were only mildly enthusiastic. Kitty recalls: "Actually, I didn't think much about Hank Thompson's song—or that it needed an answer. It used a familiar melody—it had been used for a lot of lyrics by people like the Carter Family and Roy Acuff." Still, Johnny urged her to do it. Finally Kitty agreed. "I said, 'Well, it probably won't make a hit, but we will at least get a session fee out of it.'"

The session was set for May 3, 1952, at the old Castle Studios in the Tulane Hotel in downtown Nashville. Paul Cohen had to be out of town that day, so he delegated the work to young Owen Bradley. Bradley would later joke, "That song means as much to me as it does to Kitty; it got me my start as well." The band that day was not a studio group, but the regular working band that Johnny, Jack, and Kitty used on their radio and stage show: Paul Warren played fiddle, Shot Jackson steel. Old friend Eddie Hill was added on some cuts for the trio harmony. Four songs were cut that day, but only "Honky Tonk Angels" and another answer song called "I Don't Want Your Money, I Want Your Time" (a response to Lefty Frizzell's big hit) were issued right away. The single was released in June, but *Billboard* wasn't impressed enough to review it. Kitty went about her business, thinking about the $125 scale she hoped to get for the session, when one day she ran into Hank Williams's wife, Audrey. "You've got a hit on your hands," she told Kitty. And sure enough, by June 18, the disc was selling well enough that it appeared on the *Billboard* charts.

The song brought controversy as it was played more and more on the air and on jukeboxes. NBC banned it from any of its network broadcasts, saying it was too "suggestive." Johnny recalls, "The problem was in the first verse. The song in its original form used the word 'trustful' in the line, 'It brings memories when I was a trustful wife.' That could be read two ways. So Kitty changed it and began singing, 'It brings memories when I was a *trusting* wife.' Then it was okay." After a hailstorm of criticism from DJs and music bookers, NBC relented and dropped the ban. Kitty was asked to join the Opry, and "Honky Tonk Angels" entered history as the first real women's song in country music.

The dam had broken, and for the next decade Kitty found herself with a Top 10 hit about every six months. At first, they were more "answer" songs, like "Paying for That Back Street Affair" (1953), a follow-up to Webb Pierce's "Back Street Affair," or "My Cold, Cold Heart Is Melted Now," a woman's answer to the Hank Williams song. Then the songs began to pour in from the new generation of Nashville writers like Jimmy Work, Jim Anglin, Felice and Boudeleaux Bryant, Gary Walker, Johnny Masters, and even a very young Don Everly. There was "Making Believe" (1955), "Lonely Side of Town" (1955), "Searching" (1956), "Repenting" (1956), "She's No Angel" (1958), "Amigo's Guitar" (1959), "Heartbreak USA" (1961), and "Password" (1964). There were duets with leading male singers—Red Foley ("One by One," 1954), Webb Pierce ("Finally," 1964), and Roy Drusky ("I Can't Tell My Heart That," 1960). There were LPs, and there were honors—eleven straight years recognized as Number One female artist by *Billboard*, ten by *Cash Box*, election to the Country Music Hall of Fame in 1976, and even an award from the jazz magazine *Down Beat*.

Throughout much of this time, two individuals helped define Kitty's sound and style. One was husband Johnny Wright, who sensed the kind of songs she could do and couldn't do, and knew how to find them. The other was producer Owen Bradley, who soon discovered the elements that made Kitty's voice unique. It was a delicate voice, not booming or bluesy, and one that could have been drowned out by a large accompaniment. It was also a smooth voice, with a spine-chilling liquid vibrato that hundreds of singers, from Loretta Lynn to k.d. lang, have tried to copy. One of Owen's tricks in the studio was to have Kitty sing in a higher key than she wanted to, so the songs would "come out bright."

By the 1990s Kitty and Johnny could look back on over fifty years in country music, most of them spent as headliners and trend-setters. There were temptations to rest on their laurels—things like their museum in Madison, Tennessee, a new biography in progress, a prestigious Grammy award, several new reissues of their classic work. But most days in the summer or fall, fans still have to catch them on the road, on tour as far north as Canada—long, complex, demanding tours that have been their hallmark for years. "The Queen of Country Music," Kitty's rightful title, may have started out as a press agent's ploy, but no one takes it lightly today. Kitty has won her fame the old-fashioned way—she has earned it.

PART II

From the Victrola

Fiddlin' John Carson

He always shows up at the start of any history of country music—a slack-jawed Georgia mountaineer who could sing and play his fiddle at the same time and who happened to make the recording that many people think of as the "first" country record.

It was June of 1923, we always read, and the place was Atlanta; the man was called Fiddlin' John Carson, though his friends and cronies always called him simply Fiddler. He went into a portable studio that day and recorded two songs for the Okeh record label (technically the General Phonograph Corporation). One was "The Little Old Log Cabin in the Lane" and the other was one he called, "The Old Hen Cackled and the Rooster is Going to Crow." Though the A&R man for Okeh, Ralph Peer, thought Carson's singing was "pluperfect awful," a local store owner agreed to buy five hundred copies of the record if the company would press it up. They did, and the disc soon became a best-seller. Within months, other companies were starting to go out and record this type of music they were calling "old time" or "hill country," and the country music boom was under way. Somewhere along the way, Carson—like the Grand Ole Opry fiddler Uncle Jimmy Thompson—just droped out of sight. In the colorful world of Jimmie Rodgers and the Carter Family and Charlie Poole, we don't hear much about old Fiddlin' John. But he was there—there throughout the 1920s, a major presence on the early country music scene, and he was doing a lot of other things that he deserves credit for. Let's hoist one to his immortal memory.

There are a few details that need to be added to the familiar story; it wasn't just a case of Carson wandering in off the street with a hound dog at his heels asking to put his music on the newfangled machine. The idea started in the spring of 1923 when an Atlanta furniture store owner and record distributor named Polk C. Brockman made a business trip to New York. Brockman, a young white man with big round horn-rimmed glasses, came from an old Atlanta family, and his grand-father, James K. Polk, had started a chain of furniture stores. Now, young Polk found there was money to be made from distributing some of the new "race" records through his stores around the area. He was in New York to work out more deals on this, and while he was there the Okeh people asked him if there were enough performers in Atlanta to justify a recording trip there. Brockman agreed to think about it, and a day or two later found himself in the Palace Theater in Times Square watching a movie. The newsreel that day, though silent, featured scenes from an old-time fiddlers' contest in Virginia. Intrigued, Brockman wrote a note to himself: "Record Fiddlin' John Carson."

In 1923, John Carson was far from an obscure mountain fiddler whom only a handful of people knew about. He was already pretty famous before he stepped into the recording studio. Born in 1868, just three years after the Civil War ended, he grew up in the rough, hilly area of north Georgia's Fannin County, up near the Tennessee line. "I was born in Georgia," he used to tell his audiences, "but my maw threw her dishwater over into Tennessee." His history goes too far back into the past for us to get anything but a dim outline of his musical influences. We get glimpses of him in 1879, at age eleven, playing for tips on the streets of the mining town of Copperhill, and being dubbed "Fiddlin' John" by the governor of Tennessee, Bob Taylor, himself a fiddler. We get glimpses of him plying his trade at old-time Blue Ridge dances "where the gals wore skirts to the ground and ten yards around." We get glimpses of him playing at the great fiddling conventions that became a regular thing in Atlanta starting in 1913. We know that he married in 1894, and that about the turn of the century moved to the Atlanta area, where he found work in the mills and became one of hundreds of "woolhats"—the scornful name give to country folks who were trying to survive in the mill communities.

In 1913, John and several of his children were working at the Fulton Bag and Cotton Mill, when the workers decided to go on strike to get a union in. Faced with days of free time, John made up at least some of his lost wages by busking in the streets of north Atlanta, playing his fiddle and singing his songs. By now he was also writing some songs, and one of them dealt with the murder of and subsequent controversy over a young pencil factory worker named Mary Phagan.

> Come all of you good people.
> Wherever you may be,
> Supposing Little Mary,
> Had belonged to you or me?

In these days before recording, John made his money off this song by having copies printed up on cheap sheets of paper and selling them to listeners for a nickel or a dime. Old-timers called these sheets "ballots," and they were a direct link to an even older tradition in England and Ireland. John sang this song downtown during the long trial of Leo Frank, and, like many of his fellow Georgians, was outraged when Governor John B. Slaton, the day before he left office, commuted Frank's death sentence to life in prison. For this the fiddler wrote yet another protest song in which he accused Slaton of "becoming a millionaire" by reprieving Leo Frank and asserting that he "got a million dollars from a New York bank." This was a bit much for Slayton's friends, and Carson later told Polk Brockman that they threw him in jail for singing it.

By the end of World War I, Fiddlin' John was well enough known that he could put together a band, pile them into an old 1913 Ford, and hit the road for some impromptu touring. In this respect, he became one of the first—probably the very first—country singers to try to make a living from his music. Gene Wiggins, in his excellent biography of Carson, *Fiddlin' Georgia Crazy,* talked to some of these original cronies, and they recalled that seldom did John set up dates ahead of time, such as with a modern booking agent. He would just point the car in a direction—usually north from Atlanta—and start driving. Trading on his reputation as a "busker" and on the publicity he got from appearing at the Atlanta fiddlers' conventions, he would go to a local school, work out with the principal a deal for splitting the take, and use the schoolhouse for an impromptu show. He would also, before each trip, have a stack of song sheets printed up to sell.

Carson's fame took another quantum leap when he started appearing on Atlanta's WSB radio in 1922. The first radio station in the South, WSB went on the air in March, and was desperately looking for talent. Ernest Rogers, one of the first announcers, recalled that they used anybody who could "sing, whistle, play a musical instrument, or even breathe heavily." Just a few days after the opening, John was on the air, playing and singing his distinctive repertoire. Within a few weeks he was the hit of the station. His fame expanded not only in Atlanta, but throughout much of the South; in these early days of radio, a strong signal like WSB's could carry across several states.

All this had happened before Polk C. Brockman wrote "Record Fiddlin' John Carson" in his notebook in Times Square. Brockman's idea was not to make a star out of a locally popular fiddler, but to take an already popular fiddler with a solid reputation and see if a record of him wouldn't sell. He also suggested to the Okeh people a variety of other local acts, including two jazz bands, a gospel quartet, and a couple of blues singers. John was the only one of the bunch doing anything like country music. The time came when Okeh's A&R boss, Ralph Peer, as well as a team of engineers, descended on Atlanta to set up a temporary studio in an empty narrow building on Nassau Street, in the downtown area. It was June 19, 1923.

The day before the recording, Ralph Peer decided he needed to audition John Carson, and Brockman set it up. After hearing a couple of numbers, Peer commented that he had never expected Carson to be able to sing and play the fiddle at the same time; actually, it was pretty common in traditional mountain music, and Carson managed it by holding his instrument not directly under his chin, but a little farther down on the shoulder. Peer did not at all like Carson's singing: it was idiosyncratic, nasal, oddly timed, and full of strange scoops and slurs. It was nothing like even the earlier blues singing Peer had recorded by people like Mamie Smith, which was evenly paced and well-modulated. He told Brockman that Carson's singing was "pluperfect awful"; he was willing to record John playing the fiddle, but was going to have him drop the singing. Brockman at once objected; the very thing that made Carson so popular, and so unique, he argued, was his singing; Carson was an entertainer, not just a fiddler. His singing was true, authentic north Georgia hill country singing, and that's what the people wanted to hear. Peer was still skeptical. "How many copies of this record do you think you could sell?" he asked. Brockman shot back, "I'll buy five hundred of them right now." That was enough to justify a limited printing, and Peer went on with the session.

The two songs were ones Carson himself had chosen. The first was an old minstrel show tune called "The Little Old Log Cabin in the Lane," which had been written in 1871 by the former Mississippi riverboat captain Will S. Hays. It was still circulating in various sheet music editions, but had gone widely into folk tradition as well. The second side, "The Old Hen Cackled and the Rooster Is Going to Crow," contained only incidental singing and was Carson's version of the fiddle favorite "Old Hen Cackle." Peer shipped the big wax masters to New York and had five hundred pressed up for Brockman. He was so convinced that they would never amount to anything that he did not even put a "release number" (catalog number) on them.

The records arrived in Atlanta the day of a small fiddlers' convention where John was to play, and Brockman put the crate in his back seat and drove over to Coble Hall, where the fiddling fans had gathered. In an inspired moment, he asked for John to sit out on stage with a Victrola, playing his tune live, and then playing it again on record.

"I've stopped making moonshine and gone to making records," John supposedly said. After hearing the records, the audience flooded the stage, and Brockman sold his box of records within a couple of hours. The next day he was ordering more, and within a few weeks the disc was the talk of Atlanta. Okeh re-pressed it, this time with a release number, and asked Carson to make plans to come to New York for more recording. He did so in November 1923, kicking his recording career into high gear.

There were no *Billboard* charts or royalty statements in those early days, so nobody really knows how much "Little Old Log Cabin" sold; we do know that copies of it are still found handily by record collectors today, suggesting that it sold a huge numbers of copies—probably around 100,000. Carson's really big hit, though, was his second recording, "You Will Never Miss Your Mother Until She Is Gone." It was an unabashedly sentimental song from the Victorian era, and was known under the title "Mother and Home." Here again, Carson's fiddling was not prominent; his singing was. The song was such a smash that a sheet music publisher issued a printing of it with Carson's photo on the cover. Later homiletic songs that sold thousands were his version of the 1866 piece "When You and I Were Young, Maggie," the old gospel song "Be Kind to a Man When He's Down," and "Old and Only in the Way." Carson's records were so popular that rival companies began trying to find their own country singers so they could do "cover" versions.

By no means, then, did Carson drop from history after his legendary first record. He went on to become a major presence in the old-time records of the 1920s. Between 1923 and 1934, he released over 160 sides—more than almost any other performer except for giants like the Carter Family and Jimmie Rodgers. For the first couple of years, most of these were just Carson, his singing, and his fiddling. Later he formed a full string band, the Virginia Reelers, and began adding to his oeuvre wild dance tunes like "If You Can't Get the Stopper Out, Break Off the Neck" and "Who Bit the Wart Off Grandma's Nose." Along with his daughter, Rosa Lee Carson (who recorded as Moonshine Kate), he did a series of comedy skits in which he played an old moonshiner. He also did old-time vaudeville songs, more sentimental songs, gospel songs, and even old pop favorites like "It's a Long Way to Tipperary." He did not shy away from protest songs, and he dramatized the plight of farmers in songs like "The Farmer Is the Man Who Feeds Them All." His singing style never smoothed out or became more regular; to modern ears he often sounds like George Jones, with his back-of-the-throat, partially swallowed delivery and highly ornamented style—"snaking the melody,"' as some of the old church singers used to call it. No one who listened to his singing itself could doubt that, here indeed, was the first performer to sing country music on records.

In later years, when he retired from music, Fiddlin' John was given a job as elevator operator at the state Capitol Building, a political appointment from his friend and patron Governor Eugene Talmadge. Always good for a newspaper feature, he regaled his passengers with yarns of his older days. When he died, in 1949, the Georgia State Highway Patrol served as an honor guard, and the governor himself was an honorary pallbearer.

Vernon Dalhart

September 27, 1903, dawned bright and clear in the Blue Ridge Mountain cotton mill town of Danville, Virginia. It was a warm, Indian summer Sunday, and on nearby White Oak Mountain the maples were turning to their fall colors. It was a lazy morning, and many of the mill-workers were sitting on their porches or doing chores around the house. Coming into the town from the north were the tracks of the Southern Railway, which ran down the mountain, over a wooden bridge called Stillhouse Trestle, across the Dan River, and on through Danville to North Carolina and eventually Atlanta. For over a year now, the residents had gotten used to a new fast mail train that ran the route, a train called Old 97. This morning, some of the people were glancing at their pocket watches, and wondering why Old 97 was late.

So were the Southern dispatchers. Up the line, at the hamlet of Monroe, Virginia, they had put a new crew on Old 97, headed by engineer Steve Broady. He was a young, ambitious man, and when he found out his train was running late, he determined to make up the time. He decided to "highball" it. The problem was that Broady was new to the route, and didn't know just how tricky the curve into Danville really was. As he came roaring along the river toward the trestle, his whistle screaming, something happened. Some say he lost his airbrakes; some say he was simply going too fast.

The people in Danville looked up when they heard the whistle and knew that the mail train was coming, but also that there was something dreadfully wrong. It was coming too fast. As they watched in horror, the locomotive and its five cars flew off the rails just before it reached the bridge and plunged seventy-five feet into the ravine below. Cars crashed into the timbers bracing the trestle, and the engine boilers exploded. People from the town raced over to the scene, trying to rescue anyone alive. Few people were. The conductor, the flagman, and both firemen were dead; engineer Broady was alive, but so badly scalded that he begged them to put him out of his misery. He too later died. The final toll was nine dead, seven injured.

As train wrecks go, it was by no means the country's worst or most dramatic. It was like dozens of others back in the early days of railroading. What made it such a part of history was that a week after the wreck an eighteen-year-old Danville boy named Fred J. Lewey, one of the first on the scene of the wreck that Sunday morning, began to write a song about it. He based it on an older song called "The Ship That Never Returned," and over the next few years several other local musicians contributed to the song; eventually what came out was "The Wreck of the Old 97," a song that was destined to become country music's first million-selling hit.

The singer who would be forever associated with the song was nowhere near Danville on that infamous Sunday morning, and probably didn't even hear about the wreck where he was living, in Dallas, Texas. Certainly he didn't dream that events were under way that would eventually make his name a household word in the 1920s, as he became the biggest recording star in early country music. His given name was Marion Try Slaughter, but to millions of fans he was Vernon Dalhart. Though he didn't tour much, or become the headliner of a barn dance radio show, or make his mark in films, Vernon Dalhart did amazing things in the recording studio. During the 1920s and 1930s he managed to create a discography of some 5,000 record releases, working for virtually every major label and dozens of smaller ones. (In contrast, the Carter Family amassed a total of some 350 releases, and Jimmie Rodgers some 120 songs.)

He was so popular that he often recorded the same song for as many as ten or twelve different labels, usually under one of the 135-odd pseudonyms he used. He was certainly the first country singer to sell a million copies of a record, and in 1925 he dominated the best-seller charts as no singer—including Garth Brooks—has since. Though his recording career was effectively over barely a decade after "The Wreck of the Old 97" hit, it totally dominated country music's first generation; dozens of country and bluegrass standards still heard today were first popularized by Vernon Dalhart.

In 1981, when Dalhart was finally elected to the Hall of Fame, there was some grumbling around Nashville that the singer was a "dude" and "an easterner who wore spats." In truth, Dalhart did make his later home around New York, and he did sing in a stiff, formal-sounding tenor voice; and in truth, he did start out his career as a singer in light opera. But he was hardly any dude; he had serious and deep Texas roots. Indeed, his stage name was taken from two small towns in Texas,

Vernon and Dalhart, around which he had worked as a cowboy when young. He had been born in 1883 on a large ranch in Marion County, in northeast Texas, and spent his later childhood in the nearby town of Jefferson. This was during the waning days of the frontier, and gunfights and knifings were not yet uncommon. Dalhart had a grandfather who worked as a deputy sheriff and was a member of the local Ku Klux Klan. Dalhart's biographer, Walter Haden, has also discovered that Dalhart's father, Robert Marion Slaughter, was killed in a knife fight with his own brother-in-law. Young Vernon absorbed his share of this; he learned to shoot and was good enough that he was able to kill enough robins to sell for pocket money. He also heard some of the old folk songs the ranchers and cowboys sang, and he learned to play some of their instruments, like the harmonica and the Jew's harp; he also became proficient at whistling, and would later use all these talents on record. Oddly, he apparently never learned the guitar.

A year or so after he lost his father, when Dalhart was about twelve, he was singing in public at the First Baptist Church in nearby Dallas. At the behest of his mother, he also began formally studying at the Dallas Conservatory of Music while working in a hardware store. Shortly after the turn of the century, he married and started a family. For some reason, he decided in 1910 to move to New York to try to further his music career; to support his young family, he found work at a piano warehouse, studied at night, and freelanced as a church soloist and as a singer for funerals. His voice was soon developed to the point where he was able to get roles in operas—in *The Girl of the Golden West* in 1912, and as a lead in Gilbert and Sullivan's *H.M.S. Pinafore* in 1913. Then, in October 1916, came the break that would change the direction of his career.

According to friends, Dalhart saw an ad in a New York newspaper that said: "Wanted: Singers for recording sessions." The man placing the ad was none other than Thomas Alva Edison himself, anxious to expand his commercial record catalog—though at that time he was issuing his records on cylinders as well as the newfangled discs. Dalhart had been out to the Edison studios at East Orange, New Jersey, before, making unsuccessful tests in 1914 and again in 1915. But he was always willing to give it another try; appearing at the studio, he saw it full of well-trained opera singers and decided to try a "dialect" song called "Can't Yo' Heah Me Callin', Caroline?" Dalhart's friend Bobby Gregory, who later became a well-known country songwriter, recalled what happened. "One of the office men came out, and said, 'All singers will be dismissed except Vernon Dalhart. . . . Mr. Edison wants to speak to you.' Mr. Edison was deaf . . . and had to use an ear trumpet to hear what was going on, so he asked Dalhart, 'Would you sing this song up close to my ear?' Dal told me how he leaned into Edison's hearing aid and sang 'Can't You Heah me Callin,' Caroline.' He looked down, and Edison was smiling and said to him, 'You are the man for me.'"

Dalhart's "Caroline" song—a vaudeville song often sung in black-face, à la Al Jolson—was issued in June 1917, and soon became a hit. Soon the young singer was being called back into Edison's studios every month, and was specializing in songs with southern dialects. In his first published interview, he explained the dialect. "I never had to learn it. When you are born and brought up in the South your only trouble is to talk any other way." Edison continued to bill him as "one of the best light opera singers in America" and to feature him on everything from religious songs to World War 1 topical songs like "Joan of Arc They Are Calling You" and Al Jolson covers like "Rock-A Bye Your Baby with a Dixie Melody." By 1919 he was doing occasional records for Victor, and by 1921 was recording for Columbia as well. His versatility won him dozens of studio jobs, and he soon found he could keep his family well cared for simply by doing studio work.

Then came the first recordings by country singers: Fiddlin' John Carson's in 1923, Henry Whitter's a year later, as well as ones by Gid Tanner, Uncle Dave Macon, Ernest Stoneman, and others. In May 1924, Edison asked for Dalhart to do a cover of one of Whitter's songs, "The Wreck on the Southern Old 97." They gave him a copy of the Whitter record, Dalhart learned the words as best he could hear them, and cut the Edison master. Dalhart liked the song, and three months later, in August, he asked if he could cut it for Victor. Not at all sure what this country fad was about, the Victor executives were cautious. What would you do for a B side? they asked.

Dalhart had an idea. He pulled from his pocket a penciled text that had been written, he said, by his cousin Guy Massey, who had been visiting him from Texas. It was a lament about a man in prison, and contained the line, "Oh if I had the wings of an angel, over these prison walls I would fly." Massey had gotten the core of the song from his brother, who was actually doing time in a penitentiary and had heard the song there. At the time, the song had not even been named; Dalhart later recalled that he and Massey took a break from the recording session and retired to a nearby hotel room to finish it up. They soon came back with the words written out on hotel stationery, Victor's musical director, Nat Shilkret, took it home and arranged it, and on August 13, 1924, they took it into the studio. The song now had a name—"The Prisoner's Song"—and Dalhart cut it at the same time as "The Wreck of the Old 97." (At the same time he cut "Go 'Long Mule" and "Boll Weevil Blues," two other early country favorites.)

Released back-to-back on Victor 19427 on October 3, the songs became two of the biggest hits the industry had ever seen. Some 225,000 copies were sold in just four months, and Dalhart himself would record "The Prisoner's Song" some eighteen other times, and see it released (often under pseudonyms) on sixty other labels. The popularity of "The Wreck of the Old 97" convinced the record companies that "hill country music" was here to stay, but that its audience was mainly hungry for similar topical ballads, or what they were then calling "event songs."

Further proof of this theory came in early 1925, when newspapers around the country began carrying stories about Floyd Collins, a young Kentucky caver who had gotten himself wedged into a crevice in a sand cave in western Kentucky. Okeh records commissioned a ballad about the event from one of their artists, singer-evangelist Andrew Jenkins, and had Fiddlin' John Carson record it. Sensing a hit, Columbia asked Dalhart to do a cover of it, and in May he did so, using the name "Al Craver" in deference to his Victor contract. The company backed the song with another topical ballad, one about "Little Mary Phagan," the Atlanta factory girl who had been murdered in 1913. Dalhart had another huge hit, this time for Columbia. "The Death of Floyd Collins" sold over 300,000 copies, making it the single biggest seller in Columbia's "Old Familiar Tunes" series.

For the next several months, Dalhart was constantly rushing into the studios to do more "event songs." His third big hit was another train wreck song, "The Wreck of the 1256," about a 1925 crash on the James River. Then there were songs about airship disasters ("The Wreck of the Shenandoah"); about natural disasters ("The Santa Barbara Earthquake," "The Miami Storm"); about badmen and murderers ("Kinnie Wagner," "Frank Dupree"); and controversial trials ("The John T. Scopes Trial"). For a time, the record companies had their systems down so pat that they could have Dalhart in the studio recording an event song only a couple of days after the event—and have the records in the stores three weeks later. The results were spectacular: In 1925, Dalhart had six of the top seven best-selling discs in Columbia's "Old Familiar Tunes" series, and five of these were event songs. In 1925 Dalhart records accounted for over 50 percent of Columbia's total country sales.

By now Dalhart was being called on more and more to do country material, even though he himself protested. "I am no more Hill Billy than you are," he wrote to a friend in Kansas. In addition to event songs, he recorded dozens of sentimental country favorites: "The Letter Edged in Black," "The Little Rosewood Casket," "Maple on the Hill," "Zeb Turney's Gal," "The Convict and the Rose," "The Dream of the Miner's Child," "The Roving Gambler," and "Eleven Cent Cotton." With his partner and guitarist Carson J. Robison, the Kansas songwriter and singer who had accompanied him first on "Old 97," he did favorites like "My Blue Ridge Mountain Home" and "Golden Slippers."

The thousands of dollars in royalties from his almost continual recording bought Dalhart a pair of Cadillacs, a closet full of suits, and a huge English tudor home in fashionable Mamaroneck, New York. They bought his son a Stutz Bearcat for high school graduation, and an expensive apartment suite in downtown New York. But then suddenly everything collapsed. Dalhart lost a bundle in the 1929 stock market crash, but even worse, he found his singing style was suddenly out of fashion. New, more "authentic" country singers like the Carter Family and Jimmie Rodgers were coming forth, people who lived and worked in places like Mississippi and Virginia and Tennessee. After 1928 he and Carson Robison split up, depriving him of the musical genius who crafted and wrote his best songs. By 1929 he was recording again with pop orchestras, but to little avail. Victor's famed A&R man Ralph Peer, who discovered the Carters and Jimmie Rodgers, wrote in an article in 1955: "Vernon Dalhart was never a hillbilly and never a hillbilly artist. Dalhart had the peculiar ability to adapt hillbilly music to suit the taste of the non-hillbilly population." Dalhart, in his own way, seemed to agree.

Dalhart's last Victor session was in 1939, and even then bad luck dogged him. One of his releases, "Lavender Cowboy," was banned by ASCAP as being too suggestive. By 1942 Dalhart was working as a night watchman in Bridgeport, Connecticut, forgotten by all except a few fans. He tried for a time to give lessons, but found few takers. "So far as my voice is concerned, I am in better shape than ever in my life," he wrote a friend. But his efforts to get a record deal with the companies he had enriched all failed. He died on September 14, 1948, and was buried in Bridgeport's Mountain Grove Cemetery, under a headstone that reads merely, "Marion T. Slaughter."

Riley Puckett

It is an odd story, but it is one of those country music legends that old-timers in Georgia and the Carolinas never seem to tire of telling. It was the spring of 1928, and country music as we know it was only about five years old. Jimmie Rodgers had made his debut recordings in Bristol, and had recently released his first big hit, "Blue Yodel." Jimmie, the story goes, was not happy with Victor and approached Columbia for an audition in Atlanta. Frank Walker, the head of Columbia's "Old Familiar Tunes" division, the man who would twenty years later sign Hank Williams to MGM, listened to Jimmie sing. Shrugging, he turned to his assistant Bill Brown and said, "We don't need Jimmie Rodgers. We've got Riley Puckett."

Riley *who?* To the unitiated, the name sounds like a character from a Riders in the Sky radio skit. But to those who know or remember something about country's first two decades, the name evokes one of the music's great legends: a blind singer and guitar player who was the most popular country record maker of his day, who recorded several of the music's classic songs, and who revolutionized guitar playing. Doc Watson, Bill Monroe, and Jimmie Rodgers have all acknowledged their debt to him; fans have kept many of his old records—he made more than three hundred under his own name—in print on reissue LPs and even CDs. Historians have studied his picking style and huge repertoire of songs, and have selected him for membership in the Atlanta Country Music Hall of Fame. He was there at the very start of the country music industry, making his first acoustic Victrola records just months after Fiddlin' John Carson made his. But, unlike most of these early pioneers, he adapted and survived through the changes in the music, and was doing current songs like "Take Me Back to My Boots and Saddle" at one of his last sessions, in 1939. Throughout it all, he was an enduring radio star, and had an amazing string of hit records. Frank Walker's choice of him over Jimmie Rodgers was understandable at the time; before

Rodgers came on the scene, Puckett was probably the best-selling country singer in the nation. Though the Georgia newspapers liked to dub him "the Bald Mountain Caruso," he himself sent out publicity that described him as "King of the Hillbillies"—a phrase that foreshadows Roy Acuff's sobriquet, "the King of Country Music." But back in the 1920s, when "hillbilly" was still a word used to describe the music, Riley Puckett's handle was accurate enough.

George Riley Puckett, to give his full name, was born in 1894 near Alpharetta, a hamlet about fifteen miles north of Atlanta, just off what is now Highway 19. Neither of his parents was especially musical—his father died when Riley was young—and just where he got his interest in music is not known. His blindness was not natural, but came about as a result of a doctor's mistake. When he was just three months old, he developed a minor eye infection; a local doctor misdiagnosed it and tried to treat it with lead acetate (sugar of lead), a strong astringent. The result was almost total blindness in the child (even though some friends claimed he could at least tell light from dark). His family were not especially well off, but they managed to get him placed in the Georgia Academy for the Blind in distant Macon when he was about seven. Records show that he attended there at least two years, in 1901 and 1902, and probably longer; the school taught him to read Braille, to play the piano, and probably to play the banjo. Music was one of the few recourses open to a blind man in the rural South at the turn of the century.

Nobody knows exactly what happened to Riley during the years from 1902 to 1916, when he turned into a teenager and developed his basic musical skills. A piece of publicity in an old songbook states that he had learned to play banjo at twelve, and the first newspaper accounts of his playing single him out as a banjoist. Who taught him is a mystery. Later he learned the play the guitar in a very unusual way, picking out runs on the bass strings instead of simply strumming. Many of his friends credit an older musician from the Atlanta area, Ted Hawkins, with teaching Riley the guitar. (Hawkins would later record with Riley as part of the Skillet Lickers band.) Others have suggested that he might have learned some of his style from the bottleneck blues player Blind Willie McTell, who also attended the academy in Macon. But north Georgia in these early days was awash with talented musicians, black and white, and Riley could have learned from any of them. All he himself ever said about his influences is his spoken introduction to his blues-styled version of "John Henry" (1924), where he credits an "old darky" for teaching him the piece.

Nobody ever got to interview Riley Puckett about his early life, so much of it has to be reconstructed from circumstantial evidence. His wife remembers that though he occasionally worked as a carpenter and knew telegraphy, he made his way as a musician from the very beginning. He played on street corners ("busking"), at carnivals, at auctions, at private parties, probably at medicine shows—anywhere a musician could earn a few dollars. The first mention of him in print comes from 1916, when an Atlanta newpaper describes him as "the blind banjoist" at the fourth annual Georgia Old-Time Fiddlers Convention; one of the songs he played was "It's a Long Way to Tipperary," a current pop hit from World War I. By 1917 he was a favorite at the convention, backing up other fiddlers and—for the first time—singing. These big fiddlers conventions, held in downtown Atlanta, attended by thousands, were launching pads for many of Georgia's old-time musicians, including Fiddlin' John Carson, Gid Tanner, and others. It was here that they attracted the attention of radio station WSB and, later, talent scouts from Movietone newsreels and from phonograph record companies. Such was the case with Riley. In 1924, Columbia talent scouts hit Atlanta looking for talent that could produce the kind of "old-time southern music" that Fiddlin' John Carson was doing so well for their rival Okeh. They found Riley, along with his old friend Gid Tanner, a red-haired chicken farmer from Dacula, and sent them to New York to make records.

In fact, Riley's very first record, done on March 7, 1924, was a "cover" of the John Carson hit "Little Old Log Cabin in the Lane." Riley sang and played guitar; Gid fiddled and occasionally sang. They eventually did eleven songs, including "Steamboat Bill," "Johnson's Old Gray Mule," and "Rock All Our Babies to Sleep," which unleashed Riley's ability to yodel. This had been a favorite of WSB listeners in Atlanta, this yodeling ability, and it was Riley's first ticket to fame. The records sold well, and soon Columbia was advertising:

> Hear these Tanner and Puckett records. No Southerner can hear them and go away without them. And it will take a pretty hard-shelled Yankee to leave them. The fact is that these records have something that everybody wants.

Other ads touted his "trusty guitar and silvery voice," and soon Riley's pure, clear tenor was being heard on Victrolas throughout the country. By 1925 he had made enough on royalties to buy himself a new Model T Ford, his name painted on the side for all to see. His buddy Ted Hawkins did a lot of the driving for him, and things were looking good.

Then, early in 1925, came a serious setback. Driving back home from Stone Mountain, Riley and Ted's car was somehow hit by a trolley car. The new Model T was totaled, and both men were hospitalized for long stays; Riley had injuries to his head, legs, and arms. After a stay in Grady Hospital, he was sent home for further recuperation at home in

Thomaston. It was slow and painful, but the young nurse who was hired to help out soon became a favorite of Riley's. Her name was Blanche, and soon after he recovered, he proposed to her. They were married in May, and Columbia offered to spring for a honeymoon in New York—providing Riley could make a few more records.

The next year, 1926, turned out to be an incredible year for the Pucketts. Riley's records would have dominated the charts, had there been any. In January, his record of "When You're Gone I Won't Forget," backed by "When I'm Gone You'll Soon Forget," sold over 50,000 copies; both were sentimental pop songs done in straightforward country style. Then, four months later, Columbia released two songs, "Bully of the Town" and "Pass Around the Bottle and We'll All Take a Drink." These both featured Riley's singing, but backed him with a new "supergroup" that Frank Walker had put together called the Skillet Lickers. Built around Riley, his friend Gid Tanner, young fiddler Clayton McMichen, and banjo player Fate Norris, the band quickly became the best-known string band in country music's golden age. The "Bully" record rang up sales of over 200,000 copies—unheard of at that time. A later recording of "Watermelon on the Vine," issued in September, did almost as well. Then, to cap it all off, Riley and Clayton McMichen (under the alias "Bob Nichols") released a duet version of a song called "My Carolina Home." It was the smash hit of the year, selling over 260,000 copies, making it one of the top three all-time best-sellers in the Columbia "Old Familiar Tunes" series.

For the next few years, Riley toured and recorded often with Tanner, McMichen, and the Skillet Lickers. The band played everywhere from dusky mining towns where the light was coal oil, to the stage of the Ryman Auditorium in Nashville, where they challenged the Grand Ole Opry stars to a fiddling contest. Sometimes they even put on what Gid referred to as "monkey suits" (tuxedos) to play plush hotels. They pioneered country comedy with *Hee Haw*–flavored recorded skits like "A Corn Likker Still in Georgia." Yet, according to McMichen, it was Riley who made the records sell. "Riley proved the people wanted to hear singing. And if he didn't sing on the records, why, they didn't sell much." Riley thus paved the way for the emergence of the vocal star in country music, away from the fiddle bands, the hollering, and the focus on instrumentalists.

Riley's later hits were not as big as the early ones, but they included some that became standards in the music. His version of "Ida Red," the fiddle tune later redone by everyone from Bob Wills to Jack Guthrie, became his fourth-biggest-selling disc (1927). In late 1927, he released another duet—this time with Hugh Cross, who later became famous as one of Hugh and Shug's Radio Pals. It was an old song Frank Walker had heard in upstate New York as a kid, now outfitted with new cowboy lyrics, and called "Red River Valley" (sales were 114,000). Then there was the song that Jimmie Rodgers had covered at his first session, "Sleep, Baby, Sleep"; Riley had first recorded it back in 1924, and rerecorded it in 1927, a few months before Rodgers. Then there was—all for Columbia— "Put My Little Shoes Away" (1927), "The Preacher and the Bear" (1925), and "I Wish I Was Single Again" (1925). Later on, Riley joined forces with RCA's Bluebird and even with Decca in the 1930s, producing records like "Ragged But Right" (Bluebird, 1934), "Wednesday Night Waltz" (Bluebird, 1934), "I Only Want a Buddy Not a Sweetheart" (Bluebird, 1934—a song Bing Crosby later covered), and "There's More Pretty Girls than One" (Decca, 1937). From his very first session, Riley did about as many pop songs as folk or country songs, and his later sessions for RCA were really aimed at the crossover market. He did current hits like "Oh, Johnny, Oh," Gene Autry cowboy pieces like "South of the Border," big band favorites like "Playmates," and Broadway legend Oscar Hammerstein's "When I Grow Too Old to Dream."

Riley also had a reputation as a guitarist par excellence. Though he only recorded two guitar solos, his odd style attracted attention both in his own vocal solos and as part of the Skillet Lickers sound. His style emphasized the bass strings, rather than the "Carter lick" or "sock chords." He would use long, single-note bass runs, often starting in 2/4 time but then doubling or even quadrupling his notes by the end of the chorus. He also liked to "pull" his notes, making them sound like a jug band or tuba bass. Such unusual rhythms sometimes threw off other musicians in the bands, especially the older fiddlers who were used to a simple, straight rhythm, and several of them complained that Riley's guitar almost wrecked their records. There is no film of Riley playing this style, and his friends and fellow musicians give differing explanations of how he did it. The trouble is that none of these explanations agree: They range from the fact that he played left-handed without reversing the strings, to the assertion that he played without his thumb, making the bass runs with his index finger and picking upward like flamenco guitarists. Others say his guitar was "strung hard" with high action off the bridge; still others say he simply used a steel pick on his forefinger. Possibly he used a combination of these methods; the only thing sure is the results.

In 1930, the Skillet Lickers broke up, and Riley spent several years playing at radio stations (such as WCKY in Covington, Kentucky) with various offshoots of the band. After stints in Columbus and Cleveland radio, he briefly rejoined an abortive attempt to re-form the Skillet Lickers in 1932. It failed, and Riley spent the rest of the 1930s in a dizzying round of bands and stations. For a time he worked with Daddy John Love of Mainer's Mountaineers, and with fiddler Bert Layne. He worked radio at WSAZ in Huntington, West Virginia, and in Memphis, Chicago, and even Knoxville (where he worked with composer Grady Cole, author of "Tramp on the Street"). At one time he had his own tent show, traveling through the South, and over into the oil fields of Texas and Oklahoma. His wife often had to listen to his radio broadcasts to know when he was coming home on any given night.

By 1946 Riley found himself playing over a regional station, WGAA, in Cedartown, Georgia; his efforts to keep up with pop styles had not been too successful, and the new singers he now heard on the radio—Red Foley, Ernest Tubb, Bing Crosby—were singing a new type of song. He was staying with friends in nearby Rockmart when he developed a boil on the back of his neck. His wife thought it was minor, but had the local doctor lance it. It continued to give him trouble, and Blanche insisted he go to the hospital. "I'm not gonna leave," he said, "and I'm gonna stay right here with you and the baby." Finally, she called an ambulance, and took him to Grady Hospital. There, on July 13, 1946, Riley died from blood poisoning. For the next four weeks, they say, Atlanta's station WAGA, Riley's old home base, played his records as a tribute to him. He was buried at a cemetery across from Enon Baptist Church in the Atlanta suburb of College Park; his stone says simply, "George R. Puckett," with no word or legend about his rich or complex music, nor about his momumental contribution to country music. Somehow it is symptomatic.

Charlie Poole

One day in the late 1920s a group of musicians pulled their old car up to a dusty country store in Virginia. The leader of the group was a brown-haired, jug-eared man in his mid-thirties who looked like he could handle himself in a fight. As his mates wandered around the store, he walked over to a row of watermelons. "Say, fella," he said to the storekeeper. "How much are those cucumbers?" The old storekeeper snorted back that those things were watermelons. "Sorry," said the jug-eared man. "My mistake. I'm from down in North Carolina, and we usually have cucumbers that are bigger than these things." The joker then had the temerity to ask where in blazes he could get a drink of good liquor. That was enough for this Prohibition-era storekeeper; he ordered the whole gang out of his store. As he turned to leave, the jug-eared man quipped, "Well, being as I'm Charlie Poole, I thought I might get a drink around here." "Yeah?" shot back the storeman. "If you're Charlie Poole, I'm Henry Ford!"

This stopped the young man for a moment. Then he stalked out to the car, dug out a banjo case, opened it, and began to play and sing. The storekeeper's jaw dropped. No doubt about that voice, that banjo style, that song: Charlie Poole. Red-faced, he ducked into the back room and returned with a half-gallon of prime moonshine. The jug was passed, fences were mended, and songs were sung, and Charlie Poole and his friends—who called themselves the North Carolina Ramblers—wound up staying for a week, enjoying the storekeeper's hospitality and adding five more ounces to an already heavy legend.

Even today, people around the Southeast still tell yarns about Charlie Poole, and artists from Grandpa Jones to Ricky Skaggs to Bill Monroe still sing his songs. He was one of the first really successful country singers to work with a full string band; he was a sophisticated banjo player whose work set the foundation for later bluegrass; he was a skilled songwriter and arranger of older folk songs who produced more than his share of standards. Yet he was a restless, moody, undisciplined man whose hard living and hard drinking cut short his career just as it was ready to go into high gear. Like Jimmie Rodgers, he only got to record for a few short years—in Poole's case, from 1925 to 1931. Yet the eighty-four titles that he laid down, for companies like Columbia, Paramount, and Brunswick, were ones that counted; as late as 1999, several CDs of his work were in print.

He was born Charlie Cleveland Poole in Randolph County, North Carolina, on March 22, 1892, and grew up in the rough-and-tumble textile mill towns of the area. The locale was a far cry from the cotton fields or rural cabins of so many early singers; it was a rough, dirty, smoky setting, with a lot of hard drinking, razor fights, and quick-tempered sheriffs. "I'm gonna run me a cemetery of my own," sang Charlie in his song "Coon from Tennessee." He grew up in a big family where fighting was often viewed as a spectator sport; when the Poole boys would get to fighting in the house and fearful neighbors would call the law, the local police generally refused to come—they were no match for this family. In between all this, though, young Charlie began to learn a lot of the old songs he heard in the mills and to play the banjo. His mentor was an older man named Daner Johnson, who had learned something of the so-called classical style in the 1890s. By the early 1920s, Poole was traveling the country, making music; though he got as far as Montana, most of the time he rambled around Virginia, North Carolina, Tennessee, West Virginia, and Ohio.

In 1925, Charlie went to New York to make his first records, for Columbia. He and the other members of the North Carolina Ramblers, fiddler Posey Rorer and guitarist Norman Woodlieff, were working at textile mills in the town of Spray, North Carolina. One June day, when they decided to go to New York, all three brought their instruments to work, gave their notice, and sat down on the factory floor to play a last tune for their friends. Then Poole announced, "Goodbye, boys, we're gone!" Amazingly, it worked. Columbia let them cut two records, and both became smash hits. The first was a pairing of "Don't Let Your Deal Go Down," which became a bluegrass standard, and "Can I Sleep in Your Barn Tonight, Mister?," a tramp song modeled on the "Red River Valley" melody. The first disc sold some 102,000 copies—about five times the sales for a typical hit in late 1925. Then, in October 1925, Columbia released their second disc, "The Man That Rode the Mule Around the World" and "The Girl I Left in Sunny Tennessee," and it proceeded to sell some 65,000 copies. By this time, Roy Harvey, a hot fingerstyle guitarist, had replaced Woodlieff. Columbia was convinced that Poole was their rising star, and a string of best-sellers followed: "White House Blues" (the McKinley assassination song, later revived by

Bill Monroe), "There'll Come a Time" (1927), "Leavin' Home" (a lively version of "Frankie and Johnnie," 1927), "Budded Roses" (1927) and "Hungry Hash House" (1927). Later records didn't sell as well—few did, as the Depression deepened—but did contain songs that stayed around for years and became favorites of bluegrass bands, younger folk revival bands, and traditional singers: "Take a Drink On Me," "Old and Only in the Way," "If the River Was Whiskey," "It's Movin' Day," and others. Poole even adapted jazz and blues songs for string band—pieces like the New Orleans funeral song "Didn't He Ramble."

And Poole did ramble, disappearing for weeks at a time. One famous story tells of the time he was visiting Posey Rorer and said he was going to step up the street to see a friend and would be back in fifteen minutes. Rorer didn't see him again for six weeks. He often used pickup bands on his travels. Over time, he became frustrated not only at his record sales, but at the way in which Columbia insisted on his doing the most conservative types of old-time music. Poole wanted to explore new styles: He organized a band, the Highlanders, with piano and twin fiddles, but had to record it on an independent label, and his singing anticipated western swing.

Frustration and his abusive lifestyle took their toll; he drifted into alcoholism, and by the winter of 1931 had lost much of his interest in music. There was an offer of some sort from Hollywood—either to provide music for a western, or to make a musical short—and the studio even sent him the train tickets. But by then it was really too late. On May 21, at Spray, Charlie suffered a heart attack after another marathon drinking session. He died that evening at his sister's house. He was thirty-nine years old, and his legend started that night.

The Georgia Yellow Hammers

By 1926, the success of the Skillet Lickers was proving to America's record companies that the hard-driving north Georgia fiddle band sound could be a commercial commodity. All kinds of string bands paraded through the studios in the late 1920s, each seeking a piece of the Skillet Lickers' action, and many bearing wild, extravagant names like Dr. Smith's Champion Hoss Hair Pullers, Seven Foot Dilly and His Dill Pickles, and the West Virginia Snake Hunters. Many of these groups made a handful of records and then drifted back into obscurity. One that did not, though, was an outfit from Gordon County, Georgia, called the Georgia Yellow Hammers. Unlike many other bands, the Yellow Hammers generated a distinct style of music that was uniquely their own, and they recorded extensively and successfully.

To a casual observer, the Yellow Hammers might seem merely another imitation of the Skillet Lickers. After all, both bands were from north Georgia, and both were built around a preexisting fiddle-and-banjo team. Both presented images of hard-drinking, carefree rustics, and in both cases these images were the products of record company executives. Both recorded comedy skits, as well as vocal and fiddle tunes. Both contained musicians who wanted to transcend the narrow confines of the old-time string band. Both were in a sense studio groups, with personnel shifting from session to session, and both shared a common repertoire of north Georgia fiddle tunes. Yet there were some important difference too. The Yellow Hammers were based not in Atlanta, but in rural Gordon County, some sixty miles to the northwest. The Yellow Hammers stressed singing more than the Skillet Lickers (their records are full of fine quartet work), and boasted among their ranks two formally trained musicians who were adept at reading and composing all sorts of music. Yellow Hammers members were more ecumenical in their music, recording gospel quartets, sentimental songs, blues, pop, fiddle breakdowns, and even a couple of

Sacred Harp tunes. At one session they recorded with the fine Afro-Cherokee fiddler Andrew Baxter, in one of the first integrated sessions of old-time music. While the Yellow Hammers "covered" several Skillet Lickers hits during their first year as a band (1927), they soon moved out of this shadow and established their own identity. Indeed, by November 1927 the Skillet Lickers were themselves having to record cover versions of the Yellow Hammers hit "Johnson's Old Gray Mule."

The history of the Yellow Hammers begins on a chilly November day in 1924 when banjoist Bud Landress and fiddler Bill Chitwood boarded a train at Resaca, Georgia, for a trip to New York. Bud Landress (whose given name was George Oscar Landress) was forty-two years old; he had been born in Gwinnett County (Gid Tanner's home) but since 1905 had lived in Gordon County. Bud was versatile on all stringed instruments, but preferred banjo and fiddle; he was also a songwriter and singer and was often an officer in the Gordon County singing conventions. His partner, Bill Chitwood, was thirty-three years old, lived in Resaca, and was known locally as a fiddler; he could also sing a passable bass. Both Chitwood and Landress had played for years in Gordon County. They were not necessarily known as a team, though they did sometimes play together, occasionally being joined by another Resaca luminary, Fate Norris, later to be banjoist for the Skillet Lickers. Now the duo was going to New York to record twelve numbers for a recording company just discovering country music; the results included the versions of "Whoa Mule" and "Pa, Ma, and Me" on the Brunswick label. They were the first fruits of the two most traditional members of the Yellow Hammers.

Meanwhile, two other key members of the Yellow Hammers were making music of a different sort in nearby Calhoun, the county seat of Gordon County. One of these was Charles Ernest Moody (born 1891), who had the good sense to trade a shotgun for this first fiddle, and who also played banjo and harmonica. Moody came from a family of church singers, and recalled his father and uncles debating whether the "new" seven-shaped notes would ever replace the older Sacred Harp four-shape variety. In 1916 he attended an intensive singing school in Asheville, North Carolina, where he studied formal music—harmony, voice, and even directing. Soon he was himself writing hymns, and by 1924 he had produced two of the most popular sacred songs of the twentieth century, "Drifting Too Far from the Shore" and "Kneel at the Cross." One of Moody's local friends was Phil Reeve (born 1896), a piano tuner, manager of the local music store, and director of the local brass band. Reeve, though, was interested in other music as well; as early as 1916 he was yodeling, and by 1925 he was organizing radio programs for Atlanta's WSB that featured old-time musicians from Gordon

County. It was Reeve, in fact, who was to become the central figure in the Yellow Hammers; he got them their first recording contract, maintained rather close contacts with recording executives, and looked after copyrights and royalties. (Reeve also served as manager for the Baxters, Jim and Andrew, the Afro-Cherokee fiddle-guitar team from Gordon County who recorded several classic examples of black string band music; for fiddler Earl Johnson; and for singer C. S. Brooks.)

These diverse influences were first brought together in a studio in Atlanta in February 1927; Landress recalled that a technician for the record company thought up the name "the Georgia Yellow Hammers." Soon the officers from the Gordon County singing conventions found themselves bellowing "Pass Around the Bottle and We'll All Take a Drink" as anxious engineers watched their dials. The Georgia Yellow Hammers were born.

One of the odd and delightful songs the band recorded in 1927 was "Fourth of July at a County Fair," a wild, surrealistic account of farm animals and a balloon ride. One of the early best-sellers was the old spiritual "Mary Don't You Weep," backed with the familiar "Goin' to Raise a Ruckus Tonight," later to become a favorite of the folk music revival and a featured song in the epic film *How the West Was Won.* Another ersatz gospel song that became a big seller was "I'm S-A-V-E-D," which had earlier been featured by Gid Tanner. But the real career song for the band came in the session on August 9, 1927, at Charlotte (just a few days after Peer's famous Bristol sessions). Here they recorded two sweet sentimental songs, "My Carolina Home" (which had become hit on the rival label Columbia) and "The Picture on the Wall." It was the latter that propelled the record (Victor 20943) to sales of almost 100,000 copies. Years later, in 1953, Bud Landress gave an Atlanta newspaper writer an account of its composition:

> Landress, who has spent a good deal of his life farming, said he was inspired to write the song one night after he had plowed corn one day. After going to bed, he became fascinated with a picture hanging on the wall of his bedroom and the idea to make a song about it was born. The picture, however, was not of his mother, about whom the song was written. He got out of bed, wrote the words, and "sawed out the tune" on his fiddle. Several hours later when the composition was finished, he awakened his wife and sang it to her for an opinion, which probably wasn't very good at that time of night.

Throughout the next three years Phil Reeve booked the band into a bewildering variety of recording sessions for a number of different companies. There were several sessions for one company that were issued as Bill Chitwood and his Georgia Mountaineers, and another as

Turkey Mountain Singers. Songs the group liked, such as "Fourth of July at a County Fair," "How I Got My Wife," and "Don't You Hear Jerusalem Mourn," were recorded two or three different times for different companies under different names. The personnel seldom remained constant from session to session, and the basic four of Chitwood, Landress, Reeve, and Moody were seldom all together on the same session. In later sessions, Landress took over some of the fiddling (when Chitwood wasn't present), and did a lot of the solo singing. Landress was not the fiddler Chitwood was; he was often restrained, almost polite, and pushed the group more in the direction of a Charlie Poole sound. Chitwood was a more typical north Georgia fiddler—hard-driving, a bit rough, grabbing for wild, high harmonies. Two other regulars who often played with the band include guitarist Clyde Evans, probably from Atlanta, and guitarist Melvin Dupress, from Rome, who also recorded with fiddler Bill Shores and mandolin player Fred Locklear.

The Yellow Hammers were not as successful as the Skillet Lickers in selling records; most of their records averaged 10,000–15,000 copies each—certainly an impressive figure for the late 1920s, where million-sellers were almost unheard of. The one big hit the band had—"The Picture on the Wall"/ "My Carolina Girl"—sold well over 100,000 copies, and, significantly, featured well-mannered quartet singing. In fact, the Yellow Hammers in general had fewer traditional numbers in their repertoire than did the Skillet Lickers. Reeve, Moody, and Landress were all good songwriters, and Reeve had enough business sense to see the value in using as many original compositions as possible. Thus the Yellow Hammers' forte for strong singing, and for original songs. Most of the songs, to be sure, were cast in an old-time style, but to some members, like the distinguished Moody, writing and recording pieces like "Song of the Doodle Bug" at the expense of "Kneel at the Cross" must have required considerable reserves of tolerance and humility.

The Depression ended the Yellow Hammers as a group; most of the boys "grew up" and went into other lines of work. The one exception was Uncle Bud Landress, who continued to play music in local groups up through the 1940s; one of his friends commented, "Bud had a hard time getting over show business." Phil Reeve died in 1949, Bill Chitwood in 1962. Researcher Bob Pinson got to Bud Landress about 1965, but Bud was too sick to talk very much, and he died the next year. C. E. Moody died in 1977, wryly amused and a little puzzled at the researchers who kept wanting to talk to him about his role in the Yellow Hammers rather than his life as a hymn writer.

Darby and Tarlton

Historians love to talk about the influence of the blues in early country music, and it is true that many legends, from Jimmie Rodgers to Fiddlin' Arthur Smith, featured blues in their repertoires. But when you look at the actual singing style of most of these early stars, very few sound like such singers as Blind Lemon Jefferson or Robert Johnson. One notable exception is the team of Tom Darby and Jimmie Tarlton, country music's first really great duet team. They recorded over sixty songs for three major labels in the period from 1927 to 1933, and were best known for their two-sided Columbia hit "Birmingham Jail" and "Columbus Stockade Blues." It was one of the best-selling records of the 1920s, and the first version of two songs that have become standards. In later years, acts like Willie Nelson and Danny Davis reworked "Columbus Stockade Blues," and "Birmingham Jail" became so much a part of the country repertoire that many people consider it a folk song. Built on Tom Darby's incredible lead singing and Jimmie Tarlton's pioneering slide guitar work, the duo's sound was one of the loosest, most soulful, most unpredictable in classic country music. And their repertoire was quirky, eclectic, and vast, ranging from real country blues to old Victorian parlor songs.

Jimmie Tarlton was born the son of sharecropper parents in Orange County, South Carolina, in 1892. From his mother he learned to sing old ballads; from his father he learned to play the archaic fretless banjo. He also learned the guitar, and by the time he was twelve he was playing in the open tuning and slide style he had picked up from black musicians in North and South Carolina and Georgia. At seventeen he left home, determined to make his living as a musician. Like many early country musicians, he spent time in the textile mills of the Piedmont region of North Carolina, and then took off "busking"—traveling around the country playing on street corners, in bars, at county fairs, wherever he could find listeners willing to pitch a nickel into his guitar case. By 1922 he had made it to the West Coast, and was hanging out with the famous Hawaiian guitarist Frank Ferrara. Ferrara taught Jimmie how to use a better slide, a piece of polished steel that helped him note with much greater precision. He also taught him how to adapt pop songs of the day to the steel guitar, and how to improve the instrument's sound. By the mid-1920s the young man had returned to Columbus, Georgia, and set about synthesizing all these new ideas.

In 1927, Tarlton met up with another skilled guitarist from Columbus, Tom Darby. Eight years older than Tarlton, Darby had traveled very little, and performed in public even less. Local musicians had taught him to play and sing, and his singing in particular featured a powerful blues component—a complex sense of rhythm, a fondness for improvising around the melody, and a love of falsetto. Darby's family had come from the rugged mountains of north Georgia, and he was a second cousin to guitarist Riley Puckett. His grandfather and some of his uncles were apparently full-blooded Cherokee, and he remembered them playing fiddle music at family gatherings.

A talent scout for Columbia Records persuaded Darby to team up with Tarlton, and got them an audition in Atlanta, which was then the center of the country record industry. The team soon had their first release, a send-up on Florida land speculators called "Down on Florida on a Hog." No smash hit—but it sold well enough that Frank Walker, the A&R chief, set up a second session for November 10, 1927. That was, as they say, the career session.

Two of the songs were "Birmingham Jail" and "Columbus Stockade Blues." Both songs had folk roots, in both black and white traditions, but both had been seriously reworked by the singers—so much so that even today it is not clear how much they actually wrote and how much they borrowed. In later years Tarlton liked to say that he had written "Birmingham Jail" in 1925, when he had been in the Birmingham jail for moonshining. As he sat in his cell thinking of his girlfriend, Bessie, he said, he took the old melody for "Down in the Valley" and created the song. The guards and warden were so impressed that they got a pardon for Jimmie; in fact, in 1937, when the city dedicated their new jail, Jimmie was asked to return for the ceremonies. The record sold almost 200,000 copies for Columbia, making it one of the best-selling discs in their catalog. Both singers would have been rich had they taken royalties on the song, but Darby talked Tarlton into taking a flat fee for their work—a munificent lump sum of $75 for each song.

Over the next several years, the team had a number of other hit records, but most are known today only to history buffs and folk song scholars. A follow-up to "Jail," called "Birmingham Jail No. 2" (1928), backed with "Lonesome Railroad," became their second-best seller. Others included two down-and-dirty country blues pieces, "Traveling Yodel Blues" and "Heavy Hearted Blues"; an uptempo rendering of the Victorian parlor song "After the Ball"; a Civil War song called "Rainbow Division"; a nifty guitar instrumental, "Birmingham Rag"; and an intense, almost R&B-like number called "Sweet Sarah." These lesser hits sold between 15,000 and 40,000 copies each—solid hits in the music world of the late 1920s.

During their heyday, Darby and Tarlton toured with some of the best-known figures in early country music: the Skillet Lickers, the Delmore Brothers, the Dixon Brothers. The trouble was, this heyday didn't last long. By 1929 the duo was having contract disputes with Columbia—they were bitter over not getting royalties on their first hit—and in April 1930 they did their last session for the label. In the next few years, each man did separate sessions, but the glory days were clearly over. The new slick harmony sounds of the mid-1930s, exemplified by the Delmore Brothers and the Blue Sky Boys, made the freewheeling Darby and Tarlton style seem archaic. By 1935 both men had pretty much retired.

But the music business was not quite finished with them. In the 1960s music historian and record collector Robert Nobley rediscovered them at the height of the folk revival. The young enthusiasts at folk festivals at UCLA and Newport were excited. There were a few concerts uniting the team, but it was Jimmie Tarlton who really made a comeback. He released a new album, traveled, got lots of press, and generally enjoyed his moment of delayed glory. But it was not to last long; Jimmie died in 1979, Darby in 1971.

PART III

From the Airwaves

Lew Childre

Not long ago, the late Grandpa Jones was conducting one of his informal seminars on country music history. Several old friends, and a few young ones, were gathered around the picnic table on his patio. "Today it's all about records," he said. "People remember you because of your records. But there were a lot of people in the old days that were known as big radio stars who hardly ever made any hit records. They were fine, old-time showmen who knew how to entertain you in person. Big Slim was one of them, and Blue Grass Roy up in Illinois, and Sunshine Sue, who was in Richmond, and Cousin Emmy. The best salesman we ever had on the Opry was Lew Childre. Doctor Lew, they called him. A lot of these new people never heard of him, but if you'd been around here in the 1940s, you'd sure have known who he was."

Another of the great Opry legends, Whitey Ford, the Duke of Paducah, paid tribute to Lew Childre by calling him "one of the greatest one-man shows in the business." And, indeed, Lew could entertain in a dozen different ways: He could play the guitar, both in standard and in Hawaiian style; sing; buck dance; do comedy; recite poetry; ad lib commercials; improvise dialogue; or tell fish stories. And he could do this both on the stage and on the air, and he could do it with an easy affability that made him one of the most popular and sought-after entertainers from the 1930s to the 1950s. He was one of the last—and best—of the old-time entertainers who had been trained on the stages of the old-time medicine and vaudeville shows. His career ranged from the dusty Depression-era Texas tent shows of Harley Sadler and Milt Tolbert to the early TV stages of Nashville. He worked with many of the greats, including Wiley Walker, Floyd Tillman, Curly Fox, Bill Monroe, Bill Boyd, and Stringbean. He was no instrumental virtuoso, but he had a wonderfully flexible voice that could ease into a complex yodel at the drop of a hat, as well as a rich fund of old comic songs and stories. For years he charmed listeners across the country.

Lew always reminded listeners that he was born in Opp, Alabama—a place that sounds suspiciously like Grinder's Switch or Possum Trot. But there really is an Opp, in south Alabama just a few miles from the Florida line. Lew was born there in 1901, son of a local judge who planned a normal, upper-middle-class career for his offspring. After a few years, though, the judge began to get an inkling that this might not work out: When young Lew was seven, his father found him on the corner in downtown Opp buck dancing for any stranger who would give him a nickel. He was learning that people would pay good money to be entertained—a key lesson. In high school, he acted in plays, sang the latest pop songs, and played drums in the school band.

Though his family persuaded him to spend four years at the University of Alabama in pre-med courses, he would sneak off summers and tour with various shows. Instead of going on to medical school, he wound up traveling with the famed Milt Tolbert show in North Carolina. Here he was billed as "Milt Tolbert's Most Popular Song and Dance Artist," and posters show him dressed in a tuxedo. A little later he organized a jazz band, the Alabama Cotton Pickers, in which he played drums and sang; one of his sidemen was a young accordion player named Lawrence Welk.

By 1925, the boom in "old-time" or "hillbilly" music was beginning, and for reasons that are still a little obscure, Lew decided to move into this area. He bought a guitar and took off on a solitary backwoods fishing trip, telling his friends he wasn't coming back until he learned to play it. He did, devising a style that involved playing the Spanish guitar with a Hawaiian steel—a style he would later introduce as "Poop Deck Pappy Lew Childre and his two chord guitar." Given his singing style and fund of old songs, it all worked, and by 1929–30 he was broadcasting as a solo act on radio stations in San Angelo, Texas, and Hot Springs, Arkansas. During the next two years, he teamed with Wiley Walker as the Alabama Boys, but by 1933 he had become a mainstay on WWL in New Orleans.

It was here that he won his national fame, and did one of his few recording sessions. In March 1936 he traveled to Chicago, where he recorded some of his favorites for the old American Record Company. These included his best-known number, "Fishing Blues," as well as "Hang Out Your Front Door Key," "Hog Calling Blues," and "Horsie Keep Your Tail Up." By now Lew had the reputation of being able to sell about any product he advertised on his shows, and sponsors were lining up. He also continued to tour, and for a time took his winters at the border station XERA, in Del Rio. By 1943 he had a nationwide show on the Blue Network Monday through Saturday, and was doing three daily shows over WAGA in Atlanta. Much of this schedule was facilitated by Lew's pioneering use of transcription discs. He made dozens of these for everyone from Pepsi to the Warren Paint Company. On many of them he would start off with a spiel like he used on this old ABC transcription: "Just as easy as ABC! Yes sir, Mr. Ernie Keller, that means it's time for old Poop Deck Pappy Lew Childre to hit 'em with a few ditty-wah ditties!"

There was a partner of sorts on many shows: a little white Sheltie he named "Mr. Pooch." The dog did some tricks, acted cute, and attracted kids. But, Lew's widow recalled, Mr. Pooch also had a serious function: "Once Lew got his guitar tuned before he went out to start the show, he would put it back in its case; it was Mr. Pooch's job to lay on the guitar case and guard it." In his spare time, Lew invented new fishing lures— including one that reportedly netted him thousands in royalties and helped him found a fishing supply company in Foley, Alabama.

Lew's last stop was the Grand Ole Opry. He arrived in 1945, and went out on show tours with the likes of Curly Fox, Floyd Tillman, and Bill Monroe. By 1946 he found another partner in Stringbean: Both were natural comedians, both loved fishing, and both had a fund of old songs. For three years they delighted Opry crowds, though, sadly, they never recorded. Lew continued on the Opry (except for a short stint with Red Foley and the *Ozark Jubilee*) until 1959, when he decided to retire. Before he did, he cut his first LP, for Starday, with members of Roy Acuff's band. It was his swan song. He died December 3, 1961, at his home in Foley.

The Blue Sky Boys

It was a late spring morning on June 16, 1936, in Charlotte, North Carolina. Two teenage boys sat reading a newspaper in a waiting room in the old Southern Radio Building on South Tryon Street. Inside, engineers from the Victor recording company had draped the walls with heavy curtains to create a temporary recording studio. A big moon-faced man named Eli Oberstein was in charge, and he was making records for Victor's new Bluebird label—a cut-rate record subsidiary that featured blues and country music, and sold in those Depression-era times for 35 cents apiece. He had recently discovered that Charlotte was a good location to find both kinds of talent—he had already recorded hit acts like Mainer's Mountaineers and the Monroe Brothers there—and now he was racing through another marathon session, cutting as many as twenty or twenty-five masters in a day, and hoping that lightning would strike again.

The two teenagers in the waiting room were named Bill and Earl Bolick. They were from Hickory, North Carolina, and though they were only eighteen (Bill) and sixteen (Earl), they had been playing on radio stations in Asheville and Atlanta for a year. It was an age of duet harmony singing, and groups like the Monroe Brothers (Bill and Charlie), the Callahan Brothers, and the Delmore Brothers were winning radio fans throughout the South. Soon the Bolicks too had begun attracting fans, and while they were at Atlanta's WGST an offer had come to record for Bluebird. Now that they were here, though, there seemed to be some confusion.

One hour dragged into two, and then three, and still nobody had spoken to the boys. Finally Oberstein brushed through the room and noticed Earl reading his newspaper. "What do you think this is, a reading room?" he snapped. "I don't care what it is," Earl snapped back. Oberstein than asked them what they thought they were doing there, and seemed surprised when they said their names were Bolick and they had been told to come and make records. "We understood that you had broken up," he said. He had given their spot to somebody else. "You're the boys who copy the Monroe Brothers, aren't you?" he said. Again the brothers protested; they had replaced the Monroe Brothers on WGST, but they had never even heard them, let alone copied them. "Being that you're here, I'll give you an audition," Oberstein finally said.

Oberstein went back into the little room that he had rigged up as a control room, and the brothers unpacked their guitar and mandolin. They checked their tuning, and then began singing into the big carbon microphone.

> There's a sunny side, where no ills betide,
> On the road that we must go,
> There are pleasant vales, verdant hills and dales,
> Where flowers ever grow.

After a few more lines of "On the Sunny Side of Life," Oberstein was running out of his control room. "That's enough," he said. "That's good. That's nothing like the Monroes. It's very different, and I think we'll just go ahead and record you." By now it was afternoon, and the boys began recording the material they had worked up for the session—all songs that were proven favorites with radio fans, and songs that, the boys felt, were new to records. In addition to "Sunny Side of Life," they did nine other pieces, ranging from old Victorian love songs to prison songs like "I'm Just Here to Get My Baby Out of Jail." Of the ten songs preserved that afternoon, five were gospel tunes; the resulting Bluebird records were to write a new chapter in the history of country gospel music.

After the session, Eli Oberstein debated about what name to use for his new discovery. "At that time there were a lot of brothers recording," recalls Bill. "So he suggested we use another name besides the Bolick Brothers. Eli and I sat down and kicked it around and came up with the name Blue Sky Boys, mainly because we were from the western part of the state, which was known as the Land of the Blue Sky." Thus was born the name that for many came to stand for the very essence of old-time brother duet harmony singing —the Blue Sky Boys. Thus was also born a career that would extend into the 1970s, and would reach from the lonely one-room schoolhouses of the rural South to the distinguished halls of great university campuses.

The dean of country music historians, Bill C. Malone, has referred to the work of the Blue Sky Boys as "the prettiest country music ever performed"; a record reviewer in a 1946 issue of the prestigious magazine *Saturday Review* wrote that "the Bolicks were quite probably the finest harmonizing duo ever recorded." Through a recording career than ranged from the old Victrola 78s to modern compact discs, and which included labels such as RCA, Capitol, Starday, County, and Rounder, and which included over two hundred songs, the Bolicks have preserved their unique sound and integrity. More technically accomplished than the Monroes, more soulful than the Delmores, more mellow than the

Louvins, the Bolicks have forged a unique place in American music. And while much has been written about them as preservers of old ballads and nineteenth-century songs, little attention has been paid to their equally valid role as gospel music pioneers. "About half the songs we do are hymns," Bill recalls.

The Bolicks were originally German immigrants who moved from their Pennsylvania settlement down into the Piedmont area of western North Carolina. Bill and Earl were two of a family of six born around Hickory, sons of a cotton mill worker and city mail carrier. The family was not especially musical—Mother could play a little piano, and Grandmother could sing old ballads—but the boys' father was a strongly religious man who attended local church singing schools. Every year, a traveling singing school teacher would come by to conduct a school at the Bolicks' church, the First Church of God; he would use the paperbacked seven-shape note books of companies like Vaughan, Stamps-Baxter, Morris-Henson, and Showalter. In time, the Bolicks' father became proficient at reading the shape notes, and, as he customarily bought one or two of the books used in the classes, amassed a nice collection of old songbooks. Even as a boy as young as nine, Bill Bolick pored over these books, looking at songs, occasionally asking his father for help in deciphering the melody. Later, when the boys found themselves working on radio, the old sacred songs they had heard in church, listened to their father sing, and read in the books were among the most popular requests with listeners.

By 1935 Bill was performing in a local band with fiddler Homer Sherrill, and by the late summer of that year he and Earl teamed up with Sherrill to go to Asheville, as the Good Coffee Boys, sponsored by JFG coffee. After six months of this, they moved to WGST Atlanta and became the Blue Ridge Hillbillies. Though the station was weak and tiny, and though it was direct competition with the powerhouse WSB, the brothers continued their success, and soon had the record offer from Victor-Bluebird.

Oberstein looked over the ten sides the boys had recorded, and selected as their very first release "Sunny Side of Life" backed with "Where the Soul Never Dies." It was an auspicious beginning; the record, Bluebird 6457, became an instant success, selling so fast that the company issued a seller's flier calling the duo "The New Hillbilly Kings," and asserting that in the amount of time the record had been out, it had sold more copies than any other record by any other group for a similar period. Not only did this record assure the future recording success of the brothers, but it also introduced into country gospel music two songs that soon became standards known throughout the South. The songs deserve a closer look.

"Sunny Side of Life," recalls Bill, was taken from a songbook called *The Reformation Glory*, which was a hymnbook used by the First Church of God. "I heard it from the time I was just a kid; they used to sing it there in church." The distinctive "echo" part on the refrain, Bill believes, was actually part of the written arrangement of the song, and was not added by the Bolicks themselves. The song appears to have been penned by an evangelist and publisher named Tillit Sydney Teddlie; he had been born in Smith County, Texas, in 1885, published his first of some one hundred songs in 1907, and in 1917 started doing evangelical work with the Church of Christ. Among his best-known songs were "Safe in the Harbor" and "Heaven Holds All to Me." Teddlie was long associated with Abilene Christian College, and "Sunny Side" had early appearances in two songbooks published by the old Quartet Music Company in Fort Worth—in a 1922 book called *Song Service,* and again in a 1929 volume called *From the Cross to the Crown.* The Bolick recording was the first commercial one, and set the style for dozens that would follow.

"Where the Soul Never Dies" was another one the brothers learned from their father—"I'm quite certain he helped us with that one, because it was another song that was not sung too much." The song was copyrighted in 1914 by William Golden, author of numbers like "Will My Mother Know Me There?" and "Dear Old Home." It had been recorded before, first by the north Georgia gospel singers headed by Rev. M. L. Thrasher (Columbia, 1928), and then later by a studio group called the Blue Ridge Sacred Singers (Gennett, 1929). After the Bolicks did their version, it was recorded by everyone from Bill Monroe to Skaggs and Rice.

Over the latter months of 1936, Bluebird continued to release songs from this first session, including some of the other gospel numbers. Another one destined to emerge as a standard was "Row Us Over the Tide," with its famous opening verse:

> Two little wandering orphans one day,
> Down by the lone riverside,
> Ventured at last to the boatman and plead,
> Row us over the tide.

This song had been written by Homer F. Morris (1875–1955), the well-known Draketown, Georgia, publisher and composer who cofounded the Morris-Henson Publishing Company, which emerged in the 1920s as one of the state's leading gospel publishers. The song seems first to have appeared in a 1910 collection called *Trinity Songs of Faith, Hope, and Love,* published in Cullman, Alabama, by the Southern Music Company, and edited by Morris and J. Henry Showalter. The original music bore a footnote explaining that the song was derived "from an incident in a Southern city during the great yellow fever epidemic." Bill Bolick found this song in one of his father's books, and he too noted this footnote; "my father helped me with the tune of it too," he recalls. In spite of their fascination with gospel songbooks, neither Bill nor Earl could really read shape notes at this time. Bill would take music lessons from famed Atlanta fiddler Ernie Hodges in 1937, but their earlier songs were worked up with help from their father. Though Bill and Earl didn't know it at the time, "Row Us Over the Tide" had been previously recorded in the 1920s by Kelly Harrell, by Bela Lam's Greene County Singers, and by the Ganus Brothers, Birmingham area musicians and publishers.

Another early hit was "The Dying Boy's Prayer," another song based on a true incident. Bill recalls, "This song definitely I learned from my father, but it is in a songbook; that's where I learned it mostly, but my father did go around singing it. It is a story concerning a fellow that was working with some type of construction crew in the South, and he was badly injured while he was working. He asked someone to pray for him, or read the Bible, but they couldn't find a Bible, nor could anyone pray for him." The song starts:

> Companions draw nigh, they say I must die,
> Early the summons has come from on high,
> The way is so dark and yet I must go,
> Feeling such sorrow, you never may know.
>> Only a prayer, only a tear,
>> Oh, if sister and mother were here,
>> Only a song, 'twill comfort and cheer,
>> Only a word from that book so dear.

The song first appeared in songbooks in 1898, under the name "Dying from Home and Lost," with authorship credit to S. M. Brown. Around 1900 it seemed to peak in popularity, with many songbook appearances.

Victor wasted no time in rushing the brothers back into the studio four months later for more recordings; ironically, the brothers had "retired" by then, due in part to a nose operation Bill had had right after the first session. Soon, though, they were back broadcasting in Atlanta, where they remained until late in 1939. When their first full royalty check from Victor came in November 1936, it was large enough to enable them to buy a car, with which they could tour to supplement their income. An old poster from this time describes their program as "Old Time Hymns and Mountain Ballads," reflecting just how much of their act was gospel material.

Soon they were recording about every six months, and a string of both secular and gospel hits followed. Most of the Bluebirds were also issued on the Montgomery Ward label and sold through their huge mail-order catalog. Other gospel songs the brothers helped popularize included "Take Up Thy Cross" (1936), "Hymns My Mother Sang" (1937), "I Need the Prayers of Those I Love (1938), "Only One Step More" (1940), "Whispering Hope" (1940), and one of the first recordings of Albert E. Brumley's classic "Turn Your Radio On" (1904). All featured only mandolin and guitar, and the Bolicks' incredibly close and plaintive harmony.

This golden age of Blue Sky Boys singing ended abruptly in August 1941 when both brothers entered the service for World War II. Bill found himself in the Pacific, where he was in the initial landings at Leyte Island in the Philippines; Earl went to the European theater, and was in on the initial parachute landings at Normandy. Earl was wounded several times, winning both a purple heart and a silver star. After the war, they tried to pick up their careers, starting again at WGST in Atlanta. In spite of the fact that country music had changed, that electric instruments and honky-tonk songs had replaced the older sentimental songs and acoustic instruments, the Bolicks soon reasserted their dominance of country gospel. They had huge hits with "Dust on the Bible" (some 200,000 copies sold in 1946) and J. B. Coates's "The Sweetest Gift (a Mother's Smile)" in 1949. Their biggest hit of all, though, was a sentimental masterpiece called "Kentucky." For various reasons, though, the brothers decided to reture from the business in the early 1950s and spend more time with their families. Their last RCA session was held in Nashville in March 1950, and their last recording for the company was, ironically, a remake of one of their first: "Sunny Side of Life."

In the early 1960s, during the folk revival, with groups like the Kingston Trio and Peter, Paul, and Mary popularizing the old songs and harmony singing, the Bolicks were talked into coming out of retirement. They made a series of new albums for Starday and Capitol, and began appearing at folk festivals around the country. (One of these concerts, done at the University of Illinois, has recently been released on LP and CD by Rounder Records: *The Blue Sky Boys in Concert, 1964* [Rounder 0236].) The brothers were initially reluctant to include too much of their gospel material, not knowing how young northern college students would accept it; they soon found, though, that their gospel classics continued to have a rich appeal, and that artists like Emmylou Harris and Linda Ronstadt were appreciating them even more—and recording them. The last time the brothers actually sang or played together was 1975, after which both went again into a well-deserved retirement.

Few groups did more to popularize old-time gospel songs in country music circles than these two stately singers from Hickory, North Carolina. Nor did any groups have more respect for their material; the Bolicks always tried to perform the songs as they were written, and refused to "rearrange" them extensively, or graft new words to them, or find alternate melodies. They sensed that their own singing style was eminently suited to the gospel repertoire, and that radio and records were superb media for their art. And while their career was long, fruitful, and much more complex that I have suggested in this sketch, it was in many ways based on the southern gospel repertoire—and on the values that inspired such songs.

Brown's Ferry Four

The line between classic country and classic gospel sometimes gets pretty fuzzy—witness the work of the Bailes Brothers, the Chuck Wagon Gang, James and Martha Carson, the Oak Ridge Boys, Jimmie Davis, and others. Until recently, many country listeners' polls routinely selected as their "favorite gospel group" an act led by Grandpa Jones and called The Hee Haw Gospel Quartet. Though that venerable show has drifted into a state of permanent rerun, the quartet still remains a popular feature: four men and one guitar doing the classic gospel songs of Albert Brumley, Thomas Dorsay, Vep Ellis, and others. But what many younger fans may not recognize is that this quartet is itself a continuation of an earlier quartet, one that in the 1940s made country music history and set the style for a whole generation of groups to follow: the Brown's Ferry Four.

The original Brown's Ferry Four was formed during the turbulent days of World War II, and existed in various forms until the mid-1950s. It is best known for the forty-five songs it recorded for the King record label out of Cincinnati—songs that became best sellers, records that were played to death by radio stations and even worn out in jukeboxes. This original quartet was composed of four men who went on to become country music legends: Grandpa Jones, Merle Travis, and Alton and Rabon Delmore, who had pioneered close-harmony duet singing on the Grand Ole Opry in the 1930s. Later on, the quartet included, at various times, other greats like Red Foley, Clyde Moody, Zeke Turner, Red Turner (no relation), and Louis Innis. It was the work of these men that forged the Brown's Ferry Four sound—and defined what many fans think of when they hear the term "country gospel."

The story of the group starts in June 1943, when Grandpa, Merle, and the Delmores all found themselves working at station WLW in Cincinnati. The war was well under way, and young men were being drafted right and left. The band Merle was in, the Drifting Pioneers, was so decimated that it broke up, leaving the station with a half-hour gap in its schedule—a half-hour the Pioneers had used to sing gospel songs. One day program director George Biggar commented to Alton Delmore, "We sure could use a good, down-to-earth country gospel quartet in that spot." Alton perked up—he had as a youth in Alabama taught singing schools out of old books using seven-shape notes; he had even written songs for a local publishing company. He gathered up his brother Rabon, Grandpa, and Merle, and talked them into trying out a couple of numbers. Grandpa recalls, "We left the studio and went out into the hallway and tried a couple of songs. They sounded okay—our voices blended all right. We went back in and told Mr. Biggar he had his gospel group." The next problem was what to call themselves. Up until then, Alton's biggest song hit had been the raunchy, blues-like "Brown's Ferry Blues." As a joke, Travis suggested they call themselves the Brown's Ferry Four. (Brown's Ferry was a real place, located near the Delmores' home near Athens, Alabama.) Everybody laughed at this—a gospel quartet named after an off-color song. But Alton liked it. "It's got a good ring to it," he said. The name stuck.

Thirty minutes a day eats up a lot of material, and finding songs soon became a problem. First Alton taught Merle and Grandpa how to read the shape notes that gospel book publishers like Vaughan and Stamps-Baxter used. Then, to get "spirituals" (the 1940s code name for black gospel), the group went downtown to a used record shop run by a man named Syd Nathan to buy old 78s by groups like the Golden Gate Quartet. They soon had a growing repertoire, as well as a style: Alton sang the lead, Rabon the tenor, Grandpa the baritone, and Merle played guitar and sang bass. The results were spectacular; Grandpa remembers, "We were amazed at the response we started getting from the farmers and factory workers who tuned in at such an early hour."

But just about the time the quartet got going, the war interfered again. Grandpa went into the Army, Merle into the Marines, and Alton into the Navy. Since the station owned the rights to the name, they kept a Brown's Ferry Four on the air, filling in with local singers like Rome Johnson, Ray Lanham, and Dolly Good (of the Girls of the Golden West). The original group did not get back together again until 1946, when Syd Nathan, whose used record shop had blossomed into King Records, flew them all out to Hollywood for a series of recordings. The Delmores made one of their big hits, "Hillbilly Boogie," and Grandpa did one of his, "Eight More Miles to Louisville." Then, during a break, Nathan remembered that these men used to sing gospel songs together, and asked them to try a couple. They did, and cut two of their most popular songs, "Will the Circle Be Unbroken" and "Just a Little Talk with Jesus." The pairing came out on King 530—still in the 78 era. It was an instant hit when it was issued in May 1945, and it remained in print for the next ten years.

There was a problem, though—a big one. The members of the quartet all had separate careers now, and were living hundreds of miles from each other. (Travis had moved to California by now.) The only way Nathan could keep the name alive was as a studio group—a common idea today, but radical in 1945. He soon rushed the four back into the Hollywood studio, where they cut twelve more titles, including several more hits: "If We Never Meet Again," "Rockin' on the Waves," "On the Jericho Road" and "Over in Glory Land." These sold well, but in the next few months even more happened. All the members suddenly got hot with the record-buying public, and had major hits of their own: Travis with "No Vacancy," Grandpa with "Old Rattler," the Delmores with "Freight Train Boogie."

So the sessions continued. Travis soon dropped out, due to his Capitol commitments and his location on the coast. Red Foley came in for a session (one that produced "I'll Meet You in the Morning" and "Jesus Hold My Hand," among others), as did "Red" Turner, a regular on *Midwestern Hayride*. Other Cincinnati-area singers filled in; usually Grandpa or the Delmores (or all three) were present, but occasionally only one of them was. August 28, 1952, saw the last King session for the group; a few months later, Rabon died, and everyone sensed the heart had gone out of the group. In later years there were sporadic attempts to revive the quartet, and in 1975, at Grandpa's suggestion, the long-running *Hee Haw* version was born.

Cousin Emmy

In 1943, the editors of *Time* magazine did something that for them was rare. They recognized a country music performer. In those early days, the big national periodicals preferred to ignore such topics, hoping they would go away, but in this case they could not. The particular artist in question, headquartered over KMOX in St. Louis, was reaching an audience of over two and a half million, and was recognized by most standards as the leading radio act in the nation. And this act wasn't Bob Wills or Roy Acuff or Gene Autry or any of those slick-sounding country crooners who had a band full of muted trumpets and accordions. This was a high-spirited mountain performer who sang at full throttle, frailed the daylights out of a banjo, and played the blues by squeezing a blown-up rubber glove. And this wasn't some white-bearded old mountain man, but a vivacious blonde who blazed the trail for the Dollys and Rebas yet to come. Her real name was Cynthia May Carver, but all her fans knew her by her radio name: Cousin Emmy.

In the article from *Time,* Cousin Emmy tried to explain to the reporter just what it was that made her show so popular. "First, I hits it up on my banjo, and I wow 'em. Then I do a number with the *guit*-ar and play the French harp and sing, all at the same time. Then somebody hollers, 'Let's hear her yodel!' and I obliges. And then somebody hollers, 'Let's see her dance!' and I obliges. After that we come to the sweetest part of the programs—hymns." It was the kind of powerhouse, in-your-face entertainment that never came across in records or song-books. That's why Cousin Emmy, like other country greats such as Lew Childre, Cowboy Slim Rinehart, Minnie Pearl, and Lazy Jim Day, never worried much about making records. She didn't need them, not during her heyday. Unfortunately, people who rely on records for their history of the music hear about such stars and wonder what the fuss was about. Cousin Emmy was part of that fuss.

She was born in 1903 near Lamb, a tiny town in southern Kentucky, in an area called the Barrens. The youngest of eight children, she literally grew up in a log cabin while her father sharecropped tobacco. The family made all kinds of music, from fiddle tunes to old English ballads, and as she grew up, Cynthia learned to play the fiddle, the banjo, and the guitar, as well as the hand saw, the Jew's harp, and the rubber glove. A self-described "natural show-off," she was soon skipping school and doing little shows in nearby towns; she taught herself to read by studying Sears Roebuck mail-order catalogs.

Two of Cynthia May's cousins, Noble "Bozo" Carver and Warner Carver, had a well-known string band, the Carver Boys, and in 1927 they became one of the first groups in the region to make records. Before long, they were able to make a living playing over the radio, and Cynthia May soon joined them, playing over station WHB in Kansas City. She returned to Kentucky in 1935, where her brashness and raw talent won her a spot on WHAS in Louisville. Here she became, in her own words, "the biggest thing to hit any man's radio station." She remained at WHAS until 1937.

During the next decade, Cousin Emmy became one of the most popular radio stars, moving around the South and Midwest from station to station like a wandering tornado. She soon created her own troupe—one of the first women in country music to do so—which she dubbed her "Kinfolk" (some of them really were). She hauled them around in a big Cadillac—she used to brag that she was the first country singer to own one. Linda Lou Eastwood, one of her band members, recalls that "four of us girls rode in the front and five guys and a bass fiddle in the back seat." She never had any children herself, but took under her wing numerous orphans and waifs she encountered on her travels.

By 1937 she was working at the WWVA *Jamboree* in Wheeling, West Virginia, when she met a young man named Louis Marshall "Grandpa" Jones. "She was awfully popular," recalls Grandpa. "She had them big wide teeth, you know, she'd grin and they'd just shine. And she was mighty good on the old banjo." So good, in fact, that young Jones got interested. After pestering Emmy for several weeks, Grandpa finally got her to show him how to frail the banjo like she did when she sang a song like "Groundhog" or "Raise a Ruckus Tonight." Grandpa was a good pupil and soon took custody of the style.

During the 1940s, Cousin Emmy finally got to record. Folklorist Alan Lomax got her a deal to cut an album called *Kentucky Mountain Ballads*, which included "Free a Little Bird," "Virginia Girls," and "Old Johnny Booker." But it was her one and only Decca release that became her only record hit—an original banjo song called "Ruby (Are You Mad at Your Man?)"—one that would be made into a bluegrass standard by the Osborne Brothers.

With the demise of live radio in the 1950s, Cousin Emmy's career took a different turn. She moved to the West Coast, and took a nonmusical role in the 1955 film *The Second Greatest Sex*. (She had done an earlier two-reeler called *Swing in the Saddle*.) By the early 1960s, now white-haired and still stunning, she was appearing at Disneyland; there she was spotted by members of the New Lost City Ramblers, a young old-time string band riding the crest of the folk revival. They persuaded her to join them in a comeback of sorts, and soon she was on the folk festival circuit, appearing at Newport and on Pete Seeger's TV program. In 1968 she joined the Ramblers and cut her only LP.

Cousin Emmy died in Sherman Oaks, California, in 1980. Tributes poured in, and scholars and historians were quick to note her importance as a role model for women in country music. A few dug out the old *Time* article, and read how the reporter then had described her: "voice like a locomotive whistle and a heart of gold." All in all, it wasn't a bad summary.

The Monroe Brothers

They were cheap records, designed for a Depression-wracked South, meant to be sold for 35 cents apiece. They were heavy, breakable, 10-inch 78s with about three minutes of music on each side, and sound that was surprisingly good. The labels had their own tawdry beauty: against a pale yellow background, the picture of a brightly colored bluebird in flight, with the logo proclaiming them as Bluebird Records, and asserting that they were "electrically recorded." Below the hole was the title in big capital letters—WHAT WOULD YOU GIVE IN EXCHANGE?—and under that the name of the group, MONROE BROTHERS (CHARLES AND BILL). There were no liner notes, no pictures as on a modern album, nothing about the group except that they played mandolin and guitar. There was no hint that Bill would become the founder of bluegrass music and a member of the Hall of Fame, and no indication that Charlie would become a major radio star whose songs would become standards for several generations. Yet they would become some of the most influential discs in country music history, the start of two important careers, the high point of a duet singing tradition, the lightning rod for two volatile tempers that would change the nature of the music. Years later, Bob Dylan would tell *Rolling Stone* magazine. "I'd still rather listen to Bill and Charlie Monroe than any current record. That's what America's all about to me."

On the day they started their revolution and made their first records, Charlie Monroe was thirty-three and Bill Monroe was only twenty-five. They had been playing music full time for less than two years, but their musical roots were deep and complex. Some of them were in Ohio County, Kentucky, near the town of Rosine. This is not the Kentucky of Appalachia—that's the eastern side of the state—but the Kentucky of rolling hills, riverboats, and coal mines. It's the Kentucky of Merle Travis and his thumb-picking guitar style; of the hot string band swing of the Prairie Ramblers; of the harmony of the Everly Brothers and the sardonic humor of "Sixteen Tons"; of the jazzy rhythms of Whistler's Jug Band and other groups who played at the parties for the Kentucky Derby. Just up the road from where the Monroes lived, in Henderson, blues great W. C. Handy won his spurs as a hot cornet player in a traveling minstrel band.

At home, there were eight children born to Malissa Vandiver and James Buchanan "Buck" Monroe, who owned a 655-acre farm and had his children working at plowing, cutting timber, and even doing some coal mining. Rosine was a tough town in those days—a far cry from television's Mayberry or Walnut Grove. "They'd just as soon fight you as look at you," recalled Charlie. He was born in 1903, while Bill came along in 1911; they, along with brother Birch, formed the youngest part of the family, and came of age in the 1920s. While Buck was known as a good square dancer, his wife, Malissa, was the source for much of the music. She sang old ballads like "The Butcher's Boy," played the accordion, and was a good fiddler; Charlie recalls one time when a local dance was to be held but the regular fiddler didn't show. The organizer borrowed a horse, rode back to the Monroe farm, and asked Monroe senior, "J.B., we thought we was going to have a dance . . . but the fiddler didn't show. I wonder if we could borrow Malissa." J.B. agreed, and Malissa got her fiddle. "You never heard such fiddling," recalled Charlie. "Just sawed to death. Stood upright—wouldn't sit down—just stood up, and she was a tall-like woman, and she stood up . . . and just put the music right in your feet." Malissa's brother, Pen Vandiver, later to be celebrated in Bill's song, "Uncle Pen," was also a major influence on the boys. Unlike their older brothers, Charlie, Birch, and Bill all took to the music in a serious way.

As they grew into young men, Charlie and Bill developed radically different personalities. At first, Charlie was much more confident; he was tall, handsome, open, friendly, and gregarious. Bill was more reserved, self-conscious about his crossed eyes and poor vision, aware of his role as the runt in the family. He was the one who got the smallest instrument (the mandolin), and who had to learn to sing the high tenor harmony to Charlie's lead. He was shy and uncomfortable on stage, and tended to defer again to his older brothers. As the boys began to play for audiences, it was Charlie who really enjoyed entertaining per se; he recalled, "I worked it hard. . . . I do everything that's in my power to entertain them, to make them laugh, to make them like it."

By the time they were young men, Charlie and Birch had decided to go north to find work in Detroit. "When we left, I sold my horses," Charlie remembers. He found work at the old Briggs Motor Company ("they made Ford products"), and when they returned home for Christmas, he gave his dad a hundred dollar bill for his present. J.B. had never seen one before. "My God, Charger," he said. "You don't know how much you've done for me!" But one thing was clear: The future for the younger Monroes was not on the farm in Ohio County, but in the city. By 1929 Bill had decided to move north to join Birch and Charlie; Malissa had died when Bill was ten, and his father had followed soon after. They settled around Whiting, Indiana, where they worked in the oil refineries. Bill soon built up his muscles by stacking and carrying big barrels of oil and gas.

Like many other transplanted southerners in the area, they listened to WLS's radio show, *The National Barn Dance*. Soon they had auditioned for the cast—though as dancers, not musicians. Here they worked with the great duet singers Karl and Harty (who wrote "Kentucky"); the Prairie Ramblers; Mac and Bob, the specialists in sentimental songs; and the novelty band the Hoosier Hot Shots. Impressed and inspired, the brothers decided to formally organize their own band. Charlie played guitar and sang; Birch played fiddle; and Bill chorded along on the mandolin. Throughout the early 1930s, the trio played at local dances.

This eventually led to an offer to go professional; the deal came from a company that made Texas Crystals, a patent medicine designed to promote "regularity." Birch decided music was too risky, and returned to Kentucky; Charlie and Bill decided to give it a try. They reworked their arrangements to concentrate on vocal music, and, lacking Birch's fiddle, were forced to use Bill's mandolin to play melody on instrumental passages. While their vocal duets were good, it was their instrumental virtuosity that began to attract attention: They took numbers at breakneck speed, with Bill playing the breaks and turnarounds faster and better than any mandolin player before him. In 1934, the company sent them to do radio shows in Shenandoah, Iowa (home of the Henry Field seed company and other mail-order companies), and then to Omaha, Nebraska. The fans loved them, and the company decided to transfer them to the Carolinas—first to Columbia, South Carolina, and then to Charlotte.

In an age of Jimmie Rodgers clones and country string bands, a hot duet act was something special. In places like Spartanburg, Greenville, and Charlotte, the brothers found that their radio shows drew sacks of mail. This meant they could also book out their own schoolhouse shows as well. And both were serious about these shows; once, when they noticed a group of nonpaying freeloaders sitting in windowsills, the brothers put their comedian on, went out the back door, and began jerking the freeloaders out of the windows and punching them out.

They eventually dispatched some twenty-five this way, until somebody called the sheriff. Fortunately, the sheriff sided with Bill and Charlie.

Their popularity soon attracted the attention of Eli Oberstein, the A&R head of RCA Victor and Bluebird records. He had started regularly coming to Charlotte to record acts for his new budget Bluebird label. He found the Monroes at Greenville and sent them a telegram: "WE MUST HAVE THE MONROE BROTHERS ON RECORD STOP WE WON'T TAKE NO FOR AN ANSWER STOP ANSWER REQUESTED." The brothers were not impressed. "We just sort of ignored it," said Charlie. Records didn't seem all that important to a group that had all the radio and tour work it could handle. A day passed, then Oberstein called them at their station. "And I never got talked to so straight!" said Charlie. "And I couldn't get a word in edgewise. He had the answers and the questions." Three hours later Oberstein met with them, and the contract was signed. He even promised to interrupt his recording plans to accommodate the Monroes' hectic schedule.

Thus it was that at 3:30 in the afternoon of February 17, 1936, the Monroes found themselves in a temporary studio on the second floor of the Southern Radio Corporation Building in Charlotte. "I think it was actually their warehouse," recalls Bill. "I remember there were boxes of records stacked all around. And we both had to sing into one microphone." Bill tuned his new Gibson mandolin, and they began recording. For most numbers, Oberstein allowed them only one take—to Bill's frustration. In two hours and fifteen minutes, the brothers cut ten masters. The very first—though not the first released—was "My Long Journey Home," later to become popular in folk and bluegrass circles. Known in both white and black traditions, it was sometimes called "High Sheriff" or "Deadheads and Suckers." Their second number was "What Is a Home Without Love," an old nineteenth-century song penned by Charles K. Harris, composer of "After the Ball." According to Charlie, this was one of the biggest early hits.

But the big song from the session was the third one cut that day, the one that became the career song for the Monroe Brothers: "What Would You Give in Exchange for Your Soul?" It had been published some twenty-four years before in a shape-note songbook issued by the Trio Music Company in Texas, and authored by F. J. Barry and J. H. Carr. Bill recalls he had learned the song when he was "fourteen or fifteen years old" at a local singing convention; he got it from an old James D. Vaughan songbook called *Millennial Revival*. The brothers had already been featuring the song on the radio, and the fans were ready when Bluebird made it the first Monroe Brothers release, in May 1936. Backed by "This World Is Not My Home," the record began selling within days; sales were so spectacular, in fact, that the company rushed the brothers back in the studio for a second session just a month after its release. In a 1939 songbook, Charlie would write that RCA Victor told them that "this song outsold any song ever put on record by an 'old-time' group." The brothers themselves did no fewer than four "answer" songs to it.

The February session was the start of a three-year recording career that would eventually yield some sixty sides by Bill and Charlie. Many would become favorites, others would become some of the era's biggest hits. Included were "Drifting Too Far from the Shore" (1936), "New River Train" (1936), "Roll in My Sweet Baby's Arms' (1936), "Roll On Buddy" (1937), "He Will Set Your Fields on Fire" (1937), "Little Joe" (1938), "A Beautiful Life" (1938), and "Katy Cline" (1937). Many of the big favorites—about half—were gospel songs, and many fans associated the brothers with such numbers. Virtually all of the records were done in temporary studios in Charlotte—either at the warehouse or at the Hotel Charlotte. Helped by their rich-throated announcer, Byron Parker ("The Old Hired Hand"), they continued to work their magic on the radio airwaves as well.

By 1938, though, the partnership was no longer working. One morning, when they were working in Raleigh, Charlie went over to Bill's trailer and told him, "Bill, we're not doing any good like this. We are arguing, and we're not seeing the business alike. I'm going to go back to my trailer. I've already got it jacked up. If you're not there in ten minutes . . ." Bill shouted, "You wouldn't leave me." But Charlie left and waited the ten minutes. "He didn't come, so I just backed out my trailer and pulled out." Charlie headed to Knoxville, and eventually formed his famous Kentucky Pardners. Bill, of course, went on to form the Blue Grass Boys and get a job on the Opry in the fall of 1939. The Monroe Brothers were no more.

Wayne Raney

The harmonica—that most humble of instruments—has played a surprisingly important role in country music. After being popularized in America in the 1870s, when they were sold by mail order for three dollars a dozen, "mouth organs" were especially interesting to southern musicians, who soon found they could get all kinds of special effects by "choking" them, blowing sideways into them, and creating blues sounds by cupping their hands around them. Some of the earliest country performers to record played the harmonica—Henry Whitter (the first to popularize "The Fox Chase"), Ernest Stoneman, and even Vernon Dalhart (who played one on "The Wreck of the Old 97"). The first harmonica specialist was DeFord Bailey, who featured his train piece, "Pan American Blues," on the Grand Ole Opry throughout the 1930s. But the man who was to have the greatest commercial success with the harmonica was a tall, thin young man from backwoods Arkansas named Wayne Raney. He played his harmonica on some of the biggest hit records of the 1950s; influenced people from Johnny Cash to Jimmie Riddle; sold thousands of harmonicas and instruction books by mail; worked with stars like Lonnie Glosson, the Delmore Brothers, and Lefty Frizzell; and wrote some of the most enduring songs in the genre. In later years, Raney explained: "What appeals to me about the harmonica is the sound of loneliness that fits everybody at certain times." His career was a testimony to that truth.

Born in 1921 at Wolf Bayou, a hamlet in north-central Arkansas, Raney dated his interest in the mouth harp to 1926, when he was only five; he heard a one-armed white man, a street musician, play the harmonica and choke it. "I said then," he recalled, "that I would make it sound like that." A crippled foot prevented young Wayne from doing many of the routine chores that dogged his family, and when his parents finally got him a harp, he spent much of his spare time mastering it. (Curiously, it was a fate similar to that of DeFord Bailey, whose illness kept him bedfast and led to his mastering his harmonica.) Raney's mentor was Lonnie Glosson, also from Arkansas, who had won fame in Chicago with his "talking harmonica." Raney heard Glosson over St. Louis station KMOX, and about 1936 met him in person; the two hit it off, and about 1938 they began broadcasting as a harmonica duo over KARK in Little Rock. Wayne soon figured out how to play harmony over Glosson's lead, a technique that served them well as they played together off and on for the next twenty-five years.

Like most radio entertainers in those days, Wayne and Glosson moved incessantly from radio station to radio station trying to maintain a living wage. Wayne soon sensed he had to be able to do more than just play the harmonica, and he began to try to establish himself as an on-air "personality"—someone who could do announcing and even introduce records— to become what would soon be called a disc jockey. He got some experience in the early 1940s working at the various border stations, as well as at KFWB in Hollywood. But he really blossomed when he moved in 1941 to WCKY in Covington, Kentucky, just across the river from Cincinnati. This station was a kind of funky little brother to the more powerful WLW, but it was a favorite of many of the down-home listeners in Kentucky and West Virginia. Though Wayne was a major performer on the station, many fans remember him today as a disc jockey, and as a master salesman of harmonicas. He sold the little Kratt harmonicas—the "talking harmonicas"—by mail for $1.69 each, and soon hit upon a way to extend his pitch. "We did taped shows for 230 different radio stations, and in a five-year stretch we sold over five million harmonicas," he recalled.

By 1945 he found himself in Memphis, where he reunited with Glosson. By coincidence, the Delmore Brothers had just moved there as well; though Wayne had been a big fan of the brothers when they were on the Opry in the 1930s, he for some reason had never met them while they had all been in Cincinnati. Now he felt confident enough to aproach them, and one evening showed up on the front porch of their house in west Memphis. After introductions and a few Cincinnati stories, the brothers brought out their guitars and jamming began. There was a good blend between the voices and the harmonica, and Wayne was soon invited to join the Delmores on their WMC radio show. Wayne was especially interested in a new type of song the Delmores were exploring—the country boogie. They had just recorded for King a prototype of this new genre, "Hillbilly Boogie," and it was starting to catch on.

So were their King records; at their next session, in February 1946, the Delmores invited Wayne along as a sideman, and let him cut "Harmonica Blues." Wayne was impressed and intrigued; he told Alton that the record business was changing, and that the big market would be in records designed for jukebox play. He wasn't sure he could produce them. At the next session, he went to King owner Syd Nathan and told him he would play the Delmore session for free if Nathan would let him do a solo record. Nathan agreed, and the result, "The Fox Chase," became a good seller. For the next several years, the Delmores and Wayne played on each other's records, and forged the country boogie style that would be a prototype of rock 'n' roll. It was Raney and Glosson who played twin harps on the Delmores' biggest hit, "Blues Stay Away from Me," and Wayne had his own chart hits with "Lost John Boogie" (1948) and "Jack and Jill Boogie" (1949). The biggest hit of his career, though, was "Why Don't You Haul Off and Love Me" (1949). "I got the idea one day when Lonnie's little daughter Mary got on her father's lap and said, 'Daddy, why don't you haul off and give me some lovin?'" The song was recorded by all kinds of pop and country artists.

In the 1950s Wayne experimented with a few rockabilly sides for Decca (including the bizarre "Undertakin' Daddy"), worked for a time with Lefty Frizzell (playing harp on his Jimmie Rodgers album and singing harmony on later sides), and did a brief tour with the Opry. Eventually he returned to Arkansas, where he founded Rimrock Records, and turned his attention to gospel songs. His "We Need a Whole Lot More of Jesus (and a Lot Less Rock and Roll)" attracted a lot of attention during the folk revival, and was even covered by Linda Ronstadt. Eventually, though, failing health forced him to sell his label and his studio. He was living in Drasco, Arkansas, when he died in 1993.

Karl and Harty

Ricky Skaggs's and Tony Rice's highly praised 1980 album *Skaggs and Rice* served notice to a new generation of bluegrass fans that a great deal of bluegrass singing style and repertoire comes from an era in country music history when duet singing reigned supreme. From the early 1930s until World War II, the hottest country acts were radio performers who, accompanying themselves by a mandolin and guitar and little else, crooned soft, well-crafted, plaintive harmonies into radio and record microphones. More often than not, their songs were sentimental or even maudlin, or moralistic and even religious. There was little of the uptempo, off-color, jaunty novelties that characterized the western swing bands developing in the Southwest, for the duet acts found their turf east of the Mississippi. More often than not, the acts consisted of two brothers, since many bookers and program directors felt that two brothers would have voices identical in tone and timbre. Four of the era's five big duet acts were brothers: the Callahans, the Delmores, the Monroes, and the Bolicks (who performed as the Blue Sky Boys). And, in truth, historians have been kind to these four groups, lavishing on them record reissues, magazine articles, discographies, and even books. Yet the fifth major group of the duet era, the one not composed of brothers, has been almost completely ignored by historians and reissue compilers: This was a duo that held forth for almost twenty years over Chicago radio under the name Karl and Harty, a duo that was one of the first, and most influential, of them all. And this is an attempt to tell their story.

But if historians have overlooked Karl and Harty, the music fans and the musicians themselves certainly have not. Bill Monroe remembers. So does Johnny Cash. So does Grandpa Jones. The Everly Brothers. Gene Autry. They remember the big record hits like "I'm Here to Get My Baby Out of Jail" and "I Need the Prayers of Those I Love" and "The Prisoner's Dream" and "Wreck on the Highway" and, their best of all,

"Kentucky." These hits came from a relative handful of records: Karl and Harty recorded only some 50 songs before the war, as compared to over 80 by the Callahans, over 130 by the Delmores, and over 75 by the Blue Sky Boys. True, many of these Karl and Harty records were sold through Sears, Roebuck's huge mail-order catalog operation, which meant that while the team made rather little on them, the records and the songs spread all over the country. This may be one reason why Karl and Harty songs have remained in the repertoires of hundreds of singers, while the men behind the songs have remained vague and shadowy figures.

Though they were to spend almost all of their careers in Chicago, and though they were both to retire and die there, Karl and Harty came from backgrounds rustic enough to satisfy any folk music romantic. They hailed from northeastern Kentucky, and were part of a remarkable pocket of musicians that moved en masse from that part of Kentucky to Chicago in the late 1920s: Bradley Kincaid, John Lair, Slim Miller, Doc Hopkins, and Red Foley. All of these men knew each other, played in each other's bands, swapped songs, and shared experiences; all made a substantial impact on commercial country music. Karl and Harty were not brothers, but they were childhood friends, having grown up together in Mount Vernon, Kentucky. Their full names were Karl Davis and Hartford Connecticut Taylor, and both were born in 1905. In later years, John Lair, who had gone to school with Harty's father, and who became founder of the *Renfro Valley Barn Dance,* delighted in telling audiences the story of how Harty got his name. "Harty's uncle John Taylor was a blacksmith, and he ordered all his horseshoe nails and supplies from this place in Hartford, Connecticut. The night he was born, his father looked up at the wall and saw a calendar there from this company, with the name and address, and said, 'We'll call him Hartford Connecticut.' It's a good thing he didn't look over at the opposite wall, cause there was a calendar there from Lydia Pinkham." Karl's father, who died when Karl was only ten, used to play fiddle tunes on a cheap fiddle, and his mother would sing old songs while she was hanging up clothes or doing household chores. "She knew a lot of songs," Karl recalled, "and a lot of the songs Harty and I did after we came up to Chicago were ones my mother had sung." Mount Vernon was then a hamlet of some seven hundred souls, in the foothills of the Cumberlands, and was the county seat, the meeting place on Saturdays. As young boys, Karl and Harty would watch as the wagons and mules made their way up the muddy streets, and as the hill country men took out their fiddles and banjos and played on the courthouse lawn. "I remember one boy that came in barefoot and in old overalls named

Willie St. John that played the old drop thumb banjo and sang, 'I'm as Free a Little Bird as I Can Be.'" Later Karl was to say, "Some of those songs were pretty important to us," since by this time Harty had gotten a twelve-dollar catalog guitar and Karl had a ten-dollar mandolin. Since both were shy by nature, they at first confined themselves to instrumental music. They also learned from a local piano player named Brag Thompson, who used to play mood music behind the silent movies at the Mount Vernon theater. (One of Thompson's pieces, a march, the boys adapted to mandolin and guitar and called "The Renfro Valley March," and later used as a theme song when they got onto radio.)

After graduating from high school, Harty worked in a local drugstore and then for a time was a teller in the local bank; Karl began attending Center College in nearby Danville, where he was a basketball and baseball star. In their spare time, they joined forces with a neighbor, Doctor Howard Hopkins (Doc Hopkins), an older musician who had served in the Army overseas and toured vaudeville; they formed a unique string band called the Kentucky Krazy Kats, which was performing over WHAS in Louisville as early as 1929. It was unique because it was also part of a basketball team that would barnstorm the state, play a local team, and then during the halftime go out into center court and entertain the fans with string band versions of 1920s favorites like "Five Foot Two," "Goofus," and others. "We would dress in these Spanish costumes," Karl recalled, "and I remember how hard it was to have that costume on right over my basketball uniform after we had been playing for a half hour."

In 1930 Bradley Kincaid heard Karl and Harty picking at a local pie supper and got them an audition at WLS, Chicago. At that time WLS's *National Barn Dance* was the leading country radio show in the nation, and Kincaid was its shining star; the program directors were anxious to hear any talent he could turn up, and they listened eagerly to the two harmony singers from Mount Vernon. At first they were on the *National Barn Dance* only, and had to work in area factories to make ends meet; a little later they got on the regular WLS staff for scale of $60 a week, plus $15 for each personal appearance they made in touring groups. For a time they also did the early morning show, in between the farm reports and the weather, and got to know another early WLS star just starting out, Gene Autry. In fact, Karl and Autry were roommates, and he was with Gene the night he got the call to go to Hollywood to become America's favorite singing cowboy.

The world of the *National Barn Dance* was rich and varied, and quite different from the country music radio shows located in the South. Here singing, not fiddling, dominated, and along with Karl and Harty and Bradley Kincaid, the big stars were Grace Wilson, a former vaudeville singer and soprano; Ford and Glenn, a pop singing duo; an organist named Ralph Waldo Emerson; and a "barnyard imitator" named Tom Corwine. These acts were far more pop than country, but the *Barn Dance* (which had started in 1924 with the Solemn Ole Judge Hay—later to start the Grand Ole Opry—as the announcer) had added by 1931 singers like banjo-picking Chubby Parker, singer Arkie the Arkansas Woodchopper (real name Luther Ossenbrink); guitarist and singer Zeke Clements; fiddler Tommy Dandurand, who led the show's "Barn Dance Orchestra"; and the team of Mac and Bob (Lester McFarland and Robert Gardner), two blind musicians from Tennessee who first popularized mandolin-guitar duet singing in the late 1920s with hits like "Twenty-One Years" and "When the Roses Bloom Again." Mac and Bob were strong influences on the younger Karl and Harty, and Karl referred to Mac as "the greatest musician alive." Much of the Karl and Harty style came from Mac and Bob.

The pair soon found that their daily radio grind devoured repertoire, and they began to hunt up more songs. "The first thing I did," said Karl, "was to write my mother and have her go to see some of the people we had known from back in the hills and get some of their songs." Another good source was old records by the Carter Family. "I bet we used fifty of their songs. They were a great source for real authentic, colorful songs with a punch, with beautiful melodies, and we would go to the Montgomery Ward's catalog store here and order their records." Still another source was the old gospel songbooks that their families had used; they would take songs written in shape notes and designed for gospel quartet singing, and turn them into duets. Two of these were by James D. Vaughan, the Tennessee publisher who helped popularize the idea of the gospel quartet, and they became two of the team's biggest hits when they were recorded in 1934 and 1936: "I Dreamed I Searched Heaven for You" and "I Need the Prayers of Those I Love."

But their best source of songs was to ultimately be themselves, and the songs that Karl and Harty wrote or coauthored were destined to be the ones that people forever associated with them. Karl recalled how the first—and one of the most popular—of these songs was written. "After Harty and I came here, we needed songs desperately. We wanted to stay here, and it was important that we made an impression. There was a pastor of the *Barn Dance* on WLS, Bill Vickland, who always did a little prayer at the close of the program," and one day he was sitting on a bale of hay there, and he said, 'I've got to go to Madison, Wisconsin, tomorrow.' It was 150 miles and I was lonesome, all by myself, and I had a car, and just to be a big guy, I said, 'I'll drive you up there tomorrow.' It kind of paid off, being a Good Samatarian like that, I guess, because on the way back, on those long crooked roads, I started humming this melody and began fooling with some words, and by the time I got back I had a song in mind: 'I'm Here To Get My Baby Out of Jail.'" The song, backed with "I Dreamed I Searched Heaven for You," became their first duet recording on March 22, 1934, and was soon covered by nearly every duet act in the country. The combination of two favorite country motifs—the mother "old and gray" and the young man wasting away in prison—made the song so popular that several years later the team did an "answer" song to it, "She Did Not Get Her Baby Out of Jail."

A silent partner in many Karl and Harty songs was a Chicago songwriter named Frank Johnson. Though Johnson was a Chicago native, he had an uncanny ability to weave rural stereotypes and themes into memorable songs. He always signed his songs with the pseudonym "Pat McAdory," and his many songs on prison themes won him the title "the jailhouse songwriter." The most successful of these was "The Prisoner's Dream," written with Karl and Harty in 1936 and recorded by them that same year; it was the team's second monster hit, and it became a standard in duet singing. The song's structure—a series of "what if" dreams that are always punctured by the cold gray realities of the prison cell (a device echoed in more recent years by "The Green, Green Grass of Home")—proved so effective that the duo had to come up with a follow-up song for it too.

About 1930, the WLS station management decided to organize a new string band on the station, and asked John Lair, who was then working in advertising, to help form it up. The band was to be formed around Karl and Harty, and was to be called the Cumberland Ridge Runners. After several personnel changes, the group finally stabilized to include fiddler Slim Miller; singer-composer Hugh Cross; Linda Parker, a young vocalist reared in Indiana; and a twenty-year-old bass player from Renfro Valley called Red Foley. It was quite a training school, since every member later went on to achieve fame (except for Linda Parker, who was killed in an automobile accident in 1936). After Gene Autry introduced Karl to Art Satherley, the famed record producer for the American Recording Company, then the leading company in the country and Autry's label, the Cumberland Ridge Runners began making records. Their first session was held in Chicago in April 1933, and included one of the first recordings of "Old Rattler," as well as "Take Me Back to Renfro Valley." In fact, Karl and Harty's first solo records were done as part of a Cumberland Ridge Runners session on March 22, 1934. Later, another Kentucky son, Doc Hopkins, joined the Ridge Runners and began to collaborate with Karl and Harty on songs.

By 1936 the original Ridge Runners had pretty much broken up, and Karl and Harty were having record hits on their own. They were also attracting quite a following. One was a young man named Bill Monroe. "While we were at WLS, we'd go over to Gary and Hammond, at the steel mill towns, and play barn dance shows at the theaters there. In Hammond we played the Paramount, and Bill and Charlie Monroe were young boys then working in a refinery. These boys would always come back stage and see us. I remember the first time I saw him Bill said, 'Could I see your mandolin?' and he took this mandolin and I've never heard anybody play as fast in my life, and I went across the stage and got Red Foley and Linda Parker and Harty and I said, 'Come over here and listen to this man play this mandolin.' This happened two or three times." Though Karl and Harty were hardly aware of it at the time, their songs were soon to be recorded by the Monroes, who later joined the WLS *Barn Dance* as square dancers and had even more chance to hear Karl and Harty's music. By 1940 Karl and Harty songs were also showing up in repertoires of the Blue Sky Boys, the Delmore Brothers, and dozens of other groups.

In 1937 the management of WLS fired Slim Miller, and, in a complex dispute, Karl, Harty, Red Foley, and Slim all left that station and moved over to WJJD's *Suppertime Frolic,* a new show on a rival Chicago station. WJJD was a "daylight" station, which meant that it had to go off the air by dark. It was also a directional station; unlike WLS, which was a clear channel station, heard pretty much throughout the Midwest and South, WJJD's directional antenna was aimed to the southeast, which meant that Karl and Harty's biggest audience was to be located in West Virginia and Pennsylvania. For seven years the pair worked over WJJD on a "PI" basis ("per inquiry," in which they were paid according to how many orders or letters the sponsor got for the product), selling now-obscure drugs like Peruna tonic and Acedine. "We kind of did whatever we wanted to do," Karl recalled. "We'd decide to do a song two minutes before we did it. In most stations you have to get 'em cleared. And they gave us time to plug our songbook—a minute each show—and so we rented an old building across the street and we all mailed out these songbooks and made a little extra on that for a while." Through their fan mail and their personals, Karl and Harty found that they had an audience not only in the rural South, but also that they appealed to Finns from Wisconsin, Indians from Michigan's Upper Peninsula, Pennsylvania Dutch, and the upper crust from the plush Chicago suburbs of Evanston and Deerfield.

By the end of the war, the duo was starting to experience the changes in taste that were altering all of country music. The record companies were now concentrating more on the jukebox market than on home sales, and they encouraged Karl and Harty to do more uptempo topical songs. The duo tried newer songs like "Training Camp Blues" and "Girls Don't Refuse to Kiss a Soldier" and "When the Atom Bomb Fell," the first country song about the atomic bomb. They also did more honky-tonk songs, including "Don't Monkey 'Round My Widder" (recently revived on an LP by Doc Watson and Chet Atkins), "Seven Beers with the Wrong Woman," "Don't Mix Whiskey with Women," and "Blondes, Brunettes, and Redheads." Karl recalled: "I remember once we were in Henderson, Kentucky, and we walked down the street and we heard our records—I think, 'Don't Mix Whiskey with Women'—coming out of a couple of places that were kind of wild. Well, that's what we had turned to, but on the air our best things were songs like 'Read the Bible' and 'Wreck on the Highway,' those good old substantial religious and sentimental songs." (The duo had recorded "Wreck on the Highway" in 1941, after learning it from a Dixon Brothers record; their version preceded Roy Acuff's by a year.) The gap between their records and their radio shows became greater. "We were like Dr. Jekyll and Mr. Hyde, and we didn't much like that either."

It was during the trying times of the 1940s that Karl wrote his most famous and most enduring song, "Kentucky." "I wrote the song as a tribute to my home state," Karl said simply, but it became much more than that. After the team recorded it for Columbia on January 24, 1941, the song became an anthem for lonely servicemen, regardless of whether they were from Kentucky or not, who pined for the simple rural pleasures they had left behind. In 1947 the Blue Sky Boys recorded the song, and it became even more of a best-seller, running up sales of almost half a million copies; it has since been recorded dozens of times, by the Osborne Brothers, the Everly Brothers, the Louvins, and others. Karl was never able to duplicate its success; RCA Victor producer Steve Sholes always used to greet Karl at conventions by saying, "Karl, write me another 'Kentucky.'" On the strength of its beauty and popularity, Karl Davis was made a Kentucky Colonel in 1970.

It was, sadly, one of the few tokens of recognition he received in later life. As their radio career ended in 1950, Karl kept his hand in songwriting and gradually became a "record turner" at WLS, where he had once been a star; his latter years were spent putting pop hits by James Taylor and Creedence Clearwater Revival and the Beatles onto 8-track "carts" for the DJs to play. Harty went to work for the state of Illinois, and managed a toll collecting station on a nearby turnpike. Both kept up their skills, and Karl managed to get a hit in the 1960s with his "Country Hall of Fame" and "The Good Book Song." He got a gold union card, and became the informal historian for WLS, the man who answered the questions people would send in about whatever happened to some old favorite from the *National Barn Dance*. Harty died in 1963, and Karl lived on, often attending (as a spectator, unfortunately) Chicago folk festivals, where he got to hear some of the older music he loved. He retained his skill on the mandolin, and made home tapes for his children and friends; he was gratified to see that all three of his daughters had musical talent, and that one, Dianna, became an accomplished jazz pianist. Cancer finally took him in 1979.

Before he died, Karl got to tell his story to Doug Green. When he summed up the career for Doug, Karl Davis said, "Back then we were just gallivanting around; we never gave a thought to what we were doing, whether people would like us, or why they would like us. Even today we occasionally still get letters, and then we'd stop and say, 'Maybe we *were* something.'"

Bradley Kincaid

The most popular country singer on radio during the early years was a young tenor who won fame as "The Kentucky Mountain Boy"—Bradley Kincaid. He was born in 1895, near the Cumberland foothill town of Lancaster. His father, William Kincaid, led singing in the Campbellite church, reading with ease from the old shape-note songbooks. In his spare time he liked to sing songs like "After the Ball" from the Gay '90s. Bradley's mother, Elizabeth Hurt Kincaid, sang too, but, Bradley recalls, "She went farther back. She sang the old English ballads. I learned a lot of ballads from her, like 'Fair Ellender,' 'The Two Sisters,' and any number of English ballads. . . . My mother used to sing some of the old blood curdlers to me, and my hair would stand straight up on my head." Later Bradley guessed that he had learned as many as eighty old songs while he was growing up. Most of these songs were performed unaccompanied, until the day when Bradley's father, an ardent fox hunter, traded one of his old fox hounds to a Negro friend for an old, dilapidated guitar. It was the first musical instrument in the Kincaid family (Bradley had nine siblings), and Bradley soon learned how to strum it as he sang. In later years he would make much of his "Houn' Dog Guitar," and Sears would give the name to a cheap copy that was sold by the thousands throughout the South and Midwest. In fact, there would come a time when Bradley, going deep into the mountains to hunt up new songs, would be amazed to find one of his informants proudly holding a "Houn' Dog Guitar."

As a teenager Bradley tried a little farming and seemed destined to lead the life of an average hill country boy of that time. But one summer, after working hard to harvest a crop of tobacco, he figured up that he had made only $40 for his year's work. A religious experience also caused him to want to make something of himself, and he enrolled in Berea College in 1914. There he worked toward his high school degree by working with pioneer collector John F. Smith and gained his first inkling of the history of the old ballads he knew. He also got some formal musical training and fell in love with his music teacher, Irma Foreman, a native of Brooklyn, New York. They were married in 1922 and two years later moved to Chicago, where Irma worked for the YMCA and Bradley began attending YMCA College (later George Williams College) at night. It was at this point that he auditioned for WLS's *National Barn Dance.*

Within months, Bradley became the most popular figure on the *Barn Dance.* The fan mail continued, and booking agents began to call wanting to put him on stage in the area. On the first of these personal appearances, in Peoria, Illinois, Bradley arrived to find a line of people several blocks long trying to get into the theater. "That radio singer from WLS is going to be here," a man told him. While he made only $15 a night on the *Barn Dance,* he found he could get $300 for a personal appearance. He began to think he might make a living out of his singing. He also began to print up little songbooks, which he could sell by mail and at theater doors for 50 cents each. His first book, published in 1928, sold over 100,000 copies, and from 1929 to 1934 he issued five other songbooks.

Bradley's repertoire in these early years was almost entirely composed of genuine traditional songs; his first songbook contained "Barbara Allen," which became his most popular piece. (It was so popular, in fact, that Bradley reputedly sang it every Saturday night for four years on the *National Barn Dance.*) Other songs in Bradley's repertoire included some favorite Kentucky songs like "Pearl Bryan" and "The Hunters of Kentucky" and English ballads like "Two Sisters" and "Fair Ellen." At personal appearances Bradley liked to do comedy songs that would "get the audience stirred up," and pieces like "Liza Up a Simmon Tree," "The Little Shirt My Mother Made for Me," "I Was Born Four Thousand Years Ago," and "Gooseberry Pie" became favorites. These, too, were old, though Bradley updated them. To his credit, Bradley did not abandon these old songs as his career began to flourish.

And flourish it did. In 1928 he began recording his old songs, with fair success. Sears ran up a special section in their catalog for records by "The Kentucky Mountain Boy" and sold hundreds by mail. By the end of 1930 he had recorded some sixty-two songs on a variety of labels. However, he still considered himself a "radio artist," and while he continued to record prolifically through 1934, his real success was on radio. In the 1934 Radio Guide "Star Poll," conducted on a nationwide basis, Bradley was the only male country singer to even place on this list, and while he got nowhere near as many votes as Bing Crosby, he did outpoint pop music legends like Al Jolson and Gene Austin.

By this time Bradley had left WLS, and from 1930 to 1941 he began a dizzying round-robin series of one-year stays at radio stations in the East: WKDA (Pittsburgh), SGY (Schenectady), WEAF (New York), and finally WBZ in Boston. Here he continued to do the same kind of "mountain songs" he had done in Chicago, with the same kind of success. One of the young apprentice musicians who worked with him, Marshall (Grandpa) Jones, recalled of his Boston years: "They say that people in the East didn't appreciate country music until just the last few years here, but the people in those small New England towns were as crazy about it as anybody in Kentucky or Tennessee. Lots of times up there after a show people would even invite us home to take supper with them."

Bradley continued to remain a major draw in professional country music throughout the 1940s, doing successful stints at WLW and even for a time at WSM Nashville's Grand Ole Opry. He weathered the new and different fads in country music and continued to sing what his songbooks described as "mountain ballads and old-time songs." In the late 1940s he made a couple of tentative inroads into country music, writing and recording songs like "The Legend of the Robin Red Breast" (1945) and "Brush the Dust From that Old Bible" (1950), a topical song about the atomic bomb. But he chose to retire in 1950 and run a music store rather than compete in the Nashville hit market. In 1963 he re-recorded much of his huge repertoire—162 songs—on a series of LPs for the Bluebonnet company, and often returned to his alma mater, Berea College, to participate in folk festivals and talk with students. In 1980 he was subject of a biography (still available) by Berea professor Loyal Jones, and in the late 1980s was nominated for the Country Music Hall of Fame. He spent his last years in Springfield, Ohio, and died on September 23, 1989.

PART IV

From the Shadows: Unsung Heroes

Tommy Magness

"There are three types of history for our music," said the old man. "There's mullet history—that's the kind you tell to people from Minnesota who don't know what a banjo is. Then there's book history—that's where you divide up the music into a different chapter for each legend. And then there's the shop talk history, stuff the pickers tell each other about the secret history of bluegrass. That's where you hear about people like Joe Lee, Blue Millhorn, Emmett Miller, Arthur Q. Smith, Kennedy Jones, Mac McGarr, Amos Johnson, and all the rest of those invisible heroes. And don't forget the one who may have been the best of them all—the fiddler Tommy Magness."

Bill Monroe never forgot about Tommy Magness. "Tommy Magness worked for me in 1940, and was on my first records," he recalled. "He had that fine old-time touch, rich and pure, but he was able to put a touch of blues to it. He was the first man I heard play 'Orange Blossom Special,' and he could put a lot more in it than they do today. He taught me the song 'The Hills of Roane County,' and I taught him to play 'Katy Hill' in the bluegrass way."

Through the 1940s Tommy Magness became one of the most visible fiddlers on the country and bluegrass scene; he played with three of the biggest stars of the time—Roy Hall, Bill Monroe, and Roy Acuff—and helped start the careers of Reno and Smiley. He was instrumental in popularizing two of the best-known fiddle tunes, "Orange Blossom Special" and "Black Mountain Rag." He was heard on network radio, seen in Hollywood films, spotlighted on major record labels, and toured from Maine to California. His fiddling was a complex bridge between the older Appalachian folk fiddling, the new country music styles of the 1940s, and the even newer emerging sounds of bluegrass. Yet Tommy Magness remained an enigma, never settling in any one band for more than a couple of years, restlessly moving around the South, never getting the formal recognition he deserved. Somewhere in the 1950s he just dropped out of sight, even though he wasn't that old, and only a few close friends knew what had happened. For a while people asked, "Whatever happened to Tommy Magness?" And not many people knew, so after a time people stopped even asking. Except for a few who remembered the sweep of his little bow, and the soaring drive of his old records. But something had happened to Tommy Magness, and it's a story worth telling.

The impression one gets from talking to admirers of Tommy Magness was that he was an old, colorful musician who had been born in the nineteenth century, like John Carson or Eck Robertson or Fiddlin' Cowan Powers. Yet he was, as fiddlers go, a relatively young one, and one who died relatively young. He was in fact born on October 21, 1916, near the north Georgia community of Mineral Bluff, in the mountains not far from the Tennessee line. The area had produced two other well-known fiddlers. One, by far the most famous, was Fiddlin' John Carson, who had come from Blue Ridge, just a few miles to the east. Carson recorded and broadcasted widely in the 1920s, making dozens of records for the Okeh and Bluebird labels, and was widely hailed as the first country entertainer to make records (in 1923). The other was Allen Sisson, a much less known but important fiddler who was raised in Gilmer County, Georgia, but who settled in Copperhill (Polk County), Tennessee. Born in 1873, Sisson won nationwide fame in the 1920s, when he broadcasted over NBC radio and recorded ten of his finest for the Edison Company. Though he played in a fussy, almost prissy style, his repertoire included several pieces that would later become Tommy Magness favorites, including "Katy Hill" and "Farewell Ducktown." (Ducktown is a small community in the Copperhill area, which in general is one of the South's most notorious examples of strip-mine devastation.) Tommy's family remembers that he knew and performed some with Allen Sisson, but to modern ears there's not much stylistic connection between Tommy's work and the recorded work of either Sisson or Carson.

Most of the Magness style seems to have come from family and local musicians in the north Georgia hills. Tommy's father was a farmer and gardener named Reuben Magness, whose main instrument was the banjo. This was Tommy's first instrument as well, and family legends tell of him standing at age three or four in a chair and managing to hold and finger the instrument as he tried to learn tunes. They also tell of his fascination with playing corn cobs—one acting as a fiddle, the other as a bow. His older sister Leah recalls: "When he was a crawling baby, he played with those two cobs. I would joke him, and go hide those cobs, and he would just sit there and cry. Those two cobs suited him." But finally Reuben got the boy a real fiddle—of sorts. Leah: "The way it came about, we didn't have no toys, and when Daddy was working at Copperhill, he built Tommy a fiddle, and I learned to play it. I had learned the fiddle from watching Mother pick the mandolin. Daddy just played banjo. Then I taught Tommy when he got big enough."

By the time he was nine Tommy was good enough to start playing in public with his fiddle. One of his first jobs was playing for a local celebration at Hampton's Hardware Store, entertaining customers. About this time, he and his sister had a fight over the homemade fiddle and broke it. ("The dog got that one," laughed Lena.) His parents, sensing talent afoot, replaced it, and soon Tommy was playing with local bands. He played around Mineral Bluff with a guitar picker named Bob Baugh and a man named Booney Anderson. "They made all kinds of music growing up, they'd play in those tea rooms on the ridge. They'd have dances there, they'd call 'em that, tea rooms, but I guess they had drinks, cause he'd always come back drunk," says Lena. We don't have a clear idea of what kind of music the trio was playing, but on at least one occasion this became an issue. "One time a fiddle got busted over Booney Anderson's head. He was whistling 'Farewell Ducktown'—that's Allen Sisson's tune, about the same as 'Flop-Eared Mule.' Bob was trying to learn it and was whistling it all the time. Booney told him if he didn't stop whistling that, he would cut him up. Well, Bob was Tom's favorite buddy, and finally Booney had enough. They were coming back from somewhere in a car. And Booney pushed Bob out of the car. So Tommy got out and made Bob get back in and busted his fiddle over Booney's head. That was before Tommy was sixteen."

Another local band that Tommy knew was the one led by the Chauncey Brothers from nearby Ellijay in adjoining Gilmer County. (Fiddler Chelsey Chauncey is discussed in Gene Wiggins's biography of John Carson, *Fiddlin' Georgia Crazy.*) It seems likely that this band might actually have been the source for much of the later Magness style. One of the tunes that they all seemed to be playing during these years—the late 1920s—was some kind of version of what would become one of Tommy's signature pieces, "Black Mountain Rag." Chelsey Chauncey remembered quite clearly that he won his first awards at a fiddling contest playing this tune, and Tommy's sister recalls that she and Tommy twin-fiddled the tune during this time. "We didn't call it 'Black Mountain Rag,' though—that came much later. We made up lots of tunes, and lots of times Tommy liked to retune for numbers." Like a lot of fiddlers, he retuned for "Bonaparte's Retreat." And he got to believe there was magic in it. "One time him and a bunch of musicians from Copperhill went out and got out and got to starving. They got down in

THE ORIGINAL
CARTER FAMILY,
1928. ALL PHOTOS
COURTESY OF THE
CHARLES K. WOLFE
COLLECTION.

MOTHER MAYBELLE AND
THE CARTER SISTERS.

Roy Acuff on the Grand Ole Opry, 1940.

Roy Acuff and group, 1940. Left to right: Pete "Bashful Bro. Oswald" Kirby, Jess Easterday, Acuff, Rachael Veach, Lonnie "Pap" Wilson.

LEFTY FRIZZELL. PHOTO BY
WALDEN S. FABRY.

GRANDPA JONES AND
RAMONA ON THE GRAND
OLE OPRY, 1955.

Minnie Pearl and Grandpa Jones, "Grandpa and Minnie's Kitchen," *Hee Haw,* 1975.

Pee Wee King (with accordion) and group, 1937.

BILL MONROE ON THE GRAND OLE OPRY, 1940.

LEFT TO RIGHT: KENNY BAKER (FIDDLE), BILL MONROE (MANDOLIN), UNKNOWN GUITARIST (POSSIBLY JOE STUART), JACK HICKS (BANJO), BASS PLAYER NOT VISIBLE OR KNOWN, 1974. PHOTO BY CHARLES K. WOLFE.

HANK SNOW, BOXCAR
WILLIE, AND KIRK
MCGEE, OPRY LOUNGE,
1981.

HANK SNOW ON STAGE AT THE GRAND OLE OPRY.

Left to right: Johnnie Wright, Chet Atkins (with fiddle), Kitty Wells, Smilin' Eddie Hill, c. 1948.

Fiddlin' John Carson and his daughter Moonshine Kate.

CHARLIE POOLE (SEATED) WITH THE NORTH
CAROLINA RAMBLERS.

VERNON DALHART.

RILEY PUCKETT, C. 1935.

LEFT TO RIGHT, BOTTOM: LEW CHILDRE, "MR. POOCH," MARGE TILLMAN, "UNCLE MOSE" (BLACKFACE), FLOYD TILLMAN, ACCORDION PLAYER UNKNOWN.

BLUE SKY BOYS.

BILL AND CHARLIE MONROE, 1936.

KARL AND HARTY.

ZEB AND ZEKE
TURNER, 1948.

THE ROUSE BROTHERS.

ELVIS PRESLEY (CENTER) WITH THE JORDANAIRES.

CURLY FOX AND TEXAS RUBY, c. 1936.

ALTON AND RABON DELMORE.

EMMETT MILLER, 1949.

THE LOUVIN BROTHERS.

THE LOUVIN BROTHERS WITH
JOHNNY CASH (CENTER).

THE STATLER BROTHERS, C. 1967.

MARTHA CARSON.

CLIFF CARLISLE.

STRINGBEAN (DAVID AKEMAN)
AND LEW CHILDRE, 1946.

ALBERT E. BRUMLEY BEING INTERVIEWED
IN HIS OFFICE.

RED RIVER DAVE.

MERLE AND DOC WATSON.

THE FREIGHT HOPPERS.

Atlanta, off with some show down off the mountain, and decided they would start walking back home—all the way from Atlanta—over 100 miles. Tommy, when he got down and out, he'd always tune up his fiddle and play 'Bonaparte's Retreat' and try to get some help. So they all crawled up on the bank [by the road] and he got his fiddle out and started playing. Lester, one of the boys, was quarrelsome and said, 'What in the world are you trying to play, with us starving to death?' Tommy just played right on, and sure enough, the daddy and mother of one of the boys happened to be driving along and picked 'em up and got 'em. Tommy was only about twelve at the time."

Not long after this Tommy began to get a taste of the newly developing professional country music scene. He attended a local show by Pop Eckler out of Atlanta, from WSB's *Crossroads Follies*. "They coaxed him up on stage," recalls Faye Harris, Tommy's daughter. "It took some coaxing. But he played 'The Mocking Bird' and then something else for an encore. He went back with Eckler that night, and he played a while with them." Later, Tommy made other attempts to go out on his own, most reflecting an amazing confidence in the face of the deepening Depression. His widow remembers: "When he left home he only took his fiddle and some clothes. He got so hungry he couldn't stand it, and took his fiddle into a cafe. They asked him to play a tune. He did, and said he got steaks or biscuits or anything he wanted." In between these trips, he did work at Beacon Mills, a blanket manufacturer.

During Tommy's later childhood, the family moved back and forth to North Carolina, and Tommy's mother died there when he was eight. Not surprisingly, around 1932, when Tommy was sixteen, he quit school and moved to Canton, North Carolina, near Asheville. There he began working with a family headed by Carl McElreath, who maintained a string band and a group of dancers. In between playing on the radio and at festivals, the family built rock houses around Canton. One of the McElreath children was Ruth. She was a fine guitarist and a superb musician in her own right; when she began competing against the rest of the family, she often won the trophy at contests. Eventually, the boys got to where they wouldn't let her enter; at one particular contest in Asheville, the family took off, leaving her at home. Furious, she hired a taxi, went to the contest, and won the prizes anyway. Stunts like this impressed young Tommy, and when he was eighteen he married Ruth. Two children soon resulted, although one died in infancy.

The next few years are a little confused. We get glimpses of Tommy going to work in the nearby Deacon Mill, and playing over the radio in Asheville—WWNC—free of charge to advertise himself. He must have known some of the important Asheville area fiddlers, such as Marcus

Martin or Pender Rector or John D. Weaver, but there is no documentation of this. As he sought work on the radio, in the mid- to late 1930s, the so-called golden age of old-time fiddling was in decline; there were fewer and fewer programs featuring exclusively fiddle music, even in the mountains, and the fiddle was being relegated to a backup role for the new breed of entertainers—vocalists. The typical radio show now featured a smooth-voiced singer, a comedian, duet singers, and maybe one or two short token "fiddle breakdowns." In one sense, Tommy was hitting the media just about a decade too late.

One of the new radio singers was a handsome young man from nearby Waynesville, North Carolina, named Roy Hall. Coming from a family of mill workers, Roy and his brother Jay Hugh began recording their duet singing for major record companies in 1937 and broadcasting over WSPA in Spartanburg, South Carolina. After his brother left the band, Roy organized a string band called the Blue Ridge Entertainers. It was built around Hall and dobro player Bill Brown, tenor banjo player Bud Buchanan, and Wayne Watson on bass. By the spring of 1938 Hall had asked Tommy Magness to join him on fiddle, and Tommy accepted. Soon Tommy was being heard not only over WSPA but also over WWNC in Asheville and WBIG in Greensboro. By the fall of 1938, the band had moved to WAIR in Winston-Salem, where they had a popular show sponsored by Dr. Pepper. Roy Hall's star was ascending, and within months he would become the most popular singer in the Carolinas. And listeners were paying more and more attention to the moon-faced fiddler whose rich tone and mellow double stops were adding so much to his back-up band.

It was with this band—or a version of it—that Magness made his first commercial recordings, for the old American Record Company at a makeshift studio in Columbia, South Carolina, on November 7, 1938. Sixteen sides were cut, but most were never issued; the ones that did get released included one of Hall's best known, "Come Back Little Pal" and "Where the Roses Never Fade." Among the casualties, however, was one that would loom large in Tommy Magness's career: "The Orange Blossom Special." About halfway through the session, he cut a version of the song on master number SC-93. Tommy may not have known it at the time, but this was the very first recording of Erwin Rouse's famed train piece. Though the detailed circumstances of how the song came about are still unclear, the piece was obviously becoming very popular with radio fiddlers in 1938. Just where Tommy picked it up is not known, either. But Erwin Rouse had in fact copyrighted the song by now, even though he and his brother would not make their own first recording of it until June 1939, almost nine months later. The A&R chief for the American Record Company, Art Satherley, sensed a good tune when he heard Tommy's version, and wanted to release it; some-how, though, the Rouse Brothers found out about the Magness recording and managed to block it. "Hold release, Rouse Brothers refuse to sign contract," read one note in Satherly's files. On the recording ledger itself was another note: "Don't release—Pub. prom-ises trouble." Obviously the Rouses wanted to have the first release on their song—and did so—and so Tommy Magness's version, which Bill Monroe so admired, was left to languish in the ARC-Columbia files. (In 2000, Columbia actually discovered the "lost" master and reissued it on a CD set.)

The Hall band continued to do well on the radio and in 1939 moved up to WDJB in Roanoke, a city Tommy would use as his head-quarters off and on for the rest of his career. Here they started a live Saturday night show called the *Blue Ridge Jamboree,* which attracted a wide range of guests, from the Carter Family to Roy Rogers and Gabby Hayes. The band would do two more important record sessions in 1940 and 1941—this time for RCA's Bluebird label. Tommy would be fea-tured on both of them, and he would play on the Blue Ridge Entertainers' biggest hit, "Don't Let Your Sweet Love Die," recorded in Atlanta in October 1940. His own two specialties—numbers he is still remembered for in the Blue Ridge area today—were "Natural Bridge Blues" and "Polecat Blues, " both done in Atlanta in October 1941. Both tunes are still in the modern repertoires of such Virginia fiddlers as Greg Hooven and Rafe Brady.

In 1940, though, Tommy left Roy Hall for a sabbatical with another major string band that was in the process of defining itself: Bill Monroe and the Blue Grass Boys. Monroe had gotten a slot on the Grand Ole Opry in late 1939, and was being featured on the new NBC network part of the show. Monroe was attracted to Magness's drive and loose, bluesy style. He recalled: "Now Tommy Magness had been playing with Roy Hall and they were trying to play off of bluegrass. He'd heard the way we played when Art Wooten was with me, so it was right down his alley to get somebody behind him with that, because with that kind of little bow he worked, he could move you right along." Monroe's reference to Tommy's "little bow" is revealing; it suggests that, even though he respected the so-called long bow artists like Arthur Smith and Clayton McMichen, Monroe also saw a place in his music for the older mountain "jiggy bow" style—of which Magness was one of the very best practitioners. It turned out to be Magness who backed Monroe on his first solo recording, "Mule Skinner Blues," done for the Victor company in 1940 in Atlanta. Tommy was also featured on most of the other seven songs from the session, playing some evocative blues on Clyde Moody's vocal of "Six White Horses," some greasy shuffling on "Dog House Blues," and some nice J. E. Mainer licks on "I Wonder If You Feel the Way I Do." His masterpiece of the session, though, was the soaring "Katy Hill," played at the kind of breathless tempo that was winning Monroe his reputation. "'Katy Hill' had more in it when we recorded [it] than it ever had before," Monroe recalled. "Those old-time fiddlers didn't have anybody to shove them along." Magness did. He had three of the best rhythm players in the music back then: Monroe, guitarist Clyde Moody, and veteran bass player Bill Wesbrook. Fans responded by buying the record in droves.

Curiously, most of these Bluebird records that won Tommy his reputation were done in one marathon session in Atlanta during the first week of October 1940. On the 7th he did his Monroe session, and two days later he helped out his old boss Roy Hall for the session that produced "Don't Let Your Sweet Love Die." And in between he helped out Arthur Smith by playing twin fiddles with him on a couple of his recordings. But by the next big Bluebird field session a year later—October 1941—Tommy had left Monroe and was back full time with Roy Hall. It was at that session that Tommy recorded "Polecat Blues," and watched Art Wooten record "Orange Blossom Special" with Monroe. Hall's popularity by now had grown so much that he was running two separate bands to take care of demand, and was able to pay Tommy better than the $25 dollars a week union scale he was getting with Monroe. By now Tommy's first marriage had fallen apart, and in 1942 he married a Virginia girl named Tootsie Poindexter.

Throughout the early years of World War II Tommy continued to work with Hall for Dr. Pepper at Roanoke. Then tragedy struck: Roy Hall was killed in an automobile accident on May 16, 1943. Several months before, however, Tommy had decided to leave the band anyway after two years' broadcasting, and move to WHAS in Louisville, where he appeared on the *Early Morning Frolic* show. After about a year of this, though, he received an offer to return to Nashville—not to work for Bill Monroe, but for an even bigger name: Roy Acuff.

Acuff, of course, was himself a fiddler and had in fact first won his job on the Opry as a fiddler back in 1938. But now his forte was his distinctive singing style, and as he became more and more popular in the early 1940s, he found himself doing a number of jobs: He was master of ceremonies, lead singer, bandleader, songwriter, actor, businessman, and founder of Acuff-Rose publishing, the company that laid the foundation for the modern Nashville music business. By 1944 he had decided that, while the fiddle was still a key part of the Smoky Mountain sound, he no longer really had time to do it himself; for the first time in his career, he decided to hire a fiddler. After hearing Tommy's mellow mountain style, and the way he had backed up Roy Hall's vocals, he made the offer. Tommy accepted at once.

When Tommy and his family drove to Nashville in 1944, Roy was the most popular country singer in America. His Prince Albert portion of the Grand Ole Opry was heard every Saturday night at 9:30 Central War Time over NBC from coast to coast; his Republic feature films were seen in theaters across the country; his tent shows and stadium tours played to thousands more; his Columbia and Okeh singles were constantly in the Top 10 of the new *Billboard* charts. His band was an amiable and versatile bunch that included Pete "Oswald" Kirby, arguably the best dobro player in the business; Rachael Veach, the pioneer woman banjo player whom Acuff billed as Oswald's little sister to prevent fan criticism; Jimmie Riddle, the remarkable harmonica player who had learned his trade in the bars of Memphis; Jess Easterday, a no-nonsense old-time guitar and mandolin player who became one of Tommy's close friends; and Joe Zinkan, the bass player who later became a Nashville studio regular. (Lonnie "Pap" Wilson was by now serving his hitch in the Navy.)

Tommy fit in well here, and for the next two years became probably the most widely heard old-time fiddler in the nation. Shortly after he joined Roy the band traveled to Hollywood to film Acuff's fifth Republic musical, *Sing, Neighbor, Sing,* where Tommy backed Roy in songs like "Easy Rockin' Chair." In following years Tommy appeared in two other films, *Night Train to Memphis* (1946) and *Smoky Mountain Melody* (1948). He also became a regular on Roy's records, appearing on such classics as "Wait for the Light to Shine" (12/44), "Blue Eyes Crying in the Rain" (8/45), "No One Will Ever Know" (8/45), "We Live in Two Different Worlds" (8/45), and "Pins and Needles (In My Heart)" (8/45).

Once again, though, just as Tommy was on the verge of establishing his career, fate intervened. Acuff, in a dispute with the Opry management, decided to leave the show and strike out on his own. Acuff invested thousands of dollars in his own traveling tent show, and made plans to spend far more time on the road. It would yield more income for him and his band, but without the requirement to be in every Saturday for the Opry, it would mean far more traveling. With a growing family, such a life was not appealing to Tommy, and when Acuff really quit the show—on April 6, 1946—Tommy and steel guitar player Wayne Flemming decided to return to Roanoke and WDBJ.

By June 1946 Tommy had formed his own band, Tommy Magness and the Orange Blossom Boys, an interesting band that was part western swing, part honky-tonk, and a touch of bluegrass. It included Clayton and Saford Hall (not related to Roy), Jay Hugh Hall (Roy's older brother), singer Warren Poindexter, and steel player Slim Idaho.

Slim was one of the first to use an electric pedal steel, and Tommy's announcer always referred to him as "big Slim Idaho with his strange three-necked steel guitar"—suggesting that he either made his own instrument (as did many early pedal players) or was using one of the very first Fender pedal steels. Idaho was a remarkable instrumentalist and a key innovator on the pedal steel; he later played on WRVA and became known for his stunning work on Cowboy Copas's "Jamboree" single of 1949. With Tommy, he helped play the band's theme song—"Orange Blossom Special," of course—and did take-off solos on items like "Texas Playboy Rag." Tommy, for his part, did traditional breakdowns like "Cotton Eyed Joe," but also did Joe Holley-style takeoff solos on western swing pieces. In September 1947, the band recorded its only commercial record, for the Roanoke-based Blue Ridge label: "Sittin' on Top of the World," backed with a new train instrumental, "Powhatan Arrow."

The Orange Blossom Boys built a solid reputation in Roanoke in 1946, and Tommy's use of the "Special" as his theme song helped spread the popularity of the tune in the Southeast. But then, in April 1947, Acuff returned to his niche at the Grand Ole Opry, and made Tommy an offer to return to the more settled lifestyle there. Tommy broke up his Roanoke band and moved back to Nashville. The problem was, Acuff's career was about to go into high gear again. In November 1947 there were two huge recording sessions for Columbia, stockpiling sides for the forthcoming recording ban. In July 1948, there was another trip to Hollywood, this time to film *Smoky Mountain Melody,* and in November yet another one to film *Home in San Antone.* In between was something Tommy had not expected at all: Roy Acuff's run for governor of Tennessee. He was part of Acuff's official "campaign band," which included Oswald, Jimmie Riddle, Sonny Day, Jess Easterday, Joe Zinkan, and Lonnie "Pap" Wilson. Rachael Veach even came out of retirement to play banjo. This group barnstormed the state with Roy, doing a hundred shows in sixty-four days, and managing to get back Saturdays for the Opry.

Throughout much of the campaign, Acuff had to defend himself against charges that he was only a "hillbilly fiddler" and the fact that opponents sometimes referred him as "the fiddler." This made him, if anything, defensive about fiddling, and how complex an art it really was; he came to increasingly respect Magness's fiddling skills, and soon was letting Magness use his own fiddle on the stage. In March 1948, even before the campaign had begun, Acuff had taken Tommy aside and asked him if he would privately record his old-time fiddle tunes on a home disc recorder that Roy had bought. Oswald was brought in to play backup guitar, and Tommy began to go through his repertoire. He started with some of the old Fannin County–Ducktown tunes he had known as a child—

things like "Farewell Ducktown" and "Forked Deer" and "Little Old Log Cabin" and "Liberty" (the old version). He did some of the western swing tunes from his recent stay at Roanoke as a "radio fiddler," such as "San Antonio Rose" and "Don't Let Your Deal Go Down" and "Under the Double Eagle" and the odd, haunting "Bob Wills Stomp." There was a healthy helping of Arthur Smith tunes, such as "Blackberry Blossom," "Florida Blues," "Fiddler's Dream," "Bill Cheatam," and "K.C. Stomp." There were the familiar Magness favorites like "Black Mountain Rag" and "Orange Blossom Special" and the blazing "Katy Hill" he had recorded for Monroe—but not the two great Roy Hall pieces "Natural Bridge Blues" and "Polecat Blues." Most of the southern fiddle standards were there, but sprinkled among them were a bevy of odd and unusual tunes, such as "Duck's Eyeball," "Rocky Oaks Studman," "Grandpa's Rag," "Magness' Reel," "Lady Hamilton," "Booth," and "Up Jumped Trouble" (which had been popularized by Mac McGarr on the Opry in the early 1940s). All told, Tommy laid down over 130 tunes for Acuff's recorder, but for some reason Acuff limited the length, and so few of them are more than a minute in duration. (This is probably one of the reasons they have never been issued to the public, for their sound quality is generally excellent.) The only really problem is that Tommy and Os got no real chance to rehearse, and occasionally Tommy's odder tunes throw Os off or give him chord changes he can't believe. "Sometimes Tommy had to shout out where to go," Oswald recalls today. "He would get into some of those old tunes that neither Roy or I either one had ever heard before."

(The discs had an interesting effect on Acuff. Years later, in the 1970s and 1980s, Roy began to get interested in his own fiddling again. He did so by bringing the old Magness discs up to his dressing room at the Opry, and playing them for his own enjoyment, or to impress visitors. Friends say that it was these discs that got Roy to thinking more about fiddling, and to start sharpening his own skills.)

Another effect of this set of home discs came the next year, in 1949, when Acuff devoted an entire album to Tommy's fiddle music. In January 1949, after a session where Acuff recorded his Magness-flavored version of "Tennessee Waltz," the band recorded eight fiddle tunes featuring Tommy: "Grey Eagle," "Dance Around Molly," "Black Mountain Rag," "Pretty Little Widow," "Smoky Mountain Rag," "Lonesome Indian," and "Bully of the Town." The records were released as a 78 rpm album (No. II-8, *Old Time Barn Dance*) in May. The album was part of a national fad for square dancing and square dance records in the late 1940s, but it did get some of Tommy's very finest fiddling preserved. In the process of doing the paperwork, Acuff-Rose filed a copyright on "Black Mountain Rag" in Tommy's name—a copyright that still yields the family royalties today.

Not long after the square dance album was recorded, Tommy left Acuff again. One widely circulated story was that he left because his wife had bought a new Chevy and he couldn't wait to get home to drive it. A more likely one was that Tommy had again burned out on touring, which was now being done a lot on an airplane Acuff had bought (called, of course, *The Great Speckled Bird*). By 1950 he was back at WDJB in Roanoke, and had organized a new band which he called the Tennessee Buddies. The original personnel included Tommy on fiddle, Hal Grant on mandolin, Dexter Mills on bass, Red Smiley on guitar, Verlon Reno on guitar, and Don Reno on banjo. Later on, Cousin Irving Sharpe replaced Mills on bass, and also occasionally played piano. A baggy-pants comedian known as Chicken provided the comedy.

Tommy had known the Reno family for some time. Leah Magness, Tommy's sister, was living in Canton as the Renos were growing up, and recalls that Tommy and Don Reno even played music some together in Spartanburg. "He couldn't play too good with Tommy then," she recalled. The boys, though, hung around Lena's house a lot. "I tuned Don's first banjo. His brother had bought him a banjo for Christmas, and he couldn't even tune it up. And I helped him tune it up, I learned him how all winter. He tormented the life out of it." By 1950 Don was no longer tormenting the banjo, and had in fact already served an important stint with Bill Monroe. When Tommy heard he was available, he sent for him to join his band, and soon Don was reunited with his cousin Verlon.

Before the band could hardly get on its feet, tragedy struck again. On June 20, 1950, Verlon Reno drowned while swimming in the Cowpasture River. Tommy especially was devastated by the loss. His daughter remembers: "When Verlon drowned, it just about killed Daddy. For he never did have a son and he thought the world of that boy." One of the early Tennessee Buddies songbooks has the words to a tribute Don wrote about his cousin, "A Rose on God's Shore," which Don began to sing as a duet with the group's guitar player, Red Smiley. (The pair would later record it for their first King session under their own name.)

Though the Tennessee Buddies sported three men who would later become bluegrass legends, by the middle of 1950 they were still not quite a bluegrass band. Their songbook included numbers like Hank Snow's "I'm Movin On," Don Reno's "The Talk of the Town," Bill Monroe's "I'm Blue, I'm Lonesome," Reno's "Little Country Preacher," Hank Williams's "Everything's Okay," Stuart Hamblen's "Remember Me," Hank Garland's "Sugarfoot Rag," and even a song by Reno's eighty-four-year old grandmother, "My Sunshine Home." It was not surprising that Tommy got as a replacement for Verlon a young steel guitar player named Jackie Phelps. Remus Bell played bass. The band was busy: They had a morning show from 6:05 until 7:00, and a fifteen-minute noon show for Dr. Pepper. Each Saturday night they played at the El-Tenedore Skating Rink on Highway 221 near Floyd, Virginia, where they had both round and square dances. They also played at a tent show. "If we went too far out of town," Remus Bell noted, "I know several times we had to record" so the station would have something to play for their shows.

It was this band that traveled to Cincinnati on March 6, 1951, to record what would be Tommy's last records. They were done in the old King studios, but for release on the subsidiary Federal label. Under the name Tommy Magness and His Tennessee Buddies, the group cut four gospel songs that had all been penned by Reno (three of which had appeared in the Buddies' 1950 songbook): "When I Safely Reach That Other Shore," "Little Country Preacher," "Wings of Faith," and "Jesus Will Save Your Soul." Most were done as gospel quartets, and none had a note of Tommy's fiddle. Reno recalls that Syd Nathan wanted them done as gospel quartets, and in fact wanted to put Reno's name as leader of the group. "I said, 'No,' we were working as Tommy Magness and the Tennessee Buddies and we were going to stay that way." Tommy, after all, was the one who had the contract. Tommy agreed not to fiddle, suggesting he sing bass, as he had done so often with Monroe. But again producer Nathan stepped in; he didn't want Tommy to sing, so he finally wound up playing the bass fiddle. It was an odd session: a first for the duo that would become Reno and Smiley, the last for Tommy Magness.

As it turned out, Reno and Smiley enjoyed singing together. Shortly after the Federal session they left to work with a Wheeling comedian named Toby Stroud, and by January 1952 they had formed their own band. Tommy replaced Reno with a local player named Johnny Vipperman. But the group found itself up against some new and formidible competition: In 1952 WDJB hired the hot new band of Flatt and Scruggs for a six-month engagement, and their popularity ate into the booking possibilities of the Tennessee Buddies.

There were other problems as well. About this time Tommy and the Buddies were involved in a serious car accident; Tommy had been asleep in the back seat, and in the crash he landed on a piece of luggage and injured his spine. A couple of surgeries were necessary to try to repair the damage, but neither was successful. His wife, Vada (or Tootsie), had for some time been urging him to get out of music, and now she redoubled her efforts. "My stepmother hated him playing music," recalled Tommy's daughter. "That's one reason why he didn't go further when he was in Virginia." Gradually Tommy cut back on his music and began driving a truck for a local transport company. Then, about five years after the car wreck, his wife died suddenly. This depressed him even more, and he had the first in a series of strokes—which eventually caused a numbness in his hand and seriously affected his playing.

About 1958 he returned to Mineral Bluff and remarried, to a local woman named Leah Barnes. By now his professional career was over, though he occasionally would play with local friends and neighbors. One time, Bill Monroe visited his old friend and tried to hire him to go with the Blue Grass Boys and play bass fiddle. Tired of traveling, and not at all confident in his ability to even play bass up to Monroe's standards, Tommy refused. There were more strokes, and more back surgery, and soon it was hard for him to walk. The strokes were what hurt him, recalled Leah. "It hurt him so bad, because he had played the fiddle so good, that he wouldn't even pick it up and try to play it." But there were moments of the old power; one of his last appearances was when he played a dance at nearby Ducktown. But then, on October 5, 1972, he suffered a heart attack in his sleep and died without waking. He was only fifty-six.

There was no great public notice of Tommy's death, but he had already achieved legendary status among musicians. The next Saturday night at the Opry, fiddler Tater Tate approached a guest and said, "Tommy Magness has died. I know you've heard that he died several times before, but this time he really died." His daughter reflected: "They say Tommy's fiddle playing was twenty years too early. Now Benny Martin and Richard Greene do it—on their LPs you can hear the sound of Tommy Magness." In many ways he was a musician's musician, one of the great stylists who never made it in the public eye—indeed, who never really had an album under his own name. But Tommy Magness was also a vital link between the older mountain music and the newer bluegrass, and his spirit lives on today in the work of dozens of fiddlers who never met him or heard him in person and know of him only as one of the more potent of legends.

Arthur Q. Smith

In the late 1940s, radio station WNOX in Knoxville, Tennessee, in the very shadow of the Smoky Mountains, was emerging as a major country music center. Buoyed by promoter Lowell Blanchard's *Mid-Day Merry-Go-Round* and his later *Tennessee Barn Dance,* the station hosted an impressive parade of major country performers—from the Louvin Brothers to the Carter Family, from Carl Story to Carl Smith, from the Carlisles to Flatt and Scruggs. Still others came through as guest artists. Many of them recall making that trip to the WNOX studio, enjoying the loose atmosphere and good announcers, but being a bit puzzled at something they saw just outside the main studio doors. It was a thin-faced man who slightly resembled Danny Kaye, usually looking a bit frazzled and down on his luck. In front of him were three boxes: They were songs, original songs, he had written. The really good ones, he explained, were for sale at $25 apiece; the average ones were $15; the lesser ones were $5. His name was Arthur Q. Smith, and when he sold you a song, then you got it—not only to copyright it, but to put your name on it and record it or sell it or do what you wanted with. In an era when country songs were routinely bought and sold like old guitars, Arthur Q. Smith emerged as one of the best songwriters in the business—but hardly anybody except the musicians knew that.

Like almost everything else about him, even the name "Arthur Q. Smith" is shrouded in mystery. His real name was James Arthur Pritchett, but nobody knows why he wrote and performed as Arthur Q. Smith. The music scene at that was full of Arthur Smiths—there was Fiddlin' Arthur Smith, then on the West Coast with Jimmy Wakely, and there was Arthur "Guitar Boogie" Smith from North Carolina. Some people contend that "Arthur Q. Smith" was a slang term in Alabama for somebody who was pretentious and arrogant — "Who does he think he is, Arthur Q. Smith?" Another story says that he had been performing on WNOX and using the name of his stepfather, Arthur Smith, when "Guitar Boogie" suddenly hit. To prevent confusion with the North Carolina guitarist, he added the "Q." to his name. This would make sense, because most of what we can find out about the man suggests he had a subtle sense of irony, and a sort of Br'er Rabbit sort of cleverness that allowed him to make people think they had outfoxed him.

Arthur Q. was born in Grissom, Georgia, but his family moved to Harlan, Kentucky, where he was reared. He made his way to Knoxville in the late 1930s, and began working around the radio station; one of the first songs he sold was a piece called "Stuck Up Blues" that Roy Acuff, who had then moved from Knoxville to the Grand Ole Opry, recorded as early as 1941. It was the first in a long line of "secret" hits. Not long after that, he sold "How Will I Explain About You?" to bluegrass founder Bill Monroe— one of four songs Monroe would eventually buy from Smith. (Monroe recorded "How Will I" in 1946 at his first session with his seminal bluegrass band featuring Flatt and Scruggs.) His biggest hit from this early period was "Rainbow at Midnight," sold to Lost John Miller, but made into a top hit by the Carlisle Brothers and by Ernest Tubb.

The two songs of Arthur's best known to country music fans are "If Teardrops Were Pennies" (a giant hit for Carl Smith in 1951) and "Wedding Bells" (a 1949 Number Two best-seller for Hank Williams); for each of these, Arthur had to watch the royalty checks go to someone else— and it was all legal. Hank Williams, to give him credit, recognized the kind of songwriter Arthur was, and for a time hired him to work in his tour band and to do some booking. The problem was both men had serious drinking problems, and neither was more dependable than the other; finally Hank's wife fired Arthur and his band. Arthur kept pitching songs to Hank, and one of them—"The Man in the Moon Cried Last Night"—Hank had agreed to record at his first session in 1953. Of course, it was a session Hank never made. Arthur quipped to one of his friends, "I finally got the SOB to record one of my songs, and then he goes and dies."

Some people, like Acuff, Monroe, and Johnny Wright, were in later years anxious to give Arthur credit for the songs he had written for them. Monroe considered him one of the great bluegrass songwriters, and was not surprised to see Ricky Skaggs make the charts in the 1980s with "I Wouldn't Change You If I Could." Other performers, though, adopted a "don't ask, don't volunteer" attitude. We now know that Arthur's customers included Kitty Wells, the Stanley Brothers, Johnnie and Jack, Maybelle Carter, Jim Eanes, Ernest Tubb, and Carl Butler. One letter from Jim Eanes preserved in the family archives requests some twenty-one songs from Arthur. And there are persistent rumors around Knoxville that one of Arthur's customers was Don Gibson, and that Arthur had something to do with Gibson's career song, "I Can't Stop Loving You." Gibson himself has vehemently denied this, but friends recall that after Gibson became famous, he would regularly return to Knoxville and meet with Arthur, and that afterward Arthur would be flush for a few weeks.

Arthur apparently wrote songs easily, scratching down lyrics on scraps of paper and old envelopes. For someone as talented as he was, he was curiously inept when it came to forging his own career. He actually recorded a handful of sides under the name "Arthur Q. Smith" for the King label in the late 1940s, and went north for a time to work as a writer for King records. For a time he was signed to Acuff-Rose, the big Nashville publisher, but was eventually let go because he would continue to sell good songs on the side to his old friends instead of through the company. Though he had a family of six children, his drinking continued to alienate them, and his sons recall that on more than one occasion they had to pull Arthur's head out of a gas oven when he was trying to kill himself.

A modern psychiatrist might say that Arthur had a classic inferiority complex, or some inner drive that pushed him headlong toward self-destruction. Yet we now know that, even as Arthur was enriching other singers with his unacknowledged songs, he was playing a little game with history. He kept a big notebook, and whenever he sold a song to someone, he would write at the bottom of his song lyric exactly who he sold it to, how much he got for it, and the date. He also kept letters from singers either paying him for songs or asking for them. It was an incredible archive that his children discovered only after he died, and in recent years it has helped Arthur's widow get a fair share of royalties from hits like "I Wouldn't Change You If I Could." Though he was willing to give up the composer credits on a song, it almost seems as if he were wanting to leave behind the true story, in hopes that someday history would vindicate him. And it has.

Arthur was diagnosed with cancer in 1962, and checked himself into a VA hospital; he died in 1963. In his later years he had become a familiar figure around the streets of Knoxville; one witness recalls, "He was sunburned really dark, but not like some dude who'd been out in his cabin cruiser on Fort Loudon Lake, or playing golf at Cherokee Country Club. No, he was tanned more like some poor devil who'd been pounding the concrete all day trying to bum a drink."

One of Arthur's champions is the legendary dean of Nashville songwriters, Harlan Howard. He had heard about Arthur and his song selling from producer Chet Atkins. "I failed to understand how anyone could sell a song," he recalls. "I can't imagine not having my name on a song and hearing it on the radio. . . . You shouldn't go through life being that unappreciated or unrespected." In fact, in 1991 Howard wrote a song dedicated to Arthur, "Be Careful Who You Love (Arthur's Song)," which was recorded by Hank Williams. It wasn't a big hit, but it did call attention to Arthur's sad story. Several times friends have tried to get Arthur nominated to the Nashville Songwriter's Hall of Fame, some members of the country music establishment still feel uneasy about him getting in. It is a frustration Arthur would have understood.

Zeke and Zeb Turner

It wasn't until the 1960s that the general public became aware of an odd facet of country music that musicians had known about for years: the presence on most of the hit recordings of a shadowy cadre of crack musicians who were being known as "studio pros" or "A-teams." These were artists, mostly instrumentalists, who never toured or performed on the road, and who made their living strictly by playing backup on records and radio shows. By the 1960s, everybody was talking about the "Nashville sound" and the rise of the Nashville studio system. This was a method in which the record companies insisted that an artist not record with his regular road band but with a unit of studio musicians—gunslingers who were used to the pressures of recording, who could adapt to a new song on the spot, and who could nail a cut on one take. The great Nashville A-team of that era included names like Chet Atkins, saxophone player Boots Randolph, pianist Floyd Cramer, guitarist Grady Martin, and guitarist Ray Edenton. Besides playing on the hits of others, some of them did create hits of their own, such as Cramer's "Last Date."

But there were earlier generations of studio musicians as well, and their largely uncredited contributions had a lot to do with creating the sound of modern country music.

As early as 1928, the versatile singer and songwriter Carson Robison was serving as a studio guitarist in Victor's New York studio, and by 1930 the fiddler Lowe Stokes was working on a retainer from the Brunswick Company to back up any singer or group that needed a little extra punch. By the 1940s, crooner Eddy Arnold's style was being largely defined by the mellow, elegant electric steel guitar work of Little Roy Wiggins—though his name seldom appeared on the record labels. And the first really full-time A-team was put together in the late 1940s to back up Red Foley, who was then the biggest Opry star and arguably the biggest star in the business. This band, which was with Foley from 1946 to 1948, included the steel guitar player Jerry Byrd, fiddler Tommy Jackson, guitarist Louis Innis, and an electric guitarist named Zeke Turner. Few people remember Turner today, nor his brother Zeb. Neither had any major records under their own name, but both played on some of the best-known classic country sides, ranging from those by Hank Williams to those of the Delmore Brothers. It is high time to sing their praises.

To start with, a disclaimer. Zeke and Zeb Turner have been for some time confused with another set of Turner brothers, Red and Lige, who appeared on Cincinnati radio and were primarily gospel singers. Though they all at one time did radio work in Cincinnati, there is otherwise no connection; in fact, Zeke and Zeb Turner's name isn't really Turner at all. It is Grishaw: Zeke is James Grishaw and Zeb is Eddie Grishaw. They were born (Zeb was the older) in Lynchburg, Virginia, into a family in which the father picked a little and the mother sang a little. The brothers took their acoustic guitars and broke into show business playing on "a little station there in Lynchburg," according to Zeke. By 1938, when Zeke was fifteen, he had discovered the electric guitar; though the instrument had been around in some form for ten years, it was just beginning to make its way into the big country and radio bands. "They were pretty new then," Zeke recalls. "Nobody really knew what they could do. I used to listen a lot to Zeke Campbell, an electric guitarist with the western swing band the Light Crust Doughboys. Then I heard a lot by George Barnes; he played mostly jazz in his later years, but then he was with Louise Massey and the Westerners, out of Chicago. Another early favorite was the team of Candy and Coco—I think Coco's real name was Otto Heimal. They worked with Gene Austin, and played a lot of good stuff — more jazz than anything. I got to see them in person at one time. It was a big thrill."

The old electric guitars were not easy to master. Zeke remembers: "When I was a kid playing at WIS in Columbia, South Carolina, we'd play bookings and I couldn't sleep in the daytime, though we'd been up all night. So I'd get me a long electric cord and run it way out in the back yard, in the trees, and I'd sit there during the day and work with the electric guitar by myself. My first guitar was an old electric Gibson, and my brother got an old Epiphone Elektra out of a pawn shop for twenty-five dollars. I liked his so well that I traded him even."

Both Zeke and Zeb grew up around Columbia, South Carolina, and listened to the black guitarists in the area. When he was about fifteen, Zeke met there another pioneer of the electric guitar, Arthur "Guitar Boogie" Smith, and worked for a while with his band, the Crackerjacks. (In addition to the Turners and Smith, this part of the country also yielded a third electric pioneer, Hank Garland.) About 1942, Zeke joined the Navy for a three-year hitch.

Zeb, meanwhile, was also developing as a lead singer, working as the mainstay for a radio band from Anderson, South Carolina, called the Hi Neighbor Boys. With them, he made his first commercial recordings in November 1938; the tracks sound pretty much like any western swing–oriented radio band of the time, except for two numbers that featured Zeb on guitar. One was "Guitar Fantasy," and the other was the oddly titled "Zeke Tierney's Stomp" (probably a misnomer for "Zeke Turner's Stomp"); on these, Zeb pays tribute to his mentor Coco Heimal, unleashing a series of accoustic, single-string runs that were quite unique for their time. His versatility won him work, and by 1941 he was in Hollywood, where he performed with Roy Rogers and appeared in two films, Roy Acuff's *O My Darling Clementine* (1943) and Charles Starrett's *Sundown Valley* (1941). By 1943 he was back in Anderson again, and then in 1944 spent a six-month stay at Renfro Valley in Kentucky. He made his way to Nashville in late 1944, where he got a job with Wally Fowler's popular band the Georgia Clodhoppers.

In those days Fowler was one of the hottest acts working out of the Knoxville radio scene, with an impressive series of popular Capitol releases, including the wartime "Propaganda Papa," on which Zeb played electric lead. But one of his "bands within a band" was a gospel quartet called the Oak Ridge Quartet—later to become the Oak Ridge Boys. It became so popular that Fowler decided to drop the secular band, the Clodhoppers, and direct his energies toward gospel music. At this point, Zeb took stock and realized that Nashville was developing some real opportunities for a good professional, and, along with the Clodhoppers' fiddler, Joe Carroll, he formed a new band called Zeke Turner and his Fireside Boys. Soon they had a regular gig on station WLAC and were often guests on the Grand Ole Opry. In his band were three others who were to leave their mark on the Nashville studio scene: steel player Bob Foster, bassist Marshall Barnes, and electric guitarist Jabbo Arrington. (The latter, who later won fame with Jimmy Dickens, was another wunderkind who did hot takeoff solos, but who died tragically in the early 1950s.)

Zeb was also attracting attention with new and highly influential recordings. In May of 1946, he released "Zeb's Mountain Boogie," the very first released by Nashville's new independent label, Bullet. It showcased Zeb playing a now-familiar electric boogie beat backed by a studio band put together by Owen Bradley and called "Brad Brady's Tennesseans" on the disc's label. It was not the first real country boogie: Singer Johnny Barfield had used the term, though not the guitar style, in a prewar Bluebird record, and a man named Porky Freeman had cut a guitar version, a rather simple one, in 1943. Zeke's old boss Arthur

Smith had cut his "Guitar Boogie" the previous September (1945), on yet another independent label, and watched it become a best-seller. But Zeb's cut on Bullet was a far more intense and soulful version, much more appealing than the other two. The Bullet company soon had the pressing plant working overtime to supply the demand.

It was about this time that kid brother Zeke reappeared on the scene. Zeb got him on with Wally Fowler, and began using him on later Bullet sessions. They did a blistering duet on the Bullet release "Guitar Reel," as well as five other records through 1947–48. Soon everybody was wanting their "hot guitar" sound on their records, and they rapidly became studio mainstays. One track Zeke especially was proud of was the backup on the Red Foley hit "Tennessee Saturday Night." But probably the most memorable he did was Hank Williams's original 1949 version of "Lovesick Blues." Zeke recalls that Williams's mentor Fred Rose didn't want to use the song. "The one I really remember Hank and Freddie Rose gettin' to it about is this 'Lovesick Blues.' . . . Freddie didn't want no part of it. Hank just kept singing and singing and Freddie said, 'The damn thing ain't got no pattern to it. It don't end nowhere. How you gonna end it?' We had recorded three tunes, and Hank says, 'Dammit, them people in Louisiana liked this, and I'm gonna record it.' And Freddie says, 'OK, go ahead and record it.' And that was the last one, just to get the session over with."

Zeke's playing impressed both Williams and Rose, and he appeared as lead guitarist on over thirty Hank Williams sides between 1947 and 1949, including classics like "Lost Highway," "I'm So Lonesome I Could Cry," and "Honky Tonk Blues." These were all early studio bands, assembled for session work before Williams began recording with his own road band, the Drifting Cowboys, in 1950. Indeed, brother Zeb appeared on Williams recordings like "Wedding Bells." One of the techniques Williams liked was what Zeke called the "dead string" style. "You couldn't use drums in those days, in country music, but Hank liked a heavy beat, and so I used to play rhythm for him on the electric guitar. It's done with the ball of your right hand. You hit it and then kill it with your hand. See, you can't play a rhythm on an electric and let it ring. That wouldn't sound right at all. I heard this group Maddox Brothers and Rose, and this guy played rhythm guitar on an electric. They recorded it, and to me it sounded like hell. And I thought, that would be a good deal if it didn't ring like that. So I did practically the same thing, but I'd just whop it with the base of my hand, sort of the back palm of my hand." The effect on the early Williams recordings was, both figuratively and literally, electrifying.

Both Turners soon became part of the informal band that became Nashville's very first A-team of studio pros. Zeke recalls: "When Roy

Acuff left the Opry they brought Red Foley down from Chicago. They told him to pick out himself a band. Chet Atkins had been filling in with him, so Red came to me and asked me to join his band. So me and my brother, we left Wally [Fowler] and went with Red. Then Louis Innis joined on guitar, then Jerry Byrd on steel, then Brownie Reynolds on bass, and then Tommy Jackson on fiddle—all ones he picked. There were four of us who stayed with Red for three years. And we recorded with all different ones when they'd bring them in there."

However, things tended to get a little nerve-racking with the high-strung Foley. He would occasionally tell off sponsors and lose lucrative radio show slots; he would announce that the band was going with him to Hollywood to make a movie and then abruptly change his mind. He would suddenly decide to dissolve the band, and then the next day he would hire them back. "It was a bad situation," recalls Zeke. As a result, the band took an offer to leave Foley and Nashville and to relocate in Cincinnati, where they worked under the name the Pleasant Valley Boys—the name Foley had given them. "We did what they called the 'Top O' the Morning' show; they's start about 4:30 or 5:00 and end up at 7:00 or 7:30. By now this was myself, Louis Innis, and Jerry Byrd. Tommy Jackson went up there with us, but got in a little trouble with the program director's girlfriend and he went back to Nashville. We got Ray Sosby to replace him."

Cincinnati in those days was also home to the nation's most success-ful new independent record company, King. Started in 1943 by a Cincinnati promoter named Syd Nathan, the company quickly became home for a number of country stars like Cowboy Copas, Grandpa Jones, Moon Mullican, and the Delmore Brothers, along with rhythm and blues and soul acts like James Brown. The King studios were probably busier than Nashville's in the late '40s, and both Turners found plenty of work at their sessions. There is no way to tell, even today with the King ledgers available, exactly how many sides the Turner brothers played on. Some, though, were more than memorable. One of the seminal performances of modern country and even rock 'n' roll was the Delmore Brothers' giant 1949 hit "Blues Stay Away from Me." And it was Zeke Turner who crafted the famous single string guitar riff that opens the record and sus-tains the slow rock of the arrangement throughout. That piece of work, too, was one Zeke was proudest of. So were the thousands of kids around the country who picked it up and made it a staple of electric guitar licks.

While Zeke was content to work in the background as a studio man or a member of the Pleasant Valley Boys, older brother Zeb was more interested in building his own career as a singer and songwriter. In 1947 he coauthored with Ernest Tubb a song called "I Got Texas in My Soul," which Tex Williams cut; a year later he had an even bigger hit with "It's a Sin," a monster hit for Eddy Arnold. Starting in April 1949, he began recording with his own band for the King label, releasing titles like "Tennessee Boogie" and Hank Williams's song "Never Been So Lonesome." In June of 1950 he took his wife and two children and moved east, to Silver Spring, Maryland, where he found work in the nearby Washington radio and television scene. A couple of years later he moved up to Baltimore, working now as a disc jockey as well as singer; he began to have a few minor hits like "Chew Tobacco Rag" and "Back, Back, Back to Baltimore." In 1953 he did a piece called "Jersey Rock," replete with sax and trumpets, which took country boogie in a new direction, and he even did covers of songs like Peppermint Harris's "I Got Loaded." By now he too was using King's studio band, and on occasion was pleased to see his kid brother in the studio playing lead. The records were wonderfully varied and gritty and they helped the stage for the new rock 'n' roll sound that was just around the corner, but none of them were really big hits. Zeb spent a while working with Jimmy Dean on Washington TV, then with Sunshine Sue on "The Old Dominion Barn Dance," and then doing club and radio work around Trenton, New Jersey. By the 1960s he had moved north, and was working clubs and stations in Quebec; he continued to write songs aimed for the Nashville market—he eventually did over 170 of them—but by now he was trying to catch a ride on the folk revival. Styling himself "Mister Hootenanny," he created a folk-singing trio and held forth for years over Montreal station CFCF. He died there, from brain cancer, on January 10, 1976—known as a local second stringer and not even eulogized for his contributions to country music.

Zeke, for his part, finally grew up and gave up on his music dreams. He married and took a job driving a truck, and reassumed his real name, Grishaw, and more or less dropped out. One particular night, though, he couldn't resist. "It was the last time I saw Hank. He was playing a show up here in Middletown, Ohio, about twenty-five, thirty miles from Cincinnati, and I took my wife and my mother-in-law and said, 'I'm gonna ride up there and see Hank.' He was doing a little tent show, had a tent set up there. I went up and talked to him and he got me up on stage and he got me to do a couple of the numbers that I had done with him." And that was about it. Zeke took the old Epiphone down to his basement, but kept it plugged in to an old amplifier, just in case he felt the need to practice.

Johnny Barfield

Tracing back the history of a particular style in country music can sometimes lead into strange byways. Through the 1940s, there was a fad in the music for "country boogie," exemplified by hits like Moon Mullican's "Cherokee Boogie," Arthur Smith's "Guitar Boogie," the Turner Brothers' "Zeb's Mountain Boogie," and even a "Hadacol Boogie," named after a well-known patent medicine. The original "Boogie Woogie" was a driving eight-to-the-bar piano solo by a Chicago pianist named Pine Top Smith. He had recorded it in 1928, and it became a major hit, but Pine Top didn't get to enjoy it: He was shot and killed in 1929. A big-band version of his song became an even bigger hit in 1938 when it was recorded by bandleader Tommy Dorsey, and in the late 1930s there was a renewed interest in traditional boogie woogie pianists like Albert Ammons and Meade Luxe Lewis.

Pine Top Smith's original "Boogie Woogie" described a hip-shaking dance as much as a style of music, and many country lyrics followed suit. And though stars from Hank Williams to Moon Mullican cut boogie numbers, it was a remarkable Georgia singer that hardly anyone remembers today who really was first to use the term "Boogie" in a country song, and the first to record a country version of the popular dance. This was a performer named Johnny Barfield. On August 21, 1939, Barfield reported to the temporary Victor/Bluebird studio at the Kimball House in downtown Atlanta and did four sentimental songs, such as "In a Sleepy Country Town." Accompanied by only his guitar, he then launched into something that was far from sentimental:

> Down in Atlanta, on Decatur Street,
> They got a new dance that can't be beat,
> They call the boogie woogie,
> They call the boogie woogie,
> Everybody's doing the boogie woogie now.

Decatur Street was the notorious center of Atlanta's blues and red-light district, and had been since the 1920s. And in August 1939, the national boogie fad was in full swing; it's easy to see how the Bluebird session producers, Dan Hornsby and Frank Walker (who would later start producing Hank Williams), saw this as a chance to bring the boogie fad into country music. Barfield continued singing:

I got a gal on the Jonesboro Road,
She makes more money than Henry Ford,
Cause she does the boogie woogie. . . .

When the final product was released in the fall of 1939, it quickly became a staple in the newfangled jukeboxes that were popping up in honky-tonks around the South. There were no country best-selling charts in those days, so we don't know how popular it really got, but it was successful enough that about five months later, on February 5, 1940, the Bluebird folks rushed Barfield back into the studio to do a follow-up, "The New 'Boogie Woogie.'" To the same basic chord pattern and melody line, Barfield sings:

Oh, the boogie woogie dance is a takin' the town,
I ain't no more good from the hips on down,
I keep doin' the boogie woogie,
Doin' the boogie woogie,
Everybody's doin' the boogie woogie now.

If Barfield's songs became popular in honky-tonks, there should have been little surprise. He spent most of his career performing in the rough-and-tumble corner of southwest Georgia that includes Fort Benning, Macon, and Columbus, and adjoins Phenix City, Alabama. There, a thriving music club scene developed to serve the hundreds of soldiers who went through Fort Benning, and Barfield was a part of it. His "Boogie Woogie" pieces became his best-known songs, in addition to one called "Numbers Blues," about the numbers game. (For a time, in fact, Barfield ran a numbers game when music jobs were scarce.)

John Alexander Barfield was born in 1909 at Tifton, Georgia, and grew up backing his fiddling brother Coot and busking for tips on street corners. They found their way into the Columbia studios in Atlanta in 1927, and recorded a couple of tunes, but the company didn't think they were worthy of release. He met Skillet Licker star Clayton McMichen, though, and was soon part of the loose circle that surrounded that band—a sort of old-time music version of the Rat Pack. When the Skillet Lickers broke up in 1937, fiddler Bert Layne hired Barfield to replace the legendary Riley Puckett and began playing over

Covington, Kentucky, radio. By now Johnny was a superb guitar player and sang in a warm, pleasant tenor.

By the late 1930s, Barfield was back in the Columbus area, playing over Columbus station WRBL with his own band, which he called variously the Troubadours or the Pleasant Valley Boys. He became close friends with Alabama singer Rex Griffin, who did the version of "Lovesick Blues" that inspired Hank Williams, and in fact recorded several Griffin songs during his Bluebird sessions. Between 1939 and 1941 he recorded four sessions for Bluebird—a total of thirty-two sides.

But he interrupted this promising start in November 1942, when he left to join the Army. Later in his shows, he would joke about it. "Seventeen brave men left town that day—me and sixteen MPs." It soon ceased to be funny, though; he was shipped out March 1944 and crossed the English Channel four days after D-Day. In July he was captured by the Germans, and spent eleven months in a POW camp. During his captivity, both of his parents died.

Returning to the Columbus area, he began to play the new package tours; he did road tours with the Duke of Paducah, Bill Monroe, Max Terhune, Rex Griffin, and Lew Childre. Many of these were booked out of the old Comer Auditorium in Columbus. He also played a lot at Charlie's Club, often using guitarist Lucky Ward, who would later play with Roger Miller. In 1953 the city fathers of the area decided to "clean up" Phenix City, and the easygoing atmosphere was tightened up. By now Johnny was performing some with his son, and reportedly turned down an offer to join the Grand Ole Opry. He did try some later recordings for Nashville's Bullet label in the late 1940s, and in 1959 released a single on the JB label. It did little, though, and in 1974 Johnny died.

Few of the papers at the time mentioned his passing, and today hardly any of the country music histories and encyclopedias mention Barfield's name. But one gets the impression that this would have been okay by him; he was a modest, unassuming, easygoing man who saw his role in history in perspective. In the 1950s, when rock 'n' roll was discovering the boogie, he joked with his son, saying, "I was the first to start all that."

The Rouse Brothers

This story starts back in 1965, when Johnny Cash was hotter than a two-dollar pistol. He was playing everywhere from the Newport Folk Festival to the Grand Ole Opry, and was making friends with people like Bob Dylan and Peter LaFarge. He was singing the theme song from John Wayne's new movie *The Sons of Katie Elder,* and was on the hit charts with "The Ballad of Ira Hayes." His stage shows were something else: In addition to carrying the Statler Brothers and Mother Maybelle and the Carter Family, the show used a lot of mixed media. Part of it was the show's climax, which Cash called "Ride This Train." On it he showed a film of old railroad wrecks, hobo life, railroad yards, old stations, and the like; while this played, he sang his medley of classic train songs—"The Wreck of the Old 97," "Casey Jones," "Folsom Prison Blues." And he always ended with "Orange Blossom Special," which he sang and played on the harmonica. This last song had become so popular that he recorded it, releasing it on a single in February. It started climbing the charts, and eventually got to Number Three in the nation.

One evening in 1965 the Cash show found itself in Miami, playing for a sold-out crowd. During intermission a man walked quietly into Cash's dressing room and stood with his hat in his hand waiting for the singer's attention. Cash came over and found himself shaking hands with a stocky, well-built, white-headed man of over fifty years who introduced himself as Erwin Rouse. He lived in the swamps out in the Everglades, and he had traveled most of the day across the swamps in a special boat he had built call a swamp buggy. When he got to his sister's house in Miami, he borrowed her bicycle to ride ten more miles to the concert. "A few years ago I wrote a few songs myself," he told Cash, "but you probably never heard of them." Intrigued, Cash asked the man to sit down; the name Rouse rang a faint bell. "Which songs did you write?" Cash asked point-blank. "Just a bunch of old tunes," he replied. People coming up and claiming songs are a dime a dozen backstage, but Cash felt at once that this was no pretender. With his natural sympathy for the losers and underdogs of the world, Cash immediately sensed that here was someone who had really paid dues. "I guess my biggest one was 'The Special,'" his visitor finally admitted. "Do you mean 'The Orange Blossom Special?" asked Cash. The dressing room went quiet. "Everyone in the dressing room knew as I did that this man was sincere," recalled Cash.

Later that night, Cash invited his guest to join him on stage, and to play his song for the audience. "The house was packed for two shows," said Cash. "And when he did 'The Orange Blossom Special,' they tore the house down." Afterward, in the dressing room, musing about how popular his "old song" still was, Rouse commented, "The 'Special' belongs to everybody by now, I guess, but it used to be my best number." It was the sort of thing every composer dreams of: creating a song that the people take to heart, and that becomes so widespread and popular that it becomes thought of as a folk song. And in the years to follow, Cash would cross paths with Erwin Rouse several times, and would invite him to be a guest on his ABC television show. But he never forgot the stories Erwin told, tales about the music, about trains, about hardships, about busking on street corners, playing vaudeville, making records, and writing songs. Erwin is gone now—he died in 1981—and the Rouse Brothers are receding more and more into legend. It seems time to try to piece together their story.

It's doubtful that the Rouse Brothers would ever have considered themselves bluegrass. Their heyday was long before the term had any real meaning, and they often described themselves as "buskers" or "showmen" or simply "singers." Yet at least three of Erwin Rouse's songs have become bluegrass standards: "The Orange Blossom Special," which is arguably the best-known fiddle tune in the modern bluegrass repertoire; "Some Old Day," which was popularized by both Flatt and Scruggs and the Country Gentlemen; and "Sweeter Than the Flowers," which was recorded by everyone from Moon Mullican to the Stanley Brothers. Erwin's own fiddling was a major influence on fellow Floridian Vassar Clements, as well as the legendary Chubby Wise. Their story would be worth telling even if it weren't such a rattling good yarn.

To begin with, there were three main Rouse Brothers: Earl (born 1911), Gordon (born 1914), and Erwin (born 1917). In a questionnaire they filled out in 1959 for encyclopedia writer Linnell Gentry, the brothers listed their birthplace as New Bern, North Carolina, located in Craven County, just a few miles from the coast and from Pamlico Sound. Friends recall, though, that the family really lived up around the Fort Barnwell area, a little north of New Bern, where their father had a tobacco farm. The form lists their father's name as Ernest H. Rouse, and his occupation as a farmer; his mother was Eloise Chadwick Rouse, and she was a housewife. The whole family consisted of fifteen children, eight of whom eventually took up music of some sort.

Nobody knows for sure just where the musical influences came from. The family's father doubled as a Methodist minister, and their mother herself played the fiddle. Erwin, with his little fiddle and slight frame, became a child prodigy of sorts, playing on the vaudeville stage when he was as young as five. They had to put him on a Coke bottle crate on stage because he was so small, and on some occasions he even ran afoul of child labor laws. When he was nine, he and his brother were taken on the road by a traveling preacher, who wanted them to attract attention to his street-corner sermons. "We come down to Florida and we played on the beaches and all over," Erwin recalled. "The preacher would get the people to listening and then we'd run them out with our playing. But that preacher taught us some manners we didn't learn on the farm from Momma and Papa." By 1928, when Erwin was only eleven, he and his brothers began traveling on the RKO Keith vaudeville circuit, often with a bandleader named Mary Davis. During this time, Erwin developed his skills as a showman and trick fiddler; he would play the instrument behind his head, on the side of his leg, and even between his legs; his specialty was to do the operetta favorite "Indian Love Call" while he held the bow between his legs and moved his fiddle across it.

Sometime in the 1920s the brothers moved to the Jacksonville, Florida, area, where they acquired a manager; their old-time showmanship and natural talent soon won them lucrative jobs all along the eastern seaboard, from New York to Miami. Gordon Rouse, who often functioned as Erwin's guitarist, recalled that they played "the best in New York [The Village Barn] and the best in Miami"—the Royal Palm Club. They often were on the bill with mainstream pop stars of the day, such as Sophie Tucker. For a time in New York, they were on a coast-to-coast network hookup. And for a time Erwin actually did some pop singing with the famed Glenn Miller Orchestra when they were holding forth at the Glen Island casino. The brothers also often worked Coney Island, sometimes busking for whatever nickels and dimes were tossed into their hat.

Considering how popular they were, the Rouse Brothers never really had much success at recording. They may have tried to record for the first time in New York in May 1934 for the old American Recording Company (now CBS-Columbia). There is a session listed in the ARC files containing four songs by a group known only as "the Three Floridians." The songs include "Duval County Blues" (the county surrounding Jacksonville), and "My Family Circle," which is the odd title Erwin used for his version of "Will the Circle Be Unbroken." Another title was "The Death of Young Stribling," which sounds like a local murder song, but I have been unable to trace it. The problem is that none of the Three Floridians tracks was ever issued, so we have no notion of what they sounded like. The only clue is a reference on the file sheets to a "Luther Higginbottom," who could have been a manager or a third performer.

The first session bearing the Rouse Brothers name was in June 1936, again in the studios of the American Recording Company. For it, older brother Earl joined Erwin and Gordon, and the trio recorded eight sides; unfortunately, only two were released. These were "I'm So Tired" and the bicycle song "Pedal Your Blues Away." (The latter was revived in a modern album by cartoonist Robert Crumb and his Cheap Suit Serenaders.) Among the unissued pieces was the first recording of "Some Old Day," as well as "Please Let Me Walk with My Son," both of which would be later rerecorded and released. (The original composer credits for "Some Old Day," incidentally, are to Jack Rouse, yet another brother.) The other unissued titles are "Are You Angry Little Darling," "Toll," "Dixieland Echoes," and "Under the Double Eagle." By now Erwin was doing some serious songwriting,

The general New York publishing scene, though, was not really receptive to country or "hillbilly" product. Erwin recalled: "We walked all over New York and were turned down by all of the music publishers. We were told that 'Your music will never amount to anything.' We were discouraged and encouraged to stay out of the music business. There were several times when I got so discouraged from being told that my songs would never sell that I nearly quit and returned to our home in North Carolina." Finally he got hooked up with Bob Miller, then the leading country music publisher and composer in New York. A Memphis native, Miller had moved to New York in the 1920s, married into a wealthy family, and produced major hits with "Twenty-One Years" and "Eleven Cent Cotton and Forty Cent Meat." He totally understood matters of copyright and publishing, and took Erwin under his wing; in 1935 he encouraged Erwin to join ASCAP, which the fiddler did.

In the fall of 1938 came their career song: "The Orange Blossom Special." That season the Seaboard Air Line launched what would be Florida's first true streamlined train, which would run from Miami to New York. The Rouses, along with their young friend, fiddler Chubby Wise, decided to go to Miami's Union Station to see its inauguration. In later years, Erwin offered this story: "We wrote it the same day 'The Orange Blossom Special' [train] was christened in Miami." The brothers, in fact, were on their way to New York and actually boarded the train. "We were riding with our manager, Lloyd Smith, from Miami to

New York." Impressed with the train, and the hoopla surrounding it, Smith commented that it was going to be "a famous train, like the Old 97." Gordon continued the tale. "Our manager said to us, 'You know what would be a nice thing? If you could write a song about that train.' It took us about four hours and a half, maybe five. But by the time we got to Kissimmee, Florida, it was done." They based their melody on an old local fiddle tune called "South Florida Blues," and added words celebrating the new streamliner. As they rode on up the coast they stopped over in Danville, Virginia, and had a lead sheet written out for $15. Then they took it to the copyright office in Washington, D.C. There, on October 20, 1938, they filed copyright "no. E unpub 179156" with ownership to "Ervin Thomas Rouse, c/o J.H. Smith, Kissimmee, Florida." Later the song was placed with Bob Miller's publishing company.

It was good they did. Less than three weeks later, on November 7, 1938, fiddler Tommy Magness recorded his version of the song at a session for Blue Ridge singer Roy Hall. Just where Magness learned it is unclear, though the Rouses had doubtless been featuring it on their New York radio shows and in their personals. But when Miller and the Rouses heard about the recording, they were not happy, and told ARC boss Art Satherley so. A note in the ARC files by the title reads: "Hold release. Rouse Brothers refuse to sign contract." Another note read: "Don't release—Pub. promises trouble." The brothers obviously wanted to have first recording rights on their own song, and successfully blocked the Magness version. Unknown to the brothers, though, a North Carolina radio performer named Walter Hurdt also recorded a version of the song on February 2, 1939, for Bluebird, as "Train Special." It was the real antecedent to Johnny Cash's version, and was probably supervised by Eli Oberstein, who had a nasty habit of changing the titles of songs he recorded to mask their legitimate copyrights.

On June 14, 1939, the Rouse Brothers finally got to record their version of the "Special." At 1:30 P.M. Erwin and Gordon, joined by their brother Jack, gathered in Victor's Studio #1 in New York City; their manager and publisher, Bob Miller, was present. They started off with some old vaudeville dialogue. "All aboard!" shouts one, as the fiddle bow starts the train running. "Peanuts, popcorn!" shouts another, imitating a train hutch. Then comes the famous first strain of the piece, the long drawn-out moan of the fiddle imitating the whistle. Then Gordon and Erwin sing the familiar, three-line stanza that begins, "Lookie yonder coming." After this Erwin plays the second strain, the complex double-shuffle part that was to so delight fiddlers in later years. Then comes the third part, a single-string run that sounds like a Texas fiddle tune. Next the brothers sing a second three-line stanza, "Talk about a-traveling" and celebrating "the fastest on the rail"—"on the Seaboard trail." Erwin then returns to the second strain, this time hitting his bow on his fiddle to imitate cross ties. At the end is some more dialogue. "Hey, Gordy, what's the name of this train?" someone asks. "Where you going?" "Jacksonville," says Gordon. "Miami," says Erwin. "End of the line."

The "Special" was released on Bluebird 8218 that fall, on the flip side with another from the session, "My Family Circle (Will the Circle Be Unbroken?)." Curiously, it was the B side of the single, suggesting that Victor didn't really understand they had a potential hit on their hands. And, in fact, it was not even the first Rouse Brothers release from the session. A couple of months before, the company had issued Bluebird 8197, the fine chain gang song "Some Old Day," backed with Bob Miller's composition "Please Let Me Walk with My Son." The third coupling was "Craven County Blues" and "Bum Bum Blues," two more songs by Erwin; Miller, in fact, rushed "Craven County" and "Orange Blossom" into sheet music editions, replete with a photo of a handsome Erwin holding his fiddle.

When all is said and done, though, we don't really know how many copies this seminal recording sold. It was not issued on the Montgomery Ward label, as were many of the Bluebirds, and it was not reissued on LP until 1966, when it appeared in the Vintage series LP *The Railroad in Folksong*. Record collectors do not find it frequently in the bins of secondhand stores—not nearly as often as, say, Curly Fox's "Black Mountain Rag" or Bill Boyd's "Under the Double Eagle." There's nothing wrong with the performance: It is lively, uptempo, and precise. There are rumors that for some reason the disc was withdrawn, but it appears in the June 1941 Bluebird catalog—the only one by the Rouse Brothers that does.

But regardless of sales, "Orange Blossom Special" spread like wildfire among fiddlers of the day. With its loose structure and frantic tempo, it allowed them to show off their best work—from the gimmicky range of train imitations to the western swing–like double shuffle of the bow—what some then called the "Beaumont Rag" lick. Tommy Magness continued to play it, and after he joined Roy Acuff on the Grand Ole Opry, he found a huge national audience for it. Indeed, he became so associated with it that he named his band in 1946 at Roanoke the Orange Blossom Boys and used the tune as his theme song. In 1941, Bill Monroe recorded a version (oddly enough, also for Victor) that featured the fiddling of Art Wooten, a version also issued on Bluebird in February 1942. A third popularizer was the Rouses' old friend Chubby Wise, who worked up a version of the piece for his stints with Monroe, Flatt and Scruggs, and Hank Snow. And a forth was Fiddlin' Arthur

Smith, who introduced the tune when he was fiddling with cowboy singer Jimmy Wakely in the West. Wakely recalled seeing Smith at the *Saddle Mountain Round-Up* in Tulsa playing a solo version of "Orange Blossom" in 1939; "he stopped the show." Later he featured the piece when the band played the Last Frontier in Las Vegas, and he eventually recorded it for Capitol in 1948. By the fifties it had found its way into the repertoires of the Stanley Brothers, Flatt and Scruggs, and dozens of others. There was even a recording by the Boston Pops, and a version called "The Sanctified Orange Blossom Special" by evangelist-performer Donna Stoneman. After Cash recorded it as a harmonica piece, Nashville studio great Charlie McCoy had a decent hit with it on the new Monument label. On stage, bands found out that it was an immediate crowd-rouser; "it'll sound like they made a touchdown in the last three seconds," says producer Jim Dickson, who booked the Flying Burrito Brothers in the 1970s.

Though Erwin had a legitimate copyright on the "Special," and though he had even published it as sheet music, musicians often assumed that it was an old public domain piece, an old "traditional" fiddle tune. The brothers continued to make most of their money performing—as headliners in New York's Village Barn, as intermission buskers in Washington, and as club acts in Miami. Claude Casey, the yodeling cowboy singer, worked with them during this time, and recalls playing Miami, "including all the swanky clubs like the Royal Palm Club on Biscayne Boulevard, Jeff's Night Club, Flagler Street, station WICD in Miami, and WKAT on Miami Beach." Peter Kuykendall recalls seeing the act in Washington in the 1950s, which by then included Erwin, Jack, and Jack's daughter; "[Erwin] and Jack did a trick fiddling routine (with two fiddles) that was just unbelievable."

During all this time, Erwin never really stopped writing songs. Though he would in later years claim he had only written a handful of songs, there are dozens with his name on them. Trying to follow up on his great train song, he penned "The Champion," a train song that Grandpa Jones recorded in 1955, and "The Silver Meteor," which became popular with West Coast musicians like Scott Stoneman. Other songs that made it into sheet music include "Lend Me a Buck," "When My Baby Cries," "I'm Getting Gray Hair," "A New York Boy Gone Hillbilly," and "North Carolina I'm Coming Home." Others circulated include "Little Parakeet" and "I Know." But his next real success was not to be another train song, but sentimental mother song called "Sweeter Than the Flowers."

With its famous opening lines ("Just as far as I can remember/She'll remain the rose of my heart"), "Sweeter Than the Flowers" became one of the major country and bluegrass hits of the late 1940s. Moon Mullican, "the King of the Hillbilly Piano Players," made the first recording of it, for King, in early 1948. It spent some twenty-six weeks on the *Billboard* charts and rose as high as Number Three. Roy Acuff followed with his version in 1949. In his later years, Acuff told a story that the song had been promised to him and when Erwin came to Nashville to give it to him, he was intercepted by Syd Nathan (of King Records) and Moon. They took him to their hotel room, wined and dined him, got him roaring drunk, and came away with both the song and the publishing on it (through King's publishing arm Lois Music). In the next few years, the song became a standard in the newly emerging bluegrass field: it was covered by the Stanley Brothers (on King), Carl Story (Starday), Hylo Brown (RRHB), Reno and Smiley (Wango), the Franklin Brothers, Wilma Lee and Stoney Cooper, and others. More recently it has been recorded by Jim and Jesse with Charlie Louvin.

The song seemed so autobiographical that fans and writers never tired of asking Erwin about it. Over the years, he developed a spiel he used in his performances and to inquiring journalists. "Carrying 'Sweeter Than the Flowers' was just like a woman carrying a baby," he said. "Now, a song is in your heart and soul just like a child. It's a load to write about your own mother, and our mother was a very sweet woman. She loved all her children—she had fifteen head of children—and we all loved her. And when she passed away, our main remembrance of Mama was that she was more sweeter than any flower. We sang her song to hundreds of millions of people . . . and we're mighty proud that we had life in our bodies to do that."

The trouble is, said Erwin's old crony Zeke Clements, the story is basically "baloney." "It was designed to appeal to audiences, to be part of the performance of the song. When he started that story, you could see the white handkerchiefs come out all over the audience." The real story, according to Clements, began in Cincinnati, at a little bar where Erwin and Natchee the Indian hung out. In fact, Erwin had a little room over the bar where he was living. One day Erwin asked the owner to borrow his phone so he could call his mother on her birthday. The owner said yes, but couldn't help overhearing the strange, rambling conversation Erwin was having, and he even jotted down some of the phrases he heard, such as "You are sweeter than the flowers." After the call, the owner and Rouse sat down and started recalling more phrases, and eventually wrote the song.

In 1953, their old friend Bob Miller made another attempt to get the Rouse Brothers on record. Zeke Clements remembers: "Bob Miller went down to Erwin's house in the swamp and stayed two weeks recording stuff on his new tape recorder. He got some good music, but he told me later that it was the strangest two weeks of his life." Miller actually made two trips, the first in March 1953, where he recorded two sides by Erwin and Gordon, "Lend Me a Buck" and "The Orange Blossom Special." The pairing was released on the Rockin' label, as well as the Deluxe label, both subsidiaries of King. Released in August, the disc was well received, even reviewed in *Billboard*. This encouraged Miller to do a second session in October 1953. This time he did a larger volume of fiddle tunes:

Home Brew Rag	Deluxe 2019
Flop Eared Mule	Deluxe 2019
Up Jumped the Devil	unissued
Mississippi Sawyer	unissued
Down Yonder	unissued
Under the Double Eagle	Deluxe?
Jackson Schottische	Deluxe 2007
Rubber Dolly	Deluxe 2007
Arkansas Traveler	unissued
Varsouviana	unissued

From Miller's two weeks of work, only five sides made it out. It must have been disappointing for Miller, and frustrating for the Rouses. Today it is unclear where the unissued master tapes are, if in fact they survived at all. The Rouses would never again, as far as I can tell, make another commercial studio record.

Through much of his later life, Erwin was troubled by drinking problems and, for a time, a two-year stint in a Florida mental hospital. (Gordon apparently also spent some time there.) After his "rediscovery" by Johnny Cash, Erwin was invited to Nashville by Chuck Glaser, who had promised to help him get some of the back royalties due from the "Special." He did, and Benny Martin recalls picking Erwin up at the bus station, and seeing him standing there in the middle of summer with a long coat on and a fiddle case. Erwin visited with the cadre of pickers who knew who he was, and gave a couple of interviews to the local press. While in town, he found that his old friends the Stoneman Family were playing down in Nashville's club district, Printer's Alley, and went down to see them. He borrowed Scotty's fiddle, and what resulted was a legendary set that is still talked about today.

After this last attempt at Nashville Erwin got even more frustrated, and returned to his house in the Everglades. There he could fish, hunt, and trap; there he could build his "swamp buggies," those flat-bottomed swamp skimmers powered by a giant fan in the rear. They are used all over the Everglades today, and some say that Erwin invented the prototype. In the 1970s, his health began to fail: diabetes, kidney failure, the proverbial bad liver. He didn't tour much, but he would occasionally appear at bluegrass festivals or in country bars around Miami. "He was good-natured, free-spending, the whole bit," recalled his friend Evan Carl of the South Florida Bluegrass Association. One of his last partners was Gene Christian.

In the meantime, "The Orange Blossom Special" continued to work its way into American music. Everybody from Billy Vaughan to the Boston Pops recorded it, and the Nitty Gritty Dirt Band added a version to their 1972 *Will the Circle Be Unbroken* album. It became so popular at fiddling contests that some judges started banning it from play; they argued that it was a fairly simple tune and was used by show-off fiddlers to rev up the crowd. At a contest in Athens, Alabama, during this time, contestants noticed a fire alarm case with an extinguisher and an axe in it. Some wag had stuck on the glass a note that read, "In case of Orange Blossom Special, BREAK GLASS." But none of this seemed to derail the popularity of the piece, and in 1972 it received an award as the year's most-played instrumental.

Erwin died July 8, 1981, in Miami. About a week before, Gene Christian took a group of admirers into the Everglades to pay homage to the old fiddler. Included were John Hartford, Earl Scruggs, and Benny Martin. Erwin, wearing a grizzled white beard and an old stage hat, seemed happy to see them, and they all swapped stories and memories through the afternoon. It was a fitting ending for the long and winding road that had begun so many years ago on a tobacco farm in North Carolina, that had wound through six decades of American history, and that had produced the most famous fiddle tune of our time. If fiddlers ever get satisfaction, perhaps Erwin got a measure of it.

Seven Foot Dilly

In the years I have been studying, researching, and writing about old-time music, the name of John Dilleshaw has remained a tantalizing and elusive mystery. An inquiry about Dilleshaw—or Dilly and His Dill Pickles, as the record labels read—became a standard coda to any interview I did with any older southeastern musician, and the inquiry usually drew a blank. Who was this tall, laconic guitar player who propelled such excellent, driving string band music, and talked his way through a couple of solo performances besides?

There were abundant clues: His records are full of place-names like Bald Mountain, the Dog River, Bibb County, and Kennesaw Mountain, and the names of his supporting musicians appear on several of the skits the band recorded. Yet in spite of the clues, people digging after him kept drawing blanks. Repeated research forays into north Georgia unearthed a good many other musicians, and some of these had heard of Dilleshaw, but none really knew much about him. I had started hoping for the same fate that befell Donald Nelson in his hunt for the Allen Brothers: that the word would spread, and some morning I would get a phone call from a deep-voiced man who would identify himself as John Dilleshaw and invite me to his farm down on the Dog River for some barbecue and talk about old times.

Alas, this scenario never developed, but what did happen, while not as dramatic, is about as interesting, and it does give us at least a rudimentary portrait of one of the last big mystery figures of old-time string band music.

Dilleshaw has not been a complete mystery; over the years several researchers have gotten scraps of information about him. Back in 1963 Bob Pinson, stopping over in Atlanta, contacted Raymond W. Lindsey, the "Shorty" Lindsey of the Dilleshaw records, who played tenor banjo. In an informal conversation Bob learned that Shorty's father was "Pink"

Lindsey, also on the records, and that Shorty had played tenor banjo on some of John Carson's records, as well as on Pink Lindsey's Bluebird session. Dilleshaw, he said, was an Atlanta fireman, and died in 1942 or thereabouts; Bill Kiker, the fiddler, might still be in Atlanta.

Later, Joe Wilson talked to a personnel officer in the Atlanta Fire Department, who knew Dilly and thought that he had come from the Sand Mountain area. This is not as much of a lead as it sounds, for Sand Mountain extends for miles and miles through Georgia and Alabama. The Skillet Lickers had their most devoted fans up there (and did a skit about the area), and string band music was still strong up there. The lead eventually developed some information about the Johnson Brothers Band (no relation to Earl), the boss band in the area for years, who did a memorable session for Okeh in 1928 that was never issued; but nothing about Dilleshaw.

Then, in the fall of 1979, when I was in Atlanta for a meeting, Wayne Daniel and Gene Wiggins, both of whom had been digging into old Georgia music, told me about a man named Wylie Rakestraw, who was claiming to be related to Bill Brown, the old Columbia A&R man who had "managed" the Skillet Lickers sessions and who, I felt, had helped in Dilleshaw's career. The tip was misleading in one sense but productive in another: Rakestraw, it turned out, was the grandson not of Bill Brown but of Fiddler Joe Brown, the "champion fiddler" who appears on Dilleshaw's skit "A Fiddler's Tryout in Georgia" (Vocalion 5432). His mother had known Dilleshaw and was able to lead me to a number of other people who knew him better: fiddler Glen Martin, whose father played with Dilleshaw; farmer Willie Teal, who knew Dilleshaw in his youth; fiddler Lon Newman, an old crony who had played in John Carson's band in 1922, and in Dilleshaw's early band for five or six years. Finally it was Willie Teal's wife who provided the final answer to the puzzle: When asked about Bill Kiker, she explained that while she had never heard of anyone of that name, Dilleshaw had a brother-in-law who fiddled named *Harry* Kiker. There has never been a Bill Kiker listed in the Atlanta directory, but there has always been a Harry Kiker. While I was confirming all this, Wayne Daniel, a native of Atlanta, had been systematically calling Kikers and had come upon the same Harry Kiker. To all of these people I am indebted for information used in piecing together the following account.

John Dilleshaw, then, was born about 1896 on Pumpkinvine Creek, back of New Hope, Georgia, in northern Paulding County. More hilly than mountainous, Paulding County is a somewhat remote and sparsely settled area with its county seat in Dallas, about twenty-five miles northwest of downtown Atlanta. It borders on Kennesaw Mountain to the east and Haralson County to the west.

The Dilleshaw family farmed in the northern part of the county until about 1912, when an epidemic of typhoid fever raged through the area. Apparently the entire family was wiped out except for John, his mother, and one sister. Out of either emotional or economic necessity they packed up and moved to the southern end of the county, to the southwest corner of Garnett Mountain, near the town of Hiram.

Dilleshaw's mother, Mattie, was not especially musical; she was a schoolteacher, and soon took a job teaching at a nearby rural school. John himself, a strapping boy of sixteen, made crops, hunted, and farmed. Still, tragedy dogged the family. The sister, Ruby, had another bout with typhoid fever and died. Then, a year after that, when Dilleshaw was about seventeen, he shot himself in the foot while hunting. This accident was to have more far-reaching effects, though; as Harry Kiker tells it,

> John learned to play up there by Hiram. He was in his late teens, seventeen, eighteen years old, he was in a hunting accident and shot a hole in his foot. Had the gun sittin' on his foot, crazy like, you know, and it went off. So he was laid up a good long while there with that, and there was an old colored gentleman who lived up the road named Bill Turner. He was a good guitar picker, and he liked John, and he'd come down there and bring his guitar, pick for him. John got interested in it, and bought himself a guitar. So while they [the family] was at work, Bill would come down and show him and teach him. And that's how he learned to play, from this colored gentleman named Bill Turner. I don't think Bill ever made any records or anything—he was a good deal older than John even then.

One of the tunes John learned from Turner was "Spanish Fandango," which was later to become one of his first records.

About this time, John and his mother moved off the mountain down closer to Hiram, on the Douglasville highway, near Slick Log Creek. John had begun to play a lot with a local fiddler named Dave Puckett, playing sqaure dances and entertainments. Puckett became one of John's closest friends and later worked with him on the Atlanta Fire Department. Willie Teal recalls that the last time he heard Dilleshaw play, it was with Dave Puckett:

> The last time I heard John, it was 1928, and it was down there at the end of the old car line on Bankhead in Atlanta, at the old place they used to call Center Hill. We was coming in one night, and we stopped at a cafe, went in to eat supper, and it happened

John and Dave was in there. John grabbed me and hugged my neck. Directly I told him, "Pick that thing. I ain't heard no guitar, man." And he said, "All right. Here I go," and he lit out. You ain't never heard a guitar picker—he was an old farmer boy. He wasn't no extra singer, but he was real on the guitar. Them old timers didn't go in for foolishness. They went for the sound o' them boxes.

Willie Teal, as well as other people around Hiram, remembers distinctly that Dilleshaw's first record was made with Dave Puckett. "One side was 'Sweet Fern' and the other was 'Sweet Wildwood Flower.' It come out about 1925, and it was listed as by John Dilleshaw and Dave Puckett." I have been unable to trace this record in company files, or even anything remotely resembling it. Misremembering a date would be understandable, as well as misunderstanding who played on a record, but people seem adamant about hearing Dilleshaw play his favorite piece, "Sweet Fern," and I am at a loss to explain this. Dave Puckett, incidentally, eventually stopped fiddling, and died about 1960.

After he moved to Hiram, John formed another band, this one featuring Lon Newman on fiddle and a woman banjo player whose name Newman can't recall. Newman was born about seven miles from Villa Rica, where he still lives, and picked up his fiddling rather casually. For three or four years he played in Dilleshaw's band, performing for dances and schoolhouse entertainments around Paulding County. Dilleshaw was still farming for a living, and the band was an informal affair.

Living in Hiram at that time was a family named Kiker, and one of their number was an attractive young woman named Opal. John Dilleshaw began to court her—occasionally bringing the band along for support—until in 1918 they were married. Both were in their early twenties, and John, possibly wanting to develop his music, possibly seeking a better living for the family he planned, began to think about moving off the farm into Atlanta.

Meanwhile, Opal's kid brother Harry had become fascinated by the musicians who would congregate at his sister's house or the Kiker home to make music with his new brother-in-law. "I pretty much picked up my fiddling by listening to the ones that would come to the house, first one and then the other. I'd get to fooling with it. And Dilleshaw could fiddle a little bit, make a few chords, and he helped me get started on it." Later the young Kiker got a chance to learn a lot more fiddling from one of the local masters, A. A. Gray of Tallapoosa.

As World War I—what the old-timers in Hiram call "the old war"— was winding down, Dilleshaw was getting married, and by 1922 he had moved to Atlanta and was working for the fire department. He must have made a good fireman—sturdy, tall, raw-boned. He wasn't quite seven feet tall, Kiker remembers, "but he was a good six foot seven." While many of his musician friends got to calling him "Dilly," the sobriquet "Seven Foot Dilly" was a later invention of the record companies—probably thought up by Bill Brown.

By 1925 Dilleshaw had teamed up with Charles S. Brook, a carpenter from the Atlanta area who also played guitar. Some newspaper references discovered in 1974 by Gene Wiggins, in his research on John Carson, give us some insight into what success Dilly and Brook were having. In July the two of them, billed as the Gibson Kings, were appearing on the noon shows over WSB, singing and playing their Gibsons. (There is a suggestion that the two of them were also featured in the Gibson catalog about this time, but I haven't been able to confirm this.) A further note about the duo, with a photo, appears in the August 2, 1925, Atlanta *Journal.*

A note is in order about Charles Brook. He later signed a management contract with Phil Reeve, the manager of the Georgia Yellow Hammers and a Victor talent spotter, and a copy of the contract, dated January 4, 1930, indicates that he was then working with a new partner, one Clomer Jinks, and living in Chattanooga. (The correct spelling of his name, by the way, is Brook, without the "s," since he signed it that way on the contract.)

Apparently Reeve never got him on Victor, but a year later he did manage to make a record or two for Columbia. The first, "My Mammy's Cabin"/"Baby" (Columbia 15733–D) was a solo effort; the second, "Mama I Wish't I'd Listened to You"/"Will You Love Me When I'm Old" (Columbia 15756–D), made a few days later, was a pair of duets with one Charlie Turner, with guitar accompaniment. The records, like most recorded then, were less than successful; the former sold 473 copies, the latter possibly even fewer, and Brook dropped back into obscurity. He died in Atlanta sometime before 1940.

In the Atlanta of the mid-1920s it was easier to make a date with a fiddle band than with a guitar duet, and soon Dilleshaw was working with a more traditional string band. As early as 1925 he was, with Brook, playing with the Dixie String Band, which included the seventeen-year-old Lowe Stokes on fiddle, a Dr. W. M. Powell on fiddle, and an F. G. Dearman on mandolin. It is conceivable that this band, or a version of it, was the Dixie String Band that recorded a pair of waltzes for Columbia in 1927, "Dixie Waltz"/"Aldora Waltz "(Columbia 15273–D), but there is little direct evidence to support this. Besides, by February 1926 the band's name had been changed to the Gibson Kings Dixie String Band, a combination of the two names. Also by 1926 Stokes and Dearman had dropped out, and Dilleshaw had replaced them with another Hiram area musician, Forest Mitchell.

Mitchell was a highly skilled young fiddler Dilly had apparently known from his youth. He died prematurely, in the early 1930s, from cancer of the liver. In November 1927 Dilleshaw and Mitchell appeared on a special Thanksgiving program broadcast over WSB and sponsored by Sears. Sears, then as now one of the country's leading chain stores, frequently sponsored programs featuring old-time Atlanta-area musicians, perhaps in deference to the fact that Sears' sales were drawn from rural customers; it once sponsored Lester Smallwood in a similar show. This Thanksgiving they announced an "old-time Thanksgiving party" replete with "olden songs, old-time fiddling, comic numbers, and other variety." Paul and John, "the Two Disciples of Harmony," dreadful singers who could not possibly have appealed to any sober Atlantan, were on the show, and then came "the old-time fiddling team of J. N. Dilleshaw and J. F. Mitchell rending the atmosphere with breakdown music."

By this time Dilly was beginning to form his regular band. Harry Kiker thinks it was 1926 when he first came to Atlanta to play the fiddle with Dilly's band. Kiker would have been only eighteen at the time.

> He got to calling his band Dilly and His Dill Pickles. We played for square dances all around town, all over the country, and we played a little over WSB. We had a program for some grocery store, a fellow named Wells had it, and we played for him. Shorty Lindsey played tenor banjo, and his father, Pink, played bass fiddle. I wasn't able to make a living at it—I was working as a sheet metal worker, and Dilleshaw was on the fire department.

Whether the Lindseys were with this band as early as 1926 is questionable, but they certainly were by 1929—when the recording activity starts for all parties. On March 22, 1929, Dilleshaw made his first documented record, "Spanish Fandango"/"Cotton Patch Rag," issued on Okeh 45328 as by John Dilleshaw and the String Marvel. "Fandango" features Dilly and a second guitar player; "Cotton Patch Rag" features him and a mandolin player. Thus the String Marvel must be adept at both mandolin and guitar—and have a reason for concealing his name.

At first glance it would seem that Dilly and Charles Brook would qualify as the guitar team, by virtue of their earlier association. This still may be correct, but no one recalls that Brook could play mandolin, and there would be no reason for him to conceal his name. Harry Kiker feels sure that the mandolin player is Pink Lindsey, who often played "Cotton Patch Rag" with Dilleshaw. Furthermore, Pink was able to play mandolin, fiddle, or guitar, in addition to bass. This would make it possible for him to play backup to Dilly's lead on "Fandango"—everyone agrees that Dilly played lead on that—and the mandolin on "Cotton Patch

Rag" (which is, incidentally, probably black-derived, containing a "Salty Dog" variant). Pink would also have had reason to disguise his name: he had lined up a recording date with Columbia three weeks later, under his own name. Columbia at that time was very picky about not recording artists who had already recorded for a rival company. On April 13, 1929, Pink Lindsey & His Boys did record two sides for Columbia in Atlanta, "Love Ship" and "For Old Times Sake." Neither side was issued. Did somebody from Columbia find out about the String Marvel?

There are other mysteries about Dilly's first session. Recently two test pressings were discovered in Columbia's vaults bearing the master numbers immediately preceding those of "Fandango" and "Cotton Patch." These are two vocal numbers which, though untitled, appear to be a version of "Bad Lee Brown" and a parody song that I have dubbed "Where the River Shannon Flows." The vocalist sounds very much like Dilleshaw and he is backed by a strong guitar and a rather polite fiddle. Friends recall that Dilleshaw liked to sing "Bad Lee Brown," but no one recalls anything like the parody; however, its dry irony is very much in line with the Dilleshaw humor shown on later records. Most experts who have heard the tests agree that it sounds like Dilleshaw singing, and if so it might be feasible that Pink Lindsey this time backed him on fiddle.

None of this, however, could have anticipated the direction Dilly's next recording session was to take. It was to be a year later, and under circumstances that require a little explanation.

By 1930 the highly successful, albeit highly unstable combination that was Georgia's most commercially prospering string band—the Skillet Lickers—was coming to an end. Bill Brown, who had functioned as Frank Walker's assistant during the most successful years of the Skillet Lickers and other old-time bands, left Columbia in 1929. He was quickly hired by the Brunswick-Vocalion company, and set about duplicating for them what he had managed to do for Columbia.

He was especially interested in finding a string band to replace the Skillet Lickers—a band that would have their drive and versatility but could also be used in humorous skits. For a time, he thought Dilly and His Dill Pickles could be that band, and to that end he scheduled a substantial recording session for the group in March 1930. What he didn't know, of course, and the band couldn't know, was that the deepening Depression would wipe out the market for old-time music, and that the fine records made at that session would wind up as rare collector's items.

The march session for Vocalion was to yield eighteen issued titles. In addition to the core band of Dilly, the Lindseys, and Harry Kiker (henceforth to appear on the record labels as Bill Kiker), the group was on occasion joined by two champion Georgia fiddlers, A. A. Gray and Joe Brown.

Ahaz Gray, a seven-time Georgia champion from Tallapoosa, was an older fiddler by now. Lowe Stokes recalled being intrigued by the fact that Gray could play so well holding the instrument down low on his chest. Kiker also admired Gray and learned a good deal from him. Dilly recorded four pieces with Gray. "Tallapoosa Bound" and "Streak o' Lean—Streak o' Fat" are fiddle-and-guitar duets, with a bizarre running commentary by Dilly behind Gray's fiddling: "Tallapoosa—that's the home of yellow-legged chickens . . ." On "Nigger Baby" and "The Old Ark's A'Moving" both men sing, Gray in a high, squealy harmony to Dilly's strong baritone; this was the only time Gray sang on record. *Nigger Baby,* the tune also recorded by Dr. Smith's Champion Hoss Hair Pullers from Arkansas, and others, is a splendid driving performance that shows off Gray's skill in a breathtaking way. Kiker recalls that Dilly first met Gray at one of the annual fiddlers' contests in Atlanta, and the two had presumably played together before the recording session.

Such contests were celebrated in one of the skits recorded at the session, "A Fiddler's Tryout in Georgia (Parts 1 & 2)." Of course the Skillet Lickers had recorded a takeoff of the Atlanta contests as early as 1927—it was their very first skit—and similar efforts had been made by other groups since. "Tryout" is interesting in that all the fiddling is unaccompanied, and it gives us a glimpse of some tunes Gray never otherwise recorded, "Gray's Buckin' Mule" and a delightful version of "Sally Goodin."

Also on the "Tryout" skit is Fiddler Joe Brown, whose only recording this was. At the time he was living at Burnt Hickory, near Dallas, Georgia—just as the record says. He was born, as was A. A. Gray, in northern Haralson County. He reportedly won the state fiddling championship in 1925 and frequently attended fiddling conventions. He played a lot with A. A. Gray, and, his daughter thinks, recorded with Clayton McMichen. She also recalls:

> Once Dilleshaw and my daddy broke up a fiddling convention up at Dallas. They didn't like the way they were running it, and they broke it up, standing up there and playing on a bale of cotton.

Brown died in 1951.

On the skit record Brown proves himself a skillful traditional fiddler, playing "Arkansas Traveler" and an unusual piece called "Blue Tail Fly" (which is not "Jimmy Crack Corn"). In addition, Gray and Brown twin-fiddle a chorus or two of "Leather Britches" and "Katy Hill."

On another skit recorded at this session, "A Georgia Barbecue at Stone Mountain (Parts 1 & 2)," A. A. Gray and the band play "Turnip Greens and Pot Licker," "Hog Jowls and Back Bone," "Pretty Little

Widow," "Turkey in the Straw" and "Merry Widow Waltz," the last of which Gray had earlier (1924) recorded for Okeh as a solo.

The core band of Dilly, the Lindseys and Harry Kiker did eight selections. "Bust Down Stomp" was a version of that old Georgia standard "G Rag," while their version of "Chinese Breakdown" came out as "Georgia Bust Down." (Kiker says they knew it as "Georgia Breakdown.")

Throughout each of these instrumentals Dilly offers a wry running commentary. On "Lye Soap" he sets the band up playing a dance on the Dog River; he worries about whether they will be able to ford the creek on the way out, and remarks toward the end, 'I ain't heard anybody say anything about money yet." On "Hell Amongst the Yearlings" he assumes the role of the good-ol'-boy farmer, talking about his shoats and describing a country baseball game where a player 'slid into something he thought was first base.' Such banter, along with Shorty's fine tenor banjo and Kiker's fiddle, makes the sides unique in the annals of old-time music. In some selections the boys even try some rudimentary take-off solos. Rounding out the session were two talking blues by Dilly with his guitar: "Walkin' Blues" and "Farmer's Blues."

Starting in July 1930, with "The Square Dance Fight on Ball Top Mountain (Parts 1 & 2)" (Vocalion 5419) and "Sand Mountain Drag/Bust Down Stomp" (Vocalion 5421) by the core band, the records from this session were released, one or two a month, to the financially troubled public. Willie Teal says that the records sold like hotcakes back in Paulding County, and the sales must have been enough to encourage Bill Brown to talk the company into further sessions. Meanwhile, though, problems were developing, and the original group—the working band—was breaking up.

Harry Kiker says that Bill Brown got to using Dilleshaw as a guitarist on sessions with other groups—"remember that Dilleshaw was a pretty good guitar man"—and that by the time the next session came along, Brown had decided to create a studio band with Dilleshaw in the center. None of the old band was retained for these last recordings, which took place in November 1930.

This band, introduced on Brunswick 489 as "Dilly and His New Group," included Lowe Stokes on fiddle, as well as Archie Lee, Dan Tucker, and "Pops" Melvin. Stokes, by this time effectively split from the Skillet Lickers, was doing all kinds of recording for Brown and Brunswick. 'Pops' Melvin was probably Sterling Melvin, a comedian who did other skit work for Brunswick. It is very tempting to suggest that Archie Lee is in fact Archer Lee Chumbler, the autoharp player for the Chumbler Family (who recorded for Columbia) and the Lee Brothers

Trio, who recorded their "Cotton Mill Blues" at this same Brunswick session. However, when Gene Wiggins and I played a tape of this skit for Archer Lee's sister-in-law, she did not feel the voice was his. The other personnel are unknown but must include a tenor banjo, washtub bass, and possibly second fiddle.

It was this new lineup that produced the group's only Brunswick recordings, Parts 3 and 4 of the "Bootlegger's Joint in Atlanta" skit and the excellent "Kenesaw [sic] Mountain Rag" and "Bibb County Hoedown." Brunswick files also reveal a number of alluring unissued titles from this session.

With the collapse of the old-time music recording industry in Atlanta, Seven Foot Dilly's career pretty much came to an end. Pink Lindsey and His Bluebirds did manage a final record, for Bluebird in 1935, when they did "12th Street Rag" and "The Story of Adam." Shorty Lindsey told Bob Pinson that Dilleshaw played guitar on these, but Marion 'Peanut' Brown, who did the vocal on "The Story of Adam," told me that he did not think Dilly was on the session.

Dilleshaw continued to play informally around Atlanta through the late 1930s, but about 1940 he got sick, and in 1941 he died from uremic poisoning. His son, John Jr., followed him into the fire department, and died fairly recently of a heart attack. Three other Dilleshaw children all killed themselves, and a fifth, a daughter, died recently. Opal Dilleshaw was in a rest home as recently as 1967, but Harry Kiker says she too has now passed on. Pink Lindsey died some years ago, and Raymond just a year ago, from cancer. Harry Kiker keeps his hand in by playing fiddle with a local kitchen band that includes an ex-violinist of the Atlanta Symphony, and he hangs on to a battered old flier from the Vocalion Record Company, a flier dated June 1930 and boasting a faded picture of a tall left-handed guitar player, grinning good-naturedly in front of a band he called the Dill Pickles.

The Jordanaires

It was the night of July 2, 1956, and in the New York studios of RCA Victor a young Elvis Presley had just finished his thirty-first take of a new song called "Hound Dog." Elvis had just premiered the song on Milton Berle's television show, and it looked like a sure hit. RCA had brought to New York Elvis's regular band (Scotty Moore, Bill Black, D. J. Fontana), but for this session Elvis had added a "male quartet" as well. The RCA secretary stared at the union cards the men had signed and carefully began typing the "session sheet" for the recordings. They were personable young men, these singers: one named Gordon Stoker, who sang lead, had even taken over the piano playing for the date when the regular piano player had had to leave for another job. Then there was Neal Matthews, who had a sky-high tenor, Hoyt Hawkins on baritone, and Hugh Jarret on bass. And the name of the group? She searched her memory. Some kind of "aires." It sounded like they were saying Gordonaires. Yes. That would make sense, with a leader named Gordon. The Gordanaires it must have been. She typed it on the sheets, and the bit of history that validated one of the biggest two-sided hits in music history, "Hound Dog" and "Don't Be Cruel," went into the files—wrong.

Had the secretary known country and gospel music as well as Elvis did, she would have known in a flash that the group was actually called the Jordanaires. She would have known that they were far from some anonymous backup group, even in 1955. They had been regulars on the Grand Ole Opry since 1949, and had appeared on Eddy Arnold's summer TV show. They had recorded for almost every major label, starting with Decca in 1949–50, moving to RCA Victor in 1951, and on to Capitol in 1953. They had recorded gospel hits like "Mansion Over the Hilltop" (1951), "On the Jericho Road" (1953), "Gonna Walk Those Golden Stairs" (1951), and "Tattler's Wagon" (1953). They had sung backup on records by Hank Snow, Elton Britt, Stuart Hamblen, and Red Foley.

Through their work as staff musicians for WSM in Nashville, they had also done dozens of nationally heard singing commercials. The Jordanaires—spelled with a J—were anything but an obscure "male quartette." In 1955, when they began their association with Elvis, they were one of the best known and hottest groups in country music. And they were about to get hotter.

The Jordanaires originated in Springfield, Missouri, about 1948 when two brothers named Bill and Monty Matthews decided to organize their own quartet. Both men were ministers, and had begun singing with their father, who was a traveling evangelist. After gaining fame as part of a juvenile quartet called the Matthews Brothers, Bill and Monty started their own group; Culley Holt, from McAlester, Oklahoma, was hired to sing bass, and Bob Hubbard was added on baritone. In 1949 their pianist Bob Money was drafted, and Gordon Stoker was hired to replace him. Stoker was a veteran of the gospel scene who had won his spurs playing with WSM's famed John Daniel Quartet. Stoker would soon graduate to singing lead, and would play a pivotal role in the group's development. The original Matthews brothers left the group about 1953 and went back to Missouri; Stoker then asked young tenor Neal Matthews Jr. to join up. Matthews had grown up in country and gospel music; his father (Neal Matthews Sr.) had sung for years on the Opry with the Crook Brothers band. "That was actually my first professional gig," he recalls, "playing mandolin with them on the Opry when I was thirteen." When the Jordanaires came to the Opry, Wally Fowler's Oak Ridge Quartet was already on the show, and by then Neal was playing guitar with them. Baritone Hoyt Hawkins signed on, fresh from a stint with a popular family group, the Hawkins Quartet—with whom Gordon had originally played piano. It was a complex set of changing around, but by 1955 the quartet had a stable, well-seasoned personnel and had started exploring new roles for quartet harmony in the 1950s country scene.

Their RCA singles and Capitol albums and singles soon won them a reputation as experts in "spirituals"—what the music industry then called black or black-derived gospel. Some of their best-known songs were covers of groups like the Golden Gate Quartet, who provided them with "Noah." Since most of the early 1950s lineup were as interested in pop as country or gospel, they also consciously expanded their repertoire; a 1956 press release announced that they had decided "to add country, pop, and rock & roll music to their repertoire." But it was their recording with Elvis in 1956 that really, in the words of Neal Matthews, "opened the doors for us."

Presley had used Gordon Stoker (with two members of the Speer Family) on his earlier RCA sides such as "Heartbreak Hotel." Stoker recalls: "He told me on that session, if anything from this session becomes a hit, I want the Jordanaires to work with me from now on. And just that verbal agreement was what we had with him for some fifteen years." Elvis was soon insisting the Jordanaires sing on every session, and he once even complained to his producers when he thought the company was mixing an album to emphasize his own voice too much over that of the group. When not working with Elvis, of course, the Jordanaires were available to do freelance work with others—and everybody wanted their sound. They recorded in New York, Nashville, and Hollywood, and worked for almost every major country singer of the day, from Marty Robbins to Loretta Lynn, and for pop singers like Patti Page, Connie Francis, Rick Nelson—even unlikely performers like Julie Andrews and Andy Griffith. By 1965 they were voted one of the five top singing groups in the world, and their press releases were claiming that the quartet had "initiated a new type of vocalizing by providing a background of vocal harmonizing for a lead singer." By the early 1960s the Jordanaires were hardly able to find time to do their own albums, and even diehard fans were despairing of keeping up with the full number of records they sang on. The number of hits they sang on in one year—1957—totaled over 33 million copies.

In spite of all this, the Jordanaires kept their base in Nashville. Stoker recalls: "Lee Gillette of Capitol Records offered us a fabulous deal for us to move to the West Coast. He said, 'You all would save us a fortune in vocal arrangements on our sessions. We'll guarantee you all the work in Hollywood that you can stand.' And of course I've often wished we would have done it." Even in Nashville, they soon were doing four sessions a day, six days a week. In 1969, when Elvis decided to make his live concert "comeback" and asked the Jordanaires to join him again, they had to say no: they were too entrenched in their own very profitable world of session work.

As the Jordanaires changed the sound of pop music's background, they also made an important contribution to the Nashville music scene. In the early 1960s Neal Matthews perfected a shorthand music notation system for use in studio sessions—a way of jotting down chord changes that later came to be known as "the Nashville Number system." By 1963 this system was in common use among Music Row session players, and was later subject of a 1985 book issued by Tree. The group also founded the Nashville chapter of the American Federation of Television and Radio Artists/SAG, and built the first high-rise office building on Music Row (UA Tower). Basking in numerous awards and honors, the current edition of the Jordanaires (Stoker and Matthews, along with Duane West, Ray Walker, and Louis Nunley) continues to perform and record. One of their most recent projects was a K-Tel cassette called *Memories of Elvis*.

DeFord Bailey

"My grandfather was a championship fiddler for all of Tennessee. All of my uncles and aunts played fiddle or banjo or guitar, and every year the Bailey Family Band would go to the fair over at Lebanon and play. There wasn't no blues back in those days. It was all hillbilly music—black hillbilly music. That's all I knew out there in the country. I didn't hear the blues until I came to Nashville."

The speaker was a small, seventy-five-year-old black man named DeFord Bailey. It was the spring of 1974, and he was holding forth on the porch of his apartment in a high-rise housing unit near the Vanderbilt area in Nashville. His guests are a couple of music historians and a large football player from Vanderbilt who found himself assigned the interview as part of a summer class he had to take to bring his grades up. DeFord was dressed in a dapper blue suit (in spite of the heat) and wanted to talk about his early days out in Smith County, not far from the home of Albert Gore Jr., and about sixty miles east of Nashville. As a boy, while recovering from polio, he lay in bed listening to the sounds around him and learning how to imitate them on his little harmonica. Soon he could do "The Fox Chase" and "Hen Cackle" and various imitations of the trains he heard in the distance. By 1926 he had become one of the charter members of Nashville's Grand Ole Opry, and for fifteen years reigned as country music's first African-American star.

On this day, though, and on most other days for that matter, DeFord didn't want to talk much about the Opry or the controversy over how he left it in 1941. He didn't make a big deal out of the fact that in 1928 he had appeared on the show more than any other performer, and that he drew stacks of letters—some of them with dollar bills enclosed. He didn't make a big deal over the fact that it was his performance of "Pan American Blues" one evening in 1927 that inspired WSM manager Judge Hay to rename the WSM Barn Dance the Grand

Ole Opry. He was not worried about the fact that he was one of the artists selected for the very first recording session to be held in Nashville, by Victor, in 1928. On this day he wanted to talk about the kind of music his grandfather and uncles and cousins played back in the 1800s, and how it has been all but forgotten today: black hillbilly music. To illustrate, he pulled out an old open-backed banjo, holding it upside down so he can pick with his left hand, and began to play and sing an old song called "Lost John." His picking was nothing like bluegrass, nor like the kind of tenor banjo the jazzmen from New Orleans play. It was a much older style, and with it he was reaching very deep into the roots of African-American folk music. "Do you ever use picks?" someone asked. He smiled and held up his hand to show how he had deliberately let his fingernails grow long. "Hawks' bills," he said, and chuckled.

People hearing him on the radio could not really tell if DeFord was white or black; like most of the early Opry stars, he was never allowed to announce his own tunes and talk to the audience. Of course, the lucky fans in the live audience in the Opry studio saw him come out, always dressed in a suit, climb up on a Coke carton to reach the mircophone, adjust his megaphone to better direct the sound into the big WSM carbon microphone, and wail away at "John Henry," "It Ain't Gonna Rain No More," or "Muscle Shoals Blues." On the air, George Hay sometimes called him "little DeFord Bailey" or "the Opry's mascot" or some other code word that let some listeners know that here was something unusual—a black man on this otherwise all-white radio show.

Starting in 1933, the Opry began to send out touring groups to do personal appearances during the week, and DeFord was much in demand; there was some serious money to be made from these shows, but in order to do them DeFord had to encounter the audiences first-hand and in person. Throughout the 1930s, such tour groups drove thousands of miles, in overcrowded cars, on narrow two-lane highways to ramshackle county schoolhouses and lodge halls. DeFord made the trips with almost of the big Opry stars of the day: the Delmore Brothers, Uncle Dave Macon, Arthur Smith, Sam and Kirk McGee, Paul Warmack and the Gully Jumpers, the Fruit Jar Drinkers, Lasses White and Honey Wild, and, later on, with young Roy Acuff and young Bill Monroe.

Most of the musicians gained immense respect for DeFord as a person and as a musician, and often helped him overcome the prejudice he encountered in those Jim Crow days. If DeFord was refused a room at the hotel where the Opry troupe was staying, Uncle Dave would insist that he was his personal "valet," and if he wasn't allowed to stay in his room, Uncle Dave would not stay either. On other occasions when DeFord was refused a room, his fellow Opry musicians would go with him to find some kind of private accommodation. Nobody remembers any really ugly scenes with a hostile audience or redneck violence, but DeFord did worry; he took to carrying "Old Bessie," a small revolver, as protection against robbers and what he called "wild animals."

Though he had grown up playing the banjo, DeFord had never had much of a chance to get at a guitar until these Opry tours. Often when the group would go out to eat or to drink, DeFord would stay behind and guard the instruments. To while away the time, he began to pick some of the guitars he found, playing them upside down like he did the banjo. Soon he had adapted the guitar to his old style of fingerpicking and was entertaining his colleagues backstage. He recalled: "I never will forget, Mr. Arthur Smith said, 'I don't mean anything by this, DeFord, but play just like a nigger.' We got a blues sound. A black man picks with his finger. Most white men strum, humm, humm. You got a tune, but you ain't doin' nothing." One of his favorite songs was his version of the Papa Charley Jackson hit "Kansas City Blues," which he picked and sang with the guitar, and which he even began to play some on the Opry shows and tours. "Here comes DeFord and his bulldog," Sam McGee used to say, in reference to the opening stanza.

In 1941 DeFord was fired from the Opry. While later journalists looked on this as an obvious example of the entrenched racism in country music, few on the Opry saw it that way. The musicians had worked with DeFord for fifteen years, and admired his skills and character; why only now did prejudice surface? The real truth comes from two events of the early 1940s. One was the attempt to give the Opry more general appeal, to "slick it up" so the new NBC network audiences would tune in. That meant smooth singers, slick western styled bands, even electric instruments; the older, folk-derived solo music of DeFord was considered passé in an age of Bob Wills, Gene Autry, and Benny Goodman. "It got to where I would go down there and wait around all evening and then get to play one number," DeFord recalled. He also got caught in the middle of an ugly performing rights dispute between the older ASCAP agency and the newer, WSM-sponsored BMI agency. Suddenly DeFord found he was banned from playing his best-known tunes. He left bitter, and for over twenty years virtually dropped out of any kind of professional music. He opened up a shoeshine stand in downtown Nashville—about where the present I-240 southern loop is—and played only for his friends and family.

He rejected all kinds of requests for interviews and even offers to record. He had a chance to be in a Burt Reynolds film, *WW and the Dixie Dancekings,* and to go north to the Newport Folk Festival. Those who knew of his memories, his opinions, and the dimensions of his music began to fear his story would never be told. But then things took a turn for the better. A young housing authority officer at the high-rise met DeFord and struck up a friendship; though he didn't know anything about the history of country music or the Grand Ole Opry, David Morton knew a good story when he heard one, and soon began to confirm some of things he was hearing. Throughout the late 1970s Morton often visisted DeFord, and even began to encourage him to get out and play a gig or two—such as the 1975 "Old-Timer's Night" at the Opry.

Morton also persuaded DeFord to tell his story on tape, and to preserve some of his later harmonica work, as well as singing, banjo playing, and harmonica playing. After DeFord's death in 1982, Morton began to transcribe the tapes, and eventually brought them to me. The result was a book called *DeFord Bailey: A Black Star in Early Country Music* (University of Tennessee Press, 1992). A few years later, Morton and the Bailey children made some of the music tapes public, and they were issued on a compact disc released by the Tennessee Folklore Society, *The Legendary DeFord Bailey*. It won widespread reviews, and a major article in *USA Today*. At the presentation ceremonies, in which the family was presented with the first copies of the disc, harmonica players from as far away as Chicago traveled to Nashville to pay homage to the little man in the big white hat. "I was a humdinger," he once said, and nobody has questioned that.

Emmett Miller

There are dozens of unsung heroes in the annals of country music; some are instrumentalists, like the legendary Georgia fiddler Joe Lee, who introduced the "long bow" style to greats like Clayton McMichen; some are songwriters, like the gospel singer Grady Cole, who wrote "Tramp on the Street"; others were promoters and radio personalities, like the late Eddie Hill, who helped introduce the music of the Louvin Brothers to a wide audience. But one of the most unsung, and one of the most mysterious, was a remarkable blackface comedian and singer named Emmett Miller. He flourished in the 1920s and 1930s, made a handful of records, and left an indelible impression on several generations of major country singers.

How major? Try Jimmie Rodgers, Bob Wills and Tommy Duncan, the Callahan Brothers, Hank Williams, Merle Haggard. Hank Williams had Miller's old 78s in his personal record collection; Merle Haggard dedicated his *I Love Dixie Blues* album to Miller. What kind of musician could inspire such a wide variety of imitators? Miller's story is as fascinating as his music.

Until recently, only bits and pieces of Miller's story had been known, and several of his earliest records are so rare that no copies are even known to survive. Miller himself died before historians could interview him, and it is doubtful that he even knew the extent of his influence on modern country music. He left behind, though, a number of friends and colleagues who remembered him and kept scrapbooks. Best of all, one of them preserved a "self-interview" that Miller did in the 1940s—a script he gave to local radio announcers when he was doing personal appearances in the area. In it, Miller describes himself and his partner as minstrel men. And it was this tradition, not folk music or blues or country music, that gave Miller his start.

We now know that Emmett Miller was born in Macon, Georgia, in 1903. In 1919, when he was only sixteen, he started performing as a blackface comic with a well-known minstrel troupe headed by Dan Fitch. By 1924, about the time the record companies were starting to sign their first country singers, Miller had made it to New York. Here he starred on the big-time vaudeville stage with singer Cliff Edwards (later to become famous as the singing voice of Disney's Jiminy Crickett) and the comedy team of Smith and Dale. By now Miller had developed his famous singing style; it included the trick of breaking into falsetto in the middle of a word, or even a spoken sentence, recognized today in the later "blue yodels" of Jimmie Rodgers. Through Cliff Edwards's connections with the New York recording companies, Miller made his first recordings, for Okeh, in 1924. These included Miller's then-current hit "Anytime," the old pop song that would later become a country standard when done by Eddy Arnold in 1947.

In 1925 Miller and his partner, Turk McBee, relocated to Asheville, North Carolina; here they worked in clubs and amazed some of the local country singers. The Callahan Brothers, Bill and Joe, heard Miller and based their first record hit, "St. Louis Blues," on his arrangement. McBee attests that Miller met Jimmie Rodgers (McBee called him "that damn hillbilly Jimmie Rodgers") in Asheville, and claims Rodgers also learned a lot from Miller's singing. In the summer of 1925 Ralph Peer, on one of his first field trips south to find talent, did a session of country musicians in a hotel in Asheville. Miller did four numbers here, including his first recording of another one of his favorites, "Lovesick Blues." It was not the very first record of the piece, but it was the first to use the famous falsetto breaks in the opening line that Hank Williams would later copy.

By 1927 Miller was back in New York. According to his friends, he never considered himself a country singer, and though he could play the guitar a little, most of his shows he did with either a jazzy piano backup or with a Dixieland jazz band. By 1927, he was very well known throughout the South's theater circuit, and was the headliner for the Al G. Field show.

The year 1928 saw a flurry of activity, with Miller starting to record in earnest for Okeh; usually he was backed by a studio jazz band (often the same one that backed Cliff Edwards) which Miller called the Georgia Crackers. Personnel often included later stars like trombonist Tommy Dorsey, drummer Gene Krupa, and guitarist Eddie Lang. He did new versions of his two big hits, "Lovesick Blues" and "Anytime," but added versions of "St. Louis Blues" and "I Ain't Got Nobody," with its famous descending falsetto on the opening word "I." In the following year, 1929, Miller did three other songs that became country standards: "Right or Wrong" (which western swing singers soon adopted), "Big Bad Bill Is Sweet William Now" (which Merle Haggard later redid), and "The

Blues Singer from Alabam'." Occasionally the Okeh producers tried to get him to do a slow ballad, but he resisted. All told, Miller cut some twenty-eight sides of music, plus comedy skits.

Down in Fort Worth, young Bob Wills painstakingly copied off the words to many of the Miller records and added the songs to his repertoire. When he hired Tommy Duncan, Wills tested him by asking him to sing Miller's version of "I Ain't Got Nobody." Over in Alabama, singer Rex Griffin watched Miller do a live show at a club, and then adapted "Lovesick Blues" to his own style, recording it for Decca in 1935. This recording, along with Miller's original, inspired Hank Williams to do his version in 1949. And, of course, Jimmie Rodgers used Miller's falsetto style, now dubbed "blue yodeling," throughout the late 1920s on many records.

In the meantime, what had happened to Miller? In spite of radio and movies, he remained convinced that vaudeville was not dead, and he kept at it. He did a final commercial session for Bluebird in 1936, and then spent his time booking his own and other shows in the Carolinas. In 1949, Miller took to the road with what he called "the last great minstrel show," "Dixieana." The tour led to a Hollywood film called *Yes, Sir, Mr. Bones* (1951), a remarkable collection of old vaudeville acts, including Miller. The film flopped, and soon Miller was back on the club circuit, working with a pianist named Mack McWhorter.

One memorable week they found themselves playing in Printer's Alley, Nashville's old nightclub district, and singing Emmett's "Lovesick Blues" for a few well-lubricated patrons. Just a few blocks down the street, in the Ryman Auditorium, Hank Williams was bringing the crowd to its feet again while he did another encore of "Lovesick Blues."

Tommy Jackson

The first great Nashville session fiddler, Tommy Jackson has probably been heard on more country records than any other musician. Throughout the 1950s and 1960s, he dominated the field, appearing on records by every major star of the era, from Hank Williams to Bill Monroe, from Ray Price to George Jones. He virtually invented the standard country fiddle backup style, and in the early 1950s had a string of hit albums of his own that both reflected and stimulated the square dance craze.

Born in Birmingham, Alabama, March 31, 1926, Jackson and his family moved to Nashville when he was barely one, and he grew up listening to the Grand Ole Opry and Nashville radio. He remembered being especially impressed with two of the fiddlers on the early Opry, George Wilkerson of the Fruit Jar Drinkers and Arthur Smith of the Dixieliners. Even though there was not much music in his immediate family, Tommy's father, a barber, encouraged him, and Tommy became a child prodigy of sorts; when he was seven, he went into Nashville bars and sawed out fiddle tunes for nickels and dimes. By the time he was twelve, he was going on tour with Johnny Wright and Kitty Wells. With a neighbor, he formed a group called the Tennessee Mountaineers and soon began to play over Nashville station WSIX. By the time he was seventeen, he was playing regularly on the Opry with Curly Williams and his Georgia Peach Pickers, and later with Paul Howard. But on April 17, 1944, he enlisted in the Army Air Corps, and spent the rest of the war as a tail gunner on a B-29. (He eventually won four bronze stars and an air medal for his service.)

Discharged in April 1946, Tommy returned to Nashville and did road tours with various Opry stars, including Whitey Ford and Jimmy Selph. He didn't like the road grind, though, and hooked up with Milton Estes, then starting a radio show on WSM. This job led to a similar one with Red Foley, who had just come to town as a replacement for Roy Acuff on the Opry. This band, the Cumberland Valley Boys, including guitarist Zeke Turner, steel player Jerry Byrd, and Louis Innis, became the first Nashville "A-team," and soon the four were doing all manner of studio work, for all manner of labels. Tommy's first commercial record was a Sterling session for a young Hank Williams in 1947; two months later, on another Williams session, Jackson created the famous fiddle intro for "I Saw the Light." In 1948 he backed Williams on "Lovesick Blues," and later backed Red Foley on pieces like "Satisfied Mind."

In November 1948 the band moved en masse to Cincinnati and struck out on its own as the Pleasant Valley Boys. They continued to do session work—now for King as well as others—and recorded with Cowboy Copas, Hawshaw Hawkins, Grandpa Jones, and the York Brothers. It was while he was in Cincinnati that Tommy made his first solo recordings. He was doing a backup session for Rex Allen, the cowboy singer then under contract to Mercury. In charge of the session was Murray Nash, then gaining fame as the producer for the first Flatt and Scruggs records. Allen's father was a fiddler, and he liked fiddling; he asked Tommy to make a couple of custom discs of "Black Mountain Rag" and "Fire on the Mountain." Tommy obliged, and Nash liked the songs enough to release them as singles.

Sales were surprisingly strong, and between 1949 and 1953 Tommy cut twelve fiddle standards on the Mercury label. In 1953 he signed a contract with the newly formed Dot record company of Gallatin, Tennessee, and continued to record successful singles. He first Dot release was "Arkansas Traveler"/"Soldier's Joy," one of the first Dot records to be issued on both 45 and 78 format. But the real innovation came a few months later, when Don got the idea of combining 12 of Tommy's singles onto an LP, and aiming it at the square dance audience. Square dancing was becoming a big middle-class social fad in the early 1950s, and clubs were springing up everywhere. There was a need for canned square dance music that a local caller could use when calling a dance, and a need for fiddle tunes that went on longer than the customary three-minute limit of the 45 or 78. Tommy's LPs filled this need, and they were lapped up. *Popular Square Dance Music—Without Calls* (1953) was quickly followed by *Square Dance Tonight* (1957) and *Do Si Do*, which offered detailed dance instructions on the back of the album. Before it was all over, Tommy had piled up eleven LPs for Dot, and around thirty singles.

Tommy's square dance sales made him the most heard, and most imitated, fiddler of his generation. "I always kept the tunes as simple as possible, 'cause I was selling a beat," he explained. He broke with that tradition after his first few records and added a full rhythm section: piano, bass, drums, guitar, and mandolin. His favorite backup man was

Hank Garland, the legendary Nashville guitarist, who played some lead guitar and often even mandolin on Tommy's sessions. Tommy's clean, driving, straightforward style won a lot of admirers, and some of the tunes he wrote or popularized, like "Crazy Creek," "Cherokee Shuffle," "Acorn Hill" (named after a little town where his wife's family came from) and "Bitter Creek Breakdown" are still standards among fiddlers today. A few of his records, such as his Decca version of Arthur Smith's "Fiddler's Dream," sold over 40,000 copies in the 1960s.

Meanwhile, he continued to make a name for himself in session and radio work. He, along with the rest of the Pleasant Valley Boys, had returned to Nashville after a year or so at WLW. He rejoined the network segment of the Opry, and for some thirteen years he was to have a featured fiddle solo on coast-to-coast radio, another key to his influence on other fiddlers. He broke with Red Foley shortly after Foley left Nashville to go to the *Ozark Jubilee* about 1954. He soon found dates with everyone from Roy Acuff to Ernest Tubb, and recorded with most in between. Among his favorites was Faron Young, on whose recordings Tommy popularized a double-stop backup technique.

In the 1970s, the vocation Tommy invented became filled with so many other fiddlers that he had a hard time getting work. Health problems began to develop. There was an interesting experimental rock album Tommy did with his son Mychael, and a reunion album of Ray Price's Cherokee Cowboys; but the experimental, free-form fiddle album he had always wanted to do never materialized. Tommy died on December 9, 1979, but only the sharp-eyed reader looking through the death notices in the Nashville papers would have learned about it.

Jimmie Riddle

People who have enough patience to dig beneath the hype and glitter of modern Nashville will discover that the city is an incredible nest for all manner of veteran musicians and older musical traditions. A case in point is the late Jimmie Riddle, who died on December 10, 1982. Jimmie spent most of his musical career in Nashville, was heard by thousands as a longtime member of Roy Acuff's Smoky Mountain Boys, and was seen by millions doing his hambone routines with Jackie Phelps on *Hee Haw.* Yet few realized how rare and unique a performer Riddle was; by nature, he was a retiring, easygoing man who was more content to break up his friends at a local tavern doing his great mouth music renditions of "Stars and Stripes Forever" than pursue hit records. Jimmie, indeed, made only a handful of solo records, including one incredible LP, and most fans still remember him as a piano player and harmonica player with Acuff. Not many know about his rare ability to do the odd, hiccupping rhythm singing he calls "eephing" or "hoodlin'" and few know about his imitations, comic singing, mugging, and "hand squeaking."

In November 1979 I interviewed Jimmie for the PBS series *Southbound* and he told me something about his career and his rare ability to make sounds with his hands and mouth. At the time, we made tentative plans for a second, more leisurely interview, and even talked about a new album. Unfortunately, neither of these projects ever came about, but in going over the tapes from November, I found that Jimmie had expressed himself very well, and that his own account of his career was about as succinct and impressive as anyone could ask for.

"I was born in Dyersburg [Tennessee], on September 3, quite a few years ago," he began. "My parents left Dyersburg when I was just a month old, and moved to Memphis. Old Bluff City. Shelby County. That's where I was raised, until I left and went to Texas. Memphis was a real city when I was growing up there. I used to go down and play in the taverns on Main Street, along about 1936 or so, and pass the hat. That's the way I got quite a bit of extra money back then. I was playing the harmonica mostly then, but I was also doing this other crazy thing they call eephing. But the real name of that's hoodling. That's what my Uncle Ralph told me, and I used to listen to him do it, and that's where I learned it. I'd say, 'Uncle Ralph, hoodle for me,' and he'd start in on it.

"My uncle learned that up at a dance out of Dyersburg, where somebody was doing it up on stage with the musicians. That's where he got it, and he's got to be seventy years old at least. When Uncle Ralph came to visit us in Memphis, I was just six, but I took a liking to that eephin' stuff. And I asked him to do it for me and he would. When I was younger, I never heard anyone but him do that, but since then I have heard four or five different ones that can do it.

"My grandfather used to do a lot of imitations, especially imitate boats and animals. I just picked it up by listening to them. I don't even remember starting to play the harmonica, but my mother told me I was three and a half years old. My grandfather—my mother said I was enthralled by everything he did. He was a practical joker. Did all kinds of imitations and the harmonica. Mother said one day he handed me his harmonica and I played a tune on it. His name was John Boone, and he was originally from Palestine, Arkansas, and was born in 1871.

"So that was my start in show business, playing down in Memphis on North Main, where the taverns were just coming in at the time, I was playing the harmonica, one of the boys the guitar. Boys? They were grown men, in their twenties then, one played guitar and the other played mandolin and I the harmonica. No eephing then. There was a band called Uncle Rube Turnipseed and the Pea Ridge Ramblers and I went up one day and did my harmonica and played a little guitar back then, and the first thing I knew I was playing show dates with them. Later on the Swift Jewel Cowboys invited me to come in and play on their show with them, I was about sixteen years old, I played harmonica, guitar, bass fiddle, accordion, piano, and when any of the boys would take their two weeks' vacation, they'd call on me to fill in on whatever instrument they played. I didn't really play 'em all that good, just enough to get by."

Jimmie made his first records with the Swift Jewell Cowboys at the old Gayoso Hotel in Memphis in 1939; he was twenty-one at the time, and was featured on "Dill Pickle Rag" and "Raggin' the Rails." The records show that Jimmie had absorbed a lot of the hot western swing as well as Memphis jazz. "I left Memphis in 1939 and went out to Houston, Texas; we'd started a little band out there." The "we" included ex–Swift Jewell Cowboys Jim Sanders and Curly Nolan, as well as western swing giant Tiny Moore, and the band was called the Crustene Round-up Gang. "I stayed there about three years, traveling around some to Victoria and Austin and other places. Then we formed a band called the Jolly Texans; we were all young, and we were almost too good. We played fast, hot music, and worked around Greenville and Jackson, Mississippi. There was another band in Jackson, Slim Scott, and they couldn't play anything like we could, and they were making eighty dollars a week and we were making twenty . . . if we were lucky. We didn't realize it at the time, but you had to get more down to earth with the people.

"I met Roy Acuff in Houston in 1943, and he told me that if I wanted a job with him, I could have it, and I decided to take that offer up right away. I played harmonica with him, though I started out on accordion; but the accordion wasn't liked too well, so I switched to piano, and I've been on it ever since. I went to Hollywood with Roy that first year and made that movie *Clementine*, and since then made four others with him. I didn't get much chance to do hoodlin' or mouth music with Roy, with all my harmonica work, but I kept at it just for fun. I made my first records with him in Chicago."

Jimmie's first records with Roy were probably made at the Chicago session of December 19, 1944; his name is not on the session list for August 2, 1945 (the only early Acuff session union contracts exist for), possibly because he was in the service. Jimmie also appears on a number of Acuff Opry and radio transcriptions of the early 1950s, playing breathtaking harmonica solos. He continued with Acuff through the '50s and '60s, taking time out for a rare solo LP on the Cumberland label, *Country Harmonica*, and appearing on an odd Starday LP by the Smoky Mountain Boys minus Acuff, *Smoky Mountain Music*. In the 1970s Mike Seeger recorded him demonstrating eephing, and I included this tape on a collection for New World Records called *I Am on My Journey Home: Vocal Styles and Resources in Folk Music*. Jimmie made a few festival appearances with his famous aunt, Almeda, and left a few examples of his way with a humorous folk ballad; he also left us examples of his uncanny helicopter imitations, his ability to thump out "William Tell Overture" on his throat, his tap dance on his teeth, his hamboning, and his general imitations. In 1970 he recorded and issued a great tour de force single for Decca, "Yakety Eeph" and "Wildwood Eeph," in which he did most of his great mouth sounds, and played most of the instruments, bowing only to Vic Willis on "Wildwood" for Vic's famous turkey imitation.*

---

* Jimmie had recorded an earlier Decca single in 1950, " I Found My Mama" and "Three Tree" (Decca 46239).

Jimmie was proud of his son, Steven, who has taken up his father's eephing and hamboning talents. Steve, while working as a drummer in Nashville, has already made his recording debut on a legendary LP by the Holy Modal Rounders, *Good Taste Is Timeless*, in which he eephs through a cut called "Living in the Country." During the *Southbound* taping, Jimmie and Steven got together to do some eephing duets, producing some of the funniest sounds ever recorded. (The tapes were not used in the final TV show, but I have carefully rescued them from the cutting room floor and hope to use them in some later project.) "You'll probably never get two hoodlers together again," said Jimmie. Alas, he was all too right.

PART V

From the Stage: Classic Country

Curly Fox and Texas Ruby

It was during one of the Grand Ole Opry's "Old-Timer's Night" shows from the 1980s, and it was one of the most memorable scenes in a night that had seen many. Backstage, waiting to go on, was a tall, dignified man with fine white hair, a classic ice-cream suit, and a regal manner. Under his arm he held a fiddle. Around him were a diverse group of friends, reporters, and younger musicians anxious for a glimpse of a legend. He talked about growing up in the 1920s and learning from an earlier generation of fiddlers that few at the Opry had even heard about: Uncle Jimmy McCarroll, Sawmill Tom Smith, Jess Young, Joe Lee, Natchee the Indian. A burst of applause from the front signaled that it was time for the guest to go on. He walked quickly on stage and began to entertain. First a fast, deftly played version of "Listen to the Mocking Bird"; then a comic version of "Johnson's Old Gray Mule," in which the fiddler lowered his instrument, sang a verse, pulled on his chin and gave a raucous imitation of a mule in full bray. In the wings, Grandpa Jones walked up. "Only one person can make that sound," he said. "It's the flower of the flock, Curly Fox."

Out front, the audience agreed and gave the man in the white suit a rousing ovation. Some of them realized that for three decades, from the 1930s to the 1960s, Curly Fox and his wife, Texas Ruby, were one of the best-known husband and wife duos in country music. Ruby's deep, sultry voice and honky-tonk songs, coupled with Curly's love of blues and novelty songs, had won them fans far beyond the normal arenas of country music—they played places like the Hollywood Bowl, the Village Barn in New York, and the Pump Room in Detroit. They were at the peak of their popularity in the late 1940s and early '50s, just as network radio was giving way to the new medium of television. And though Curly and Ruby made their mark in both areas, they were among those many country stars who made it big without ever having very many hit records. Their remarkable career was still in full flight when tragedy ended the partnership in 1963.

Curly was born Armin LeRoy Fox in 1910 in a little town called Graysville, Tennessee, up in the mountains between Chattanooga and Knoxville. Curly's father was a fiddler, and he taught young Curly tunes like "Shoot the Turkey Buzzard" and "Smoke Behind the Clouds." Once he had the tunes nailed, young Curly would stand in front of his mirror and try to improve his posture and appearance, a foretaste of what would become one of his most important qualities—his sense of showmanship. After the eighth grade, Curly took off rambling to see just how far he could take his music; he joined an outfit called the White Owl Medicine Show, traveling around the Midwest, learning more fiddle tunes, listening to black section hands play the blues, finding out ways to play the mouth harp, and learning how to mix Chief White Owl's Miracle Pain Balm.

For a time Curly led his own band, the Tennessee Firecrackers, over WSB in Atlanta, but soon found he could make more money entering fiddling contests. At first he entered legitimate contests held by local civic clubs and organizations; then, after proving himself at a contest in Ohio, he hooked up with promoter Larry Sunbrock. Sunbrock would go around the country with a set of musicians like Curly, Natchee the Indian, and Clayton McMichen, pull into a town, hire a hall, and announce that there was a "world championship" fiddling contest scheduled for that week. Local fiddlers were invited to try their hand at defeating the touring champions. They seldom won, though, and the "showdown" was inevitably between somebody like Curly and Natchee. Regardless of how many times he won or lost, Curly was paid a straight salary by Sunbrock—$250 a week.

By 1937, Curly had established himself as a premier fiddler and had recorded on Decca Records with the Shelton Brothers. While playing in Fort Worth about 1937, he met Ruby Owens, "Texas Ruby Owens," they called her, "radio's original cowgirl." She was a real Texan, coming from a ranch near Decatur, Texas. By the time she was three, according to family legend, she was singing to cowboys around her father's corral. Often she sang with her two brothers, straightforward arrangements of old songs, but with a fine rich harmony brought about by Ruby's unusually low voice. One day the three accompanied their father on a cattle drive to Fort Worth; while waiting for the business to be finished, they whiled away the time singing for the other cowboys. A meat packer and radio station owner from Kansas City was in the crowd, and soon young Ruby was off on a singing career.

Curly and Ruby married in 1939 and began work on some of the country's biggest radio stations. From 1940 to 1944 they were featured on the *Boone County Jamboree* over WLW Cincinnati and later that decade on the Grand Ole Opry. In 1948 the William Morris Agency brought them to New York to pioneer an early television program over WNBC, but after several months they decided to accept an offer to return to Texas, where they starred on the Texas Quality Radio Network out of Houston.

During their stint at the Opry, Curly and Ruby recorded their best records, a series for Columbia in 1945 and 1946. Most of these featured Ruby's singing, Curly's hot fiddle, and the innovative electric guitar work of Jabbo Arrington. "Blue Love," "Don't Lie to Me," and "Nobody Else But You" attracted the attention of musicians everywhere, but were not exactly hits. In November 1947, the pair went into the King studios to do a long session. "We were doing eighteen sides at this one session," recalled Curly. "And Ruby was getting as hoarse as a horse. King's owner, Syd Nathan, said, 'Curly, haven't you got a fiddle tune to throw in?'" Curly did—one he had been playing on the Opry called "Black Mountain Rag." Curly's guitarist then was Mose Rager, the legendary Kentucky fingerpicker who helped teach Merle Travis; Mose worked out a solo, and the band raced into the song. When the King side was issued in 1948, it became Fox's biggest hit—in fact, it became what is probably the biggest country instrumental hit of the decade.

In later years, Curly and Ruby returned to Nashville, where they did an album for Starday in 1963. Not long after, Curly left Ruby in their mobile home to play the Friday-night Opry. While he was gone, a fire broke out, and Ruby died in the blaze. Devastated, Curly returned to his hometown and drifted into semiretirement. By the late 1970s, though, he was playing again and even recording some of the rare tunes he later played backstage at the Opry on that "Old-Timer's Night." He died in 1995, and his home at Graysville is now a small museum.

The Delmore Brothers

To the casual fan, the Delmore Brothers might be seen as just another duet act from the 1930s, along with the Callahan Brothers, the Monroe Brothers, the Shelton Brothers, the Rice Brothers, or the Bolick Brothers (the Blue Sky Boys). But the Delmores were far more than just another duet act: They were one of the first of these acts, and they retained their popularity longer than any of the others. They sang original songs, and sang them in such a unique musical style that they influenced generations of country and bluegrass performers. Today they are seen as a vital transitional group in country music development; they link the blues, ragtime, and shape-note sacred singing of the rural nineteenth-century South with the polished, complex, media-oriented styles of the 1930s and '40s. The Delmores are also transitional in another sense, for they were among the first country acts to appeal to a wider audience—they enjoyed two of the first "crossover" hits with "Beautiful Brown Eyes" and "There's More Pretty Girls Than One." In their singing you can hear echoes of the Carter Family and Jimmie Rodgers, to be sure; but you can also hear touches of Paul Whiteman's Rhythm Boys, the early Mills Brothers, and even the Boswell Sisters. The Delmores were wide-ranging in their own musical taste, and their broad-minded creativity helped expand the definition of country music for millions of listeners.

Though much of the Delmores' success came from their own innate skill and drive, part of it also derived from their being in the right place at the right time. In the 1920s it was necessary for the Carter Family or Riley Puckett to generate volume enough to be heard under rather primitive staging conditions, but by 1930 radio had made it possible to sing softly and still be heard. The first generation of country music stars—Rodgers, the Carters, the Skillet Lickers—could not depend on radio to establish their reputations; in many cases their artistic style was not suited to the new radio medium. But the second generation of country stars sensed the absolute need to fit their art to the medium, and the Delmores were among the first of this group. On radio, their carefully crafted harmonies could be appreciated and their strikingly effective lyrics understood.

Both Delmore brothers were born in Elkmont, in northern Alabama—Alton on Christmas Day, 1908, Rabon on December 3, 1916. Their parents were tenant farmers who struggled to eke out a living in the region's rocky red clay, and for much of their lives the brothers saw little but hard times.

Musical talent ran in the family; the boys' mother and uncle were both skilled gospel singers who could read and write music. Uncle Will was a well-known gospel music teacher who had composed and published several hymns. Often, the entire Delmore family would sing at revival meetings and "all-day singings" held at tiny churches throughout the South. As a young boy, Alton was taught to read the old shape-note music by his mother. He also attended various summer singing schools held in rural churches.

By the time Rabon was ten, in 1926, the Delmores were playing together and singing the close harmony they later became famous for. They sang informally around the community and at local fiddling contests. Alton admitted later in life that the amateur gospel quartets that flourished (and still flourish) in the rural South were a major influence on their style. The brothers were soon hauling down more than their share of first-place awards in singing, and local newspapers began to praise them in print. Encouraged by this success, Alton began writing to radio stations and record companies asking for a tryout; he got firm but polite refusals. In 1931 they got a chance to cut a single record for Columbia, but it was the depth of the Depression, and it sank like a stone.

Alton next approached Harry Stone, manager of Nashville radio station WSM. The station's *Saturday Night Barn Dance*, which had been rechristened the Grand Ole Opry only four years earlier, was quickly gaining popularity throughout the South. Alton recalled later: "We all knew that the Grand Ole Opry was the greatest show on the air at the time. Or at least people in the South thought so, and we were southerners." But for a year Stone wrote back offering little encouragement. The brothers hung on. "We brought home some money nearly every time—precious money that kept some food on the table, along with Daddy's help. We were treated almost as celebrities at our home in Limestone County, Alabama, but we didn't have the money to make the thing real." Finally, in 1932 the boys auditioned successfully for the Opry and were given a regular thirty-minute slot, replacing the Pickard Family.

The Delmores' stay on the Opry was stormy and controversial at times, but it gave them the exposure and the national audience they needed. They became popular with listeners right away. Soon they were receiving more mail than any other Opry performer except Uncle Dave Macon. The brothers actually read their mail, made up lists of numbers that were requested, and even sent personal letters in reply. They had an unusual rapport with their audience, but were disappointed at being unable to get good tour bookings. To the early Opry artists who were trying to work at music full-time, personal appearances were necessary to supplement the meager wages paid them by the station. In April 1933, the brothers went to Chicago to make their first Bluebird records for Victor. They drove up with another popular singing group from the Opry, the Vagabonds. Eli Oberstein, who did so much of Victor's hillbilly and blues field recording in the 1930s, was in charge of the session. He was to supervise the Delmores' recordings throughout most of their stay with Bluebird. The seventeen sides from this Chicago session (which included two of their most enduring numbers, "Brown's Ferry Blues" and "Gonna Lay Down My Old Guitar") gave them even wider exposure.

By 1936 and 1937, the Delmores were the most popular group on the Opry as well as the show's only really successful recording act. Their Bluebird records sold well, and soon they had cut over eighty sides, many of which were also issued by the famous mail-order calalog company Montgomery Ward. Their best-seller was "Brown's Ferry Blues." By mid-1937 it had racked up sales of over 100,000—an astounding figure in that Depression-wracked economy. Other hits included "Southern Moon," "When It's Time for the Whippoorwills to Sing," "Gonna Lay Down My Old Guitar," "The Girls Don't Worry My Mind," "Weary Lonesome Blues," and "Fifteen Miles from Birmingham." The brothers often toured with Fiddlin' Arthur Smith, the Opry's most popular fiddler, and with him they recorded some of the era's most enduring songs: "Beautiful Brown Eyes" (1937), "There's More Pretty Girls Than One" (1936) and "Walking in My Sleep" (1937). Soon the radio waves were full of other artists covering Delmore songs; a 1937 WSM press release reported, "In every nook and corner of the land, one can hear recordings of The Delmore Brothers being played—in corner drug stores, at church festivals, in private homes, wherever the charm of the folk-tunes or hillbilly songs penetrates."

A disagreement over booking practices caused the Delmores to leave the Opry. In September 1938, they formed a new band (featuring Milton Estes from Pee Wee King's band) and drove out of Nashville. On the whole, it was a bad move; the Delmores were free to play all the theaters they wanted, but they had a hard time finding a new radio base. They found themselves moving almost every few months; starting in Raleigh, North Carolina, they then went to Winston-Salem, then to Greenville,

South Carolina, then to Washington, then to Charleston, West Virginia, then to Birmingham. In Birmingham they organized a hillbilly union and met Hank Williams, whom Alton described as "a sad boy." Finally they landed at WLW, the new powerhouse station in Cincinnati.

By 1943 WLW was at 50,000 watts, but it was still heard all over the Midwest. At this point the station decided to increase its country music programming to ten hours a week and add the popular *Boone County Jamboree*. This move attracted a number of bright young musicians besides the Delmores, including Grandpa Jones and Merle Travis. As the war began to take its toll on various bands, program director George Biggar (formerly of Chicago's WLS) told Alton Delmore he needed "a good, down-to-earth gospel quartet" to replace one of the decimated bands. Alton commented that he used to teach gospel music singing schools in Alabama, and Biggar told him to try to put one together.

Alton got together his brother, Grandpa Jones, and Merle Travis and talked them into trying out. Grandpa recalls: "We left the studio and went out into the hallway and tried a couple of songs out. They sounded okay—our voices blended all right. So we went in and told Mr. Biggar he had his gospel group. 'Okay,' he said. 'Start in the morning. Go a half-hour.'" Back in the hallway, the boys began to wonder just what they had let themselves in for. The quartet didn't even have a name, so they began to think of one. Travis recalled that the Delmores' biggest hit had been "Brown's Ferry Blues," named for the Alabama hamlet where the brothers had grown up. He suggested they call themselves the Brown's Ferry Four. Everybody laughed at the joke—a gospel quartet named after an off-color song like "Brown's Ferry Blues." But Alton began to think, "You know, that's not a bad name. It's got a good ring to it." So, Travis later recalled, "We went on and called ourselves the Brown's Ferry Four, and nobody ever connected it to Alton's bawdy 'Two old maids lying in the sand' song."

The quartet would, of course, become the most popular country gospel group of the decade. It took to the air in 1943; because they had to have enough material to do thirty minutes a day, Alton taught the others how to read the shape-note gospel songbooks put out by Stamps-Baxter, James D. Vaughan, and others. They also liked to do "spirituals"—the old-time name for black gospel songs. To learn these, the four went down to a used record store in downtown Cincinnati to buy used records by groups like the Golden Gate Quartet. Merle picked guitar and sang bass; Grandpa sang baritone; Rabon, tenor; and Alton, lead. Soon the show was drawing stacks of mail. Grandpa recalled, "We were amazed at the response we started getting from farmers and factory workers who tuned us in at such an early hour."

About the time the quartet got to going good, though, the draft struck: Merle went into the Marines, Grandpa into the Army, and Alton into the Navy. Since WLW owned the name Brown's Ferry Four, the station continued to run the show, filling the spots with whatever singers were available who could sing gospel. For the first time in their careers, the Delmores were not singing together. Before they had split up, though, the Delmores, Merle, and Grandpa had made a handful of records for a Cincinnati businessman named Syd Nathan. (It was his used record store they had haunted looking for black gospel records.) Nathan's label was called King, and during the war King records took off. By war's end, the company was more than a regional label, and in March 1946 Nathan flew the Delmores, Grandpa, and Merle to Hollywood for a big recording session. Each act did some specialties, and then Nathan asked them to re-create the Brown's Ferry Four for a couple of records—"Will the Circle Be Unbroken" and "Just a Little Talk with Jesus." To everyone's surprise, the quartet was a smash hit.

The Delmores, on their own, had started out recording for King the same kind of acoustic, old-time duets they had been doing for Bluebird (and later Decca). Then, at the famous Hollywood session in early 1946, they tried something new: Adding a third guitar, played by Jethro Burns, and a strong bass, they did a piece Alton had written called "Hillbilly Boogie." In the interim the Delmores had moved from Cincinnati to the more heady atmosphere of Memphis, where the blues and rhythm and blues were flourishing. The brothers' longtime interest in the blues found new inspiration. At the same time, a new style known as "country boogie" was producing hit records for Porky Freeman and Arthur "Guitar Boogie" Smith. Syd Nathan was anxious to get a piece of the action. With "Hillbilly Boogie," he did, and the Delmores found themselves riding the crest of yet a third career.

Soon the Delmores were cutting uptempo boogie records at almost every King session. One of their first big boogie hits was "Freight Train Boogie," in 1946, on which the acoustic sound was enhanced by an electric guitar—the brothers' first step into "modern" country. Next came "Mobile Boogie," "Peach Tree Boogie," "Pan American Boogie," "Sand Mountain Blues," and "Blues Stay Away from Me." The latter, cut in 1949 as an example of what Syd Nathan called "a hillbilly Hucklebuck" (a popular rhythm and blues dance), became the biggest hit of all. Worked out by the brothers and Henry Glover, King's black studio pianist, the song featured one of the most memorable guitar riffs in modern music: It was invented, and played, by Zeke Turner, the Cincinnati session man who played some of the hottest licks heard on Hank Williams's records. Another fixture on the boogie sides was harmonica player Wayne Raney, who had teamed up with the brothers in late 1945 and worked with them off and on for the next six years.

Sadly, the Delmores seemed unable to take full advantage of the spectacular success of their King records. They moved restlessly around the South during this time; from Memphis they went to Chattanooga in 1947, then to Jackson, Mississippi, then to Athens, Alabama, then to WCKY in Covington, Kentucky, then to Fort Smith, Arkansas, then to Del Rio, Texas, and finally to Houston. Here they finally broke up. The country boogie fad had spent its force, and the newer rockabilly and honky-tonk styles were starting to emerge. Though Alton was interested and able to embrace this next generation of music (he, in fact, cut a couple of rockabilly-flavored singles in the later 1950s), Rabon couldn't. With Rabon suffering from lung cancer, the brothers reunited for a final few months. There was time for one more recording session, in August 1952; they decided to do a set of Brown's Ferry Four sides, and one under their own name. One of these, "The Trail of Time," became the final hit in a joint career that encompassed over two hundred sides. On December 4, 1952, Rabon died.

Alton Delmore, the more creative of the two, who had written most of their songs, continued to dabble in music, but with little success. His songs were recorded by artists like Tennessee Ernie Ford, and he enjoyed modest royalties; but he finished out his life working as a postman, bitter about the new Nashville scene. He channeled some of his creative energy into writing fiction, and completed most of an autobiography titled *Truth Is Stranger than Publicity*. The Delmores' music still lives today in the work of artists like Doc Watson, Bill Monroe, Jim and Jesse, Ricky Skaggs, Emmylou Harris, and others, and in the work of Alton's son, Lionel, whose "Swingin'" was a huge hit in the early 1980s. Their legacy is one of country music's richest, a link between the music's past and its future.

Don Gibson

In 1965, when Don Gibson was on Knoxville's WNOX *Tennessee Barn Dance,* the venerable announcer and emcee Lowell Blanchard used to introduce him by saying, "Here's the young man with the fine voice and fantastic phrasing. He came to the *Barn Dance* four years ago to see if he could find his niche in life. He's still looking—and still singing. He adds the modern touch to our music here."

Surrounding Gibson on the show were fiddlers, bluegrass banjo pickers, old-time duet singers, and mandolin pickers, and though it was the age of Jim Reeves and Eddy Arnold, Gibson was beginning to feel out of place with his smooth singing and sophisticated guitar playing.

"I was amazed that they even hired me," Gibson recalls. "When I went in there, singing like I sing, smooth sound and everything, I thought, 'I'll never go over in there.' And sure enough, when we tried playing out—playing schoolhouses and auditoriums and such, like the old-time and bluegrass groups did—nobody would ever show up."

Don Gibson was twenty-three years old in 1955, and he had been in the music business for six years. During that time, he had always assumed that if he was going to make it, he would do it as a singer or, at worst, a rhythm guitar player.

"A lot of people at WNOX remembered Don best for his unusual rhythm guitar work," recalls Archie Campbell. But in the summer of 1965 neither talent seemed to be doing much for the man. That was the summer that WNOX radio moved from its longtime location on Gay Street in downtown Knoxville out to the new digs at Willow Springs. The new place had a big empty basement with interesting acoustics.

"One day I had to do the noonday show, and after it was over I started walking down the steps and found myself humming a tune," Gibson recalled. "About a year before I had written, sort of by accident, a song called 'I'm Glad I Got to See You Again,' and Hank Snow had picked it up and recorded it. Now I was humming another melody. It wasn't because of any lost love or anything like that. I just got thinking: I wrote one song, maybe I can write another. Maybe I could be a songwriter."

Down in the basement, he started fitting a chord progression together (C-D7-G7) and working out two very simple stanzas and a bridge. He never wrote any words down, nor any music, but if any of the secretaries upstairs at the radio station on that sleepy summer afternoon had been listening to the music wafting up the stairs, they would have heard the first tentative strains of a song that millions of listeners today recognize as "Sweet Dreams."

Three decades later, Don's Willow Springs opus is still making him money, and his questions about what path he should follow in the music business have been pretty much resolved. "I consider myself a song-writer who sings, rather than a singer who writes songs," he says. "And my guitar playing is really incidental to my career—though I'm occa-sionally termed a musician's musician—whatever that means." Yet there are impressive statistics to validate his success in each of these three roles.

Songwriting. "Don has one of the largest catalogs of standards in the country field," says booker Buddy Lee. Don Gibson estimates he has between 150 and 175 "working" songs, songs that continue, year after year, to make him money. Long after his own recordings of his songs have dropped off the charts, other artists pick them up and give them new leases on life—artists as diverse as Count Basie ("I Can't Stop Loving You"), Emmylou Harris ("Sweet Dreams"), Ronnie Milsap ("I'd Be a Legend in My Time"), Ray Charles ("I Can't Stop Loving You"), Connie Smith ("Just One Time"), and Johnny Cash ("Oh Lonesome Me"). According to Gibson, "I Can't Stop Loving You" has been recorded over seven hundred times worldwide, and it, along with "Oh Lonesome Me," has sold over 30 million records in various forms.

"Don probably has influenced more young singers—pop and coun-try, white and black—than any other country singer," says Danny Davis, who produced Gibson for RCA in the late 1960s. The busy accountants at Gibson's publishers, Acuff-Rose, nod in agreement.

Singing. For a songwriter who happens to sing, Gibson has built up an impressive discography. Between 1949 and the end of 1986, he recorded some 513 titles on a range of labels that includes Mercury, Columbia, RCA Victor, Hickory, Warner Brothers, MCA, and K-Tel. Not all of these were issued, of course. Some were buried in albums, and on the B sides of singles. Some that should have been released were. But thirty-five of his singles made the Top 20, and his original version of "Oh Lonesome Me" earned a gold record. His vocal stylings were strong enough and appealing enough to allow him, in his later career, to make hits out of other writers' songs—such as Gary Paxton's "Woman, (Sensuous Woman)" (1972), Eddy Raven's "Country Green" (1972), or Gene Thomas's "Rings of Gold" (1969).

"He is the master of country soul," says his onetime singing partner Dottie West.

Picking. From the dawn of Nashville session picking, in the late 1940s, there has been a strong but unspoken interest in jazz and blues guitar traditions. Men like Jabbo Arrington, Grady Martin, Hank Garland, Chet Atkins, and Zeke Turner knew the work of jazzmen like Les Paul, George Barnes, Barney Kessel, and Django Reinhardt.

From his early days in Knoxville, where he often sat in with a jazz-oriented studio band, Don Gibson was attracted to challenging instrumental music. Though he played rhythm guitar, he knew and respected the lead work of others, and on his sessions as well as his road bands, he tried to get the best.

Two of his best LPs, *Girls, Guitars, and Gibson* (1961) and *Don Gibson with the Spanish Guitars* (1966), were built around guitar work. The former brought together jazz legend Johnny Smith, Hank Garland, and Harold Bradley for a three-guitar backing, while the latter was originally designed for the Brazilian duo Los Indios Tabajaros but later redone with ace Nashville session men providing the Spanish guitars.

In 1974, Gibson made news when he added to his own collection of ten guitars a rare Maccaferri instrument originally designed by and owned by Django Reinhardt. Reinhardt, a French Gypsy guitarist who died in 1953 after making a long series of superb jazz records in Europe, had become Gibson's "all-time favorite musician." "Django was a master's master," Gibson recalls, "and his music has always reached me." Some have even argued that Gibson's love of guitar styles has influenced his singing and songwriting, and that one can hear echoes of Django Reinhardt in both.

Though Don Gibson has been celebrated as one of the inventors of the Nashville sound, and though he is generally recognized as the quintessential Nashville songwriter, he never moved to the city until long after he was rich and famous.

He was born Donald Eugene Gibson on April 3, 1932, in Shelby, North Carolina, in the same area that produced banjoist Earl Scruggs. He was one of four sons and two daughters born to a local railroad man and his wife, neither of whom had much special interest in music. Don did, though, and he began picking it up when he was fourteen.

He remembers: "I bought myself a cheap guitar and started sitting on the back porches where local musicians gathered. The older fellows would teach licks and runs to us younger guys. I had a good buddy who knew most of the basic chords, and he was a lot of help as well. Then I actually began playing music when I was sixteen or so. As a teenager, I used to hang out in pool halls a lot, and one day this boy named Ned Costner came along and asked me if I played. I said I did and he said, 'Well, let's go down to my house and pick some.' I think I knew two or three chords then, but we started up and before long we had put a band together. We called it the Sons of the Soil. They had every instrument except a bass, so I got a bass and learned how to play it."

At first, the Sons of the Soil played local dates for groups like the Kiwanis and the Lions, and for private parties. As their name indicated, they were very much in the mold of the Sons of the Pioneers, who by 1949 were influencing everyone in country music. Gibson's band liked to feature the sort of smooth harmony singing popularized by the Pioneers. Even this early, Gibson's voice was distinctive, and he was soon featured on most of the band's solos, accompanied by two local boys, Howard Sisk and Jim Barber, on the trios. Barber also played fiddle and trumpet; Sisk played rhythm guitar; Hal "Pee Wee" Peeler played electric guitar; and Milton Scarborough played accordion.

By 1948 the band was good enough to land a regular job playing over Shelby station WHOS, and this allowed the boys to announce dances, concerts, and bookings they had set up—though the station job itself paid next to nothing. All the members kept their day jobs; Gibson worked for J&K Music, moving jukeboxes and restocking them with records.

One of the hungry new record labels that started up after the war was Mercury, which released its first sides in November 1945. By 1949, anxious to get into the lucrative hillbilly market, Mercury had named Murray Nash as its new country A&R chief, and with much ballyhoo was announcing that Nash would be touring the South on an extensive talent hunt, recording acts on location, à la Ralph Peer and Frank Walker in the early days of country music in the 1920s.

Nash had heard the Sons of the Soil and set up a session with them. On his way to Shelby, though, he stopped over at WBT Charlotte, where he did some more recording and visited veteran radio and film star Claude Casey. Casey's stardom had mad him a target for song pluggers and songwriters, and just before Nash arrived he had received in the mail a song called "Cloudy Skies" from two writers named Dahle and Mulligan. "It was a beautiful trio song," recalled Casey. "I played it for Nash and he begged me to let him take it up to this new band he was recording in Shelby." Casey agreed, and later added a second song, "I Lost My Love," to Nash's briefcase.

Thus Don Gibson's first recordings came about in the spring of 1949 at radio station WBBO in Forest City, N.C. In addition to the two songs

Nash brought, which were done as trio sides, the group did two featuring Gibson's vocal solos, "Automatic Mama" and "Why Am I So Lonely."

Nash first decided to change the group's name to the Highlighters, and the original Mercury master acetates still bear that name. Later though, before the session, the name Sons of the Soil was restored. Gibson even got label credit for his two solos. "Why Am I So Lonely" also mark Gibson's first attempt at songwriting—one that he wasn't too proud of. "It's really silly," he recalls today. "But everybody tries to write a song once in their lifetime and that was my first."

Mercury had high hopes for "Cloudy Skies," but when it was released a month or so later it fizzled. The second Mercury pairing, featuring Merle Travis-sounding "Automatic Mama," did the same, and before long the Sons of the Soil had broken up.

Later that year, Gibson struck out on his own, and by 1950 he had a manager, Hal Houpe, who also managed the local Rogers Theater in Shelby. Gibson was a regular on a Saturday night jamboree show broadcast over the new FM station in Shelby. He had formed a new band, the King Cotton Kinfolks, that included fiddler Jim "Blackie" Lunsford (related to the famed folk singer Bascom Lunsford, and later to be known for his work with Roy Acuff and other stars), Summie Hendrick (a fine steel guitarist from Shelby who would remain with Gibson for seven years), and D. C. "Sed" Addis (a Shelby guitar player). The Shelby radio show went out over a network of twenty-five stations around the Southwest, and this fact made it easier for manager Houpe to set up another recording session. This time Houpe contacted Steve Sholes, RCA Victor's A&R man. Sholes liked what he heard and set up a session for October 17, 1950, in the studio of WSOC in Charlotte.

"Steve came down from New York," Gibson remembers. "He had a tape machine with him—the first we had ever seen." Four more sides were out, two of which were instrumentals: "Wiggle Wag" was Summie Hendrick's steel guitar specialty, while "Carolina Breakdown" was an old-time fiddle and banjo tune. Since it seemed so much at odds with Gibson's characteristic smooth and modern sound, this record has long puzzled fans and historians alike. Was Gibson experimenting with bluegrass or what?

Gibson laughs, "That was all Steve Sholes's idea. Two of the guys who played on the Shelby radio station were the Davis brothers—Pee Wee and Hubert. Pee Wee was a fiddler, and Hubert played banjo. They weren't even members of my band; I had never played with them before and never did after. But Steve had heard them and wanted to record their old-time music, and so he sort of ran them in on my session, just for that one number."

(The Davis brothers had grown up in Cleveland County around Shelby, often performing with a young Earl Scruggs; Hubert would later join Bill Monroe and then have his own band, the Season Travelers.)

The session also yielded another Gibson original, "Roses Are Red," a well-crafted song with sophisticated chord changes that reminds one of George Morgan. Unfortunately, the RCA Victor sides sold about as well as the Mercury sides and, like the Mercuries, were not even noted in *Billboard*'s review columns.

Don Gibson was becoming frustrated. He recalls: "There was an announcer at the station there in Shelby named Butler, a good friend of mine, and he kept saying, 'Don, if you're gonna make anything out of yourself, you better get out of here because you'll never get any recognition here.' I agreed with him. But I said, 'Where will I go?'

"At first I went down to see Arthur Smith at Charlotte—he was big then, with 'Guitar Boogie' and all that. But we didn't see eye to eye. He wanted to hire me, but he didn't offer me too good a deal. And I wanted to go out on my own. He [Butler] had been checking around on his own. He checked first at Bristol, Tennessee, WCYB. He came back and said, 'They have a couple of shows up there, and Flatt and Scruggs are up there, and some of the other bluegrass people are.' I thought it over and said, 'Well then, I don't want to go up there.'

"So the next day he came back again and said, 'I've got the right thing for you. A station in Knoxville has a thing called *Tennessee Barn Dance* and *Mid-Day Merry-Go-Round*. If you can get on that, it would be the best place to go.' He went there and I was still on RCA—the records hadn't done anything but I was on the label—and he told 'em that his singer was on RCA so they said, 'Send him up here Saturday night, and we'll audition him.'"

When Gibson got to WNOX and heard the amount of bluegrass and old-time country on the station, he despaired. "I'm really gonna stand out there," he recalls thinking. "When I started in there, with my smooth sound and everything, I thought, 'I'll never go over in here.' But they hired us—I was soon getting $30 a week."

Gibson brought four of his Shelby band to Knoxville with him: Summie Hendrick, Jim Lunsford, Sed Addis, and bassist Bill Kirby. He went over well on the radio show, which soon joined a national network hookup, but ran into trouble "playing out" at concerts. "I finally figured out I had too smooth an outfit," Gibson says.

He was, in truth, finding himself astride a great watershed in country music history: the shift from the old-time concert venue of the country schoolhouse and small-town auditorium to the nightclub and dance hall. The shift had already taken place in the Southwest, and was now changing musical patterns in the Southeast as well. Gibson sensed this. "I said to myself, 'You'd better get off finding a club and working it.' And I found one. It was out by Alcoa, just across from the old airport, a place called Esslinger's. I worked there for about four years. And that's where Wesley Rose heard me and signed me."

Before then, though, there were more dues to pay. A second RCA Victor session—held in Nashville in October 1951—yielded a modest hit in "A Blue Million Tears," but at the end of that year his RCA contract was not renewed.

Don Law signed him to a Columbia contract on June 26, 1952—for a 2 percent royalty—and set up sessions in 1952, 1953, and 1954. These were mostly hard country sides with backing by such fiddlers as Kenny Baker and Marion Sumner. For them, Gibson drew on the talented community of songwriters that was developing in the Knoxville area. These included the enigmatic Arthur Q. Smith (not the fiddler or guitarist, but the composer of Hank Williams's "Wedding Bells"), Johnny Masters, Carl Butler, H. McMahon, Harry Kaye, and Speedy Krise.

During this time, Gibson recorded only one of his own songs, "Many Times I've Waited" (1954). So much was he convinced that his success lay in singing that he even earned extra money cutting demos for the Valley Publishing Company that had been founded in Knoxville in 1953.

Evenings he honed his art at Esslinger's and occasionally at other local nightspots like the Duck Inn. His warm, lazy baritone was quite a change from the high, tense Roy Acuff/Webb Pierce school so much in vogue then, but it was finding its audience. By the summer of 1955 he was featuring it on his new song called "Sweet Dreams."

"I had a friend over there, a record plugger, named Mel Foree," Don Gibson recalls. "He had been working for Acuff-Rose for years, working Knoxville, and that summer Wesley Rose came over to a celebration they used to have every year in Maryville. On the way back, Wesley said he wanted to get a beer, and Mel said, 'I know just the place. There's a guy at this club named Don Gibson, and he's got a song I want you to hear.'

"So he brought Wesley in that night, and he heard me sing 'Sweet Dreams.' I hadn't copyrighted it yet. Then Mel came up and said, 'I've got Wesley Rose here tonight and he wants that new song you're singing for his publishing company.' So I went over to his table and we talked, and I said, 'I'll let you have the song, but you have to take me with it—sign me and get me a recording contract.' 'Well, I don't know,' he said. 'I'll see what I can do.' So he took the song, and Acuff-Rose got me a new contract with MGM."

On September 12, 1955, Don Gibson traveled to the old RCA studios in Nashville to cut his first sides for MGM—a session that included

"Sweet Dreams" and another Gibson original called "I Must Forget You." Again, the public response was underwhelming. "Those records were awful," Gibson admits. "I wasn't singing in my natural voice. They wanted me to sing up real high, like Webb Pierce, and in order to get on, I had to do it. Even some of those earlier records were better."

Meanwhile, Acuff-Rose got "Sweet Dreams" to Capitol star Faron Young, and in June 1956, just days after its release, the song hit the best-seller charts for a run that was to continue seven months. Gibson's career was at last on the move—but as a songwriter rather than a singer. Four later MGM records, released at the height of Young's "Sweet Dreams" run in 1956, had little impact, though they encouraged Gibson's songwriting efforts.

Buoyed with the royalty checks rolling in from Acuff-Rose, Gibson quit his job on the *Tennessee Barn Dance* and struck out for a try on WWVA's *Wheeling Jamboree* in West Virginia in the fall of 1956. Wheeling didn't work out, though, and by early 1957 Gibson was back in Knoxville, determined to try his hand at full-time songwriting. That spring he turned out "Too Soon to Know" and "Blue Blue Day," good songs that were eventually to prove themselves. But a couple of months later—Gibson thinks it was June 1957—he had "the kind of day I could use a few more of." In one afternoon he wrote "Oh Lonesome Me" and "I Can't Stop Loving You."

"I was living in the Shilom Trailer Park, up on the Clinton highway north of Knoxville, up there back in the woods," Gibson says. "I was sitting in the trailer feeling low. When you're sitting in a trailer and don't have a job, you're low and down. They had come and got my TV one afternoon, and even the vacuum cleaner, started carrying things off, and I wrote those songs because I felt bad.

"I sat down to write a lost love ballad, and that was 'I Can't Stop Loving You.' I jotted down some of the lyrics before I sang them into my tape recorder, and saw the line 'I can't stop loving you' and said, 'That would make a good title.' Then I did 'Oh Lonesome Me'; sang that into my tape recorder. I usually compose on my tape recorder and so when I sent the tape off to Acuff-Rose, whoever transcribed it misunderstood it. I had originally titled it '*Ole* Lonesome Me,' but when it came out on sheet music and all, they had it '*Oh* Lonesome Me,' and it was too late to change it then."

For years a popular Nashville place-name legend has held that Gibson wrote "Oh Lonesome Me" at the Biltmore Courts Motel, not far from the Acuff-Rose offices, and some tour buses still mention this. Gibson isn't sure how this tale got started.

Acuff-Rose promptly got Kitty Wells interested in recording "I Can't

Stop Loving You," but by this time Gibson was gearing up for yet another crack at record-making himself.

For years Gibson had known and worked with Chet Atkins, who had strong Knoxville connections. In fact, Atkins had worked on one of Gibson's 1951 RCA Victor sessions. Now Atkins had been named RCA's head producer in Nashville. Atkins recalls, "One of the first artists I decided I wanted was Don Gibson." Gibson had gone to Nashville in February 1957 to do a session with Atkins.

Gibson remembers: "We tried a session using nothing but straight-out country, steel guitar, fiddle and all. They put them out, and pretty soon Chet called and said, 'Don, they're not selling. Let's try one more thing. Let's put the voices behind it, and get rid of the fiddle and steel guitar.' That was right when rock and roll was starting, and some of the artists had started using the Jordanaires, dropping the steel, not sounding so country. So we did 'Blue Blue Day' that way, and it sounded pretty good."

Before "Blue Blue Day" was even released, though, Don Gibson sent Atkins a demo tape with "Oh Lonesome Me" and "Loving You" on it. Another session was set, this time for December 3, 1957, in the newly built RCA Victor studio, at 9:30 A.M.

On his demo recording of "Oh Lonesome Me" Gibson had used an unusual bass drum to create a novel effect. "I had a boy from Knoxville named Troy Hatcher playing drums," Gibson explains. "We all came over from Knoxville the night before the session, stayed up all night, got loaded, and straggled into the session the next morning. Chet set a microphone right in front of the bass drum and off we went. I didn't tell Troy to use that beat. In fact, he put it in there in a way that we didn't even hear it clear until we were in the booth listening to the playback. He told me later on that he had picked up that beat by listening to a black jazz band, one led by Coleman Hawkins."

Even at that, the session almost didn't come off. "When I had sent 'Oh Lonesome Me' down ahead of time to Wesley Rose, I had told him to give it to George Jones," muses Gibson. "I didn't think it was that much of a song, and George was just getting started then. I brought 'I Can't Stop Loving You' as a ballad I wanted to do on the backside. Chet and Wesley looked at it, and said, 'Well, it's not much of a song.' And I said, 'Well, it's gonna be on the B-side, so what difference does it make?' They finally let me cut it as the B-side to 'Oh Lonesome Me.' Over the next three years that record sold about 600,000 copies."

It did more than that. After it hit the charts in February 1958, for a thirty-four-week stay, it stimulated sales for "Blue Blue Day," which had been done in the same sparse "Nashville sound" style six months earlier but had been largely ignored. In May 1958, nine months after its release,

"Blue Blue Day" hit the charts as well, and, like "Oh Lonesome Me"/"Loving You," it hit Number One. In fact, for a few weeks in mid-1958, Gibson had three Top 10 hits on the country charts, with two ("Blue Blue Days" and "Oh Lonesome Me") crossing over to the pop charts.

It would have been an impressive feat at any time, but coming on the heels of the rock-induced depression country music was suffering in the mid-'50s, it was stunning. It showed that country could compete with the new pop sounds, and it helped establish the sharp, clean "Nashville sound" as a viable commodity.

It also validated Don Gibson as a singer. For the next eight years (1959–1966), he produced a consistently good series of singles and albums for RCA, managing to place three, four, or even five singles in the Top 20 each year. These included even more country standards such as "Who Cares" (1959), "Lonesome Old House" (1959), "Don't Tell Me Your Troubles" (1959), "Just One Time" (1960), "Sea of Heartbreak" (1961), "Lonesome Number One" (1961), "Yes, I'm Hurting" (1966), and "Funny, Familiar Forgotten Feelings" (1967). These same records also nibbled around the bottom of the pop charts, attracting even more interest by pop singers and producers.

The big breakthrough here came in 1962, when Ray Charles included "I Can't Stop Loving You" in his legendary country and western album for ABC, and when his producers pulled the song to be released as a single. For weeks it was a Top 10 hit. Gibson found himself winning industry awards by the carload and, not surprisingly, was asked to join the Grand Ole Opry in 1958. By the fall of 1959, he had married, settled into a modern split-level home in Knoxville, and was the proud father of a baby girl named Autumn Scarlet.

Coping with the sudden success, after years as a journeyman musician, took its toll. Always a shy man who preferred the solitude of his home to the concert stage, Gibson now found himself being asked to do an increasing number of television shows, radio shows, and concert tours, often involving long stints of traveling. He began having weight problems, and sometime in 1960 he began taking pills to help him diet. Soon he was taking twenty-five of them at a time.

"I got hooked on pep pills and tranquilizers," Gibson admits. "Never the hard stuff or pot, but the pills were bad enough. They were trouble, and I lived with trouble. I knew I was getting hooked—and I liked it at the time. But it was the worst thing that ever happened to me. I let my career go, said good-bye to my career, because I simply didn't care. They couldn't find me to record. They tried to find me, and I'd be back in those hills. Victor was pulling their hair out, Chet didn't know where to find me. I used to be on planes and I didn't even know where

I was at. My songs I wrote then weren't as good—the only good one I did while I was on pills as 'I'll Be a Legend in My Time.'"

He was fired from the Opry in 1963—"I was emceeing a Prince Albert show one Saturday night and I showed up two hours late"—and his records that used to make the Top 10 were now peaking out at rankings like 37, 51, or 71. Things had gotten so grim that he found himself going back home to his parents' home in Shelby in 1966, leaving behind him a trail of missed appearances and angry bookers.

His marriage had dissolved, and while home in Shelby he met a local girl, an attractive bookkeeper named Bobbi (Barbara) Patterson, and they began dating. One June 4, 1967, they were married, and Bobbi began helping Don get his career reorganized. It was not dramatic turnaround, though, and pill problems continued.

"Around 1969 I did a show in South Carolina," Gibson recalls. "My mother, my wife, everybody was there, and I made a complete fool of myself. I had gotten tired of falling down, though, and when I got home I told my wife, 'I'm not going to do that anymore.'" Things were not going well between RCA Victor and Don, either, and when their relationship ended in 1969, it seemed a good time for Don and Bobbi to finally move to Nashville and start all over.

A fresh start with records came with a new contract with Hickory, Acuff-Rose's label, in January 1970. Producer Wesley Rose seemed determined to rebuild Gibson's career on his singing. Of his first forty Hickory sides done in 1970, only seven were Don Gibson songs. The rest were by the cream of Nashville's songwriters—from Dallas Frazier to Tom T. Hall. The plan worked: By 1971 Gibson had his first Top 10 hit on Hickory, Eddy Raven's "Country Green." And people began to talk about Gibson's "natural" singing voice.

"My idols were really Red Foley and Eddy Arnold and George Morgan. And when you listen to some of the songs I do, especially the older ones and the sacred ones, you can hear some of Foley," says Gibson.

Critics began to speak of his "weathered honky-tonk" voice, and in 1979 a review for the prestigious *New York Times* hailed Gibson's working by saying, "Technically, he doesn't have much of a voice, but his bluesy, improvisational style makes the lyrics he writes sound remarkably fresh. His embellishing moans and cries are exquisitely musical, so perfectly are they laid into the rhythm, and his entire presentation rings with the sort of sincerity that can't be faked."

Dottie West, who recorded a number of duets with Don during his last years at Victor, agrees. "Everything stays stored up in him until he gets to the microphone, and he runs as soon as it's over. You don't know Don Gibson until you hear his songs."

Thousands of new fans did, as Don Gibson began another string of best-sellers for Hickory. By 1972, he was back on top again, with a new Number One effort, "Woman (Sensuous Woman)," a record that sold over 200,000 copies. It was not penned by Gibson, though, but by Gary Paxton. Other Hickory hits during the 1970s would be written by people like Paxton, Eddy Raven, Bobby Bond, and Mickey Newbury ("If You Ever Get to Houston Look Me Down").

Soon Gibson's creative juices were flowing again, though, and he was weighing in with chartmakers like "Is This the Best I'm Gonna Feel" (1972), "Bring Back Your Love to Me" (1974), and "I Wish Her Well" (1975). Respectable, if not blockbuster, successes continued throughout the decade on ABC/Hickory (1977–78), MCA (1979), and Warner Brothers (1980).

By the end of the '70s, Gibson was being recognized as a major force in Nashville music, and young songwriters listened closely to his rare explanations of his own songwriting philosophy.

"My songs are simple, and just about all of them are about love. I write about people, not things. I never had a lot of education, and I don't feel easy with words. Most of the words to my songs are real simple. I just make them up to put to some tune on the guitar I've come up with. It's the sound of the guitar that I've always been interested in," Gibson stated.

If this sounds like a textbook definition of a country song, it probably is . . . at least a modern country song. Gibson's elemental two-chorus songs, which look so stark and terse on paper, form simple and memorable statements when sung. They cross musical genres with ease and appeal to all sorts of fans—which is fine with Gibson. "It is so idiotic to like only one thing, one way," he says. "People should listen to all types of music. They should be concerned with whether the song is any good, not with what type of music it is."

In 1986, Don Gibson began recording again with the man who helped produce his first hit: Chet Atkins. Both Atkins and Gibson could, if they wished, rest on their laurels; neither needs to prove anything. But the same impulse that produced two of the age's most popular songs in a trailer park on one lonely East Tennessee afternoon thirty years ago is still very much alive, and the rich legend of Don Gibson has chapters yet to come.

The Louvin Brothers

On the morning of Friday, January 25, 1955, Charles and Ira Louvin, from Henagar, Alabama, arrived in Nashville to see about joining the Grand Ole Opry. They were no star-struck kids, but veterans of over ten years in the music business; their songs had been recorded by some of the biggest names in country, and they'd had their own Capitol contract for four years. Recently, though, their career had stalled, and from a phone booth in Birmingham they called their Capitol A&R man, Ken Nelson, to see if he could help. "We told him we wanted to get on the Opry," Charlie Louvin remembers. "We had auditioned before eight different times without any luck. Ken told me he'd get back to us next week. But I told him that we didn't have enough food to last until next week, and we needed to know something now. We had to give him the phone booth number and wait by the booth until he could call us back."

The call finally came, and the boys were told to be at the Opry office three days later. It was only later that they found out that Nelson had bluffed them onto the show: He had told Opry boss Jack Stapp that the *Ozark Jubilee* also wanted the Louvins. For now, though, they were just happy to have their shot. As four o'clock neared, they climbed the hill to the National Life Building on Seventh Avenue. Their meetings with Stapp and music clearance man Vito Pelletieri were cordial; then Vito said, "Come on, I'll introduce you to the stage manager, Jim Denny."

The brothers exchanged nervous glances. Denny was the man for whom they had auditioned those eight times in the past, a brash and seemingly cynical individual who had little use for the Louvins' gospel hits like "Love Thy Neighbor." Later they would learn that at this time Denny really had no authority to hire anyone for the show, but now they were not sure if he was their final roadblock. As the late afternoon sun began to set, they entered Denny's office. Charlie remembers: "We sat there for ten minutes and were completely ignored. Ira had this attitude that, even if they throw us out, I'm gonna say this anyway. So he finally said, 'Well, Mr. Denny, we've got to go. We'll see you on the *Friday Night Frolic*.' [That's what they called the Friday night Opry in those days.] And Denny looked up over his hornrims and said, 'Boys, you're in tall timber. You better s——t and get it.' And Ira said, 'Well, we got the saws, you just show us where the woods are.'" A couple of hours later they were on the Opry stage, singing "Love Thy Neighbor" and getting called back for an encore. The tall timber was starting to fall.

There was a time when close-harmony duet singing dominated country music. In the mid-1930s the sounds of the Delmore Brothers, the Blue Sky Boys, Karl and Harty, the Monroe Brothers and the Callahan Brothers filled the airwaves and the recording studios. That era passed, though, and by the 1950s many thought the duet style was about as trendy as a Model A Ford. Then came the Louvins; in the space of a few years they single-handedly reinvented the duet style, sharpened the old harmonies, and crafted new songs that became country standards. Though their career in the big time lasted only about eight years, and though they only had ten charting records, their sound and style were to haunt singers for decades to come. Many consider them the finest of the country duet singers, and artists from Emmylou Harris to Vince Gill have revived their songs and kept their style alive. Songs that hardly charted at all during the Louvins' career have managed to remain in print and have become standards. "When I Stop Dreaming" spent exactly one week on the *Billboard* charts, but is today considered a masterpiece of hard country harmony. "How's the World Treating You" spent one week as a best-seller; "Love and Wealth" didn't even do that well. Dozens of country singers have covered Louvin songs, as have folk and even rock groups: the Byrds had a memorable version of "The Christian Life," and Nicolette Larson did a moving reading of "Satan's Jeweled Crown." Not surprisingly, the Louvins have been nominated for the Hall of Fame; also not surprisingly, as an act that sang its last notes forty-two years ago, they haven't made it. But Charlie Louvin, still a soloist on the Opry, takes consolation in the fact that hardly a day goes by without somebody asking him about the times when he and Ira were riding the wild horse and changing the face of country music.

The long climb to the top started on Sand Mountain, in northeast Alabama. It is a huge plateau, running over a hundred miles into the central part of the state, with rough, steep sides that discouraged much contact with the outside world. The people who lived on the plateau had few radios, and were rich in older musical traditions like Sacred Harp singings and fiddling contests. In the 1920s one of these families was headed by a Colonel Monero Allen Loudermilk, an old-time banjo player who enjoyed a regional reputation as a pretty decent frailer. The Colonel and his wife had a total of seven children, who needed to help with the cotton, the cane, and the corn; two of them were named Ira Lonnie and Charlie Elzer, born in 1924 and 1927 respectively. The brothers grew up hearing their father's old-time music, but were just as interested in their mother's ancient ballads like "The Knoxville Girl" and "Mary of the Wild Moor." Their family was active in the Sacred Harp singings and knew of the newer shape-note gospel songs published by companies like James D. Vaughan and J. M. Henson. When the brothers were around eleven or twelve, the Colonel decided they would benefit from gospel singing lessons offered by an itinerant singing school teacher. He gave them their $12 tuition, and sent them on their way. They never made it, though. They stopped by a country store, used some of the money to buy candy and cigarettes, and laid out in the woods until school was over. As a result, Charlie and Ira never learned to sing from those shape-note gospel books, but they learned something of the wrath of their father. Charlie recalls: "He whipped us for not going; he whipped us for lying; he whipped us for spending money; he cleaned our plow good."

Nevertheless, the Colonel was proud of the way his two boys could harmonize together, and had them sing for neighbors and at church. By now they were listening to the Delmore Brothers, who had grown up a couple of counties away from Henagar, as they sang every Saturday on the Grand Ole Opry. As a child, Ira had crafted a homemade mandolin out of a syrup bucket and corn stalks, and a little later traded his bicycle for an old beat-up guitar. Eventually he got a mandolin, and learned to play it by listening to old Monroe Brothers records. On July 4, 1940, the brothers were paid for performing for the first time, at a hamlet called Flat Rock. About the same time they saw their first touring show—a visit by Roy Acuff and his troupe at a local schoolhouse. Charlie remembers standing in the field hoeing crops and seeing a huge old air-cooled Franklin drive up the road with the legend "Roy Acuff and the Smoky Mountain Boys" on the side. "We knew at that point, when we saw Acuff pass in his car that day, that's what we wanted to do. It was just a matter of how to do it."

It was a struggle. Ira got married while still a teenager, and had to take a job at a mill in nearby Chattanooga to support his family. Still, the boys persisted, and eventually won the chance to do their own radio show over WDEF in Chattanooga in 1942, where they appeared as the Radio Twins and featured songs like "There's a Hole in the Bottom of the Sea." Soon, though, Ira was drafted; Charlie despaired and returned home, but some three months later he received interesting news from

Ira: He had injured his back during training at Fort Bliss, and was being discharged. They returned to Chattanooga, where they spent the next two years working with the area's most popular radio band, Bob Douglas and His Foggy Mountain Boys (not related to the later bluegrass band of the same name). In 1945 it was Charlie's turn to be drafted; he enlisted instead and landed at Lowery Air Force Base. Ira took a lob with Charlie Monroe and his band, and played the mandolin on several hit records by him, including "Bringing in the Georgia Mail."

By the fall of 1946 the brothers were reunited again and found work in Knoxville at WROL. It was here they changed their names to Louvin. "People had trouble with Loudermilk," says Charlie. "They pronounced it wrong, spelled it wrong, sometimes even laughed at it. So we took the first three letters of Loudermilk and added the v-i-n to it." It was also at Knoxville that they met a veteran promoter and musician named Smilin Eddie Hill, who was to have a major effect on their career. Soon he landed them all a job in Memphis, where they were to spend the next four years, from 1946 to 1950. For a time they did three shows a day over WMPS. Though they did everything from comedy to western swing, they soon found their niche with gospel songs. "Ira and I would get 6,000 letters a week from people requesting hymns," Charlie said. Hill was still skeptical—until he went with the brothers to a church concert and watched them collect a "love offering" of over $200.

Ira had continued to write songs, and through Eddie was able to get them published by Acuff-Rose. Fred Rose wasted no time in placing Louvin songs with major recording stars of the day: Within months Red Sovine, Charlie Monroe, Johnny and Jack, Wilma Lee and Stoney Cooper, Carl Smith, and Jim and Jesse had all cut Louvin songs. Rose also got them recording contracts on their own, first with Decca and then with MGM. It was with Decca that the Louvins had their first release under their own name, a lilting tribute called "Alabama," backed up by "Seven Year Blues" (1949). The MGM sides included a set of influential gospel numbers like "Weapon of Prayer" (a special favorite during the Korean War). The records, though, didn't translate very well into touring and radio success, and the early 1950s became a frustrating round-robin of gigs in Knoxville, Greensboro, Danville, and Birmingham. A low point came in late 1951 when the team decided to split up and get out of the music business. But then Fred Rose called with some good news: He had talked Ken Nelson at Capitol into giving them a try on his label. By late September 1952 they were in Nashville cutting their first new sides, including the popular "Love Thy Neighbor." And it was Nelson they called a couple of years later, in 1955, from the Birmingham phone booth, asking about the Opry.

When they started on the Opry—their first assignment was the Prince Albert show with Red Foley—the brothers were known primarily as a gospel act. Sensing that this would limit them both in record sales and in touring, they asked Nelson to let them start cutting non-gospel material. He was reluctant: One of his other big acts, Martha Carson, had tried to switch into straight country and failed. Finally, though, he agreed, and the brothers came up with a non-gospel song they thought would work: "When I Stop Dreaming." Charlie recalls, "We sang that song for a year, messing around with it. We felt that if we were gonna change with anything, we could get by with using that song." They were right. Cut on May 25, 1955, the single was rushed into release in July, and shot to Number 13 on the charts.

The gamble had paid off, and now the hits started coming: "I Don't Believe You've Met My Baby," "Hoping That You're Hoping," "You're Running Wild," "Cash on the Barrelhead." By the end of 1956 the brothers were winning awards for Best Singing Group as well as Best Sacred Group. Nelson managed to hold on to their gospel audience by putting out gospel songs in album form, and using the best secular stuff for singles. Neither brother lost interest in gospel, even when they toured with the hottest act in show business, Elvis Presley. Both Presley and his mother had been fans of the Louvins since Memphis days, and the Louvins could have had a major relationship with him but for an incident backstage on a 1956 tour. As was his custom, Elvis began playing gospel tunes on the piano and remarked, "This is really my favorite kind of music." Ira, standing nearby, took offense. "If that's your favorite music," he shouted, "why don't you play that out yonder, instead of that trash!" Presley lamely responded, "When I'm out there, I do what they want to hear. When I'm back here, I do what I want to do." Things almost came to blows. Charlie remarked: "If Elvis ever had any ideas about doing a Louvin Brothers song, he dropped them then."

Success was also tempered by Ira's increasingly turbulent lifestyle. He soon won a reputation as the best tenor singer in Nashville, and as perhaps the best post–Hank Williams songwriter. He was also very much a ladies' man, between and during his four marriages. He was also a driven man, capable of manic intensity one moment and wild humor the next. He was a major-league drinker, one given to sudden tantrums and outbursts of violence. More than once he trashed his mandolin on stage, and a fight with his third wife, Faye, led to a shooting. Ira was rushed to a Nashville hospital—three bullets, lodged too close to his spine for surgery, he carried with him to the day he died. "It was sort of like walking on eggs," commented a band member who worked with the brothers during the latter days.

Many think that the Louvins' partnership broke up only with Ira's death, but in fact they had split up two years earlier. Both planned on pursuing solo careers with Capitol, and Ira was already working on a solo album and a single called "Yodel Miss Molly"; Charlie, whose sense of business and responsibility had served as ballast for the group from the first, had his first solo hit with a fine Bill Anderson song, "I Don't Love You Anymore." He had recruited Tommy Hagen, a North Carolina singer, to do Ira's harmony parts. Despite their split, the brothers were not estranged, and Ken Nelson was still hoping the two would get back together.

But then, early one Sunday morning on June 20, 1965, as Ira and his new wife, Anne Young, were returning to Alabama from dates, there was a grinding head-on crash near Warrensburg, Missouri. Six people died, including Ira and Anne. Charlie heard the news while he was doing a date in West Virginia, and he grimly began making his way back to Nashville. It was a long, long drive.

The Statler Brothers

One summer day shortly after the Civil War ended, two young men made their way up a dusty road toward a village called Singer's Glen in the Shenandoah Valley of Virginia. Their names were Aldine Kieffer and Ephriam Ruebush, and they had met in a Union prisoner-of-war camp; both were lovers of music, and Kieffer's grandfather had operated a songbook-printing company before the war. Now the two friends had in mind resurrecting the company, but as they got into the town and looked over the scene, they found the printing presses broken up, overgrown with weeds, the type jumbled and spilled. Determined, though, they set to work, cleaned up the print shop, picked up the spilled type, and were soon publishing new books of gospel songs.

These books used a system of shaped notes rather than the round ones generally used by northern and European publishers, and it quickly spread throughout the South. To help encourage it, the two friends decided to organize the Virginia Normal School, which began to dispatch singing teachers throughout the South. One of the pupils was a Tennessean named James D. Vaughan, who eventually started his own publishing company, and hit upon the idea of promoting his new songs by sending quartets of well-trained singers on the road to give free concerts in local churches. Within a generation, these male quartets were becoming more popular than the songs they were singing, and by the 1920s they had become synonymous with gospel singing itself.

In the early days of country music, many of the ideas of what consitituted good singing came from this gospel tradition. A lot of early singers got their training in harmony, meter, and tone from the old-time "singing schools" and early quartets. Opry pioneer Kirk McGee attended them as a child, as did the Delmore Brothers, Bill and Charlie Monroe, A.P. Carter, and others. Members of the old colorful string bands like the Red Fox Chasers, the Georgia Yellow Hammers, and Dr.

Smith's Champion Hoss Hair Pullers were trained in quartet singing, and even wrote songs for the little shape-note songbooks. They helped to make quartet singing a legitimate part of country music, and by the 1930s the radio airwaves were full of the rich harmonies of bands like the Prairie Ramblers and the Sons of the Pioneers. When the Ramblers sang about "Riding Down the Canyon" or the Pioneers did their trademark "Tumbling Tumbleweeds," listeners were transported on waves of nostalgia for a earlier, simpler America. The rich, four-part close harmony became evocative in itself, like the barbershop quartet, and soon every country radio show had its singing group.

Flash forward a hundred or so years. It is now 1980, and the Shenandoah Valley still echoes with the sound of quartet singing. This time it is not at Singer's Glen, but in a town just to the south called Staunton. There the center of attention is a big music festival called "Happy Birthday USA," staged every year by country music's most popular singing group, the Statler Brothers. Natives of the valley, the Statlers had grown up in the gospel quartet tradition, and all of them still lived and worked in the Staunton community. Once a year, they gave back—in a big way. For days, fans, reporters, songwriters, musicians, and assorted music business types would descend on the small picket-fence town to revel in nostalgia, apple-pie values, and small-town ambience. Reporters got to visit the old schoolhouse that the Statlers had bought and turned into their national booking and promoting offices; they got to see the little-league baseball fields where the Statlers coached, and the nearby farm one of them owned. By 1980 some 75,000 people were descending on the town for the celebration. "It's old-fashioned," admitted one of the Statlers. "It looks like some pages out of a 1901 calendar."

Which is fine with the Statler Brothers. For over three decades the Statlers have found their niche in country music by developing a new, modern sense of nostalgia and tradition. Back in the 1920s and 1930s, the nostalgia in the music was for the "good ol' days" of the nineteenth century, for the rural bucolic South or the idealized West of Hollywood movies and Zane Grey novels. The Statlers realized that their generation really didn't remember any of this; their youth was full of Saturday afternoon matinees, poodle skirts, letter sweaters, knock-knock jokes, and soda shops—the flotsam and jetsam of the 1950s. With the unexpected success of their record "Do You Remember These" in 1972, the group began developing a musical counterpart to the new Trivial Pursuit games, creating a series of songs that were heavy on harmony, and long on the kinds of details of daily life that struck home with a huge audience. One of the founding Statlers, Don Reid, said, "Nostalgia by itself is real nice—it gives you a warm feeling and everything—but you can't eat it."

But in fact, for a number of years the Statlers did eat nostalgia. They fully embraced the old country music values of family, patriotism, religion, and small-town life. Another founding member, Phil Balsley, notes that "there are a lot of people out there who, to a certain extent, think like us. Believing in the country or the government for good or bad, and working a day for a dollar. I guess that's what it means to be Statlerized." Cynics and jaded journalists, to be sure, began to call the group "the Nostalgia Brothers," but no less a figure than respected novelist Kurt Vonnegut praised their songs, referring to them as "America's poets." And though the individual members of the Statlers continued to raise their families and participate in Staunton life—three of them were elders in the Olivet Presbyterian Church—their records sold as well as those of rock stars. Between 1965 and 1980, no fewer than thirty-eight of their singles got onto the *Billboard* best-seller list, with almost half of them making the Top 10. For years their television series was the most popular music show on the Nashville Network.

The history of the Statler Brothers begins with the man who was one of the quieter members, Lew DeWitt. It was Lew who was the cornerstone for the original group that became the Statlers, it was Lew who persuaded them to break out of gospel and try pop songs, and it was Lew who wrote their first big hit, "Flowers on the Wall." Born in Roanoke on March 12, 1938, Lew learned singing from his mother, who played guitar and sang; before he was eight, she had him singing on local radio shows and talent contests. By the time he was a teenager, it was the 1950s, and he was playing his guitar and singing in a series of country and rock 'n' roll bands in the Valley. Though he soon had a job as a psychiatric aide at Western State Hospital, he continued to do music part time, and began singing tenor in several of the many amateur gospel quartets in the area.

In 1955 Lew found himself singing in a pickup quartet at the local high school graduation, and a nearby organizer and businessman named Joe McDorman heard him and was impressed; he asked Lew is he would join him in organizing a new quartet. Lew agreed, and promptly recruited two of his boyhood friends, Harold Reid and Phil Balsley. Harold had been born in Augusta County, Virginia, on August 21, 1939, and had known Lew since they were in the fourth grade at Staunton. As boys, the two would occasionally make music together, but it did not play an especially large part in their lives. They were like most small-town boys, interested in baseball, Saturday afternoon matinee movies, working part time in the local apple orchards. In later years,

Harold would work this apple business into his onstage jokes; he wondered how they ever made it big in country music, since they had never picked cotton. "We did pick a lot of apples, though." To be sure, they did find they could harmonize well together, and as they grew older they began to sing for the fun of it. Harold graduated from high school in 1957—a date that would later play an important role in the Statlers' most famous song—and married his sweetheart, Brenda; soon he was working at a Staunton clothing store.

Phil Balsley, the second friend Lew asked to join the quartet, had been born out in the countryside near Staunton on August 8, 1938. He grew up a baritone, and was singing in various vocal groups as well as the Olivet Presbyterian Church, where more than half the choir were members of the Balsley family. He bagged groceries as a teenager, practicing when he could during his lunch hour. Thoughtful, quiet, systematic, serious, Phil got a job keeping the books for his father's sheet metal business.

Now they were all brought together under the direction of Joe McDorman, and they found their voices blended very well. After a few weeks of rehearsing, they felt confident enough to make a public appearance at a Methodist church in Lyndhurst, a hamlet about eight miles south of Staunton. Phil remembered the occasion. "There were only about forty people there. I'm sure it sounded terrible, but the people seemed to like it." Harold agrees. "Everybody at the church thought we were great. I never figured out whether the congregation thought we were great because we were great, or because we were free."

For the next four years this quartet worked its way through a succession of small-church Wednesday and Friday night "sings," pie suppers, tent meetings, homecomings, all-night gospel conventions, and shows on the flat roofs of concession stands of drive-in movies. They were sticking exclusively to gospel music, but there was little to distinguish them from hundred of other small-time, shiny-suit groups. "I guess if you're talking about direction, we didn't really have any," recalls Harold. "We were just plodding along."

The plodding finally trailed off to nothing in 1959, and the quartet disbanded. McDorman left to persue other business interests in Florida, and the rest of the guys continued to work at their day jobs and to look after their growing families. Then, about 1961, Phil recalls, "Harold got to talking things up again, and said, 'I'd like to sing some more.'" As it turned out, Harold's younger brother Don, who was then sixteen, "was coming along pretty good with the singing. So Harold kind of popped him out there in the middle, and things haven't been the same since." Young Don, born in Staunton on June 5, 1945, had the reputation in school as a creative, "artistic," personable boy with a great appetite for reading history. Even before he graduated, he had become the master of ceremonies and lead singer for the revived quartet. They renamed themselves the Kingsmen, and set about modeling their music on that of the two hottest southern gospel groups then going—the Statesmen and the Blackwood Brothers.

These groups were changing the face of gospel music by adapting modern harmonies and popular singing styles to the music, and this appealed very much to the young Statlers. One day they worked out an arrangement of a non-gospel song, Ferlin Husky's "Gone," and liked the sound. Gradually they began to integrate a few such songs into their programs, and found that this helped them expand their audience appeal. Harold laughs: "If they had $50, we did their type of music; if they had $25 or even $10, we sang. Finally, we had three different shows we'd do. One night we'd be at a church singing gospel, one night at a banquet singing pop, and the next day at a country music park singing country." They never charged for singing gospel music—except for the traditional voluntary "love offering" where the plate was passed—and they are proud to say that, even in later years, they never sang gospel music professionally.

Before long, setting aside just their weekends to take dates was not enough time to accommodate their growing popularity. Says Don, "It got to where we were singing in surrounding states three to four nights a week. We would get in at two or three in the morning from performances and would have to get up at eight and go to work." The stress began to show in their personal lives and in their day jobs. At one point Harold and Phil were working at a clothing store in Staunton; Harold was the assistant manager. "It was a pretty nice job for somebody who didn't particularly want a job," Harold remembers. But then came one weekend when the Kingsmen decided to enter a talent contest over in Maryland. The elderly clothing storeowner, angered at their lack of zeal for their jobs, refused to give them the time off they needed. "We left a couple of part-time guys there to help the old man, and he got mad. When we got back Monday morning, he made me turn over the keys to him. He got pretty upset, and it was a pretty bad scene."

Episodes like this, combined with the growing realization that the Kingsmen had "sung everything out in our part of the country," convinced them that it was time to try going at their music full time. Harold now jokes that they were "too young and too dumb" to realize the odds against their success in show business. They did have enough sense to realize they needed a new name; already there was a gospel group called the Kingsmen (from Asheville, N.C.) and a rhythm and blues group called the Kingsmen. One afternoon they were meeting in Don's front room at Staunton to discuss it. Don recalls: "Harold saw a box of Statler tissues across the room and said, 'How about Statler? That's as good as anything.'" At the time, Statler was not exactly a nationally known name; it was a regional brand. "We might have made out even better as the Kleenex Brothers," jokes Don. "The Statler people even sent us a box of free tissues a few years ago, so I guess they're happy about our borrowing their name."

With a name in place, the foursome faced other, bigger obstacles. Quartets had not been big in country music since the singing cowboy phase of the 1930s, and modern country promoters and bookers were skeptical. Don explains: "At the beginning, when they saw that we were a group, they thought we were a gospel quartet. I don't think there was an up-front country quartet before us. We always had it in our minds that we would be the first quartet to step out front. You don't see quartets out front; you see them singing background."

In August 1963 their big break came, sooner than any of them expected. They got a call from Carlton Haney, a prominent bluegrass and music park promoter in Virginia, who had booked a Johnny Cash show for an upcoming fair at Roanoke. Haney invited them to come backstage, and introduced them to Cash himself. "I've got a group I want you to hear," he told Cash. "Okay," Cash replied. "Can you come to Berryville Sunday?" Harold allowed as they could. Sunday rolled around, and the Statlers reported to Cash. Instead of auditioning them, Cash stunned them by inviting them to go on stage on his show that night. As the serious Statlers went through their set, Cash sat by the side of the stage and listened."After the show, he said he really liked us," says Don. Harold, in his usual brashness, blurted out, "Could we go to work?" "Yeah," said Cash, "I'd like to have you." Harold replied, "When?" and Cash said, "I don't know."

Nobody else seemed to either. The Statlers returned home to wait, but one week rolled over into the next, and soon seven months had passed. That fall of 1963 Cash was riding the crest of his biggest nationwide popularity, appealing not only to his normal country fans but to thousands of new urban folk music fans caught up in the trendy folk music revival. And he was a very busy man, as Harold found out when he started trying to get hold of him. "I went home and called him twice a week . . . for four months. I called him one night in California, New York, and Texas, and finally ran him down in Hollywood on the set of *Hootenanny*. I got to talk to him. We had to go to work for him to pay the phone bill." Cash did finally come through with a bona fide offer, and the Statlers joined him on March 9, 1964, in Canton, Ohio. With nothing more than a handshake for a contract, they joined an organization where they would spend the next eight and a half years.

The Johnny Cash Show at this time was, in essence, a microcosm of country music history. It included Mother Maybelle Carter and the Carter Family, whose style and repertoire dated back to the 1920s and the very dawn of the music. Carl Perkins, whose electric guitar style and rockabilly songs had helped define rock 'n' roll, was a regular. Cash himself had a repertoire full of country laments, gospel, rockabilly, blues, sentimental songs, patriotic favorites, protest songs, and insane comedy pieces. The Statlers fit into the show well, often opening with gospel songs and their own arrangements of current country hits. They also supplied background vocals for other singers later in the show. They soon learned to be versatile, and Cash's grueling schedule gave them ample opportunity to perfect their style. Still, press releases always talked about their gospel flavor, and they often topped off their part of the show with their rendition of "How Great Thou Art."

Less than a month after they first walked on stage with Cash, he got them a record contract with his label, Columbia. Soon they were in Nashville, cutting their first two sides. One of the first released was a version of "The Wreck of the Old 97," the classic country ballad about a train wreck not far from Staunton. Another was "Hammer and Nails," where Cash himself did the recitation. They also began to get part of Cash's national spotlight; they made *The Tonight Show* with him and went with him to San Quentin for his famous concert there. They also got roles on Cash's ABC variety show in 1969 and 1970.

Gradually the Statlers began to establish their own identity, and in March 1965 they recorded an original song by Lew DeWitt called "Flowers on the Wall." It was a springy, uptempo catalog of the ways a victim of loneliness and estrangement deals with the time on his hands: counting the flowers on the wallpaper, playing solitaire with a short deck, watching the kiddie television favorite *Captain Kangaroo*. It was an old country theme, but Lew's sharp details and familiar references struck a responsive chord in listeners. Released as a single, by September it had made both the country and pop charts. By year's end it had garnered the group nominations for four Grammy awards, two of which they won: Best New Country Group and Best Contemporary Performance by a Group. In the latter category, they beat out such competition as the Beatles and the Supremes. More awards and a string of albums and singles followed, as well as more national television spots. Three years after they had joined Cash, they could look back and feel satisfied that they had proven to everyone that quartets were not just for background anymore.

They were not, however, fully satisfied with their music. Columbia had taken them on at Cash's insistence, but its executives were still nervous about the quartet format; even after "Flowers on the Wall," they were nervous about the Statlers using more of their own material, or even choosing their own producer. "We were their albatross," Don recalls. "They didn't know what to do with us, and they didn't care." Columbia's attitude was reflected in the record sales: Throughout the 1960s, only a handful of the Statler singles made it onto the charts, none rising higher than Number 10. Columbia producers kept pushing them to do material by journeymen Nashville songwriters—the country equivalent of Tin Pan Alley hacks. Wilma Balsley, Phil's wife, reflected on this point in their career: "They played a kind of music that was between pop and country. They didn't want to commit themselves to a definite style."

Two events in the early 1970s changed this. One was an amicable parting from the Johnny Cash Revue in 1972, though the Statlers and Cash would continue to appear together on "special occasions." The Statlers wanted to take advantage of the increasing number of requests they were getting for separate bookings. Cash understood. "We left the best of friends," says Don.

The other change was a move to Mercury Records when their Columbia contract expired in 1970. At the new label, according to the Statlers' own press release, they "were granted more artistic freedom"— a common enough cliché in the politics of modern country label-hopping. In this case, though, it turned out to be true. They were assigned a young producer named Jerry Kennedy, a Louisiana native who had cut his teeth as a guitarist for *The Louisiana Hayride;* his first advice to the Statlers was to forget about trying to sound pop, to concentrate on doing good country, and to come up with more original songs— suggestions with which the group totally agreed. Kennedy then put together a team of crack Nashville session men for the studio dates, and the results were so pleasing to everyone that the same basic formula— indeed, the same basic group—was used for the next three decades. One of the studio band's unique sounds was the bunching of two or three rhythm guitars, usually played by Ray Edenton, Chip Young, and Kennedy himself; a six-string bass guitar (usually Harold Bradley); an electric lead guitar (Kennedy); a pedal steel guitar (Pete Drake); and a bass (Bob Moore). Rounding out this team were Pig Robbins's piano, Buddy Spicher's fiddle, Bobby Thompson's banjo, Buddy Harman's drums, and Charlie McCoy's harmonica. The first fruit of this new collaboration was an original by Harold called "Bed of Roses," released as a single in the fall of 1970. Though it did well as a country side, it also did well on the pop charts.

The Statlers' real breakthrough did not come until their second Mercury album, *Pictures of Moments to Remember* (1971). It was a concept album, with all the songs revolving around nostalgia. The cover was a montage of personal snapshots, and the liner notes, by rockabilly great Carl Perkins, began: "Memories, my friends, are treasures; whether good or unpleasant, our tomorrows will be filled with memories of yesterday." Six of the songs were old-time chestnuts such as "When You and I Were Young, Maggie," "I Wonder How the Old Folks Are at Home," "Moments to Remember," and "Faded Love." The other five songs, though, were new ones by Don, Harold, and Lew. These too focused on nostalgia, and two of them, Lew's "Things" and Don and Lew's "Pictures" were catalog songs—detailed lists of items or events from the past. The album sold well, and yielded two successful singles.

This encouraged the Statlers to continue in this vein. In 1972 they had two even bigger hits, "Do You Remember These" and "The Class of '57." The former was yet another trivia catalog, but the latter was far more: It chronicles people instead of things. It was a bittersweet account of the faded hopes and dreams of a small-town high school class of some fifteen years earlier, a litany of failed marriages and stalled careers. "Where Mavis ever wound up is anybody's guess," read one line. Harold himself had indeed graduated from high school in 1957, but both he and Don insist that this event was not the primary inspiration for the song. That came from one night when Don and Harold got together at Don's home for a songwriting session. Harold had been leafing through a TV listings magazine and had noticed an episode of the detective series *Ironside* that was entitled, "Class of '57." The episode did not interest him very much, but the title did. He pitched it to Don, and within minutes the two were putting together a song. Don later admitted, "Some of the people in the song are real, but we had to embellish the truth on others. We've had people come up to us and say, 'Hey, you guys included me on your last record.' Then we'd get to thinking and say, 'That's right.'" One of the real people who wound up in the song was a fellow graduate of Harold's who "took his life."

"The Class of '57" became the biggest hit yet, and with it the Statlers finally found a sense of identity and direction that was to characterize their work for the next three decades. Journalists began calling them "the Nostalgia Brothers," and noting that their records happened to come along at a time when a mania for trivia and nostalgia and the 1950s was sweeping the nation. But the Statlers protested that they had been interested in nostalgia long before it became fashionable. "We're genuinely nostalgic," Lew told an interviewer in 1972. "It has nothing to do with trying to get on the bandwagon. We love it and we try every way we can to visit it temporarily. We feel like we were some of the first to get on it." Throughout the 1960s, for instance, the brothers had indulged in their love of 1940s Hollywood films, especially the old two-reeler cowboy films, and had even begun buying old prints of them to show on their bus while traveling. (It was a collection, in those pre-videotape days, that would eventually number over five hundred films.) The Statlers began to sense that the mellow, simple, easygoing melodies and barbershop harmonies of their nostalgia songs were appealing in the post-Vietnam/Watergate era. "Our music was not right for the period of the '60s," said Don in the early 1970s. "Today the people want to hear music that recalls memories of better times, and we inspire their good emotions."

In the thirty-plus albums they have released since "Class of '57" hit the charts, the Statlers have been careful to include one or two "good ol' days" songs on almost every set. As late as 1993, in their *Home* album, they were adding songs like "My Past Is Looking Brighter (All the Time)" and the old Red Foley hit "Chattanoogie Shoe Shine Boy." Throughout the years, a good many of these nostalgia songs—such as "Child of the Fifties," "Love Was All We Had," "Carry Me Back," "Whatever Happened to Randolph Scott," "Silver Medals and Sweet Memories," "The Movies"—became hits. A mellower Statler style emerged, one built on easy tempos, clean melodies, and four-part harmony. "We do know that audiences seem to like harmony singing," says Don. "Perhaps because it's hard to sing good harmony." This, along with Kennedy's patented backup style, has created one of the most stable and distinctive sounds in country music. The Statlers of the 1990s continued to sound very much like the Statlers of the 1970s—much to their fans' delight. And fans have responded by buying over 30 million of the records and CDs since.

What's more, as hundreds of skeptical reporters have learned over the years, the Statlers themselves really believe in the patriotic, small-town, old-fashioned Norman Rockwell values they sing about. Harold once told a cynical writer for *Country Music* magazine, "We just don't have no *hook*. We're patriotism and nostalgia and Mom and apple pie, and that's *it*. What more can I say? We'll try to do something daring, but I don't guarantee it, you understand. We're the Bland Brothers." The singers have resisted the temptation to move their offices to Nashville or New York, and their headquarters for years has remained in their hometown. "Staunton is a college and church town," says Don. "We still live here because it's home. It's a great place to come back to after a concert tour, a place to be normal and be who you really are. I don't think you can really do that if you live in Nashville or L.A. It's great to get your head on straight."

"It's important to maintain your perspective," Harold adds. "One night you're getting a police escort into a 15,000-seat hall, the next night you're home asking, 'What's Mama been up to?' and throwing the ball with the kids." The Statlers have been a real part of Staunton life—three of them have served as elders in the Olivet Presbyterian Church; one works with the YMCA; another owns a fifteen-acre farm; and all appear regularly in local parades and celebrations. From 1969 to 1994, they founded and starred in a "Happy Birthday USA" festival over the Fourth of July in Staunton, a three-day charity event and concert that started with an audience of 3,500 and had grown to almost 100,000 by the time the brothers decided to let someone else take it over in 1994.

All the Statlers are strong family men; the original four members have a total of fourteen children. "We plan our schedule around the kids," says Don. This means that many road tours last no more than ten days, and the group seldom tours at all in July or December "because we don't want to miss the kids growing up." They eagerly share their old films, antique cars, and Wurlitzer jukebox with their children. "We feel like we're giving our kids something that we grew up with and treasure," says Don.

This doesn't mean the brothers do not see themselves as professionals: They have created one of the best support organizations in the business. They were years ahead of their time in seeing the importance of controlling as much of their business as they could. Their efficiency and organization are admired by many in the music business as much as their songs or style. One of their former booking agents, Dick Blake, noted, "We've got a group that's so organized they'll tell you today what time they're going to leave their office three months from now." Another of the promoters, Lon Varnell, scheduled their concerts using a set of scientific charts developed while he was working for Lawrence Welk in the 1960s; even before the age of laptop computers and modems, he could tell just when the Statlers had played a city before, and avoid revisiting cities too soon. Borrowing techniques they learned from their tours with Cash, the Statlers try to retain total control of their road shows. "On the road we rent each auditorium and promote each show ourselves," says Don. "We hire all the talent that's on the show, pay any stagehands, carry our own emcee, our own lights and sound equipment, the whole thing. That way we don't have to go into a different situation every night, wondering who's gonna mess up where." (Such total packaging soon became common with the big rock band tours.) In the 1980s, the group more and more turned to their own songs, or those by their children, and in 1992 formed their own publishing company, American Cowboy Music, and later merged this into Songs of All Nations. And in an age when show contracts often have pages and pages of detailed ego demands, such as what color M&Ms have to be in the dressing rooms, the Statlers still offer a simple one-page agreement that specifies where they appear, how much they get, when they appear, and where on the stage they want the piano. "We come to work, not to party," says Harold. Bookers and promoters appreciate this, and the Statlers have over the years built up an amazing amount of goodwill. The stage shows themselves are fresh, well-organized, and brought off without a hitch.

The Statlers are also known for their sense of humor, a quality that delights their fans and helps them keep their work in perspective. "On stage we stay loose, kid around a lot, have a good time," says Harold. "We work better that way." Harold himself is responsible for much of the stage banter, which often treads the narrow line between the sacred and the profane, between the idealistic and the topical or political. For years the show featured a "Harold and Don" segment, with Don acting as the straight man. The audience heard things like, "Did you hear Ted Kennedy and Billy Carter have teamed up to run for office? Yeah. Their slogan is, 'You drink, I'll drive.'" During a question-and-answer segment, a woman asks Don, "Will you go home with me?" and Harold yells, "Ma'am, I don't want this to sound bad, but he's gone home with harder-looking women than you." They consider their onstage jokes important enough that they assign one of the group—usually Don—to keep a record of each one that's told.

The Statlers' humor can be infectious, extending beyond the confines of their stage show. When Barbara Mandrell gave them a new movie projector for their bus, they reciprocated by giving her a beautifully restored jukebox, loaded with forty old 45 singles—each one a copy of their hit single "Bed of Roses." The brothers are half serious when they call themselves "the Marx Brothers of country music," and they demonstrated their penchant for manic parody with their creation of a hapless small-time country band called Lester "Roadhog" Moran and the Cadillac Cowboys. This surfaced first in 1973, with an album skit called "The Saturday Morning Radio Show." Here was a seedy, raggy, pretentious, out-of-tune ensemble, trying to do covers of '50s hits, broadcasting from station WEAK, and improvising ads from Buford's Barber Shop. The whole thing caught on, and the "Roadhog" (who bore a strange resemblance to Harold) soon found himself the center of a cult following; Mercury even had to release a press photo of the band. Soon an entire LP emerged, *Live at Johnny Mack Brown High School*, which carried the joke even further. But the brothers realized that they were creating a Frankenstein monster, and wisely pulled back so they could concentrate on their more serious work.

In fact, the group's first real crisis was looming in the early 1980s. For years, Lew DeWitt had been suffering from a type of intestinal problem that was eventually diagnosed as Crohn's disease; as far back as the days with Cash he had suffered from long bouts of pain and nausea, and now, with increased traveling and touring, it was getting worse. In November 1981, he was hospitalized and temporarily replaced in the group. By 1982 it was obvious that he could not continue with the Statlers, and, in an emotional press conference, the group announced that he was retiring. Throughout the '80s he fought through surgeries and therapy, and while the disease was in remission even began forging a solo career. In 1985 he had a minor hit with "You'll Never Know," an old big-band ballad, but the disease came back; he died on August 15, 1990, of heart and kidney failure. His last album with the group had been *The Legend Lives On* in 1982.

In a sense, Lew chose his own replacement. Even when his absences were temporary, he recommended to the group that they hire another young Virginia singer named Jimmy Fortune. He was from Nelson County, about thirty miles from Staunton, and had grown up singing gospel quartet music, just like the other Statlers. By the time they met him, he was leading a band at a local Holiday Inn and working for a car dealership during the day. The brothers at once liked his youth and enthusiasm—he was a good fifteen years younger than most of them—and they were seriously impressed with his soaring tenor; on certain gospel numbers he was fond of kicking the key up on the final chorus, like the old quartets in the '50s had done, and winging up at some impossibly stratospheric level a full octave above the other singers. Coming from a background similar to that of the Statlers, he had little trouble fitting into the group. "Jimmy had so much in common with the rest of us," Harold quips, "we were bored with him the second day."

Even with the revitalization that Jimmy Fortune brought to the group, the Statlers began to see that they couldn't sustain their career on songs about nostalgia and songs that featured cute wordplay like "Charlotte's Web" and "Don't Wait On Me." During the 1980s, they began to reinvent themselves, exploring new directions but at the same time preserving the style and the values that their fans wanted to hear. Their longtime producer, Jerry Kennedy, has noted, "When we're in the studio, and we could go one way or another with a song, their first thought is always for what they think the fans want to hear." One of their unexpected directions was the songwriting ability of Jimmy Fortune; he broke away from the nostalgia and catalog themes almost at once, and created in "Elizabeth" (1983) the group's first Number One hit since "Do You Know You Are My Sunshine" five years before. He followed it up with pieces like "Forever," "My Only Love," "Too Much on My Heart," and others.

The Statlers also found ways of rebottling old wine, and during the 1980s began singing their own versions of vintage songs from the 1940s and '50s. Their big hit of 1982 was "Oh Baby Mine (I Get So Lonely)," which had been a top hit for the Four Knights in 1954; in 1985 they had a Number Three reading of Ricky Nelson's classic "Hello Mary Lou." They echoed the Platters in "Only You" in 1986, and in 1992 refurbished the Ames Brothers' 1958 favorite "It Only Hurts for a Little While." This, as well as newer songs like "Atlanta Blue" and "More Than a Name on a Wall" (about the Vietnam veterans monument), kept the Statlers on the charts through the 1980s. Indeed, they enjoyed about as many hit records in the Jimmy Fortune era as they had in their heyday of the 1970s.

They also tuned into the new media sweeping the music. In the 1990s they combined some their earlier gospel tracks into a special set to be marketed through direct TV sales. The results were stunning, and set a precedent for other artists wanting to find ways to resurrect their back catalog. In 1982, their syndicated television special *An Evening with the Statler Brothers* won a number of awards for the best show of its type, and there had been rumblings about a regular series. The brothers had resisted, though. Harold said, "We'd seen television suck people in, spit' em out, and they were never the same afterward." But in 1991, the Nashville Network approached with a deal in which the brothers would be given the best time slot on the schedule—nine o'clock Saturday night—and complete creative control over their show. It was hard to resist, and in October 1991 they took the plunge. At first they were assigned a team of professional writers, but the group felt at once that they were not capturing the feeling they wanted for the show. Somewhat reluctantly, they realized they would have to write the scripts themselves, and began gathering in their schoolhouse offices in Staunton to grind them out.

The show took on the look of an old-time 1950s live variety show. There were minimal sets, bantering with the guests, comedy, and a lot of music. One of the favorite segments that soon emerged was where the brothers would group around an old upright piano and sing old gospel favorites—a feature that further stimulated sales of their gospel mail-order packages. Throughout the 1990s, the show was one of the highest-rated on the Nashville Network, and was obviously successful in appealing to a substantial audience of listeners who were turned off by MTV. With the chart hits starting to dry up, the Statlers' longtime label, Mercury, released a huge thirty-year *Anniversary Celebration* set in 1994—

a collection of the big hits and favorites from three decades of brilliant music. Reflecting on it all, Don Reid recalls that one important secret is to keep from getting in a rut. "Sometimes you write a song and you say to yourself, 'I wrote that same song five years ago, that same message, I said it the same way.' You can't do that. You've got to stay away from what you have done in writing lyrics and arranging songs. We never try to shock people by being too different, but we try to be a little bit different." It is an appealing and effective strategy, and one that has become emblematic of much classic country music.

Martha Carson

Few country singers have mastered such a range of styles, from old-time string band to duet to country gospel to novelty, as Martha Carson, the dynamic redhead from Neon, Kentucky, whose music has won her fans from creaking country schoolhouses to posh Las Vegas lounges. Martha spent much of her career fighting to carve out a solo career in the male-dominated world of country music. Born as Irene Amburgey (she pronounces the name with the accent on the *Am*) on March 19, 1921, Martha grew up traveling rural Kentucky with her family's gospel quartet and playing string band music with her two sisters, Opal and Bertha. Later the sisters would record together, as Mattie, Minnie, and Marthie, for King, and as the Amber Sisters for Capitol. The sisters won their initial fame on the old *Renfro Valley Barn Dance*, and then moved to WSB in Atlanta. There Martha teamed up with James Roberts, taught him some of the old shape-note gospel songs she had known as a child, and watched as the pair gained a following throughout the South and a contract with Capitol Records.

But in 1950, while working at WNOX in Knoxville, James and Martha split up—both personally and professionally. Martha wanted to pursue a solo career, but at once ran into problems. "I was under contract with Capitol from the duet days for seven more years," she recalls. "And about every week, I'd get a call from Dee, or a letter from Capitol, or he'd show up, with someone new for me to team up with. Once he wanted me to team with Archie Campbell; or this man, or that one. But I said, 'Nope, I'm not going to sing another duet with another man.'"

About this time Martha wrote "Satisfied." Stung by some caustic criticism aimed at her by a WNOX listener upset over her divorce from James, Martha left for a tour into the Great Smoky Mountains crying and upset. "I cried more than halfway up the mountains," she recalls. "One of the reasons for all the suffering I had gone through was that I didn't want to disappoint our audience; they thought we were the Barn Dance Sweethearts: they named children after us. All this emotion came out. Then all of a sudden a whole new world came down on me, and I knew it was an inspiration from God, and I thought, 'I'm satisfied, and God is satisfied,' and all of a sudden these words started coming to me. I found one of Bill Carlisle's old blank checks in the floor of the car and wrote out the words on the back of it."

When Martha went to Nashville with Bill to record "Too Old to Cut the Mustard" in 1951, she met Hank Williams's manager, Fred Rose, and sang her new song "Satisfied" for him. "Gal, who are you recording for?" he asked, and after Martha explained that Capitol would not let her record solo, Rose got on the phone and began burning up the lines between Nashville and Hollywood. A few days later a solo contract from Capitol arrived in Knoxville for Martha, and in November 1951 she traveled to Nashville to do her first solo session—with Bill Carlisle, Chet Atkins, and her sister Opal, now known as Jean Chapel, backing her up. It included "Satisfied," and the record became her best-selling hit—a hit that would make the song a standard, to be recorded by everybody from Elvis Presley to the Blackwood Brothers.

From 1951 to 1954, Martha recorded over two dozen songs for Capitol, all of them done in Nashville with a small group of studio regulars. She joined the Opry, and toured widely with the likes of Jimmy Dickens, Faron Young, Ferlin Husky, and Elvis Presley. "Elvis went on tour with me when he had only one record out on the Sun label," she recalls. "We toured Georgia and Florida. Every time we got to the auditorium a little early, he'd say, 'Martha, come back here and let's sing some of those good old gospel songs.' He later recorded a version of my song "Saints and Chariot."

Martha during this time met and married Xavier Cosse, a pop booker and promoter who had come to Nashville to learn country music and work with Hank Williams. During the early 1950s there was a nationwide fad for what the trade publications called "religioso" music—souped-up pop gospel represented by pieces like "This Ole House" and "Give Me That Old Time Religion." Both Cosse and Steve Sholes felt that Martha could use this to expand her audience appeal; when she signed with RCA, the company tried one session in Hollywood, and then decided to move her to their New York studios. The William Morris Agency began to get her bookings on network TV shows and at hotels and lounges. Martha and Cosse moved to New York in early 1957.

One of her first live television appearances was on *The Steve Allen Show* on NBC. "On the night the show was telecast, I stood behind the curtains, and I never prayed so hard in my life," recalls Martha. "I was just a country girl from Kentucky, and here was this New York audience. I went out, and started doing a song called 'Let the Light Shine on Me.' I had written it years before when Jimmy Dickens and I had done a tour in the Midwest.

"That night on the Allen show, I got about halfway through it, and the audience just froze. About halfway through it, the arrangement had a modulation in it, and I had asked Mr. Allen if I could go off the stage into the audience. He said sure, it was the job of the cameramen to follow you. So when we hit that modulation, I went down into the audience, and soon they were rocking with me. The next week Steve Allen took out a whole page in *Billboard* that said, 'Martha Carson is not a girl: she's an explosion.'"

Martha's managers and arrangers tried to get her to do pop material, but they soon found that the audiences—and Martha—needed the kind of heartfelt spirituals that Martha excelled in, spirituals made even more dramatic by big-band backing and slick arrangements. Her RCA recordings reflected this mix, as Steve Sholes brought her song after song to try out. Two, "Now Stop" and "Just Whistle or Call," were by Elvis's writer Otis Blackwell. Others, such as "Be Not Discouraged" and "Get That Golden Key" were popular favorites in her club act. "Saints and Chariot" was Martha's dynamic closing to her stage shows, while "I'm Gonna Walk and Talk with My Lord" was the song that Martha ranks as her second most popular, just behind "Satisfied."

By 1958, Martha and Xavier had returned to Nashville to start yet another chapter in their career: a return to the gospel roots she started with. Today Martha still lives in Nashville and, after a period of semiretirement following the death of Xavier, has returned to occasional performances of her exuberant "happy spirituals."

The Carlisles

For over four decades now Bill Carlisle and the Carlisles have been known as one of the zaniest and most colorful groups on the Grand Ole Opry. In recent years, their fans have been treated to the antics of octogenarian Bill Carlisle racing on stage in a green wig, urging the audience on to a "standing ovation," and leaping as high as the WSM microphone in the midst of songs like "Too Old to Cut the Mustard." What leader Bill Carlisle seldom tells the audience is that he and his group have one of the longest pedigrees of any act on the Opry—a pedigree that extends back to the very dawn of country music and embraces some of the raunchiest blues ever cut, rich gospel songs, outrageous novelty songs, and lively tunes that pointed the way to rockabilly and rock 'n' roll.

Before there was the Carlisles, there was Bill Carlisle and his brother Cliff, two of the biggest stars of the 1930s. Born in Wakefield, Kentucky, in 1908, Bill followed in the footsteps of older brother Cliff, who helped pioneer the Hawaiian guitar and dobro and backed Jimmie Rodgers on several records. In July 1933, Cliff managed to land Bill a record contract with the old American Record Company, and soon the younger Carlisle had a major hit with a song called "Rattlesnake Daddy." The ARC publicist was soon promoting "Smilin' Bill" as a successor to blue yodeler Jimmie Rodgers, and was urging fans to see him as a hot young singer of white blues. And as Franklin Roosevelt struggled to get Americans off of soup lines, Bill Carlisle entertained them with off-color blues like "String Bean Mama," "Copper Head Mama" and "Sally Let Your Bangs Hang Down." By the end of the decade, Bill had switched to Bluebird and then Decca, and was demonstrating his versatility by recording hits like "The Heavenly Train" and "A Shack by the Side of the Road."

Though he made dozens of records, Bill was like most of the other country singers of the time: He made his true living from radio. For a time he was at WLAP in Lexington, and then moved on to stations in

Charlotte, Greenville, Atlanta, Winston-Salem, Shreveport, Memphis, and Knoxville. It was at Knoxville, in 1946, that Bill and Cliff had their last—and biggest—hit as a duet, combining their talents on a haunting Arthur Q. Smith song called "Rainbow at Midnight" for the new independent King label. The following year Cliff decided to call it quits and retire, and Bill was left on his own. After working a time with KNOX/Knoxville veterans like Archie Campbell, as well doing a comedy act as "Hot Shot Elmer," Bill decided to form his own group, the Carlisles.

It was the spring of 1951, and three separate events conspired to create this new group. First, in April, gospel greats James and Martha Carson split up; Martha went with publisher Fred Rose to try to make it as a country songwriter and as a soloist. Second, in June, the trade papers announced that Cliff Carlisle was bored with retirement, and was reuniting with Bill to become part of the Carlisles. Within a matter of weeks, Martha Carson had decided to join forces with them as well, giving the new band three of country music's most distinctive singers. The third event occurred when W. D. ("Dee") Kilpatrick, the former country A&R man for Capitol Records, took over the reins of the Nashville office of Mercury Records, one of the new, up-and-coming companies that had started in 1945. Kilpatrick began looking for new acts, and found the Carlisles. In early July 1951, he gathered them in Nashville, along with a backup band that included Red Foley's bass player, Flatt and Scruggs alumnus Benny Sims on fiddle, and Chet Atkins on guitar. Atkins, who would become an assistant producer for RCA the following year, had played on the Carlisles' King session that produced "Rainbow at Midnight" some five years earlier, and had in fact held his first professional job playing for Bill Carlisle and Archie Campbell over Knoxville radio years before. Even though he would soon become closely identified with RCA, he would do the electric lead guitar work for most of the Carlisles' Mercury recordings through 1955.

Bill, Cliff, and Martha each had a new song for the session, but it was Bill's "Too Old to Cut the Mustard" that made the session—and the group. The phrase itself came from an old saying of Bill and Cliff's father, and Bill had been using it in a story he told in his act. Dressed up as Hot Shot Elmer (a rube character who jumped over chairs and tables on stage—the source of Bill's jumping today), Bill told a tale about an old mule getting too old to work who ran away into the woods to form a community with other old, "useless" farm animals. The expression "too old to cut the mustard" meant too old to work, and it seemed a natural song title. The Carlisles' version was issued in September 1951, and while it did well enough, it was soon covered by five or six other acts. One of them, Red Foley and Ernest Tubb, released a version three months later that soon rose to Number Five on the *Billboard* charts. The song went on to become a country standard, and Dee Kilpatrick set about getting the Carlisles a hit record of their own. The new group was getting plenty of bookings, and in early 1952 they became the first Mercury act to appear on the NBC network segment of the Grand Ole Opry.

The next two Carlisles sessions—in March and April of 1952—featured Cliff, Martha, and Bill, but yielded no real hits; indeed, most of the third session was never even released. Career changes conspired against the band: Cliff went back into semiretirement; Bill found himself moving from Knoxville in August 1952 to take a job at WDOD in Chattanooga; and Martha joined the Opry as a solo act in April 1952. Still, Martha and Chet Atkins were able to join Bill in the studio in September 1952 to cut "No Help Wanted," a Bill Carlisle original that would become the first record by the Carlisles to hit the *Billboard* charts. It stayed there for eighteen weeks, eventually reaching Number Two. Roy Sneed was singing bass with the group by that time, and after the "No Help Wanted" session, Betty Amos (who would later become a Mercury and Starday soloist in her own right) replaced Martha Carson, who was becoming very busy leading her own band on the Opry.

From January 1953 came the next session, this one probably featuring Sneed, Amos, and Atkins's guitar; it included "Leave That Liar Alone," a traditional gospel song that had been recorded by Frank Luther in 1934, and by black gospel quartets as far back as 1928. It was also the model for Ray Charles's "You Better Leave My Woman Alone." "That Little Difference," another Bill Carlisle original recorded around this time, was never released on 78. It's an "anti-love" song that recalls some of Bill's 1930s songs like "Onion-Eating Mama." "Knot Hole" was the next hit, though, rising to Number Eight on the charts in April of 1953. This too was Bill's song, though the name "Suber" appears as coauthor. Explains Bill, "Tillman Franks was managing me then, and I gave him half the royalties in his wife's name. That's his wife, Suber."

By late 1953, in fact, Tillman Franks was also playing bass for the band, and Tommy Bishop had taken over on lead electric guitar. Betty Amos continued to help on guitar and vocals. (The instrumental work in the studios continued to be led by Chet Atkins.) On the strength of his recent hits, Bill and his group were also invited to join the Opry as regulars, and his move to Nashville put him in touch with a bevy of other talented musicians and, especially, with good songwriters. One was Ira Louvin, who came to Bill that year with a song called "Is Zat You Myrtle," which the Louvins had apparently been using in their own comedy stage show in the segment in which Ira dressed up as a character named Sal Skinner. "We had an agreement that he would give me cowriter's on anything he wrote that I would record," recalls Bill. "But after Ira had the wreck and got killed, I turned all my royalties back to them for their children." The record became the group's third chart hit, rising to Number Nine. In December 1953, the band was back in the studios doing a follow-up to "No Help Wanted" called "I Need a Little Help." "Me and Tommy Collins's name is on there," says Bill, "but Tommy Collins wrote that." Chet Atkins's guitar and Tommy Jackson's fiddle propel things along, as does a newly added studio drummer.

The next few years saw even more personnel changes; Kenny Hill came on board to sing and play bass, and ace guitarist Luke Brandon added his electric lead guitar. Mercury releases like "Busy Body Boogie" and the strange "Female Hercules" no longer made the national charts, but became favorites of the high-powered stage shows, and of their spots on the Opry. One of their sides from 1954 was a version of "Honey Love," first done by R&B singers Clyde McPhatter and the Drifters—one of the first instances of a country act covering a black hit. In the late 1950s the band added Robert Lunn Jr. (son of the famed "Talking Blues" man) and Dottie Sills to do the female leads. By 1960, Bill's own children were starting to perform with him. The Carlisles had their last big hit in 1965, with "What Kinda Deal Is This?" on Hickory. They continued to record for a variety of labels, including Columbia, Hickory, Vanguard, and Chart.

In recent years, their Opry band has included Bill and his son Billy, his daughter Sheila, and the fine singer and bass player Marshall Barnes. Joe Edwards from the Opry stage band often plays the hot guitar leads for the uptempo songs. Recent heart surgery has curtailed Bill's famous jumping somewhat, but he remains the oldest active member of the show. When he sings, as he often does, "Too Old to Cut the Mustard," his audience knows exactly what he means, and laughs right along with him.

Albert E. Brumley

In the years shortly before he died, in 1977, songwriter Albert E. Brumley took great pleasure in hosting his Hill and Hollow Folk Festival on the grounds of his publishing company in the hamlet of Powell, in southern Missouri. One day, the story goes, a group of locals were sitting with a group of visitors at a picnic table, exchanging small talk about the crops, the weather, and music. Finally one of the older men, dressed in khaki pants and baseball cap, muttered good-byes and wandered off. Talk continued for a while, and finally one of the visitors remarked, "You know, I came here hoping to meet Albert Brumley in person, but I haven't seen a thing of him." Another, more experienced visitor looked up and said, "Why, woman, that man who just left was Albert Brumley. He's been sitting here talking to you for an hour!"

It is a typical Albert Brumley story. While many can easily recognize the legends of country singing, far fewer can recognize the great song-writers. And Brumley was certainly that; in the last decade of his life, he was honored about as much as any songwriter could be. He was in the first group of inductees to the Nashville Songwriters Hall of Fame, and was an early member of the Gospel Music Hall of Fame. Festivals and singings were named in his honor, and his songs had been recorded by everybody from Elvis Presley to Ray Charles. Yet throughout all the hoopla, he remained an essentially modest man, with a gentle smile and mellow friendliness that made him look more like an accountant or a postmaster than the creator of classics like "I'll Fly Away" and "Turn Your Radio On."

He worked far from the glitter of Nashville or the bustle of New York's Tin Pan Alley, choosing instead a beautiful little valley about seventy miles west of Springfield, Missouri, just a few miles from the Arkansas line. It was a place he could play checkers at the local gas station, or take an afternoon off to go fishing. It was this down-to-earth quality that also made his songs so memorable, that made them sound like they were ancient folk songs that had been sung for generations. It was this that made his songs more popular than those of any other gospel composer of this century. Throughout the 1930s, 1940s, 1950s, and on to the modern age, they have become standards. And many contemporary singers echo the praise of Nashville's Larry Gatlin: "I wish I was half the songwriter Albert E. Brumley was."

The Brumley story started back on October 29, 1905, when Albert was born into a family of tenant farmers near what is now Spiro, Oklahoma. This was two years before Oklahoma had even become a state, and Spiro was very much a part of the frontier. Young Albert grew up in the "little pine log cabin" he would write about, listening to his father's old-time fiddling and his mother's singing of parlor songs. When he was seven, Albert attended an old-time singing school—rural gatherings where singers in a community were taught the "rudiments" of singing from church songbooks. "That set me afire," he recalled later. He determined to learn to create his own melodies from the little scales and notes he had seen up on the blackboard, and in the 1920s he left the dusty cornfields of his father's farm and went off to study. He did not go to a formal college, but to the Hartford Music Company in nearby Hartford, Arkansas, near Fort Smith. Headed by a veteran composer named E. M. Bartlett ("Victory in Jesus"), the company served as a publisher, a music college, and a retailer, and was sending its salesmen and songbooks all over the Southwest.

Here Brumley met some of the era's best-known gospel composers, learned the craft of songwriting, and even toured as a piano player with one of the Hartford quartets. (Though he was a competent musician, he would never really be known as a performer.) His stay there was extended, and extended again—eventually to last five years. By 1927 Hartford had actually accepted his first song, "I Can Hear Them Singing Over There," and he saw it published in one of the little paperback songbooks the company issued. It would be the first of some six hundred songs he would publish. Soon he was writing on a regular basis for Hartford, though he seldom got any real money for his efforts; more often than not, he was "paid" with fifty or a hundred copies of the songbook his latest work appeared in. In truth, as he went around to singings and singing schools, he could sell these books for 15 or 25 cents each, but even by Depression standards, that didn't put too many potatoes on his plate. It was a start, though, and soon he married and moved to the small town of Powell, were he worked in the store of his new father-in-law.

It was here that his talent suddenly blossomed. In a span of thirteen years, he created most of his greatest songs—and some of country's greatest gospel classics. These included "I'll Fly Away" (1932), "Jesus Hold My Hand" (1933), "I'd Rather Be An Old-Time Christian" (1934), "I'll Meet You In the Morning" (1936), "Turn Your Radio On" (1938), "Did You Ever Go Sailing?" (1938), "Rank Strangers to Me" (1942), and "If We Never Meet Again" (1945). At first, the songs were spread not by hit records or radio stars, but by the people themselves—people who sang them over and over at church singing conventions. It was only after 1937, when he signed with the powerful Stamps-Baxter company, that Brumley songs were routinely pitched to radio singers. Then artists like Grandpa Jones, Bill Monroe, the Blue Sky Boys, the Chuck Wagon Gang, and Whitey and Hogan began picking up Brumley songs and getting sacks of mail cheering them on.

In later years, Brumley recalled how some of his best songs came about. "I'll Fly Away" came to him as he worked in an Oklahoma cotton field; it was derived from the old Vernon Dalhart song "The Prisoner's Song," with its famous line "if I had the wings of an angel." It was first recorded in 1940 by evangelist Rex Humbard and the Humbard Family. Albert had started working on the melody to "Jesus Hold My Hand" when he was still at Hartford; years after, when he had married, an old friend visited him and asked what had ever become of the "old Negro song" Albert used to hum. After he left, Brumley got the old song out and began working it out. "Turn Your Radio On" came about as a result of station KWTO in Springfield (later home of the *Ozark Jubilee*), the nearest big station to Powell. Quartets and singers on the station loved Brumley songs, and often did them; by 1938 friends were always calling him up and saying, "Turn your radio on, Albert, they're playing one of your songs." He recalled: "I heard that so many times I decided to use it as a song title." Brumley dedicated the song to the famed Stamps Quartet over KRLD in Dallas.

One could go on for pages about the various stories connected to Brumley songs. There's the one about how Ralph Stanley made "Rank Stranger" into a bluegrass standard in the late 1950s; or the one about how Hank Williams "borrowed" the melody and lyric pattern for "I Saw the Light" from Brumley's 1939 "He Set Me Free." Or how Elvis Presley used to claim that "If We Never Meet Again" was his mother's favorite song, and how it was sung at her funeral. Even in a more modern age, Brumley's songs about his rural home, his family values, and the past endured; he became a musical equivalent to Norman Rockwell. In later life he said, "There are people who criticize me because I write about my mother and the old home. But if it comes to a place where mother and dad and the old home's not sacred, I'll take my sign down. I'll quit."

Fortunately, he didn't have to quit. When the Hartford Company, who owned so many of his song copyrights, got into trouble, he stepped in and bought them out, and started the Albert E. Brumley and Sons Publishing Company, which still functions today in Powell. His children have carried on his legacy; son Tom Brumley has won fame as a steel guitarist with the likes of Buck Owens and Rick Nelson, and currently heads a Brumley Family show in Branson. Son Bob manages the music business in Powell, issuing new songbooks and collections of his father's work. Albert himself died in 1977, and is buried in his beloved valley.

Stringbean

November 10, 1973. The newspapers are full of Watergate; President Nixon has just appointed Leon Jaworski, a conservative Texan, as special prosecutor in the case. Vice President Agnew resigned a month earlier. In Nashville, the Grand Ole Opry is beginning its last winter at the old Ryman Auditorium before moving in the spring to its new million-dollar home at Opryland Park. This Saturday night, the second show is under way, and veteran cowboy star Tex Ritter is the host for the Union 76 portion of the show. Tex is mellow, very much at ease, basking in the glow of a long career in Hollywood and, for the past eight years, in Nashville. He doesn't know it, but this is one of his last nights on the Opry; within two months he will die of a heart attack. But tonight he is full of fun, and he likes to kid the guest he's about to bring on. He has always been amused at the strange, corny costume the guest wears: a long shirt that stretches down a lanky frame to meet a tiny pair of trousers at about the kneecaps. The guest's name is David Akeman, but for years and years everyone has known him as Stringbean.

As he waits in the wings for Tex to introduce him, String kids with a friend about the earlier show this night. "Tex finally got me on after about fifteen minutes of introduction," he gripes. Tex had as much trouble getting him off; Stringbean had done an old Kentucky "shout" song called "Y'all Come" and had gotten a good number of the 3,000 members of the audience to sing along with him. "I had to bring him back for an encore," Tex recalled later. "A lot of young people were screaming." College kids interested in old-time banjo playing, and television fans of _Hee Haw_, are threatening to make a new hero out of Stringbean, a laid-back, nature-loving, gentle humorist who is given to pronouncements like, "A man who plays the five-string banjo has got it made. It never interferes with any of the pleasures in his life."

Tex continues his introduction as the clock drags on toward 10:25. String yawns. He has an early fishing trip planned the next morning with his old friend and neighbor Grandpa Jones, and they like to start early. Tex says, "Since being on *Hee Haw,* his price has gone up and his pantaloons have gone down a little." The audience laughs, and String takes a step foward toward center stage. He stops and backs up; Tex isn't finished. "I understand since he's become so successful, String now has a new chauffeur. This is Kirk Gibson here, he's driving him around and playing backup for him." Finally Tex gets him on, and String starts a funny, duck-waddle walk toward the microphone. Fans start screaming again, and flash bulbs start popping from the crowd standing at the edge of the stage; when it all subsides, String cuts the air with his hand and delivers the old Jackie Gleason line that he has made his own: "How sweet it is." He does two songs, and before the second one he reaches for his old gray hat with the turned-up brim, tips it at the audience, and begins singing:

> I come out of old Kentucky, early in the spring,
> Headin' for the Grand Ole Opry, boys, to make myself a name.

And then it's over. String has sung the last song of his career. Two hours later he is dead, gunned down in his front yard by robbers.

Robert Akeman, String's youngest brother, likes to have the chance to talk to writers about him. "There's a lot been written about him, some of it by String himself, that wasn't exactly so," he says. Setting the record straight starts with String's birthdate, which is usually given in histories as 1915; "we've checked the family records, and it shows it on June 17, 1914," says Robert Akeman. "We don't know how it got to be 1915. String had four brothers and three sisters, and he was about middleways in the pack. There was one other brother besides String who was musical; his name was Alfred, and he could play about anything, but he never would keep it up." The Akeman clan hailed from the small town of Annville, in Jackson County in east-central Kentucky, about halfway between Corbin and Richmond, in a fertile breeding ground for old-time music. The region produced banjoists like Marion Underwood, Buell Kazee, B. F. Shelton, Dick Burnett, and Lily May Ledford, and dozens of good string bands and singers. String's father planted corn and tobacco in the daytime, and played the banjo at neighborhood dances at night. Young String was suitably impressed. "He used to go around before he got a banjo and he would get an old shoebox and some of my mother's sewing thread, and thump around on it, and pick up one of those legs and flop on it like he was playing the banjo, and he'd say, 'Boy, you'll hear me over the air one of these days.'" By the time Stringbean was twelve, he was ready for his own banjo, but the common story that his father made him one isn't quite true, according to Robert. "His first banjo was a homemade banjo, all right, but our father didn't make it. String traded a little banty hen and a little banty rooster for it. Now once he had his banjo, Dad, he helped him a little bit with it."

Young David Akeman dropped out of school after the sixth grade and began to work regularly with his father on the farm. As the country tumbled into the Depression in 1930, times got increasingly hard for rural families, and the large Akeman family was one of the first in the area to qualify for the new government relief programs. In later years String liked to tell friends about this experience; Kirk McGee recalls, "For some reason, the first food they got from the program was a whole case of macaroni. Just that. Nothing but a case of macaroni. String said, 'We even had it for breakfast. By God, it tasted like the best stuff that ever was!'" In March 1933 the New Deal Congress authorized the Civilian Conservation Corps (CCC), and by May there were over 100,000 camps springing up in the rural areas of the country, offering to young men out of work the gainful employment of planting trees, doing landscaping, building roads. Young David found himself working in one of these camps in 1934 and 1935, and earning enough to hold his head up. In his spare time he continued to play the banjo, but not to sing much; he was genuinely shy and by nature a quiet lad, and singing did not come easily to him.

Sometime about 1935 Asa Martin, a local radio star and well-known singer associated for years with fiddler Doc Roberts, held a "talent contest" in McKee, the county seat of Jackson County. Martin was well established as a figure on Lexington radio by then, and held these talent contests throughout the area as part of his personal appearance circuit. The one in McKee was held right in the courthouse, right in the courtroom. David, then still in the CCC camp, entered, and impressed Asa Martin, who was looking then for a banjo player. "He didn't actually win first place," recalled Asa years later, "but I really wanted to hire him. The next morning he showed up with his banjo, ready to go to work. I never did figure out just how he got out of that CCC camp, but I hired him." When Asa got ready to introduce his new band member on stage, he couldn't remember David's real name, but he looked over at the long, skinny young man, and announced him as "String Beans." The name stuck, and within a few weeks the new banjo player was known by this name; later on, on the Grand Ole Opry stage, the name was to be changed to the singular form, "Stringbean." It was an appropriate name; not only did Akeman physically resemble a specimen of the *Stringus phaseolus*, but he dearly loved to eat string beans. His brother recalls, "Our mother used to have green beans on his birthday, and he'd always come and visit just to get there and to have some green beans. He loved 'em, them and that good old country ham."

Still, Stringbean (or String Beans) was not really doing anything except clawhammering the banjo on Asa's shows. But as he traveled with the show he began to watch the comedian, and in his spare time entertained the boys with imitations of his jokes and routines. As Doc Roberts recalls it, "One night this comedian got sick down in Hazard, when they had a big show lined up that night in Hindman. Acey insisted that Stringbean go on as the comedian—in fact, he said he'd fire him if he didn't. String had never sung in public, and he didn't think he could make people laugh, but he went backstage and got himself fixed up. When he came on stage, the crowd gave him the awfullest hand you'd ever want to see. He straightened up right then and made the best comedian Acey had ever seen. When they got into the car that night, Stringbean said, 'Well, you can fire me if you want to, but I'll never play nothing but comedian again.'"

For the next four years, String worked with several bands around the Lexington area, and was often heard over station WLAP. For a time he was with a band called Cy Rogers and His Lonesome Pine Fiddlers, during which time he picked up a lot of the tunes that were to become favorites in later years: "Pretty Polly," the old Kentucky murder ballad; "Mountain Dew"; Get Along Home, Cindy"; "Suicide Blues"; and "Crazy War," a variation of an old Spanish-American War protest song that String later updated and performed as "Crazy Vietnam War." He also continued to work a lot with Asa Martin, and by 1939 was enough of a star to get personal billing in the ads for Asa Martin's Morning Round-Up Gang; he was billed as "String Beans and his Old Banjo."

During these years, String was following another occupation that gave him as much pleasure as playing the banjo: baseball. For several years he played semipro ball in his spare time with various sandlot teams around central Kentucky. "He was a pretty good ball player, I'll tell you," says his brother. "He was a pitcher, and one that never could be struck out. They might catch him out, or they might walk him, but they never could strike him out. He'd always hit it." In fact, says Robert, String's ballplaying ability was what first attracted Bill Monroe to him. "Bill come up here and got him when String was playing on WLAP and living at Winchester; Bill went up there to get him to play baseball for his team. He first hired him as a baseball pitcher. As far as I know, Bill didn't even know he played banjo when he hired him. After he found out he could play, he went to playin' a little with Bill's band. Then he left Bill to go with Charlie [Monroe] and then went into the service, and then he came back and went with Bill again."

The years between 1939 and 1942 are confusing ones in String's history. We do know that sometime in late 1939 String moved to Charlie

Monroe's show at WBIG in Greensboro, North Carolina, where he did rural comedy and even some blackface. Also for a time in 1940 or 1941 he had his own band, String Bean and His Kentucky Wonders. In July 1942 he joined Bill Monroe on the Grand Ole Opry in Nashville; Bill recalls that String had written him from Kentucky asking for a job, and he hired him. George Hay, the Solemn Ole Judge, first introduced String to the Opry audiences.

"Stringbean was the first banjo picker with me," recalls Monroe. "What I wanted was the sound of the banjo, because I'd heard it back in Kentucky, and I wanted it in with the fiddle and the rest of the instruments. So Stringbean gave us the touch of the banjo and he was a good comedian." The term "touch of the banjo" aptly describes String's role in the band, for the banjo was anything but featured in the early Monroe band. The band that String joined in 1942 included Bill Wesbrook ("Cousin Wilbur") on bass, Howdy Forrester on fiddle, and Clyde Moody on guitar, in addition to Monroe. Photos of that era show that String seldom posed in any kind of comic garb—mostly he is dressed like any other Blue Grass Boy, with shirt and tie and baggy pants. In some shots he is sporting a new Vega Tuba-Phone banjo. On Monroe's very first solo records, done a couple of years before String joined, there is no banjo at all; and on the early 1945 records he made for Columbia, which were String's first, the banjo is barely audible on some songs. By listening carefully one can hear delicate fingerpicking by String behind "Footprints in the Snow," but on most of the hot numbers it is Monroe's mandolin and Chubby Wise's fiddle that take the lead. This first Columbia session by the Blue Grass Boys was done in February 1945, at the end of String's time with the band. Within a few months he was replaced by Earl Scruggs, whose style was more in line with the new band's style.

While traveling with Monroe's tent shows in 1942 and 1943, String and Cousin Wilbur worked out double comedy routines. One of the skits involved String and Wilbur trying to outbrag each other about which one grew the tallest corn, or the biggest beans; to localize the joke, one would pretend to be a farmer from the town where the tent show was playing, the other from a nearby town. "String could never remember the name of the town we were in," recalls Bill Wesbrook. "Right in the middle of the act he'd get the audience laughing and then he'd ask me out of the corner of his mouth, 'What's the name of this town?' and I'd tell him. One night in Arkansas I really fixed Stringbean up. The name of the town was Rector, Arkansas. And Stringbean asks out of the corner of his mouth, 'What's the name of this town,' so I told him it was Rectum, Arkansas. That's what Stringbean up and said, 'Right here, folks, right here in Rectum, Arkansas.' And he like to wrecked the audience. They must have laughed for fifteen minutes. And I got so tickled that Stringbean got broke up. . . . I looked backstage, and there was Bill Monroe and Honey Wild—Honey was a big fat guy—and they were backstage of the tent lying down on the ground just holding their stomachs."

After he left Monroe, String began a three-year partnership with Lew Childre, working on the Opry and doing tent shows. "Doctor Lew" was an old veteran minstrel man who was as fast-talking as String was laconic, but who shared with String a love for old songs and comedy numbers. He also shared with String a passion for fishing—one of his featured numbers was "Fishing Blues" ("Everybody's Fishing, I'm a Goin' Fishing Too"), which String later featured himself. The team was an immediate success on the Opry—so successful that WSB in Atlanta tried to hire them away from WSM, but they elected to stay. By this time Stringbean had devised his famous "short pants" costume, and was making it his trademark. Kirk McGee says, "String once told me that he borrowed that idea from an old comedian somewhere up north, I don't remember his name, who had worn a costume like that and String had seen him. When he retired and didn't use it anymore, that's when String started working with it."*

During this time, String also came under the influence of the Opry's premier banjoist-songster, Uncle Dave Macon. When String met him in 1942, Uncle Dave was seventy-two years old, and was still going strong in a career that had begun in 1923 in vaudeville shows and primitive recording studios. He was still a headliner for the Opry, and the show's most beloved comedian; he came from an age when banjo picking and comedy were not separated, and utilized a bag of jokes, tricks, bits of poetry, and other baggage he had preserved from the nineteenth-century stage. String became fascinated with Macon's stage style; he later remarked, "Uncle Dave was the greatest entertainer I've ever known. He would play to an audience forty-five minutes and then go back for seven or eight encores. It takes a hoss to do that."

"String got to where he worshiped Uncle Dave," recalls Kirk McGee. "He would stand in the wings watching him, watching him real close, trying to get down every little move he made. We used to kid Uncle Dave about it, say, 'Uncle Dave, he's gonna steal your stuff, you better watch out,' and he didn't think much about it, but one night while he was on stage, he turned around and looked back over to us, and String was right in the middle of imitating him, and String just

---

* John Lair later argued that string had modeled his costume on that of fiddler-comedian Slim Miller, of the *Renfro Valley Barn Dance*.

stopped dead in his tracks, and Uncle Dave turned back and snorted, 'Oh hell.'" Cousin Wilbur used to try to get String to break up on stage, to break up his deadpan expression: "I'd reach over and say something to him that Uncle Dave had said, and it would always break him up." Gradually, Uncle Dave accepted String as a pupil and began to help him by showing him licks and teaching him songs that he had made his own—"You Can't Do Wrong and Get By," "Eleven Cent Cotton and Forty Cent Meat," "Mountain Dew," "Chewing Gum," and in time these became Stringbean favorites as well. One story is true: When he died in 1952, Uncle Dave did will String one of his banjos, and String used it a lot on later records; it was an old Gibson that Uncle Dave himself had used a lot in the 1940s.

By 1950 String was getting national recognition as a banjoist and singer. He became a regular on the Red Foley portion of the Opry that was broadcast nationwide over NBC, and was on many of the Opry's AFRS (Armed Forces Radio Service) shows that were recorded and sent around the world to military bases. On these programs, he shared the stage with Red Foley, Hank Williams, the Old Hickory Singers, and comedians Rod Brasfield and Minnie Pearl; he seldom did any comedy routines himself, but would specialize in old banjo songs like "Going Down the Country," "Lonesome Road Blues," and "Mountain Dew." A listener would hear Williams or Foley finish a number, hear applause, and then suddenly String's driving clawhammer banjo would start up, vamping while Foley would introduce him to the crowd. Foley thought enough of String's crowd-pleasing that he even coaxed him into following him to Springfield, Missouri, for the *Ozark Jubilee* television show in 1955.

It wasn't until about 1960, after some twenty-five years in show businesss, that Stringbean began to make any serious solo recordings. His first album, done about 1960 for Starday, was *Old Time Banjo Pickin' & Singin'* (SLP 142), and was pitched to the popular folk revival market that was then thriving. The liner notes stressed the songs String had learned from his folks back in Kentucky, some of which dated "back to the 16th century." Included were some of his favorite stage pieces like "Barnyard Banjo Pickin'," his own version of "Hot Corn, Cold Corn," an old Kentucky moonshine piece, the autobiographical "Stringbean and His Banjo," as well as a handful of Macon songs like "Give Me Back My Five Dollars," "Keep My Skillet Good and Greasy," and "Polly." Later albums for Starday followed in 1963, 1965, and 1966; one of them—the only one currently in print—was a full-fledged tribute to Uncle Dave that was for years the only way Macon fans had of hearing some of their favorite songs. On many of the Starday sessions, String was backed by a small studio band that on occasion included Tommy Vaden on fiddle and Hoss Linneman on dobro; it gave the recordings a nice balanced sound, but there were few instances where one could really hear String all by himself, whipping it out like he so often did on stage. For this sound, one has to turn to a set of five rare 45 recordings on the Cullman label that String did in the late 1960s; these recordings are probably String's best (and ironically, his least known) and feature him doing such fine old banjo pieces as "Cold Creek March" (his version of the classic Kentucky picking exercises "Coal Creek March"), "I Bought Me a Mule and a Little Red Wagon," "Shake That Little Foot Sally Ann," and "Going to the Grand Ole Opry." It is on these Cullman 45s, produced in Nashville by veteran Hal Smith, that one begins to realize just how well Uncle Dave's lessons took, and just how good a clawhammer banjo player String could be when he got serious about it.

The last album that String himself saw out was a session for Nugget recorded with Fred Carter and Josh Graves on February 16, 1970, and released as *Me and My Old Crow*. It was a delightful mixture that ranged from "Nine Pound Hammer" to String's oddly effective version of "Long Tall Sally." A last album, on the Ovation label, was issued in 1976, three years after String's death.

In the summer of 1969 Stringbean became a charter member of a new CBS television show called *Hee Haw;* along with Archie Campbell, Junior Samples, and Grandpa Jones, String brought generations of country comedy tradition into living rooms across the country. String's droll, laconic wit and Chaplinesque figure added ballast to the barrage of one-liners that punctuated the show. His "cornfield crow" quickly became a favorite part of the show, a fact that prompted him to write his "Me and My Old Crow, We Got a Good Thing Going," with the line "I used to hunt the old crow, from him all around, now he helps me out on *Hee Haw,* best friend I ever found." Stringbean's crow and his great one-liners—the most famous being, of course, "Lord, I feel so unnecessary"—became an integral part of *Hee Haw.* He was so much a part of the show that his gut-wrenching groan on the "Gloom, despair, and agony on me" feature still remains a taped feature of that weekly number today.

Even before *Hee Haw,* String was achieving national popularity. Bob Hope once quipped that when he had landed in Nashville he was surrounded by fans wanting his autograph because they had mistaken him for a big country star—Stringbean. He played Las Vegas, was on big talk shows and dozens of syndicated country shows, and toured with Ernest Tubb and Hank Williams Jr. But he always came back home to the country. He bought a 134-acre farm up near Goodlettsville, north of Nashville—"After all," he told a reporter, "a fireplace man needs a lot of wood"—and spent his spare time doing what he liked best, hunting and fishing. Most mornings, after several cups of coffee and several pipes, he and his wife, Estelle, would lift their boat onto the station wagon and head for a nearby lake. It was a good, sane life.

They tell a story about the time String was pursuaded to go on a deer hunt with a bunch of other musicians; one of them was a real greenhorn who had somehow gotten hold of a new high-powered rifle. He was shooting at anything that moved, and finally String cautioned him to be careful, and managed to keep as much out of his way as possible for the rest of the day. Finally, as the late afternoon sun was warming an old field, the greenhorn came upon String sitting quietly on a stump smoking his pipe. "String," the man asked, "are all the boys out of the woods yet?" "Yep," said String. "They're all safe." "Praise be," said the greenhorn, "then I guess I've shot a deer." String just stared at him for a long, long time. "I made up my mind right then," he said later, "that from then on I was going to hunt alone. I don't much take to the idea of being shot at."

PART VI

From the West

Girls of the Golden West

Six decades before the Judds, five before the Parton-Ronstadt-Harris *Trio* album, four before the Davis Sisters, there were two sisters named Millie and Dolly Good. In the 1930s they made history as country music's first successful female harmony duet: the Girls of the Golden West. For a generation, they held forth over the big radio stations in Chicago and Cincinnati. Fans by the thousands wrote to them, sent them gifts, bought their records and used their gentle, haunting harmonies to weather the Depression. Almost by accident, they created a musical style that has echoed down the years, and their struggle to find their place in what was then an all-male profession blazed a trail that women singers today still follow.

The public got their first chance to really see the Girls of the Golden West in 1933, when WLS radio (Chicago) issued its annual promotional book, *WLS Family Album.* Earlier that year, the girls had joined the cast of *The National Barn Dance,* which was, in 1933, the biggest and best country music program in the nation. The page for the Girls pictured them in their knotted neckerchiefs and fringed skirts, and announced that they were genuine cowgirls from the hamlet of "Muleshoe, Texas." It was the start of a legend that would persist for years and get into dozens of reference books. "We didn't really even know where Muleshoe, Texas, was," recalls Millie. "It just seemed like such a funny name to us." The girls in reality were born in Mount Carmel, Illinois, a town some 300 miles south of Chicago on the banks of the Wabash, right on the Indiana state line. The girls grew up in Mount Vernon, and then later East St. Louis, where their father worked in a local plant. They grew up listening to their mother sing old songs, learning from her the rudiments of the guitar and the basics of harmony; after her daughters became famous, their mother even occasionally sang with Millie on the radio. As Millie and Dolly grew into teenagers, they found that harmony singing came naturally; Dolly would sing lead, and Millie harmony. "I'd never sing solos," Millie explained, "but when I hear a note, I hear the harmony note to it. I got that gift from my mother."

Soon the girls were broadcasting over St. Louis station KNOX. At first, they used their real family name—Goad, not Good—but found that it was easily garbled over the air, everything from "Goat" to "Gold." A radio executive named Walter Richards came up with the name Girls of the Golden West, derived from an old cowboy story by Bret Harte and a subsequent popular opera by Puccini in 1910. They spent a short time in Kansas working on the notorious "border station" XER (which then had its studios in Kansas and transmitter in Mexico). Here they began attracting bushels of mail, but left when they learned that a male act on the same show was getting ten times more salary than they were. They returned to Illinois, found a manager who sensed how unique their music was, and soon got a job on WLS in Chicago.

Though they were barely out of their teens, the Girls felt at home in the family-type atmosphere of the Chicago station. And though there were precious few women acts in the budding world of professional country music, WLS had more than its share of them. "WLS was a big country station then," recalled Millie. "They had the Three Little Maids—the Overstake sisters—and Linda Parker, and another trio named Winnie, Lou, and Sally, and then Lulu Belle, and later Patsy Montana." Though the sisters had grown up singing old pop and sentimental songs as opposed to cowboy songs, they soon began adopting a western image—one that seemed to be working so well for fellow WLS singers Gene Autry and Smiley Burnett. They toured with Gene, and on some of the tours, Smiley, who helped Gene with a lot of his songs, would help the Girls try their hands at originals. Millie specifically remembers Smiley helping her with the first song she ever wrote, "Two Cowgirls on the Lone Prairie." Along with the name and songs came a series of lovely custom-made cowgirl costumes. "We did make them ourselves," says Millie. "They were made out of velvet, and then we had more of a drapery fringe on the bottom of the skirt." They copied from movie cowboys "since there were no cowgirls at that time that I knew of." Over several years, the outfits got flashier and flashier. There were real boots, fringed vests, white hats, big belts with MILLIE and DOLLY spelled out in bright studs, and a gun and holster. The guns were real, too, "but they never had any bullets in them." The costumes became famous not only at the Washington Boulevard headquarters of WLS, but also at the countless state fairs and small-town theaters where the WLS road show toured.

Dozens of records—at first for Victor's Bluebird and later for the huge American Record Company—preserved the best songs from the Girls' repertoire. There were genuine old cowboy ballads like "Old Chisholm Trail" and "Cowboy Jack" and Belle Starr's "My Love Is a Rider," but soon originals followed, written by the Girls or by a small cadre of women writers they knew, like Lucille Overstake. These were songs like "Home Sweet Home in Texas" and "Lonely Cowgirl" and "I Want to Be a Real Cowboy Girl" and "Give Me a Straight-Shootin' Cowboy"—songs that captured the sunsets and cactus of the West, but did so from a woman's point of view. When the Bluebird A&R man complained about these original songs and insisted the older ones sold better, Millie and Dolly moved to a different label. Their style remained the same whatever they sang: lilting guitar, achingly pure and close harmony, harmony yodels, and verses of high, wordless falsettos that sounded like a Hawaiian guitar.

By the mid-1930s, both girls had married men from WLS's music staff: Dolly to fiddler Tex Achison from the Prairie Ramblers and Millie to Bill McCluskey, an announcer and promoter. Toward the end of 1937, the Girls joined Red Foley and Lily May Ledford in a special program for Pinex Cough Syrup; it did so well that the sponsor moved them to Cincinnati. Eventually this move led to both the Girls and Bill McCluskey relocating to WLW, which was just starting John Lair's *Renfro Valley Barn Dance*. When Lair moved the program to Renfro Valley, Kentucky, the Goods stayed on at WLW, eventually joining the *Boone County Jamboree*. The Girls worked together until 1949, and then reunited in 1963 for a series of albums on the Texas-based Bluebonnet label. Dolly Good died about 1967, but Millie and Bill McCluskey still live in Cincinnati, with their friends, their scrapbooks, and a sense of accomplishment that comes only to true pioneers.

Billie Maxwell

Throughout the 1930s, the image of the singing cowgirl was dominating popular old-time music. Millie and Dolly Good, the Girls of the Golden West; Patsy Montana; Texas Ruby—all dressed in fancy cowgirl outfits and sung of their love for the range or for cowboys. Few of these performers, excellent though they were, could really be called as authentic as the first singing cowgirl, a slim, dark-haired beauty from Arizona named Billie Maxwell. Though Billie only made a handful of records—in 1929—they are prized as examples of authentic western singing, and as instances of a woman creating her own highly personal and highly successful songs.

Until recently our knowledge of Billie Maxwell has been pretty much limited to the pages of the *Victor Master Book* and two old photos that were uncovered in an old Victor warehouse in New York and later published by Robert Shelton in his *Country Music Story*. Some recent research, however, has led to the discovery of Billie's family, and telephone interviews have helped to piece together the story of this fascinating performer.

Billie Maxwell was born in February 1906 and died in 1954. She was raised near Springerville, Arizona, then very much a part of the real frontier, and part of the last vestige of the American West. Her father was E. Curtis Maxwell, known throughout the area for his fiddling. Curtis, in turn, learned many of his tunes from his father, William Beatty Maxwell, who had come originally into Nevada from Illinois; later in the 1800s he moved down into the old Arizona Territory. Curtis formed a band called the White Mountain Orchestra, and played throughout the country for cowboy dances. His son-in-law recalls: "He could play any tune those old cowboys called for," and he often played at ranch dances that went on all night. Often the band had to travel to dances on horseback.

In addition to playing a lot of older fiddle pieces, Curt Maxwell was known for tunes he himself composed, including "Frolic of the Mice" and "Escudilla Waltz." (The latter number he preserved for posterity on one of his four Victor recordings.) He also had "his own" quadrille and "his own" schottische, neither of which was preserved.

Billie was a member of the White Mountain Orchestra from her teens. She was remembered as an excellent guitar player—often she and her father rode horses into the backcountry to play alone at remote dances—but was only incidentally considered a singer. Billie's brother Marion usually played mandolin in the band as well.

In 1929 Billie, who was then twenty-three, married Alvin C. (Chester) Warner, a young schoolteacher from the area, and the pair settled down to start raising their family. But then in June of that year Billie's uncle, Frank Maxwell, a lawman from Silver City, noticed an advertisement in the local paper: A field session was to be held in El Paso by Victor Records, and people in the area were invited to audition for a possible recording opportunity. Curt Maxwell took his family band down to Silver City to audition. When they got there, it was decided that Frank Maxwell, who was described as a "good lawman but a sort of mediocre one-man band" (playing guitar with a harp on a rack), should play with the band as well. Thus the augmented four-piece band auditioned, only as a string band, not with Billie's vocals, for the Victor representative (who was not Ralph Peer). They won a slot in the forthcoming El Paso session.

About two weeks later, on July 2, Chester Warner drove his in-laws down to El Paso to make the recordings. Here they did meet Ralph Peer, the famous Victor scout who had recorded so many early country music greats. On this trip, Peer was recording a lot of Mexican numbers for release in Victor's special ethnic series, but he was also recording important old-time artists like the Lewis Brothers and M. S. Dillehay. Peer listened to the White Mountain Orchestra record four string band numbers: "Gooson Quadrille," "Leather Britches," "Maxwell's Old Rye Waltz," and the aforementioned "Escudilla Waltz."*

After the instrumentals were made, Peer, who was quite taken with Billie, asked her if she could sing. Surprised, she said she had sung a little, and he asked for a sample. She tried out a few verses of an old traditional cowboy ballad, "Billy Venero." Peer loved it, and loved her

---

* There is a bit of a discography problem here. The Victor files for the string band session list Curtis Maxwell as playing fiddle, "F. L. Maxwell" (Frank, the uncle) and "F. M. Maxwell" (Marion, the son), as playing guitars, and "Mrs. A. C. Warner," who would have been Billie, as playing banjo. Mr. Warner recalls that Billie played guitar on the session, and that Marion played mandolin. On the old records, it is difficult to determine if the instrument is a banjo or mandolin, or whether, indeed, both are present. Billie apparently could play tenor banjo some, though she seldom did.

voice, and at once demanded that she record it. Backed by her father's fiddle, Billie recorded her powerful version of this lonesome ballad; the song was so long that it extended over both sides of the 78 record. Billie and her father performed it in an archaic manner, with the fiddle playing unison to the vocal.

Peer was happy with this, and asked Billie if she could work up any other songs. (Peer, remember, was getting copyrights on many of these songs, and was especially interested in original material. In fact, he often told prospective recording artists during this time that unless they had original material, he couldn't use them.) Billie said that she thought she could, and he asked her to go back home, work up some more songs, and return in a week.

Billie prepared four new songs. One was a rare version of a strange, eerie western ballad called "Haunted Hunter." Two others were older pop-oriented songs, the chesnut "Where Your Sweetheart Waits for You, Jack," and a piece called "The Arizona Girl I Left Behind Me." The fourth, and most unusual, was a strange minor-key piece called "The Cowboy's Wife." This song (which was reissued on Rounder's *Banjo Pickin Girls* LP) is recalled as either an original, or a piece Billie coauthored with a friend. Billie's husband recalls that they had to get a letter of permission from the composer before Peer would record the piece. But the tune is almost unique in the annals of old-time music in that it is a song distinctly from a woman's point of view: a graphic account of the cowboy's wife going about her chores as she waits for her husband to get in.

On July 7, 1929, she and her father returned for the second session. After a morning's work, Peer pronounced himself satisfied with the session, and asked to make some photos of Billie and the band. Billie, "who was quite retiring as a person anyway," was also by now several months pregnant, and was embarrassed to have her photo made. Finally they made a satisfactory photo, of her looking over a horse, that pleased everybody. (It was this photo that was to surface in the New York warehouse some thirty-five years later.)

Peer took his masters and returned to New York; Billie and her folks went back to Silver City. Their paths were destined not to cross again. The records that were released from the session were adequate sellers, but not spectacular sellers: not well enough, at any rate, to justify bringing the Maxwells to New York or Atlanta, or to justify another field trip to El Paso. ("Billy Venero," the best-selling record from the session, sold 3,125 copies when it was issued on November 22, 1929; "The Cowboy's Wife" (Vi V-40188) sold 2,641, and Vi V-40241, issued on May 16, 1930, and containing "Haunted Hunter," did barely 1,300.)

Billie continued to play with her father's band for a time; they moved into central New Mexico next to Fort Beard and played in a place called the Smokehouse. Soon after the birth of her first child, Billie began to drop off from playing music, and spent most of her time raising her family. She was to have two children, and both carried on their mother's interest in music (though neither was especially interested in old-time music).

The elder Maxwell continued to play, often with his son Marion helping him. Once he was invited to play for the governor of Arizona and on the way down to the governor's mansion he lost his bow. Some friendly cowboys heard of his plight and chased down a horse so he could make a new bow out of the tail. Curt Maxwell continued to play until a month before his death in December 1944.

The string band tradition of the Maxwell family was carried on through Marion's side of the family. Marion himself still lives near Springerville, Arizona, and still plays quite well on a variety of instruments. He spends most of his time as a hunter in the upcountry. "He can play all of his father's old tunes," recalls his brother-in-law, Chester Warner. Both of his sons, one of whom teaches college, also play well.

Billie herself never received any money, nor much recognition, from the six recordings she released, but they preserved for posterity her fragile, unusual singing, and gave us a glimpse of a musical tradition that was as rich and distinctive as the southern mountain tradition that has received so much attention.

Red River Dave

One of Red River Dave McEnery's favorite stories is about a time back in the late 1970s in Nashville when he was at a banquet with a lot of singers and music industry executives. By chance Dave and his wife overheard a conversation between two "experts" on country music discussing the classic song "Amelia Earhart's Last Flight." (The song, a tribute to the pioneering flyer who disappeared in the Pacific in 1937, had been popular in the 1930s and had been revived during the 1960s by groups like the Greenbriar Boys, Jim Kweskin, Spanky and Our Gang and, more recently, Kinky Friedman and His Texas Jewboys.) One of the "experts" was saying that the song had been written by the legendary old cowboy singer Red River Dave, who had been dead for years. Dave and his wife finally stepped into this talk—one way to get a rise out of a man is to call him dead—and protested. The "legendary old cowboy singer" was very much alive and performing as well as ever. It took some time, but the two experts were finally convinced: Red River Dave was indeed alive and well and living in Nashville.

But it's hard not to think of Red River Dave as a legend. He was one of the first great radio cowboys, and his strong, clear baritone voice introduced country music to thousands of northerners and midwesterners who had never heard of Jimmie Rodgers or Riley Puckett. Dave began his career in Texas during the Depression; he sang over local San Antonio stations as well as the "border stations" in Mexico. He learned many of his songs and tales directly from old trail drivers and cowboys in the ranch country around his home. He also won Texas championships in rope spinning and yodeling. In 1938 (at age twenty-four) Red River Dave was in New York broadcasting his own coast-to-coast program for the Mutual Network, and the next year he was also heard on NBC. Dave recalls that there were four big cowboy singers broadcasting nationally out of New York in those days: Wilf Carter (Montana Slim), Texas Jim Robertson,

Elton Britt, and Red River Dave. "Most of 'em were pure cowboy people—they were sincere and they loved those songs. They weren't something some advertising agency thought they could promote." Singers like these, coming from genuine folk backgrounds, forged vital links between folk music and commercial country music.

In 1939 Red River Dave, with his Swift Cowboys, participated in a television experiment at the World's Fair, and Dave gained the honor of becoming the world's first television "star." His "Amelia Earhart's Last Flight" had become a big hit, and he landed a recording contract with Decca. (His discography was eventually to include over two hundred sides, excluding transcriptions and reissues.) After service in World War II, Dave relocated to Hollywood and appeared in films with the likes of Rosalie Allen, Jimmy Wakely, and the Hoosier Hot Shots. Later Dave had a long-running TV show in Texas, and finally went into semiretirement in the 1960s, when he became a real estate broker. But in 1975, Dave, now a widower, married writer Lee Reynolds, moved to Nashville, and decided to get back into the music business full-time.

In addition to performing, Red River Dave has always been a natural and prolific songwriter. In 1946, as a publicity stunt, he wrote some fifty-two songs in twelve hours—while handcuffed to a piano. Dave has over a thousand songs to his credit, and they have been recorded by dozens of major country singers. One of his specialties is the "event song," or as Dave calls it, the "saga song." Basically a topical ballad about some current event, it is one of the oldest kinds of country song. During the 1920s songs like "The Death of Floyd Collins," "Wreck of the Old 97," "Freight Wreck at Altoona," and "The Sinking of the Submarine S-51" were country music's first big sellers. In fact, in the days before phonograph records, ballad singers roamed throughout the South, writing and singing such songs, selling them on printed broadside "ballet" cards. Red River Dave is one of the few remaining masters of this folk art of the topical ballad. He got much of his training from Bob Miller, one of the finest of the old event songwriters; and Vernon Dalhart, one of the finest event song singers, recorded one of Dave's pieces, "Johnnie Darlin'," at his last session in 1939.

A catalog of Dave's event songs reflects nearly every aspect of modern American history. He has written about gangsters of the 1930s, World War II, James Dean, the civil rights movement, the Kennedy years (the Bay of Pigs, the assassination), Vietnam, the moon landings, the Manson murders, Watergate, and the Patty Hearst story. Keeping in the ancient tradition of the event ballad, Dave's songs are clear, factual, and often have a moral.

In an age when the idea of a topical song is often equated with political ideology, the songs of Red River Dave resist classification into simple liberal or conservative categories. On the one hand, Dave has produced songs like "I Want to Give My Dog to Uncle Sam" and "Vietnam Guitar," which reflect conservative notions of patriotism; on the other hand, his "Ballad of Emmett Till," written well before Bob Dylan's similar song, created a furor when he sent it to radio stations in the South. An ordained preacher, Dave responds to the world through his own value system rather than through any one political ideology.

Dave is also steeped in another American tradition, that of the cowboy song. He has written "Is the Range Still the Same" (his theme song), "Westward Roll the Wagons" and "I Won't Care a Hundred Years from Now," and his repertoire includes songs by Wilf Carter (Montana Slim), such as "Love Knot in My Lariat," and by his pal Carson Robison ("When the Bloom Is on the Sage"). He also performs songs first popularized by Vernon Dalhart, such as "The Prisoner's Song" and "The Letter Edged in Black."

During his years in Nashville, Dave connected with younger musicians who were fascinated with the singing cowboy tradition. One he helped teach and inspire was Douglas Green, who was shortly to become Ranger Doug of Riders in the Sky. In recent years, Dave returned to Texas, then moved to California, where he continues to write topical songs and to appear at Knott's Berry Farm. In 1991, following an incident of ill health, he sent *Country Music* magazine the manuscript to an event song based on the Persian Gulf War, inspired, he said, by a vision of Amelia Earhart. He remains reluctant to claim the title "Last of the Singing Cowboys"—in this he still defers to Montana Slim—but he is certainly one of the last links with a very special tradition, and a very special magic.

Skeets McDonald

Greenway, Arkansas, is a small town nestled into the extreme north-eastern corner of the state, next to the Missouri boot heel; eighty miles to the west is West Plains, Missouri, home of Porter Wagoner; eighty miles to the southeast is Memphis, home of the blues. It is an interesting musical climate, and was the home turf for one of the most underrated country singers of the 1950s, Skeets McDonald. Born on October 1, 1915, as Enos William McDonald, into a cotton-picking family of three brothers and three sisters, Skeets grew up on his father's farm at a hamlet called Rector.

Early in life he acquired the nickname that would stick with him throughout his life. "We raised cotton down there," brother Lynn McDonald recalls, "and he was the baby in the family, but he always wanted to go out with us. There was one day when we were out hoeing twenty acres of cotton, and he wanted to come and help; we said it was too hot, though, and the cotton was too tall—it was about as tall as he was. But he insisted, so we took him. Well, the mosquitoes were really bad that day, and they started getting after him. After a little of this, he shouted, 'I got to go home! Skeets bite!' My brother-in-law was with us, and he got a kick out of this, and started calling him Skeets. Skeets didn't like the name at all, didn't like to be called that, but it stuck and after a while he couldn't do much about it. It was Skeets McDonald."

Though none of his immediate family was a notable musician, Skeets learned traditional Ozarks music at the local "music parties" that still characterize Ozarks grassroots music. The older generation of pickers Skeets listened to included mandolin player Charlie Dodd, and guitarists Carol Hasty and Scott Bradford. By the time he was five, Skeets had a homemade cigar-box fiddle, and was trying to saw out the fiddle tunes he heard from the region's premier fiddler, Elvin Burns. (In later life, Skeets would often call a set of square dancing on a stage show in

California or Texas, drawing on his skills honed with Burns and other fiddlers.) The family also had a Victrola, and through this Skeets heard his first singing influence, Jimmie Rodgers, whose popularity peaked when Skeets was thirteen. A well-worn family story recounts Skeets at age twelve getting his first guitar; "he traded a red hound dog for a guitar and six dollars," recalls his brother Lynn, "and a farm boy became a musician. In the evenings he would sit for hours, picking guitar and singing." In between, there were hard chores to do, especially when the Depression hit and money in rural Arkansas was almost nonexistent; still, there were the music parties, the coon dogs and hunting trips, good fishing, and good friends; "it was a great and happy life," Skeets reflected in later years.

Like many young southerners in the Depression, Skeets's older brother Steve went north to Michigan to work in the auto factories, and in 1933, when Skeets was eighteen, Steve returned to Arkansas for a visit. He brought news of an entire transplanted "cracker" culture in Michigan, where so many southerners had moved, that the bars and roadhouses and radio stations around Detroit were filled with the sounds of string band music. Though Steve was not a musician himself, he had contacts in a band led by the Buffington brothers called the Lonesome Cowboys, and when he heard how good his little brother had gotten on the guitar and how well he could sing the old songs, he invited Skeets to return with him and promised to get him a job. Skeets went, and had no trouble fitting into the band; for the first year, he worked in the factories during the day and played music at night; but by 1935 he was able to make music full-time, and began a career that was to last until his death in 1968.

The Lonesome Cowboys hit the radio waves over station WEXL in Royal Oak, about halfway between Pontiac and Detroit, and Skeets's vocals were popular enough that he soon began thinking of organizing his own band. He called on several of his Arkansas buddies from Rector, and soon they joined him: Junior Waddington on accordion, Shug Doughtery on lead guitar, brother Durwood Dougherty on steel, Les Thomas on piano, and Willie Burns on guitar. With this band he joined WFDF in Flint, and then moved on to WCAR in Pontiac. He did the club scene as well, including a legendary stint in Detroit on the Seven Mile Road, where he was such a success that the owners had to enlarge the building to make room for more customers. But World War II intervened; for an unmarried twenty-six-year-old, enlistment looked like a good deal. He found himself attached to the Medical 69th General Hospital, operating in North Africa, India, and Okinawa, and came home with the bronze star.

Returning to Michigan after the war, he took a variety of jobs in the local music scene, including a TV spot in 1948 over WKHH in Dearborn, and a spell playing bass in clubs for a colorful character named Chief Red Bird. Shortly after his marriage to an attractive young woman named Jo in May of 1948, he joined forces with a fiddler named Johnnie White in a band called the Rhythm Riders; with this group, he made his first records in 1950, for the Detroit-based Fortune label. They included two original compositions, Skeets's "The Tattooed Lady," and "Mean and Evil Blues," songs that reflected the increased amount of songwriting the young artist had been doing since his return. The Fortune sides were modestly successful, and Skeets decided to make a serious run at the record business. Within months he had done sessions for London (four sides) and Mercury (two sides), but he was beginning to sense that his location was working against anything but a minor league career. In February 1951 he packed up his wife, his songs, and his Maltese cat Boo Boo, and lit out for Los Angeles, where one of his booking pals "had contacts."

The California scene in 1951 was dominated by Capitol Records, which had enjoyed an impressive roll of Top 10 artists in 1950: Tennessee Ernie Ford, Margaret Whiting and Jimmy Wakely, Tex Ritter, Leon Payne, Hank Thompson. Though heavily weighted toward a music style derived from western swing, Capitol was starting to sense the growing importance of honky-tonk singing. Ken Nelson had just replaced Lee Gillette, who had started Capitol's C&W division, and he continued to work closely with Gillette's A&R man, Cliffie Stone. Stone was Skeets's contact, and he soon auditioned the young singer in the studios of KXLA in Pasadena; Stone signed Skeets on the spot to be on his *Hometown Jamboree,* a pioneering country television show done in Pasadena, and then phoned Ken Nelson at Capitol to work out an audition there. Nelson was equally impressed. Lefty Frizzell was tearing up the charts with his Texas soul sound, and here was a possible answer to Lefty: a remarkably expressive singer who came from the same general area, and who could write songs like "Today I'm Movin' Out" and "Ridin' with the Blues." Skeets's contract came through in two weeks, and on April 5, 1951, he was in the Capitol studios doing his first record, "Scoot, Git, and Begone."

His stay with Capitol lasted until the end of 1958, and produced some eighty-five recordings, including what is probably his best work. Only one ("Don't Let the Stars Get in Your Eyes," from his sixth session, in 1952) actually got onto the *Billboard* charts, but several others sold well or were very influential: "Scoot, Git and Begone," "I'm Hurting" (which was also recorded by Nat King Cole), "Bless Your Little Ol'

Heart," "Big Family Trouble" (written before he left Detroit), "Baby Brown Eyes" (written for Jo), "Wheel of Fortune," and "I've Got to Win Your Love Again." Skeets's earliest Capitol sessions featured slower songs like "Bless Your Little Ol' Heart," "Today I'm Movin' Out" and "The Love That Hurt Me So," and he delivered them in a highly mannered style suggestive of Lefty Frizzell, to whom he has often been compared. These performances are full of Lefty-like octave drops and syllable splitting. By 1952 and 1953, Skeets was showing he could do a passable imitation of Hank Williams—as in "Look Who's Crying Now" and "I Need Your Love," where he lets his voice nasalize and ride on top of the beat. But Skeets's own unique style emerged in August 1952, with his recording of "Don't Let the Stars Get in Your Eyes." This was defined by uptempo songs set off with a barrelhouse piano, a Cajun-style fiddle, and a strong electric guitar doing lead-ins; the vocals were characterized by long melodic lines, often ending in a high, sustained note that the Capitol engineers sometimes enhanced with an echo chamber. Listen to how similar "Stars" is to numbers like "I've Got to Win Your Love Again," "Let Me Know," "Looking at the Moon," and "I Can't Stand It Any Longer." The last cut, done in January 1955, shows that Skeets and his producer Cliffie Stone were still trying to clone another "Stars" as long as three years after the original hit.

Skeets's career did not end, of course, when his Capitol contract expired in 1959. His work on *Town Hall Party* soon won him a new contract with Capitol's arch rival, Columbia, and for them he continued to record regularly from 1959 until 1966. His 1963 hit, "Call Me Mr. Brown," was the most successful in terms of chart action since "Don't Let the Stars Get in Your Eyes." In later years, he began to break away from the West Coast, traveling to Nashville to record and appear on the Grand Ole Opry and to Dallas to guest on the *Big D Jamboree*. He resisted efforts to modernize his sound, and in the 1960s reviewers were saying that "he belongs to another age. Listening to him sing is like playing a record you liked twenty years ago. It's the plaintive sound from a thousand beer joints along highways from Altoona to Albuquerque." This sort of thing didn't seem to bother Skeets, though, and he was still doing his classic songs in a straightforward way when he died from a massive heart attack on March 31, 1968.

PART VII

New Fogies

Hazel and Alice

When the original edition of the LP *Hazel and Alice* was released in May of 1973, nobody involved in the project knew exactly what to expect. Hazel and Alice themselves had been singing together for about ten years, and their only other album that had been released was a Folkways effort with a heavy bluegrass feel to it. The new record, though, was not exactly bluegrass: Some of the songs came from old-time repertoires, but others were new songs by country or folk writers, and half were originals by Hazel and Alice. Rounder itself was still a "collective" with a staff or three or four, depending on the time of the year, and had been in operation for barely three years. In Washington that summer, everything was Watergate, and down in Nashville builders were working on a new Grand Ole Opry house. The Number One hit that May was Roy Clark's "Come Live with Me," a typical Nashville record that was like most country and bluegrass records back then—safe, well-crafted, slick, and eminently predictable. Like most commercial records, it was a well-packaged product, aimed at a specific audience, designed for a well-worn track.

Whatever anyone felt about *Hazel and Alice,* it was not destined to be this kind of a safe, neatly pigeon-holed effort. It was to go places where no Rounder record had gone before, to audiences no bluegrass or old-time or folk record had reached. Like the underground best-sellers college students were creating, it would find its wonderfully diverse audience by routes no Music Row sharpie could have predicted. It would appeal to the folk and bluegrass fans that already knew about Hazel and Alice, but also to the members of the growing women's movement, the experimenters of the country rock bands, the fans of the outspoken new Nashville songwriters and singers who were starting to come together as the "Outlaw" movement. It was an album that rode the cusp of a vital moment of time, and, like a stone thrown into a quiet lake, its ripples spread to shores far beyond.

The public had first seen Hazel and Alice at the Galax, Virginia, fiddler's contest in 1962, when they donned guitar and autoharp to do songs of the Carter Family. Hazel Dickens had grown up in the coal mining towns of West Virginia; her father was a strong old-time singer who taught his children to sing the old songs "hard." Like many of her family, she migrated to Baltimore in the 1950s, where she met Mike Seeger and got plugged into the developing folk revival movement. Alice Gerrard came from Seattle, and grew up on a farm near Oakland, California, before attending Antioch College. Her musical background had been focused on classical and pop music until she too found herself in the Washington-Baltimore area in the late 1950s. There she met again Jeremy Foster, whom she had first encountered at Antioch College. He was also a high school friend of Mike's, and he introduced her to the round of music parties that were then going on in the area; at one of these parties she met Hazel. Hazel by now already had a following, and was known for her singing and bass playing. Alice would later marry Jeremy, and they would have four children, though he would be killed in an auto accident in 1963. That same year, Hazel and Alice cut their first LP, *Who's That Knocking,* on the Vervel Folkways label—on a production budget of $200, and with a big aesthetic assist from veteran bluegrass fiddler Chubby Wise. A second Folkways LP, *Won't You Come and Sing for Me,* was cut a couple of years later, but shelved for eight years by Folkways owner Moe Asch.

The Rounder album came about after the collective had seen and admired Hazel at Smithsonian folk festival workshops on coal mining songs, and seen both women perform as a duet at Gloryland Park. "They were interested in the kind of material I was doing, and in me," recalls Hazel. "We had a conversation, but I was still skeptical. They were these weird hippies, and I didn't know if it was somebody I wanted to be connected with. Then we had another meeting, and I said the only way I would do something would be with the woman I was singing with [Alice], and they said fine. So we set up a meeting with them at a festival up in Pennsylvania or Delaware where they were selling records. We went over to their Volkswagen bus which was loaded down with records, and we sat around and had a little meeting on the lawn there. We agreed to do it, and we came back home and started getting material together. I finished up some songs I had been writing that looked like they might work. The Rounders didn't provide any real input—it was all our own picking of the songs and arrangements. We produced it ourselves."

Both women had been writing songs for some time. "We knew each other as friends before we started singing together," reminds Alice. "It was during these times that I sort of considered that I was learning a lot from Hazel. She was older, the more all-wise one. And that balance continued after we started singing together, but then it kind of balanced out more as I brought things to the musical relationship. But there weren't many models for what we wanted to do. There was certainly not much that way happening in bluegrass, certainly not for women. That was our primary thing, that's how we got into it in the first place, through the bluegrass door. Going to festivals and stuff, we did hear other people writing songs, but I don't recall anybody specifically in our genre." It was in part because of this that they decided to divide the album into two sections: one side devoted to older songs, the other to new original songs. "It was more updated stuff," says Hazel. "Some of the newer ideas we were having. We weren't writing for the women's movement, for we didn't even know that it existed. But we had been out on the scene a little bit, and we saw a little more about what it was like to be a woman in the business." Songs like "Don't Put Her Down," "My Better Years," and "Custom Made Woman Blues" had been written from these experiences.

By late 1972 things were ready, and the album was cut at Dick Drevo's Urban Recording Studio in Bethesda, Maryland. "It was really done in his basement," recalls Alice. "He had a little setup down there, very small." Drevo was in fact a local banjo player who had done several other early Rounder albums by people like Del McCroury, Ted Lundy, Buzz Busby, and the Morris Brothers. "We really did produce it ourselves," says Hazel. "The only feedback we got from Drevo was whether or not it was off pitch, and then we'd just do it again until we got it right. But mostly it was like a little homemade record, one of the nicest experiences we had had recording."

The result, too, was a powerful new type of harmony that was like nothing heard from women singers at the time. The Hazel and Alice harmonies were not "sweet" or cloying, as with so many women's duos of the time, nor did either singer try to pitch their songs artificially high, as did the singers of the Baez-Collins school. It was what Hazel calls "hard" singing—full-throated, sparse, expressive, and with an edge to it. "Give it that old lonesome sound," Hazel's father once told her, and Hazel always tried to, emulating the singing of artists like Bill Monroe, George Jones, Loretta Lynn, Wilma Lee Cooper. "That's the only way to sing it," says Hazel. "If I couldn't do it that way, I wouldn't sing it." In a technical sense, part of what made the Hazel and Alice sound so distinctive was the fact that they basically had a woman (Alice) singing a man's part, with a second woman singing over it as a tenor. "Alice's voice was low enough so she was singing virtually what the men do, and I am doing what the man tenor does over that," says Hazel. "It was a sort of mountain soul," recalled one of their fans at the time. "You could feel the hurt, the anger, the sadness."

And so the album was launched. The Rounder front office was savvy about promoting albums to bluegrass and old-time fields, but they weren't really geared up to do anything on a national level. What they didn't realize until later was that the album was appealing on several fronts in addition to the old-time and bluegrass ones. The women's movement was just then starting to develop its own support culture, and the album became one of the few—very few—sources of songs by women and about women. Though neither Hazel nor Alice had created the songs from an ideological stance—they were simply writing from the emotion of their own experiences—many women heard their songs and at once identified with them. The fact that both were skilled musicians who were singing with power and emotion was an added appeal, especially to other women struggling in the male-dominated field of bluegrass and old-time music. Artists as diverse as Cathy Fink, Emmylou Harris, and Wynona Judd found inspiration and encouragement in the album, as did dozens of lesser known performers who were struggling along as "girl singers" in local bands.

Hazel and Alice were still doing most of their own booking during this time (Alice drawing most of the duty when Hazel could talk her into it), and while they were distressed at how little the record was reviewed, they began to notice that at concerts, when people brought their LPs up to be signed, a lot of them had given or received the albums as gifts. "There was a lot of news spread by word of mouth," remembers Hazel. "People happend to get a copy of the record somewhere, and were giving it to others as Christmas or birthday presents." Some of the songs were printed in *Sing Out* and there were TV appearances on shows called *Woman Alive* and NBC's *Sounds of Summer.* There were some festival appearances, but, says Hazel, "we did not know what the general public was like."

The first indication of just how important the duo had become to women came less than a year after the album came out. Hazel and Alice came to Boston to play a concert for the Folk Song Society of Greater Boston. This was a group that had earlier frustrated Mike Seeger by insisting on singing along with him, and Hazel and Alice were not sure what to expect. The members had routinely sent out notices on their mailing lists and put up fliers around Cambridge, assuming that mainly their own singalong members would come. When the night came, though, and Hazel and Alice reported to the appropriate room on the Harvard campus, they found it jammed—not so much with Folk Song Society types, but with women who had seldom come to the other "hootenannies." "The whole room was full," recalls Hazel. "They were sitting on the floor where there were no chairs. It was mostly women, but there were some men—there was one guy who baked some brownies for us. It was just an incredible audience. We couldn't have done anything wrong that night. And they really loved the newer songs. They were screaming and yelling and clapping, and these two other women were sitting right at our feet and they got really infuriated and I heard one of them say, 'They're treating them like stars!' They wanted us to be just like them, close to the earth. Another one of the society members said, 'Where did these people come from? Who are these people?'"

Alice recalls another concert about the same time in New York. "It turned out to be a women-only thing. They literally were not letting men in the door. And they hadn't told us this. We kind of got upset; we wanted this music to be accessible to everybody, and we didn't have a lot of sympathy for the idea of a place where just women went." It was only later that they learned that the record had made an impact as far away as Japan; at a Japanese bluegrass festival years later, Japanese women came up to Hazel and held her hand, literally in tears. They too had had no other role models.

Through the years, the album has continued to sell, eventually running up impressive sales of over 20,000 copies. Had Rounder had the kind of promotion system that commercial companies had, they feel certain it could have even reached more markets—that it might well have been a female counterpart to the legendary *Outlaws* album that renewed the careers of country singers Willie Nelson and Waylon Jennings. In 1977, when Hazel and Alice delivered the second Rounder album (*Hazel Dickens and Alice Gerrard*), there was talk of a national promotional campaign. By then, though, for various reasons, the two singers had decided to split up.

In later years, each would continue to make major contributions to the music, and the two would on occasion reunite for special events. It was only later, too, that it became apparent just how much their duet work had opened the door to a new generation of women in bluegrass: artists like Laurie Lewis, Allison Krauss, Lynn Morris, and others. It is harder to judge their effect on generations of women who heard and cherished their songs, and who saw them as tough, intelligent, humane role models who were willing to put their art on the line for the right cause.

Doc Watson

The story of Doc Watson, the man many consider to be the finest flat-pick acoustic guitarist alive, has more than its share of dramatic moments, but a good one to start with dates from Labor Day weekend in 1960. It was in the waning months of Eisenhower's presidency, and John F. Kennedy and Richard Nixon were coming down to the wire in a hard-fought election campaign. Kids all over the East were dancing to a new fad called "The Twist," and country fans were listening to Cowboy Copas's nifty flatpicking on "Alabam'." Up north in Boston and New York, the folk music revival was in full swing, and while most young fans were content to listen to Joan Baez and the Kingston Trio, a few were trying to hunt up some of the veteran performers who had first recorded many of the old songs in the 1920s. One of these young fans was a college student named Ralph Rinzler, and one of the veterans he had found was Clarence Tom Ashley, who had recorded songs like "The Coo Coo" in 1928. Somewhat reluctantly, Ashley had agreed to let Rinzler make some new tapes of his singing, and on this Labor Day, Rinzler, accompanied by his record collector pal Gene Earle, found himself driving into the Appalachians toward the hamlet of Shouns, Tennessee, just a few miles from the North Carolina line. There Tom Ashley was to meet them, with a band he would collect.

They finally arrived at Ashley's house, and the older singer introduced them to the man most people in the area considered "the best guitar picker around," a tall, good-looking, thirty-seven-year-old blind man named Doc Watson. Ashley had decided that he didn't want to play himself on the new tapes, but that Doc would be great. When Doc got out his instrument, Rinzler and Earle looked at each other. It was a Fender solid-body electric with a Woody Woodpecker decal stuck on the front: not exactly a staple in folk revival circles. Rinzler was taken aback, and said he hadn't come all that way to record the legendary Tom

Ashley with an electric guitar. "Doc made it clear that he had his own professional standards," Rinzler later recalled. "He owned no acoustic guitar, and if he were to borrow one, he wouldn't be accustomed to it." Doc told him, in essence, "That's all I own and that's all I play." Rinzler later learned that Doc had a considerable reputation in the mountains playing rockabilly, honky-tonk, and straight country music, but for now he just saw Doc as another modern country picker. The recording session with Doc was summarily canceled.

The story—and Doc's career—might well have ended there, but it didn't. The next day Rinzler went with Doc and a group of musicians to the house of Ashley's sister to do some recording. Sitting in the back of the pickup, Rinzler began playing some old mountain tunes on his banjo. Within a few minutes, the truck stopped, and Doc, who had been riding in the cab, got out and hopped up into the truck bed. "Let me see that banjo, son," he said, and Rinzler handed it over. Doc launched into a local variant of the then popular "Tom Dooley," picking the banjo and singing in a warm, languid voice. Surprised, Rinzler spent the rest of the ride talking with Doc about old-time music and folk music and the way it was becoming so popular around the country. Doc listened with interest, and began to see that what his visitor wanted was what Doc called "the old music"—the folk ballads of the area, and the kind of songs sung by Grayson and Whitter, the Carter Family, and the like. And Doc also explained that if he liked this kind of music, Rinzler should meet his family, who lived at Deep Gap, North Carolina. He agreed, and also made Doc's first recordings, several banjo pieces like "Keep My Skillet Good and Greasy." Everybody seemed satisfied, and when Rinzler mentioned returning later for more recording, Doc began seriously thinking about honing his skills on his old Martin D-28 acoustic guitar. As he headed home, he began wondering if maybe there was some way he could make a living with this "old music" after all.

The hamlet of Deep Gap, North Carolina, is located just under the west bank of the Blue Ridge, directly off the Blue Ridge Parkway, in the extreme western part of the state. A few miles south is the Tweetsie Railroad; to the northeast is Mount Airy, the model for Andy Griffith's Mayberry. The region is a center for classic Appalachian string band music, and greats like Pop Stoneman, Tommy Jarrell, Henry Whitter, G. B. Grayson, the Red Fox Chasers, and George Shuffler hail from it. Arthel "Doc" Watson was born there in the Stoney Fork township on March 3, 1925, one of nine children in the family of farmers. An eye disease left Doc blind at the age of two, and he began turning his attention to the music and sounds around him. "As far back as I can remember," he says, "I've been fascinated with anything that had a musical sound.

There were a couple of old cow bells and sheep bells lying around the house, and I remember how interested I was in the different tones of the bells, and I also remember how Mama would scold me for making so much noise." Both sides of Doc's family had roots running deep into the mountains, and he also grew up hearing church songs, old ballads, and his father's banjo.

Doc's first real instrument was a little harmonica his father bought him. Once he had mastered it, he added to it by stringing a wire to the door of a nearby shed, plucking the wire, and "tuning" it by moving the door back and forth as he played the mouth harp. Though he called it "crude," such instruments have been known among African-American musicians in the South for years and are called "diddley bows." When he was eleven, Doc got his first stringed instrument, a hand-carved maple-necked banjo his father made for him. "The head was made of cat skin, which my father tanned in a very special way, taking the hair off, of course, but not weakening the unbelievable strength of the skin." Though it was fretless and not easy to play, Doc was soon working up local tunes like "Down the Road" and "Rambling Hobo."

By this time, the guitar was becoming more popular in the mountains, and the younger musicians were starting to replace the old open-backed banjo with it. While Doc was attending the Raleigh School for the Blind, he heard a classmate play one, and learned a few chords. Then one day, when he was thirteen, one of his brothers brought home a borrowed guitar—it was an arch-top Harmony—and Doc began fooling with it. At breakfast next morning, his father said, "Son, if you can learn to play a tune on that thing by the time I get home, I'll go with you to town this coming Saturday . . . and we'll find you a guitar."

The boy set to work, and by that evening had worked up a passable version of the current Carter Family hit, "When the Roses Bloom in Dixieland." Impressed, his father bought him a little Stella flat-top; "it was pretty hard to fret," Doc recalls, "but Lord, I thought I had the King's treasure." Armed with the treasure, Doc now listened even more intently to the family radio and stash of Victrola records, quickly mastering the basic "Carter Family" lick and then moving on to the newer styles coming from the 1930s Opry: the guitar work of Jack Shook and His Missouri Mountaineers, of Burt Hutcherson, and especially of the show's hottest group, the Delmore Brothers. He was amazed at the dense, bluesy guitar breaks he heard on the Delmore performances, not realizing at the time that they were using two guitars, a standard and a tenor. Still, Doc managed to work out his own version of the breaks, and added a bunch of Delmore songs to his repertoire—where they remain to this day. After a couple of years, he ordered a flat-top Harmony from

Sears, and with it came a pick and a Nick Lucas instruction book. It was then that Doc became a flatpicker.

It took him a while to figure out how to make money with his new skill. One was to do what area musicians had done for years: go "busking" on street corners and courthouse lawns. His older brother Linney would take Doc into town on Saturdays; "In the summertime I'd get out there on the street when I'd be home, and pick some. I didn't feel guilty about it at all. Some people looked down on you for it in those days, but I didn't care. I needed a little spending money, and my daddy was a poor man." Often Doc would find a store or barbershop and ask if he could come in and pick; it would almost always draw a crowd, and with requests and donations, he would often come home with a dollar or so. Other money he made by working with his brother cutting timber for a local tannery. Just before his twenty-second birthday, Doc met a young local girl named Rosa Lee Carlton, the daughter of a well-known local fiddler named Gaither Carlton. They were married in a year, and Doc found himself with a new bunch of in-laws that were as full of music as his own family. And by 1949 he had his first son, Eddie Merle—named after two of Doc's heroes, crooner Eddy Arnold and picker Merle Travis.

It was a little before this time that he got his nickname "Doc." He was working a local job at a furniture store, and the show was counting down to a live radio feed. While they were waiting to go on, the local announcer began having trouble with Doc's given name, Arthel: "What kind of name is that? That's a little stuffy for this show." A woman from the audience called out, "Call him Doc!" and the announcer obliged. The name stuck. It's a term often used in the mountains to refer to someone who is special or who has mysterious, special talent; friends always used to call A.P. Carter "Doc."

In spite of what folk song collectors thought, the music in the mountains never stood still, but it was changing more dramatically than ever in the 1950s, as Doc and Rosa began to rear their family. To get work in local bands, Doc soon found he had to make his peace with the electric guitar—even though his own homestead didn't yet have electricity. He first tried amplifying the D-28 Martin he had bought, but wasn't satisfied with the sound. For a time he had a Les Paul electric ("with all those little knobs on it") and then settled in with a solid body Fender Stratocaster, which had just been introduced in 1953.

So armed, Doc was able to make some serious money playing in a local rockabilly-country band headed by neighbor Jack Williams, often at a VFW hall in nearby Johnson City—a gig that often brought the group some $50 a night. He played for a time in another band headed by electric steel player Bryan Adams, and yet another headed by Frog and Carl Green. He did everything from "Honky Tonk Angels" to "Steel Guitar Rag," but he especially became adept at picking fiddle tunes on the guitar. At first, Doc told the folk fans he did this because none of these new bands had a fiddle and they needed an occasional tune; later, he admitted that he had really been inspired by listening to some of the Nashville pickers, like Joe Maphis. "And Hank Garland and Grady Martin had done some of those tunes on the electric guitar with Red. Foley. They really inspired me to try," he explained.

In later years, Doc would celebrate these days by featuring a medley of "Tutti Frutti," "Blue Suede Shoes" and "Whole Lotta Shakin' Goin' On" in his shows, and eventually, in the 1990s, an entire album entitled *Docabilly*.

All of which gets us back to that meeting with Ralph Rinzler and his interest in the "old music." When the young man returned in 1961 to make more tapes, Doc had dug out his D-28 and was regaining his skill as a flatpicker. He soon recorded pieces like "The Lone Pilgrim," "I'm Troubled," and ancient pieces like "The Coo Coo Bird." Overjoyed, Rinzler took the tapes to New York and tried to shop them to a major label: no luck. The only company that really seemed interested was tiny Folkways, and in 1961 they issued Doc's very first sides, as *Old Time Music at Clarence Ashley's*. At about the same time, Rinzler arranged for Doc and Ashley's group to come to New York to do a concert; it was well-received (though the band was puzzled about why the youngsters were not dancing), and the *New York Times* singled out Doc as the hit of the show.

From here his reputation began to soar. He soon had climbed aboard the burgeoning folk music coffeehouse circuit, playing early dates at the University of Chicago folk festival, the famous West Coast club the Ash Grove, and the prestigious Newport Folk Festival. Under Rinzler's guidance, Doc did a series of dates with bluegrass patriarch Bill Monroe, re-creating some of the old classic Monroe Brothers sides. The two worked so well together that Rinzler went to Monroe's label, Decca, to see if he could "borrow" Bill for an album of duets on Vanguard, but Decca turned him down. In 1967, Doc did succeed in forging a splendid album with bluegrassers Flatt and Scruggs, *Strictly Instrumental*, which became his best-selling effort up until then. As a soloist, he began a long string of albums for Vanguard: the first was called simply *Doc Watson*, and featured many of his signature songs: "Black Mountain Rag," "Deep River Blues," "Omie Wise," and "Sittin' on Top of the World." By the time of his third album, *Southbound* (1966), Doc was starting to assert his true (and eclectic) repertoire— good Nashville songs by Mel Tillis and John D. Loudermilk, as well as old-time country songs like the Delmores' "Blue Railroad Train." He also introduced on this album the lead playing of his teenage son Merle.

For the next twenty-one years, Merle appeared with his father on concert stages and bluegrass events across the country. The money was coming in pretty well now, and Doc was pleased to write the government and tell them he didn't need their support anymore for his family. Record deals flourished; from Vanguard he went to the Chicago-based Flying Fish, then to a series on Liberty, to a heavily produced sound (with drums and electric bass) for United Artists, to Poppy, to the classic *Will the Circle Be Unbroken* set for the Nitty Gritty Dirt Band and to his current label, Sugar Hill. The run was broken in 1985, when Merle was suddenly killed in a tractor accident on his farm. Stunned and grieving, Doc thought about giving it all up—after all, Merle had been playing about half the lead work in the arrangements. But friends encouraged him to keep on, and after friend Jack Lawrence stepped in to replace Merle, Doc's innate creativity reasserted itself, and soon the Watson music was rolling again.

Roy Harper

Most people do not exactly consider Nashville a mecca for old-time music. At fiddlers' contests in Alabama, bluegrass festivals in Virginia, and back-step dances in North Carolina, "Nashville" has become synonymous with everything that old-time music stands against. Yet when you get beyond Music Row Nashville, and get to Nashville the town, or Nashville the community of musicians, a different picture emerges. From as long ago as the 1920s the rolling hills around Nashville have produced an impressive stream of traditional musicians, and over the years more than a few of them were drawn into the periphery of the Nashville music industry. It is still possible in Nashville or its suburbs to find people who toured with the Delmore Brothers, played bass for Uncle Dave Macon, jammed with Arthur Smith, picked with the original Coon Creek Girls, or crossed bows with Fiddlin' Cowan Powers. Go out a little further from Nashville, down to Tullahoma or Tracy City or Manchester or Dickson, and you'll find even more remnants of old-time music, and hear tales about an old-time music culture that existed, and still exists today, in the very shadow of Nashville's bizarre glamour. This is a story about a part of this culture. It is about a man that many people consider the best old-time singer in the state: a lean, lanky, easygoing man named Roy Harper.

Roy's commitment to the old songs he sings is not superficial, nor is it academic, nor is it a matter of family heritage, nor is it a matter of aesthetics. "I want you to tell people that I live in the past," he said recently, "and that I dwell on and thrive on memories of the past. If I had my way, we'd still be driving Model A Fords and listening to Jimmie Rodgers on the Victrola." As a matter of fact, Roy does have an impressive collection of 78s—Jimmie Rodgers as well as others—which he does listen to and which he does learn songs from. And as a matter of fact, when Roy shows up for a job, he does arrive in his cherry-red 1948

Aero Fleetwood Chevrolet, which looks just like it came off the floor. (Roy is used to it attracting attention, and likes to startle young onlookers by proudly announcing, "Two more payments and it's mine.") Roy doesn't favor the spangled coats on sale at Nashville's Alamo, nor the 1960-chic flannel-shirt-and-jeans mode of so many young revivalists. He dresses the way he remembers the serious singers of the 1920s and 1930s dressing: well-polished boots, dark coat, gambler's vest, floppy bow tie or string tie, all topped off with a dark gray cowboy hat or his old railroad cap. He's likely to come on stage carrying an old ladder-back chair, take his seat, adjust his guitar, organize his harmonica rack, and then address his audience with a quiet poise and dignity born of some forty-odd years in the business. His songs range from the ancient ballads like "The Butcher's Boy" and "The Soldier and his Lady" to cowboy songs like "Little Joe the Wrangler" or "Rainbow on the Rio Colorado," from old-time protest songs like "Cotton Mill Blues" and "Roll Down the Line" to venerable radio favorites like "The Prisoner's Dream" and "I Lost My Love in the Ohio Flood" and Lum and Abner's well-known "They Cut Down the Old Pine Tree." Roy sings these straight and true and sincere, in a voice that sounds like a mixture of Rex Griffin, Jimmie Rodgers, and Ernest Tubb. "I guess you could call me a dinosaur," he says, "one of the few dinosaurs living who still has the nerve to perform these old songs and take them seriously."

Roy was born in 1925 in Manchester, a town about halfway between Nashville and Chattanooga, in south-central Tennessee. As a boy, Roy recalls being fascinated with two things: music and trains. He liked to climb up under the trestle of the local railroad and brace himself just a couple of feet from the roadbed "so I could look right up into the engine and see those drivers work." By 1943 or so Roy began working as a brakeman on different railroads in the Southeast and West, and he continued with this career, off and on, until 1959. During this time he did a lot of singing, much of it in the rough-and-tumble bars of the South and Southwest. He very quickly became adept at imitating the style of Jimmie Rodgers, then dead only a decade but already a legend among the old railroaders who felt a special tie to his music.

Also as a boy, Roy got a schooling in the string band music heritage of southern Tennessee. He especially admired two local string bands, those of W. B. Jacobs and Nathan Barger, who won a local fame of sorts by playing on the radio at nearby Chattanooga. Roy also learned from the two most famous old-time acts in the area: Uncle Dave Macon, the banjo-playing star of the early Grand Ole Opry, and the Allen Brothers, Lee and Austin, from nearby Sewanee, who recorded prolifically their repertoire of blues, rags, and hits like "Salty Dog" in the late 1920s. He added songs from both acts to his growing repertoire, and found in both role models for anyone wanting to become an entertainer as well as a musician. "Once Uncle Dave was entertaining on the courthouse square in Manchester," he recalls. "That was when the old highway U.S. 41 went right through the center of town, and everybody going down to Chattanooga had to go right through Manchester. Well, one night about dusk a sharp-looking car with New York plates came up, and rounded the square several times, and it was obvious they were lost. Finally one of the men in the car stuck his head out, and in one of those rude, brash New York accents shouted to Uncle Dave, 'Say old man, can you direct us to the road to Chattanooga?' And Uncle Dave looked up and shouted back, 'Well, you didn't have any trouble finding it in 1863!'" Two local auction companies routinely hired Uncle Dave to play for sales in the Manchester area—a type of musical advertising that Roy would later do himself. "Frank Patch was one of the agents that worked with the auction companies back in the 1930s," recalls Roy. "He told me that when he came down for a job, Uncle Dave would worry them to death wanting to have them hear him try out new songs. They got to where they would even stay in separate hotels so Uncle Dave couldn't find their room and come up late at night and bother them to hear some new song he was working up. But some of Uncle Dave's jokes were too clever for city folks anyway. He liked to tell one about his brother Bob, and how much his brother Bob loved music. 'Why the other day,' he'd say, 'my brother Bob was out working in the field and there was a splinter over there on the fence, and a wind came up and started hitting that splinter, and Bob liked to have laughed himself to death.' Folks who haven't been around one of those old rail fences and don't know what kind of a sound they make when the wind causes them to vibrate can't really appreciate that."

There were other local musicians around Manchester that Roy recalls as well. "There was a good black fiddle band that used to hang out and play on the square, right in front of Basil McMahon's store. They used a fiddle, guitar, and a tater bug mandolin, and liked to play things like 'St. Louis Blues.' Then there were other groups that came through on a sort of regular circuit, setting up and playing for spare change. I remember another black string band that featured a sort of rough guitar player, who played in a high banjo tuning and made bar style chords with his forefinger. They had a yazoo [a large kazoo attached to a horn], a Hoover bass [i.e., washtub], and a washboard; they sounded a little like those old Memphis Jug Band records, and I found out that they traveled as far south as Florida."

Roy was especially interested in this sort of music, since his father had given him a harmonica when he was six, and he was learning to use it as his first instrument. He was also starting to work with the guitar, and listened when he could to the premier guitar player around, another black musician, one named Coaly Streeter. "He was another Josh White on guitar," Roy remembers. "He wasn't just a straight blues picker—he could work in all different styles, including fingerpicking. He was from down at Wartrace, but he was well-known in Shelbyville and Murfreesboro. He was a favorite of the upper crust there, well-to-do white folks. They'd get him to play for their card parties or card games, and even for their rooster fights." Some of the blues and guitar numbers in Roy's repertoire can be traced, indirectly, to Streeter.

As he traveled around the country as a young man in the early 1940s, Roy continued to hone his style and enlarge his repertoire, and to work as a brakeman on the Santa Fe and other lines. "Back then being a brakeman was considered the third most dangerous job in the country," he said. "But I did enjoy it, and I got to see a lot of country." About 1945 Roy returned to Manchester and met a man who was to have a lasting impact on his career: guitarist and dobroist Blake Bynum. Bynum was several years older than Roy, and had been born in the community of Beech Grove, a few miles north of Manchester; he and his family moved to Enid, Oklahoma, when he was a boy, and then back to Tennessee when he was a teenager. He was a small man, and suffered from epilepsy, but he was totally consumed by his music. He was married, had a family, but music always seemed to take first place. "He was amazing, the way he could learn guitar pieces," recalls Roy. "Once back in 1927 he saw Sam and Kirk McGee at a schoolhouse concert at a little town called Noah. Sam did his version of his specialty, 'Buck Dancer's Choice.' Blake watched him like a hawk, and in a week he had it down to where he could play it. Another time I remember him listening to records by Blind Lemon Jefferson and Blind Boy Fuller and Josh White. One time I was at a friend's house with Blake, and this friend played a record of Josh White's 'Homeless and Hungry Blues.' Blake loved it, and listened to it twice, and then he went home and came back next week and played along with the record, note for note."

By 1946 a lot of medium-sized towns like Manchester were starting to get their own radio stations, and since many of these were too small or too poor to affiliate with one of the big networks, there was a renaissance of sorts in the kind of live, regional, independent programming that had characterized broadcasting during its golden years of the 1920s. In middle Tennessee this meant that there was now a place for up-and-coming local string bands to ply their trade in a series of new stations that began to flourish in the very shadow of Nashville's giants WSM and WLAC. These stations were at Manchester, Tullahoma, Murfreesboro, Crossville,

Cookeville, Dickson, Springfield, Clarksville, Fayetteville, and others; for about ten years this informal circuit provided work for the young bands who hadn't made the big time, and for the traditional bands whose older style and repertoire was appealing to the people of rural Tennessee, if not to the slick talent bosses in Nashville.

Blake Bynum had become a part of this circuit. About 1944 he had formed a radio band called the Sand Mountain Boys; Chief Red Bone (aka Taylor Jones) was a real Cherokee Indian who was a fiddler and the front man; Jack Bailey played the accordion; Marvin Wilson played the five-string banjo. One day a mutual friend named Clarence LeFevre met Roy on the square in Manchester and introduced him to Bynum. Blake liked Roy's Jimmie Rodgers imitations, and soon invited him to join the band as their singer. Roy gave it a try, and made his radio debut one hot afternoon in the cramped Manchester station. As Roy stepped up to the mike to sing his first solo, a fly lit on his nose and proceeded to make himself at home. Nervous to start with, Roy now found himself trying to sing, to keep rhythm on the guitar, and to wriggle his nose to dislodge the fly. The rest of the band members watched with a strange combination of awe and and hilarity. Roy worked his way into the third chorus of his song, and the fly worked his way down to the end of Roy's nose. By now both Roy and Blake were wondering about whether it was possible to sing on key if a fly actually got into Roy's mouth. Finally the last chorus came, Roy hit his final chord, and made a grab for the fly. He caught it—and passed his audition.

By the early 1950s, the Sand Mountain Boys had become one of the most popular radio bands in the area. They were heard so much on midstate radio that Blake Bynum was able to copy the booking technique pioneered by Uncle Dave Macon back in the 1920s: He would go up to area schoolhouses, pretend that the band happened to be in the area that afternoon, and ask the principal if he could visit one of the classes. In class, Blake would ask the kids how many of them listened to the Sand Mountain Boys on radio. A lot of hands would immediately shoot up, and Blake would look at the principal, who was usually impressed by this show of fame, and start talking about a booking for the school (the school would get a cut of the gate). Kids would then run home and tell their parents about the celebrities they had met that day, and spread the word about the upcoming schoolhouse show. Since few of the regional radio stations could afford a band full time, the band would play only two or three days a week at, say, the station in Cooksville; here they would advertise their nearby dates and schoolhouse concerts, and "play out" in that town's area for that week. The next week they would move on to a different town on their circuit, perhaps thirty or forty miles away, and repeat the procedure. Blake and Roy also got a lot of work playing for auction companies. Roy explains: "On the morning of the auction, we would go into town, around the courthouse, get on a wagon or maybe a flatbed truck, and play some lively music. When we had a crowd, we'd get on the PA system and tell 'em to come on out to the place, that there was a big sale on. Then during the sale itself, we would play during breaks, or when they wanted to get some hot bids lined up in the crowd. We would get a flat five dollars a day—not much by modern standards but a lot of people back then were jealous of us for it." In 1949 the Sand Mountain Boys auditioned for the Grand Ole Opry; unfortunately they chose the same week that the Opry signed Hank Williams, and while the Opry personnel asked the band to return later, they never did. Roy, eternally nervous and insecure about trying to make a living with his music, found himself with an offer to return to the railroad. Some friends told him to go for the railroad job and its pension and benefits; others said that if he turned down the Opry shot now, he would be giving up the golden ring. Unable to decide, he flipped a coin; the railroad won, and Roy went back to being a brakeman. Ironically, though Blake Bynum never returned for the Opry audition, a year later Hank Williams drove his Cadillac up to Manchester to hunt out Blake to play in his band. Unimpressed, Blake hid behind the curtains of his cabin while Williams walked around his yard calling his name.

About 1959 Roy decided to retire from the railroad for good, and embarked on a second career as a traveling salesman. For a time he sold encyclopedias door to door, then worked for a photographer who restored old photos, then for a company that made home safes. A natural talker with a healthy curiosity and a love of people, Roy really began to hit his stride in this work. Yarns he heard and things he experienced helped him hone his ability as a raconteur and a storyteller, and the steady travel was an adequate substitute for his old railroader's wanderlust. He also had more time for music, and the chance to befriend other musicians and learn new songs. He was attracted to some of the veteran Opry performers in the area, especially Sam and Kirk McGee, and Fiddlin' Arthur Smith, who in his later years ran a music barn down south of Manchester. Soon Roy was performing with these men, jamming with them, and learning their songs. "Sam and Kirk were two of the best men on that Grand Ole Opry," Roy recalls. "But WSM wouldn't let 'em play anything but the same three or four tunes over and over—'Chittlin' Cookin' Time,' 'Milk Cow Blues,' none of that great flat-top pickin' that Sam could do. They were on Hank Snow's Coca Cola segment of the show, and I finally said to Sam one day, 'Why don't you just flat out do one of those guitar pieces like 'Drum Watch' or 'Buck Dancer's Choice'? The people would like it. And he tried it, and people did like it, and Hank Snow got to where he wanted to feature them each week doing an instrumental."

By the mid-1960s, Roy and Blake were pretty much working as a duet, and had been together about twenty years; they had seen their radio work pretty much dry up, and were wondering about the possibility of making records. Their chance came when Ben McCloud, a former DJ whom Roy had known while selling encyclopedias, came into some money and decided to get into the record business. He set up in 1965 a place called Varsity Recording Studio on Church Street in downtown Nashville, and began issuing singles under the label of Map Records, and LPs under the Varsity label. It was an interesting label—one of the few Nashville labels geared to older forms of country music—and it would eventually record a number of good records by fairly well-known artists, including the first sides cut by the Kendalls. In 1966 McCloud offered a record deal to Blake and Roy, and the pair cut their first single: "Hawaiian Wiggle," a guitar number featuring Blake, and "The Old Hitching Post," an obscure western song that Roy liked. On it Blake used an old Weymann guitar that Roy had acquired; the guitar meant a lot to Roy because it was the same brand used by his idol Jimmie Rodgers. "I had gotten it through a local man named E. W. Anderson. It didn't have any kind of name on it, and about 1930 he had sent it in to the Gibson people to be fixed up. The Gibson people did a fine job on it, and sent a note back saying that it was really a beautiful instrument, but it wasn't one of theirs. Then about 1956 when Mr. Anderson died, a friend of mine got it from his estate for me, and paid a whole $35 for it. Blake used it on almost all of the records we made, and it's now in a museum up at Manchester."

As he traveled around the South, Roy took copies of his new 45 single with him, and managed to get it quite a bit of radio airplay and jukebox distribution. This led to a second Map single a few months later, Roy's version of an old Cowboy Copas song called "Doll of Clay," backed with Blake's version of the old fiddle tune "Carroll County Blues" which he called "You Guessed It." This kicked up even more dust, and "Doll of Clay" became a regional hit; it remains one the favorites in Roy's repertoire today. Two more singles on Map soon followed ("Hobo Bill's Last Ride"/ "New Missouri Waltz" and "Blake's Chimes"/"Reflections of a Fool"), and Roy and Blake began to sense that there was a developing market for their music on records.

In the fall of 1967 Roy found himself in Barbourville, Kentucky, and looked up gospel singer–record company owner A. L. Phipps. Phipps had begun his career as a passionate fan of the Carter Family and the Carter-style music, and had begun a record company called Pine Mountain devoted to recording and distributing this sort of music. Phipps listened to Roy's singles, bought a stock for his retail sales company, and then offered Blake and Roy a contract to do a series of LPs on Pine Mountain. The first of these, *Very Countrified,* came out in 1968, and it was in short time followed by *Echoes of the Past, Country as Can Be,* a gospel LP, *Hear Them Again,* and *More Old Time Favorites.* In the late 1970s, Roy did a seventh Pine Mountain LP, *Sounds of the 1920s and 1930s,* as a solo effort.

The Pine Mountain LPs not only helped spread Roy's name around as a fine singer, but crystallized his commitment to the old-time repertoire of the Carters, Rodgers, and even more obscure singers like Buster Carter, Wilmer Watts, Blind Jack Mathis, Rex Griffin, and others he heard on old 78s. Unfortunately, about the time the Pine Mountain LPs really began to take off, Blake Bynum got sick. He died on May 17, 1973. Roy's partner, mentor, and friend of almost thirty years was gone, and Roy suddenly found himself trying to make it as a solo act.

He began to adapt. He had learned to play the harmonica at an early age, and now he rigged up a rack and began to accompany himself on harmonica as he did solo spots. (Though he didn't realize it until years later, he had learned to play the harmonica backward, and still does today; "when I found out about it, I turned my harp over and tried to play it right, but I can't. So I just play it the way I learned.") He also had a big kazoo (a yazoo) he had bought in 1938 for 39 cents ("it was the deluxe model"), which he mounts on the side of his rack for variety.

He also found new musical companions. One was veteran blackface comedian and medicine show veteran Goober Buchanan, a fixture in middle Tennessee since the 1930s and a bandleader who worked with Riley Puckett, Lowe Stokes, and Slim Rhodes. Roy and Goober did a series of appearances in the late 1970s—including one at Renfro Valley—in which they re-created some of the classic rube skits from the medicine show days. Roy also began appearing with the Cove Hollow Boys, a band from the Smithville area, and performing with fiddler Billy Wommack, a Woodbury, Tennessee, barber who used to play with Uncle Dave Macon's son Dorris; he often works with younger dobro players like Johnny Bellar, Fred Duggin, and Ricky Rigney.

Some of these men are heard on some of the newer records Roy has done since leaving Pine Mountain. In 1987 he released *I Like Mountain Music* on Old Homestead, a set that got good reviews and better sales, and included such items as a topical ballad Roy wrote about the flea market at Tullahoma, Tennessee, as well as some rare ballads like "The

Murder of Tom Slaughter" and "I Lost My Love in the Ohio Flood." Roy has also contributed to anthology albums put out by the Tennessee Folklore Society, the Clarksville fiddling contest, and the Cumberland Valley reunion organization. He estimates that his total discography includes about 110 recorded songs—probably a fourth of his total repertoire. He often makes custom cassettes off unissued master tapes for fans and friends, so a complete Harper discography might be almost impossible to compile. Roy is also one of the most knowledgable singers around today, and often prefaces his songs with remarkable histories and backgrounds—more testimony to how seriously Roy takes his songs. "You can't sing it if you don't know it," he says.

For the last twenty years, Roy has routinely won or placed in most of the old-time singing categories at fiddling contests in Tennessee and Alabama, and was one of a handful of Tennessee artists to represent the state at the 1986 Smithsonian Festival of American Folklife in Washington. He is often used by the Country Music Hall of Fame in their folk music educational programs in middle Tennessee, and has become a popular feature at the Country Music Elderhostel classes held every summer in Murfreesboro. His paintings, which he began doing again about five years ago, have proven irresistible to collectors of folk art and, especially, to railroad buffs. (Roy's train pictures are not of vague generic trains on generic landscapes, but of specific trains at specific locations.) But the facet of Roy's work that has been attracting most attention recently has been his remarkable re-creations of the Jimmie Rodgers style; many Rodgers fans say that nobody today sounds as close to Rodgers—both in blue yodel and in singing style—as Roy, and his appearances at Rodgers festivals in Texas, Nashville, and Mississippi have won rave reviews and letters from fans all over. One of his most prized ones comes from Hoyt "Slim" Bryant, the great guitar player who actually recorded with Rodgers, who urges Roy to keep up the good work and keep Jimmie's tradition alive. Roy keeps the letter in his guitar case, brings it out when he needs to impress some young whipper-snapper, and keeps doing his best to follow Slim Bryant's admonition. That too is one of the ways of the past.

The Freight Hoppers

By the late 1950s, as country music moved into its post-Elvis era, the old-time string band tradition that dominated the music in its first generation was almost dead. Local square dance bands still held forth, playing at the local Moose club or country school auditorium, but in the commercial world there were only a handful of real, veteran string bands still working regularly. J. E. Mainer still had his Mainer's Mountaineers, and Steve Ledford still had his band in North Carolina; on the Grand Ole Opry stage in Nashville, bands like the Crook Brothers and the Fruit Jar Drinkers still took to the stage every Saturday night, usually playing for a rowdy troupe of square dancers. In Georgia, Gordon Tanner, son of the legendary Gid, kept together his band, the Junior Skillet Lickers, though they too played mostly for dances. Most of the younger musicians who liked accoustic music had gone into bluegrass, and what string bands were left were busy imitating Flatt and Scruggs.

Then, starting about 1960, an odd thing happened: There emerged a self-conscious revival movement of the old Charlie Poole–Skillet Lickers sound. It was almost certainly an offshoot of the so-called folk revival movement of that time, spurred on by the success of groups like the Kingston Trio, and it was unique in that it transferred the venue of string band music from the country schoolhouse to the concert stage and the college campus. Its flagship band was one formed in 1958 called the New Lost City Ramblers—the name being a witty play on the old colorful names from earlier days. Its original members were Mike Seeger, a masterful collector and singer and son of musicologist Charles Seeger; Tom Paley, a mathematics teacher; and John Cohen, a Yale-educated veteran of the New York folk club scene. None of them was from the South (in fact, all of them were born in New York City), and all approached the music from a historic and even academic point of view. Their first record, on the "scholastic" Folkways label in 1961, was quite different from the latest Kingston Trio or Harry Belafonte LP: Inside a rather plain-looking cover with an old WPA photo on the front, one found an inserted booklet of notes. They were not slickly printed, but crowded onto the page like some fussy professor's lecture notes. Here the Ramblers explained who played what, where they learned the song, what the words they sang were, and suggestions for further reading. The vast majority of the songs had been borrowed from old-time 78s from the 1920s and 30s, or from obscure field recordings in the Library of Congress, and the Ramblers did their best to emulate these sources. Over the following three decades, the band produced some sixteen such albums for Folkways, and played thousands of concert dates. (Tom Paley was replaced in 1963 by another gifted young musician, Tracy Schwartz.) Their records and concerts were immensely influential, and to "validate" their music, they began performing and recording with some of the older veterans like Cousin Emmy and Maybelle Carter. Soon amateur bands all over the country were trying this "new" style, and some of the best of them began to win national reputations. The movement created some exuberant music, but it also set off an interesting debate as to just how younger generations should approach the music.

The New Lost City Ramblers were faithful to the performances they had heard, and copied them, at times almost note-for-note. This was nothing new; young revivalists in blues and jazz had been doing it for several years—copying a Bix Beiderbecke solo exactly, or a Robert Johnson guitar run. But this offered little compromise to an audience schooled in bluegrass and country; some bluegrass pickers, angry at hearing such bands show up at bluegrass festivals, sarcastically referred their product as "cave music" and looked on it as little more than a primitive form of bluegrass. Some way to translate the energy and beauty of old-time string band music into more accessible terms was needed if the new bands were going to actually get enough work to keep together. And during the 1970s, several bands emerged that sought, in different ways, to do just that.

Just how complex their challenge was can be seen by a metaphor from an outside source. In John Ford's classic western film *She Wore a Yellow Ribbon,* John Wayne plays Captain Nathan Brittles, a grizzled cavalry officer who is just days from an enforced retirement. Toward the end of the film, Brittles's troop has to seek out and engage a hostile party of renegade Apaches; but before they leave the fort, the soldiers present Brittles with a gold pocket watch, with an inscription on the back: "To Captain Brittles—Lest We Forget." The captain is visibly moved, and the troop rides off. But Captain Brittles soon rejoins them, and in the film's most dramatic scene stands with his soldiers on a hill overlooking the Apache camp. His plan is to have his men gallop down the hill at top speed, race through the camp, and run off the enemy's horses. But before he gives the signal to charge, he pulls out his new watch with its inscription of "Lest We Forget." Then he gives the signal to charge. What results is one of the most breathtaking, dangerous, and exhilarating scenes in a western film. It becomes the symbolic and literal climax of one of American film's masterpieces.

There are two ways of dealing with the sentiment like "Lest We Forget." One is to assume that it is a sentimental tribute to the past and to tradition, and to respond to it with a sort of genteel appreciation. Or you can do as Captain Brittles did, and respond to the past with a hell-for-leather charge that will make your mark on the world even if it isn't cleanly executed and carefully planned. And these are basically the two ways that the new generations of old-time string bands deal with their sources. Some try to copy the old 78s lick for lick, and take the music as seriously as if it were a Schubert quartet. Others make the charge, using the old 78s as a general guide and inspiration and then following their own instincts as musicians. "We don't sound like the people who made those records," said one such young musician, Suzanne Edmundson. "We don't try to. We try to capture the spirit that's in those grooves."

Edmundson's band, the Hotmud Family, was one of the first of the 1970s bands to deal with this problem. Formed in 1970 around the Dayton, Ohio, area, the band was built around the singing and guitar work of Edmundson, the fiddling of her husband, Dave, and the banjo work of Rick Good. They began recording for the Cincinnati label Vetco, and did an early album with a fine local fiddler named Van Kidwell.

Though all the group knew and loved old-time music, they also knew that in order to get work at bluegrass festivals they had to had to use bluegrass harmony and singing styles; thus they would do an old Uncle Dave Macon song like "Over the Mountain" with clean, classic, Osborne brothers–style harmony. Though they often were at odds with their record labels as to how much "bluegrass" they should include on an album, they routinely featured old-time songs in their live shows. After a long string of good albums, and after a series of frustrations in the commercial market, they disbanded in 1983. Suzanne Edmundson remarried and became Suzanne Thomas, and began a successful solo career in the 1990s.

The two other bands that laid claim to the old-time title in the 1970s were the Red Clay Ramblers, from Durham, North Carolina, and the Highwoods String Band from upstate New York. The former was created about 1973 by banjoist Tommy Thompson and fiddler Bill Hicks, and quickly established itself as a crowd-pleasing but very eclectic band, whose repertoire included old jazz tunes, blues, Irish, early country, original songs, ragtime, and even Sacred Harp in addition to old-time country. Recording on the well-circulated Flying Fish label, they also added a piano (Mike Craver) and even a trumpet ("the bluegrass three," as Thompson used to introduce it to skeptical audiences).

The Highwoods, on the other hand, used as their model the hell-for-leather style of the Skillet Lickers, with twin fiddles to drive their performances. The title of their 1976 Rounder album was *Dance All Night with a Bottle in Your Hand,* and their music was both sold and received as good-time old-time dance music, capable of bringing even the most jaded festivalgoer to his feet.

By the 1980s all of these bands, except for the occasional shows by the New Lost City Ramblers, were history. A number of third-generation groups tried to fill the voice—the best of them was a Nashville band called the Still House Reelers—but the commercial music industry was simply not able—or willing—to support them. But then in the early 1990s emerged a new band that seemed poised to take up this mantle, and to hold its own in the contemporary festival and concert scene. This was a dynamic young outfit from North Carolina who rode old-time music like it was a mud bike rather than a restored Model A, and who went by the name of the Freight Hoppers.

The original four-piece band began performing together not on college campuses or coffeehouses, but at a well-known mountain tourist site, the Great Smoky Mountains Railway, in 1993. Their first time there, they came in second in a talent contest with a field of 492 entries; their reward was a guest appearance on Garrison Keillor's legendary PBS show *Prairie Home Companion.* They soon signed a contract with Rounder, the largest and most visible of the various independent labels, and their first CD (*Where'd You Come From, Where'd You Go?,* 1996) scampered up the Gavin Americana charts and the *Bluegrass Unlimited* Top 20—something even Gid Tanner never did. There were shows to packed houses everywhere, and showcases for the annual meeting of the Folk Alliance and International Bluegrass Music Association, and the word began to spread that here was a hard-driving band that played with the kind of reckless abandon and good humor of the original bands of the 1920s. Everywhere people lined up to buy one of the band's T-shirts featuring the legend "Gid Is My Co-Pilot," a tribute to Gid Tanner and the Skillet Lickers.

By 1998 the Hoppers were playing a dizzying round of tours and personals. In one tour they started out in the urban mountain city of Asheville, North Carolina, and moved directly up to the old coal-mining town of Pikeville, Kentucky, in deep Appalachia. They then moved on to the Merlefest in North Carolina (named in honor of Doc Watson's son Merle) and to a similar festival at Olathe, Kansas, just outside of Kansas City; then to Pennsylvania, upstate New York, British Columbia, Oklahoma, Telluride (Colorado), and Berkeley; they even ventured onto the strange, haunted mesa that is Branson, Missouri. Unlike many of the earlier revival bands, the Freights were able to appeal to a surprising number of audiences: bluegrassers, folkies, lounge lizards, students, old farts, on-the-edge accountants, bikers, chicken farmers, tourists ("mullets," they call them in Branson), Internet gabblers (they have their own web site), and alt country types. Individually and collectively, they had by 1999 released three home videotapes as well as a second CD, the appropriately titled *Waitin' on the Gravy Train*.

For most of the 1990s, the Freights were built around three individuals. Much of the lead singing and the solid rhythm guitar was done by Cary Fridley, who grew up in Virginia and listened closely to the mountain singers she heard, such as Dellie Norton and Dolly Greer, and to the old records of the Carter Family and Alfred Karnes. But she also holds a master's degree in music education and has taught music at the high school level; she can speak articulately and with authority on the technical end of mountain singing. "You have to sing wide open, with your full voice," she notes. "There's not many dynamics in old-time singing."

Banjoist and singer Frank Lee is a Georgia boy whose father bought him his first banjo when he was in a hospital recovering from a broken leg; the dynamic lead fiddler, David Bass, loves Skillet Lickers records as much as apples, but honed his skills playing for tips in the subways of New York City. James O'Keefe, whose booming bass helps drive the Freight Hoppers rhythm, is a more recent member of the band, having joined in 1998.

Like most innovators, the Freight Hoppers walk a thin line between tradition and creativity. If one's creativity gets too far out of hand and out of balance, then the result is what Bill Monroe once described as "no part of nothing." Stay too traditional, and you get carbon copies of songs that were recorded better in 1928. This is good for winning fiddling contests, but otherwise won't put too many taters on your plate. The band members talk about this issue a lot, and have become thoughtful and articulate about it. Frank Lee says, "I always feel bad because the way I'm playing ths banjo is definitely not in line with what Fate Norris or Kyle Creed were doing. But while I really like listening to those old recordings, and the people who were making them, I still don't feel they were concerned with playing like somebody a few decades before them. They were taking all the influences and playing the best music they could. And I'm thinking that's the same thing we're doing."

Cary Fridley agrees. "I think the most authentic thing about our music, what we get out of the old recordings, is the spirit in them, and the drive in them. We all try really hard to understand, though we can't possibly completely understand, that they're singing from the bottom of their souls and it was hard times, and they had a nothing-to-lose type of approach." The band began to realize this when they started listening closely to Uncle Dave Macon records and looking at his career as an entertainer. Frank says, "Uncle Dave had his audience just where he wanted them, and that impressed us. I said, all right, he's like I am, his voice isn't perfect, and he was never a star in a big sense. But he had this spirit. So even if I don't have a great voice, maybe there's something else I can get across." When he shared this insight with the rest of the band, there was a dramatic reaction. "The entertainment value of the group changed drastically after we realized you didn't have to have a perfect voice, or whatever. And people started going crazy over it."

True enough, but when people ask what makes the Freight Hoppers so different from other young old-time bands, the subject of their singing always comes up. Far too many young bands look on singing as a minor inconvenience, but the Freights pay close attention to their harmonies, whether they are Carter Family or falsetto Gid Tanner. They also listen to the singing on those old records, and know it is more complicated than it sounds. Few other acts can show an across-the-board versatility that can range from unaccompanied mountain styles like "My Love Has Brought Me to Despair" to pungent Mississippi fiddle tunes. (There are some two hundred songs in their active repertoire.) And no band captures the on-the-edge, in-your-face excitement of the Freights. Says Cary, "It's a music where you've stripped it down to the very bareness of rhythm and simple melody. So what's left to come out is basic human expression—the singing."

Acknowledgments

Many of the profiles in this collection were first published in the following publications (all copyrighted by Charles K. Wolfe, except where noted):

The Journal of the American Academy for the Preservation of Old-Time Country Music, published by *Country Music* magazine:
"The Carter Family," No. 1, February 1991
"The Carter Family on Border Radio," No. 20, April 1994
"The Carter Sisters and Mother Maybelle," No. 41, February 1998
"Roy Acuff I," No. 1, February1991
"Roy Acuff II," Volume II, No. 3, June 1992
"Lefty Frizzell," No. 4, August 1991
"Grandpa Jones," No. 29, October 1995
"Pee Wee King," Volume II, No. 4, August 1992
"Bill Monroe," No. 16, August 1993
"Hank Snow," No. 2, April 1991
"Kitty Wells," No. 5, October 1991
"Vernon Dalhart," No. 27, June 1995
"Charlie Poole," No. 16, August 1993
"Darby and Tarlton," No. 18, December 1993
"Cousin Emmy," No. 33, June 1996
"The Monroe Brothers," No. 35, October 1996
"Wayne Raney," No. 36, April 1997
"Bradley Kincaid," No. 4, August 1991
"The Jordanaires," No. 22, August 1994
"Emmett Miller," No. 21, June 1994
"Tommy Jackson," No. 26, April 1995
"Curly Fox and Texas Ruby," No. 13, February 1993
"The Delmore Brothers," No. 5, October 1991
"The Louvin Brothers," No. 25, February 1995
"Martha Carson," No. 27, June 1995
"The Carlisles," No. 28, August 1995
"The Girls of the Golden West," Volume II, No. 6, December 1992

"Red River Dave," No. 15, August 1993
"Skeets McDonald," No. 30, December 1995
"Doc Watson," No. 45, October 1998

Bluegrass Unlimited
"Lew Childre," May 1979
"Karl and Harty," March 1978
"Tommy Magness," April 1997

Precious Memories
"Blue Sky Boys," July-August 1989
"Brown's Ferry Four," November-December 1989
"Albert E. Brumley," May-June 1991

Old Time Music, No. 26, Summer 1981
"Seven Foot Dilly"

Country Sounds
"Don Gibson"

Rounder Records, *Hazel and Alice,* liner notes, copyright 1995. Used by permission.
"Hazel and Alice"

Old Time Herald, 1982
"Roy Harper"

First-time publications
"Fiddlin' John Carson"
"Riley Puckett"
"The Georgia Yellow Hammers"
"Arthur Q. Smith"
"Zeke and Zeb Turner"
"Johnny Barfield"
"The Rouse Brothers"
"DeFord Bailey"
"Jimmie Riddle"
"The Statler Brothers"
"Stringbean"
"Billie Maxwell"
"The Freight Hoppers"

Index

Ford, Tennessee Ernie, 202, 270
Ford, Whitey, 94, 185
Ford and Glenn [vaudeville act], 41, 120
Foree, Mel, 209
"Forever," 234
"Forked Deer," 139
"For Old Times Sake," 171
Forrester, Howdy, 251
Fortune, Jimmy, in Statler Brothers, 233, 234
Foster, Bob, 148
Four Knights, 234
"Fourth of July at a County Fair," 87, 88
Fowler, Wally, 15, 148, 149, 150, 176
Fox, Curly, ix, 94, 96, 160; on Grand Ole
    Opry, 196; marriage to Texas Ruby, 57,
    195; profile of, 194–96
"The Fox Chase," 114, 116, 178
Foxton, Kelly, 55
Francis, Connie, 177
Frank, J. L., 38, 39, 40, 41
Frank, Leo, 66
"Frank Dupree," 74
"Frankie and Johnnie," 84
Franklin Brothers, 162
Franks, Tillman, 241
Frazier, Dallas, 32, 213
Freeman, Kinky, 265
Freeman, Porky, 148, 201
"Freight Train Boogie," 105, 201
"Freight Wreck at Altoona," 266
Fridley, Cary, 298, 299
Frizzell, Alice, 27, 28, 29, 30
Frizzell, Allen, 31
Frizzell, David, 31
Frizzell, Lefty, vii, 19, 49, 59, 114, 116, 270,
    271; profile of, 27–32
Frizzell, Lois, 27
Frizzell, Naamon, 29
Frizzell, William Orville. See Frizzell, Lefty
"Frolic of the Mice," 261
Fruit Jar Drinkers [band], 179, 185, 294
Fuller, Blind Boy, 288
"Funny, Familiar Forgotten Feelings," 212

Gabriel, Charles H., 6
"Galveston Rose," 53
Ganus Brothers, 101
Gardner, Robert, in Mac and Bob, 120
Garland, Hank, 140, 147, 187, 205, 283
Gatlin, Larry, 244
"A Georgia Barbecue at Stone Mountain," 172
"Georgia Breakdown," 173
"Georgia Bust Down," 173
Georgia Clodhoppers [band], 148
Georgia Crackers [band], 183
Georgia Mountaineers, 87
Georgia Peach Pickers, 185
Georgia Wildcats, 40
Georgia Yellow Hammers [band], 169, 221;
    profile of, 85–88
Gerrard, Alice, 275. See also Hazel and Alice
"Get Along Home, Cindy," 250
"Get That Golden Key," 238
Gibson, Autumn Scarlet, 212
Gibson, Don, 21, 144; on Grand Ole Opry,
    212, 213; picking by, 205; profile of,
    203–14; singing by, 204–5, 213; songwriting

by, 204, 210, 211–12, 214
Gibson, Kirk, 248
Gibson Kings, 169
Gill, Vince, viii, 216
Gillette, Lee, 177, 270
"The Girl I Left in Sunny Tennessee," 83
"Girls Don't Refuse to Kiss a Soldier," 123
"The Girls Don't Worry My Mind," 199
Girls of the Golden West, 40, 104; profile of,
    258–60
"Give Me a Straight-Shootin' Cowboy," 260
"Give Me Back My Five Dollars," 253
"Give Me Love," 17
"Give Me More, More, More (of Your
    Kisses)," 31
"Give Me That Old Time Religion," 237
"Give Me the Roses While I Live," 13
Glaser, Chuck, 163
Glosson, Lonnie, 114, 115, 116
Glosson, Mary, 116
Glover, Henry, 201
"God Is My Co-Pilot," 297
"Goin Back to Texas, 11
"Going Down the Country," 253
"Going to the Grand Ole Opry," 254
"Goin' to Raise a Ruckus Tonight," 87, 107
Golden, William, 100
Golden Gate Quartet, 104, 176, 200
"Golden Rocket," 54
"Golden Slippers," 75
Golden West Cowboys [band], 38, 39, 40, 41
"Gold Rush Is Over," 54
"Gold Watch and Chain," 6, 12
"Go 'Long Mule," 73
"Gone," 225
"Gonna Lay Down My Old Guitar," 199
"Gonna Walk Those Golden Stairs," 175
Good, Dolly. See also Girls of the Golden West
Good, Millie, 258–60, 261. See Girls of the
    Golden West
Good, Rick, 296
"The Good Book Song," 123
Good Coffee Boys [band], 99
Goodman, Benny, 19, 40, 180
"Goofus," 119
"Gooseberry Pie," 126
"Gooson Quadrille," 262
gospel music, ix, 3, 6, 148, 200; of Statler
    Brothers, 224, 225, 234
gospel songs, in country music, 98, 99, 100,
    102, 113, 141, 218
"Got Texas in My Soul," 150
"G Rag," 173
Grand Ole Opry, x, 9, 15, 19, 79, 139, 142,
    154, 281, 290, 294; Arthur Smith on, 179,
    290; Bill Monroe in, 44, 45, 113, 135, 179;
    Bradley Kincaid on, 127; Carlisles on, 239,
    241, 242; Carter Sisters on, 16–17; close-
    harmony singing on, 103; Crook Brothers
    on, 176; Curly Fox and Texas Ruby on,
    196; DeFord Bailey on, 114, 178–80, 181;
    Delmore Brothers on, 115, 179, 217; Don
    Gibson on, 212, 213; early days of, 57, 185;
    Eddy Arnold on, 41; Grandpa Jones on,
    33, 37; Hank Snow on, 54, 55, 290; Hank
    Williams on, 54, 253, 290; Jimmy
    Thompson on, 64; Johnny Cash on, 155;

Jordanaires on, 175; Kirk McGee on, 221; Kitty Wells in, 60; Lefty Frizzell in, 31; Lew Childre in, 96; Louvin Brothers on, 215, 218–19; Martha Carson on, 237; Minnie Pearl on, 253; move to Opryland Park, 247, 274; "Old-Timer's Night" at, 181, 194, 196; Pee Wee King in, 38, 39; Red Foley on, 146, 219, 253; Roy Acuff on, 19, 26, 136, 137, 138, 139, 144, 150, 179, 190; Skeets McDonald on, 271; Stringbean on, 249, 251, 252; Tommy Jackson on, 185, 187; Tommy Magness on, 160; Uncle Dave Macon on, 179, 252, 286; Wayne Raney on, 116; Zeke Turner and his Fireside
The Grand Ole Opry [film], 21–22
Grandpa Jones, ii(photo), ix, vii, 14, 82, 92(photo), 94, 104, 105, 117, 127, 150, 161, 186, 194, 200–1, 235, 248; in Brown's Ferry Four, 103, 104; in Country Music Hall of Fame, 33, 37; in Grand Old Opry, 33; on *Hee Haw*, 254; marriage to Ramona, 37; profile of, 33–37
"Grandpa's Rag," 139
Grant, Hal, 140
Graves, Josh, 254
Gray, A. A., 168, 171, 172–73
Gray, Ahaz, 172
"Gray's Buckin' Mule," 172
Grayson, G. B., 280
"The Great Speckled Bird" [song], 20, 22, 23
Green, Carl, 283
Green, Douglas, 124, 267
Green, Frog, 282–83
"The Green, Green Grass of Home," 121
Greenbriar Boys, 265
Greene, Richard, 142
Greene County singers, 101
Greer, Dolly, 298
Gregory, Robert, 72
Grey, Zane, 222
"Grey Eagle," 139
Griffin, Rex, 154, 184, 286, 292
Griffith, Andy, 177, 280
Grishaw, Eddie, 147. *See also* Turner, Zeb
Grishaw, James, 147, 151. *See also* Turner, Zeke
"Groundhog," 107
"Guitar Boogie," 143, 149, 152, 201, 208
"Guitar Fantasy," 148
"Guitar Reel," 149
Guthrie, Jack, 79

Habershon, Ada R., 6
"Hadacol Boogie," 152
Haden, Walter, 72
Haggard, Merle, viii, 28, 182, 183
Hall, Clayton, 137
Hall, Jay Hugh, 134, 137
Hall, Roy, 130, 134, 135, 136, 137, 139, 159
Hall, Saford, 137
Hall, Tom T., 56, 213
Hall, Wendall, 35
Hamblen, Stuart, 51, 140, 175
Hammerstein, Oscar, 80
Handy, W. C., 110
Haney, Carlton, 226
"Hang Out Your Front Door Key," 95

"Hank, the Singing Ranger," 52, 54
"Hank, the Yodeling Ranger," 52
Harmon, Buddy, 228
"Harmonica Blues," 115
Harper, Roy, 285–93
Harrell, Kelly, 101
Harris, Charles K., 112
Harris, Emmylou, 4, 102, 202, 204, 216, 258, 277
Harris, Faye [Magness], 133
Harris, Peppermint, 151
Hart, Freddie, 28
Harte, Bret, 259
Hartford, John, 164
Hartford Music Company, 244, 245–46
Harvey, Roy, 83
Hasty, Carol, 268
Hatcher, Dynamite, 21
Hatcher, Troy, 211
Hauer, Doc, 20
"Haunted Hunter," 263
"Hawaiian Wiggle," 291
Hawkins, Hawshaw, 186
Hawkins, Hoyt, 175, 176
Hawkins, Ted, 77, 78
Hawkins Quartet, 176
Hay, George D.: as Barn Dance founder, 120, 178; as Opry founder, 21, 22, 23, 40, 120, 178–79, 251
Hayes, Gabby, 135
Hays, Will S., 67
Hazel and Alice, profile of, 274–78
"Heartbreak Hotel," 176
"Heartbreak USA," 60
"Heaven Holds All to Me," 100
"The Heavenly Train," 239
"Heaven's Decision," 17
"Heavy Hearted Blues," 91
Hee Haw Gospel Quartet, 36, 103
Hee Haw [TV show], 34, 79, 105, 188; Stringbean on, 247, 248, 254
Heimal, Otto (Coco), 147, 148. *See also* Candy and Coco
"Hell Amongst the Yearlings," 173
"Hello Mary Lou," 234
"Hen Cackle," 178
Hendrick, Summie, 207, 208
Henson, J. M., 217
"He Set Me Free," 245
"He Will Set Your Fields on Fire," 113
Hicks, Bill, 296
Higginbottom, Luther, 158
The Highlanders [band], 84
The Highlighters [band], 207
"High Sheriff," 112
Highwoods String Band, 296, 297
Hill, Kenny, 242
Hill, Smilin Eddie, 59, 182, 218
Hill and Range, 51
"Hillbilly Boogie," 104, 115, 201
hillbilly music, 75, 77, 95; of African Americans, 178
"The Hills of Roane County," 24, 130
Hi Neighbor Boys [band], 148
"Hobo Bill's Last Ride," 291
Hodges, Ernie, 101
"Hog Calling Blues," 95